THE

U.S. NAVY

Other books by Nathan Miller

War at Sea: A Naval History of World War II

Theodore Roosevelt: A Life

Stealing from America: Corruption in American Politics from Jamestown to Whitewater

Spying for America: The Hidden History of U.S. Intelligence

FDR: An Intimate History

The Naval Air War, 1939–1945

The Roosevelt Chronicles

The Founding Finaglers: A History of Corruption in America

Sea of Glory: A Naval History of the American Revolution

The Belarus Secret (with John Loftus)

The U.S. Navy
A History

Third Edition

Nathan Miller

Naval Institute Press
Annapolis, Maryland

Library of Congress Cataloging-in-Publication Data

Miller, Nathan, 1927–
    The U.S. Navy : a history / Nathan Miller. — 3rd ed.
        p.   cm.
    Includes bibliographical references (p. –) and index.
    ISBN 1-55750-595-0 (pbk. : alk. paper)
    1. United States. Navy—History. I. Title.
    VA55.M55 1997
    359′ .00973—dc21   97-26244

Printed in the United States of America on acid-free paper ∞

04 03 02 01 00 99 98 97   9 8 7 6 5 4 3 2

First printing

To the officers,
men, and women of the
United States Navy

CONTENTS

Author's Preface

ANaval power . . . is the natural defense of the United States."
So said John Adams, who most deserves to be called "father of the
American Navy." Yet no nation ever was more reluctant to
create a navy or, eventually, had a more effective one than the United
States. Events forced the American people to take to the sea in pursuit of
their liberty, and the force they built in anxiety and reared in parsimony
played a compelling role not only in winning their independence but in
helping to maintain that freedom for two centuries by valor and arms.

This book is the history of that force—its ships and men, from the
raggle-taggle Continental Navy to the ballistic-missile submarines of today. Ships and weapons, tactics and strategy have undergone quantum
changes, but the mission of the navy remains unchanged: to ensure safe
passage for those who do business on the great waters. Today, the scope
and importance of the U.S. Navy's operations remain undiminished despite the end of the Cold War because the world remains a dangerous
place.

Recent events have reemphasized the fact that the United States is
basically an island nation, dependent on foreign sources of raw materials.
It is well to recall that more than 90 per cent of all our foreign commerce
is shipborne. Control of the sea permits the navy not only to safeguard that
commerce but to project our power abroad in defense of the allies who
constitute the advanced line of our defense. Such is the significance of sea
power. To understand and appreciate the vital role of the navy, the nation's
instrument of sea power, it is necessary to know how that service took
form and developed.

The purpose of this book is to provide the present generation with the story of the navy, its people, and the role they played in the creation and protection of the United States. For the most part, I have relied on the research and writings of others. In the text and in the notes, I have tried to acknowledge the debt I owe to those who have sailed these seas before, and if I have overlooked any, it is not by intention.

One thing more. Many people contributed to the making of this book and I am grateful to them all: Mark Gatlin, senior acquisitions editor of the Naval Institute Press, who expressed continuing confidence in the author; the late Mary Veronica Amoss—"Ron"—whose deft use of the blue pencil and sense of humor made working with her a delight; Frank Uhlig, Jr., former senior editor of the Naval Institute, and the late Professor Neville T. Kirk, former chairman of naval and diplomatic history at the U.S. Naval Academy, both of whom generously lent their time and extensive knowledge of the navy to reading an earlier version of the manuscript, catching mistakes, and suggesting changes that make this a better book than it would have been; and the staffs of the Library of Congress and of the Nimitz Library at the U.S. Naval Academy. And above all, my wife Jeanette, who willingly put up with a husband who was physically present but whose mind was often on distant stations.

May they all enjoy fair winds and following seas.

1

A NAVY IS BORN

"You Abraham Whipple on the 10th of June 1772 burned his majesty's vessel the Gaspée *and I will hang you at the yard arm!"*
— Captain James Wallace, RN, HMS *Rose*

"Sir, Always catch a man before you hang him."
— Abraham Whipple

Rising and falling on the long swells rolling in from the Atlantic, eight small ships huddled in the mouth of the Delaware estuary on the morning of February 18, 1776. Guns poked from their sides like stubby black fingers, and a strange new flag that combined the British Union Jack with alternating red and white stripes flew over them. All eyes were fixed on the *Alfred*, the largest of the vessels, as the order to make sail was tensely awaited. Ten months had passed since news of the fighting at Lexington and Concord had raced through the colonies, but only now was the Continental Navy's first fleet ready for sea. At about 1:00 P.M., the *Alfred* cast loose her foretopsail and sheeted it home. The long-awaited signal had come. Topmen scrambled aloft and, amid a bedlam of shouted orders and twittering boatswain' pipes, sails blossomed on the masts of the other ships. Propelled by a freshening breeze, they followed the *Alfred* around Cape Henlopen and over the horizon.[1]

Esek Hopkins, a fifty-seven-year-old Rhode Islander with considerable experience as a merchant seaman and privateersman, had been chosen by the Continental Congress to command its new fleet. An aggressive, outspoken man with a hot temper, he was described by General Henry Knox, George Washington's chief of artillery, as "an antiquated figure" who might have been mistaken for an angel, "only he swore now and then." Hopkins had been ordered to sail to Chesapeake Bay where he was to "attack, take or destroy" a small armada led by Lord Dunmore, the deposed royal governor of Virginia, that was spreading havoc in the area. If adverse weather conditions prevented these orders

11

from being carried out, Hopkins was to use his own discretion.[2] Having received information that the British had stockpiled a large amount of powder and arms on New Providence (now Nassau), in the Bahamas, he selected that island as his target instead of the Chesapeake, without informing Congress of the change.

Hopkins' fleet of converted merchantmen consisted of the *Alfred* and *Columbus*, now rated as frigates and both mounting 24 guns; the 14-gun brigs *Andrew Doria* and *Cabot*; the sloops *Providence*, 12, and *Hornet*, 10; and the schooners *Wasp* and *Fly*, of 8 guns each. Heavy gales struck the fleet the second night out, and the *Hornet* and *Fly*, after fouling each other, drifted off in the darkness. With his fleet reduced to six vessels, Hopkins abandoned any pretense of heading for the Chesapeake and pressed on to the established rendezvous at Great Abaco, an island in the Bahamas about fifty miles from New Providence, where he vainly awaited the missing vessels for two days.

Seizing two island sloops and cramming them with marines and sailors, Hopkins planned to send the vessels into the harbor of New Providence to take the fortifications by surprise. The rest of the ships were to remain out of sight until the initial advantage had been gained, but the plan miscarried when Hopkins showed his hand too soon. Instead of remaining below the horizon, the fleet was bowling along in the wake of the sloops when a puff of smoke appeared at an embrasure of the fort. There followed the thud of a heavy gun and the splash of round shot. With the chance for surprise lost, Hopkins diverted his ships to the opposite end of the island. Under cover of the guns of the *Wasp* and *Providence*, about 200 marines and 50 sailors splashed ashore on an empty beach on March 3, 1776, thus making the first amphibious landing by American forces.[3] Marching overland, they took the defenders from the rear, compelling their surrender after a parley. Eighty-eight cannon, fifteen mortars, and other military equipment of immense value to George Washington's army were captured. But the islanders, forewarned by Hopkins' blundering attempt at surprise, managed to spirit away most of the gunpowder that had attracted his attention to New Providence. Nevertheless, the booty was so great that it took two weeks to load it aboard the American vessels, and the expedition was undoubtedly the most successful Continental Navy operation of the war.

As the heavily laden vessels wallowed homeward, smallpox and fever raced from ship to ship. The epidemic raged unchecked and the daily routine of the ships was broken by the grim business of burials at sea. The *Wasp*, whose crew were ravaged by sickness, disappeared during a three-day storm off the coast of Georgia and only with difficulty made her way back to Philadelphia. Early on the morning of April 6, 1776, the remaining ships encountered the 20-gun British frigate *Glasgow* off Block Island. She should have been easy prey for the Americans but escaped after badly cutting up her opponents. During the four-hour melee and chase, Hopkins did not issue a single order except to recall his ships. "Away we all went Helter, Skelter, one flying here, another there," wrote Nicholas Biddle, the disgusted captain of the *Andrew Doria*.[4] Although the depletion of Hopkins' crews by sickness and their inexperience were extenuating factors, this inept action made it all too clear that patriotism was not enough to create a navy. Experience, training, and a heritage of victory were all required.

George Washington put it best: ". . . whatever efforts are made by the Land Armies, the Navy must have the casting vote in the present contest."[5] This remark was made after the timely arrival of a French fleet had resulted in the British surrender at Yorktown; but almost from the first musket-shot of the Revolution, Washington understood the vital role sea power would play in the winning of independence. Both the Americans and British relied on supplies shipped across the sea to support their armies in the field. Without a steady flow of arms and other equipment from Europe and the Caribbean, the American cause would have soon collapsed, while a substantial part of the men and supplies required by the British forces in America were also brought in by sea. After France entered the war, the king's troops were always in danger of being isolated and destroyed if the Royal Navy lost command of the sea off the American coast—as occurred at Yorktown.

The launching of the Continental Navy was a long and tortuous affair—"the maddest idea in the world," according to Samuel Chase, a Maryland delegate to Congress.[6] However, the pressure of events finally forced the Americans to try to wage war against Britain on the sea. Trouble had first flared between England and her colonies because the mother country's policies threatened the substantial seaborne commerce of the colonists. This was particularly true in New England where, because the thin, boulder-strewn soil was so unsuitable for farming, many Yankees had become sailors, fishermen, whalers, and slavers. Soon, their ships dominated the coastal trade that, in the absence of good roads, was the natural link between the colonies, and they enjoyed a brisk commerce with the sugar islands of the Caribbean, the African slave coast, and the Mediterranean. "No sea but is vexed by their fisheries," said Edmund Burke. "No climate but what is witness to their toils."[7]

Shipbuilding became one of the major industries of colonial America almost as soon as the first settlement had been established. By the outbreak of the Revolution, colonial yards had become so efficient that it cost only about half as much to build a ship in America as in Britain, and one-third of all the vessels employed in British commerce had been launched in the colonies. The colonists had demonstrated considerable skill and craftsmanship in the construction of armed vessels and had been turning out ships of up to 44 guns since 1690.[8] There was also an ample reserve of seamen. Large numbers of American sailors had served in expeditions to Canada and the West Indies or in privateers during the running series of wars between Britain and France for control of North America. Lamenting the conflict brewing with the Yankees, a member of the House of Lords described America as "a great nursery where seamen are raised, trained and maintained in time of peace to serve their country in time of war."[9]

In 1763 Britain had emerged victorious from the Seven Years' War and the Union Jack flew without rival from Hudson's Bay to the Florida keys. This vast empire had to be protected against any attempt by the French to regain it, but Britain was financially exhausted by the war. She decided to shift a share of the cost of defense to the Americans, reasoning that inasmuch as they derived most of the benefit, they should help pay for it. Successive British ministries resorted to new taxes and to strict enforcement of the existing Acts of Trade and Navigation to provide sorely needed revenues. The enforcement of these laws— designed to subordinate the economic interest of the colonies to those of Britain—had been notoriously lax and the Americans had grown used either to ignoring or evading them.

To the shock of the colonists, the Royal Navy was pressed into service to collect duties and to suppress smuggling. As a result, the Americans, expecting less—not more—interference from Britain now that the French were no longer a threat, were increasingly drawn into conflict with the king's ships and officers. The high-handed methods adopted by the Royal Navy to put an end to smuggling and the widespread use of impressment to man shorthanded ships transformed it from a welcome symbol of defense to an instrument of oppression.

Yet for all its power, the British navy was stronger on paper than it was on the seas. In 1775 Britain had 131 ships of the line and 139 smaller craft, such as frigates, sloops of war, schooners, and cutters. But in the dozen years since France had been expelled from North America, Britannia's trident had grown rusty. Believing in the justice of the American cause, some able officers refused to serve against fellow Englishmen, and politically acceptable incompetents were appointed in their places. The Revolution also deprived the Royal Navy of access to its primary source of masts, the forests of New England. As a result, many British ships were crippled at critical phases in the struggle.

In the early months of the war, some British officials suggested that since the army would never be able to subjugate the colonies, the task of subduing the rebellion should be left to the navy, which could impose a blockade that would cost little in blood and treasure. Just such a blockade was feared by the wiser of the American leaders, but the Royal Navy was too weak to impose it. While an admiralty official calculated in July 1776 that a minimum of fifty ships would be needed on the American Station, Vice Admiral Samuel Graves, the commander in American waters, had but twenty-nine vessels to patrol some 1,800 miles of coastline—and many of them were all but unfit for service at sea.

The first formal movement for the creation of an American navy came from Rhode Island, a colony that had been severely harassed by British cruisers because of the widespread smuggling activities of its merchants. The State Assembly passed, on August 26, 1775, a resolution instructing its delegates to Congress to introduce legislation calling "for building at the Continental expense a fleet of sufficient force, for the protection of these colonies, and for employing them in such a manner and places as will most effectively annoy our enemies. . . .''

The rebels had already been flexing their muscles at sea. On June 12, 1775, a group of Maine backwoodsmen under the command of Jeremiah O'Brien had seized the Royal Navy schooner *Margaretta* in a brisk, bloody battle off Machias. The same day, the Rhode Island authorities commissioned two small vessels and placed them under the command of an old privateersman named Abraham Whipple. Putting to sea with his pygmy squadron on June 15, 1775, Whipple captured a tender, or auxiliary vessel, serving the British frigate *Rose*. And all through the summer of 1775 fast-darting whaleboats manned by willing Yankee oarsmen swarmed out of hidden coves and creeks to harry the British warships at anchor in Boston Harbor. The rebels burned lighthouses, removed navigational aids, and swept forage and cattle from the nearby islands.

The Rhode Island resolution for a navy was introduced in the newly convened Congress on October 3, 1775, but was brushed aside.[10] There were several reasons for this refusal to act. For one thing, sectional jealousies made cooperation difficult. Some southerners were convinced that a navy was a venture that would profit only New England. The creation of such a force was also regarded as a radical gesture, for independence was as yet the goal of only a few delegates. Most members considered themselves loyal British subjects fighting the tyranny of a corrupt ministry and did not regard the break with the mother country as final. Sending a navy to sea would denote sovereignty—and independence. Widespread fears were also expressed that should any Yankee skipper be so bold as to fire a popgun from his deck, the Royal Navy would visit a terrible vengeance upon defenseless ports from Maine to Georgia.

Unknown to Congress, General Washington had already taken steps to begin the war at sea. His troops were so short of powder that he would not fire salutes for fear of provoking a British barrage that could not be answered. With growing desperation, he watched the steady and unhindered passage into Boston of British transports and supply ships. "A fortunate Capture of an Ordnance Ship would give a new life to our camp and [an] immediate Turn to the Issue of the Campaign," he observed. Acting upon his own authority as commander in chief, he launched a fleet with the hope of making such "a fortunate Capture."[11]

The first vessel he commissioned, the tiny schooner *Hannah*, put to sea on September 5, 1775. She was commanded by Captain Nicholson Broughton and manned by a crew recruited from a regiment of Marblehead sailors and fishermen who had joined the army. Although the first ship of what became known as George Washington's Navy failed to capture any significant prizes, Washington pressed ahead with his project. Over the next two years, he commissioned seven lightly armed vessels, which captured a total of fifty-five ships. John Manley, a rough-and-ready Boston shipmaster who had served in the Royal Navy, was the most successful of Washington's captains. On November 27, 1775, he captured the British ordnance brig *Nancy*, which turned out to be a floating arsenal. She carried a supply of muskets, shot, and other military equipment, including a huge 13-inch mortar that proved to be invaluable in the Continental Army's siege of Boston. Four troop transports, carrying between them about 320 British soldiers, were also taken by Washington's raggle-taggle fleet before it was disbanded in 1777.

On October 5, 1775, Congress, which had not yet been informed of Washington's seaborne activities, learned that two transports loaded with supplies for the British army in Quebec had sailed from England. Unarmed and sailing without escort, these vessels were an inviting target. If they could be captured, reasoned the supporters of a naval effort, their cargoes would be a priceless asset to Washington's army. A motion requesting the appointment of a committee to prepare a plan for intercepting the store ships was introduced.

"The opposition . . . was very loud and Vehement," John Adams later recalled. "It was . . . represented as the most wild, visionary, mad project that had ever been imagined. It was an Infant, taking a mad Bull by his horns." By a narrow margin, Congress appointed Adams, Silas Deane of Connecticut, and John Langdon of New Hampshire to draft a plan for dealing with the Quebec-bound ships. The committee must have had some prior understanding of the action it was to take, for it quickly recommended that Washington be informed of the sailing of the ships and instructed to apply to the Massachusetts authorities for permission to use the armed vessels that had been recently placed in commission by that state. If these ships were not available, he was authorized to fit out such craft as were needed to capture the vessels—an authorization that could have been used to justify him in forming his own little fleet, had he not already done so.

The committee proposed the fitting out of two armed vessels but its report was tabled for a week. In the meantime, heated debate took place on the Rhode Island resolution. The walls of the Pennsylvania State House resounded to attacks upon the proposal. "Its Latitude is wonderful," thundered Maryland's Samuel Chase. "We should mortgage the whole Continent." Realizing that the time was not yet ripe for the launching of a full-scale navy, supporters of the resolution shifted ground. Debate on the ambitious Rhode Island plan was postponed, and the more limited proposal was pressed instead.

On October 13, 1775, Congress took a step that the U. S. Navy today regards as marking its official birth. It approved the plan for purchasing and fitting out two vessels that had been recommended the week before and ordered them to be armed and sent in pursuit of the transports en route to Canada. They became the *Andrew Doria* and *Cabot*. Having cleared the first obstacle, the navy's supporters moved ahead with greater assurance. Two larger ships, which became the *Alfred* and *Columbus*, were authorized on October 30. Significantly, the mission of these last two vessels was not limited to intercepting the British store ships. They were "to be employed . . . for the protection and defense of the united Colonies."

To carry out this objective, a seven-member Naval Committee was organized and it laid the foundation for the Continental Navy. Meeting in the evenings at a waterside tavern after the regular congressional sessions, the committee accomplished a remarkable amount of work in a short time. Merchant vessels were purchased and converted into men-of-war: their sides were strengthened, gunports were cut, and they were armed. Officers were chosen and sailors and marines recruited. Regulations for the governing of the navy were drafted by John Adams and adopted by Congress on November 28, 1775. Although based on the British naval statutes then in effect, these regulations called for more humane treatment of seamen. For example, the amount of flogging that a captain could order was limited to a dozen lashes. With minor changes, these regulations remained in effect throughout the Revolution and were readopted in 1798, during Adams' presidency.[12]

In selecting the ranking officers of the Continental Navy, Congress unfortunately followed the principles of patronage and nepotism traditional in the Royal Navy. Esek Hopkins was the brother of Stephen Hopkins, a member of the Naval Committee. The senior captain, Dudley Saltonstall, of Connecticut, was a brother-in-law of Silas Deane, another member of the committee. Then came Abraham Whipple, who had married into the Hopkins clan; Nicholas Biddle, whose brother Edward represented Pennsylvania in Congress; and Esek Hopkins' eldest son, John Burroughs Hopkins. John Paul Jones, a Scots sea captain whose antecedents were shrouded in mystery, was named first lieutenant of the *Alfred*, probably through the influence of Joseph Hewes, of North Carolina, who was also a member of the Naval Committee.

With these preliminaries out of the way, Congress at last was ready to turn its attention to the long-delayed Rhode Island resolution. Southern reluctance to support this proposal was overcome by the effect of the raids launched by Lord Dunmore along the shores of the lower Chesapeake Bay. On December 13, 1775, Congress authorized the building of thirteen frigates within the next three months—which would indeed have been record time—at a cost of $66,666.66 each. This ambitious building program called for five ships of 32 guns, five of 28 guns, and three of 24 guns. With Esek Hopkins' fleet being fitted out in the Delaware, vessels being purchased at other ports, and contracts let on the frigates, the new nation had launched a significant naval effort.

Congress next set about establishing an administrative framework for the navy. The Naval Committee was absorbed by the Marine Committee, consisting of one member from each of the thirteen colonies. Like its predecessor, the Marine Committee met in the evenings after the work of the regular congressional sessions was done.[13] Five members constituted a quorum and its officers were a chairman, vice chairman, and secretary. Several clerks assisted in its work. The Marine Committee appointed local naval and prize agents—often the same man—to handle the details of refitting and manning naval vessels and to dispose of prizes. When the increasing complexity of naval administration forced the committee to provide an arrangement for handling day-to-day affairs, naval boards were established at Boston and Philadelphia. These arrangements continued until October 28, 1779—a period which saw the rise and decline of the Continental Navy.

Under fire for alleged inefficiency, the Marine Committee was replaced in 1779 by a five-member board of admiralty made up of two congressmen and three public members. The fortunes of the navy had sunk so low, however, that few men were willing to serve on the board. On February 18, 1781, the office of Secretary of Marine was created to centralize operations under a single executive. No one could be found to accept the post and it fell by default to Robert Morris, the secretary of finance, who had considerable experience in maritime affairs. The appointment was made official on September 7, 1781, when Morris was named Agent of Marine. He held the job until November 1784, by which time, for all practical purposes, the Continental Navy had ceased to exist. Throughout the entire war, the navy was faced with shortages of men and material. At times, it was so short of funds that its administrators were forced to pledge their own credit to get the ships to sea.

The outcry in Congress after the escape of the *Glasgow*, and southern criticism of Esek Hopkins for failing to follow his orders to rid the Chesapeake of Lord Dunmore, overshadowed the success scored in the raid on New Providence. After considerable maneuvering, Hopkins was suspended from his command in 1777 and formally dismissed from the service at the start of 1778. Most of the ships of his fleet swung uselessly to their anchors in Narragansett Bay, unable to get to sea again as a unit because of sickness, a shortage of seamen, and a British blockade. From time to time, some of the vessels, the *Andrew Doria* under Nicholas Biddle, the *Columbus* under Abraham Whipple, and the *Providence* and *Alfred*, successively commanded by John Paul Jones, who had been promoted to captain, made successful cruises on their own. Sailing off Cape Breton Island in the *Alfred* on November 12, 1776, Jones captured the armed transport *Mellish*, whose rich cargo included 10,000 winter uniforms, which were dyed and issued to Washington's troops.

Success in the war effort depended on such lucky captures and the ability of fast-sailing Yankee ships to elude the loose British blockade and return from Europe and the West Indies with vital cargoes. Ninety per cent of the gunpowder available to the American forces before the end of 1777—or about 1.5 million pounds of it—was brought in by sea. Britain's failure to stop the ships of the Continental Navy, the navies of the individual states, and the privateers from harassing her long supply lines, and to cut the flow of seaborne supplies to

Washington's army preserved the American cause until the intervention of France—and French sea power—brought about the eventual independence of the United States.

Eleven of the thirteen states—Delaware and New Jersey were the exceptions—had raised navies of their own. Massachusetts, Connecticut, Pennsylvania, Maryland, Virginia, and South Carolina all had a number of vessels, but the Massachusetts navy was the only one composed almost entirely of sea-going craft. The total number of ships commissioned by the states was greater than that commissioned by the Continental Navy but the former were, in general, smaller and less well armed than the latter. Most of the state craft were shallow-draft galleys and armed barges because the state navies were primarily intended to defend the states' seaports and coastal waters. For example, the mission of the Pennsylvania navy was to guard the mouth of the Delaware—a task in which much of it was lost in November 1777, after the British had captured Philadelphia. The major aim of the Maryland and Virginia navies was to drive off British vessels preying on the rich commerce of the Chesapeake. Larger ships, such as those sent out by Massachusetts and South Carolina, engaged in commerce-raiding, as did the vessels of the Continental Navy and the privateers—and with the same mixed success.

The thirteen frigates authorized on December 13, 1775, had checkered careers. Throughout most of the following year, the construction and fitting-out of these vessels proceeded with agonizing slowness at yards from Portsmouth, New Hampshire, to Baltimore. Poor planning and lack of priorities for the use of scarce materials resulted in costly delays. There was a shortage of skilled labor. Just as experienced seamen found it more profitable to join privately owned commerce-raiders than to enlist in the Continental Navy, so shipwrights preferred high-paying jobs building privateers to working on naval vessels. Only seven of the frigates ever got to sea—all to be eventually captured or sunk—while the remaining six were destroyed to keep them from falling into enemy hands. Perhaps the strangest fate befell the *Hancock*, one of the five 32-gun ships. Under the command of John Manley, who had left George Washington's fleet and secured a commission in the Continental Navy, she joined with the *Boston*, 24 guns, to capture the British frigate *Fox*, 28, on June 7, 1777. A month later, the *Hancock* was captured by a British squadron, which also retook the *Fox*. The *Boston* fled, after failing to support her consort. Renamed the *Iris*, the *Hancock* was taken into the Royal Navy and, in 1781, captured the *Trumbull*, 28, the last of the thirteen frigates in American hands.

The captain of each ship was responsible for gathering his own crew, and in the first flush of revolutionary fervor, the task of recruiting men for the Continental Navy had been comparatively easy. Usually, a junior officer would set up a rendezvous at a popular tavern, print broadsheets giving a glowing account of his vessel and then, with the hope of attracting volunteers, send out a detail of sailors and marines to march through the town behind merrily rattling drums. Joshua Barney, master's mate of the *Hornet*, outfitting in Baltimore at the end of 1775, reported that he managed by this method to drum up a crew in a single day.

Later, patriotism had little appeal and sailors became more wary. They were reluctant to join a service in which discipline was strict, conditions were harsh, the share of prize money was only a fraction of that offered on privateers, and pay was low—$6.67 a month for an able seaman, paid in depreciated Continental currency. John Trevitt, a marine lieutenant in the *Columbus*, said several months' salary "would pay for 2 pair of shoes." And despite the new regulations urging humane treatment, there were also complaints of brutality and mistreatment. "We are used like dogs," protested the crew of the *Providence* to Esek Hopkins. "We hope you will find us a new Captain or a new Vessel." John Hazard, the captain of the *Providence*, was court-martialed and dismissed from the service.[14]

Some captains tried to outbid the privateers for crews by offering bonuses and advances on wages. As often as not, the volunteers took the money and deserted at the first opportunity. Desperate measures were taken to fill out crews. Large numbers of inexperienced landsmen were enlisted. One captain reported that most of his crew of "green country lads" were seasick as the ship went into action. The army sometimes got rid of hard cases by sending them to the navy, and criminals were offered their choice between prison or naval service. In emergencies, captured British seamen were hustled on board in irons and put to work. One such group plotted to seize the frigate *Alliance*, murder her officers, and sail her to a British port. Luckily, the plot was thwarted. Upon several occasions, the recruiting of seamen for privateers was embargoed until Continental ships could be manned, and on others, exasperated naval officers seized deserters from the decks of the privateers to which they had fled. In a few extreme cases, naval officers resorted to impressment, much to the anger of civilian authorities ashore.[15] All these efforts were of little avail, however. In a time of critical need, the ships of the Continental Navy were often unable to go to sea because they lacked crews.

Just how effective were the privateers that consumed so much of the infant nation's maritime resources? Congressional records list 1,697 vessels with Continental commissions. Several states and American agents in Europe and in the Caribbean also issued commissions. Taking duplications into account, the best estimate is that more than 2,000 commissions were issued by the various authorities. Lloyd's of London estimated that not counting those that were ransomed or recaptured, 2,208 British ships were taken by Yankee privateers. Placing an average value of $30,000 on the prizes, as suggested by one authority, the loss to Britain amounted to more than $66 million, a significant sum at that time.[16]

Trade with the West Indies was especially hard hit by the activities of the privateers. As early as 1777 a resident of Grenada reported that only twenty-five ships of a convoy of sixty carrying provisions to Britain's Caribbean possessions had arrived safely. "God knows, if this American war continues much longer we shall all die from hunger," he declared. Insurance rates soared and the Royal Navy was bombarded with demands from the merchants for protection. The privateers also provided arms and stores for the American cause. When a French fleet arrived at Boston in 1778, after being battered by a hurricane and by a British fleet off Newport, its needs could not have been met had it not been for the timely arrival of prizes captured by privateers. Fear that swarms of privateers might snatch up straggling troop transports and supply ships sometimes caused delays in reinforcements being sent from England to America.

Privateering was a double-edged sword, however, for, as pointed out, it siphoned off men, ships, and weapons that could have been used by the Continental Navy. The damage inflicted by the privateers upon British trade was considerable in the aggregate, but it was not disabling, and despite the lamentations of the merchants, it had little effect on Britain's will to continue the war. Nevertheless, considering the limited resources available to the Americans, John Adams was probably close to the mark in describing privateering as "a short, easy and infallible method of humbling the English."

While attention was focused on the war on the high seas, a naval campaign unfolded on Lake Champlain that helped to determine the future of the United States.[17] Late in 1775 an American army invaded Canada with the hope of making it the "fourteenth colony." Initial success turned to failure, and in the spring of the following year, the arrival of a British fleet sent the Yankees fleeing in headlong retreat. The American colonies then lay open to a British army proceeding down the inland water route that led from the St. Lawrence through Lake Champlain to the Hudson River. If the invaders—whose major aim was to prevent a recurrence of the attack on Canada—were not checked, Washington's army at New York would be open to attack from the rear.

Lake Champlain was the key to the invasion route and General Benedict Arnold held tenuous control of it with three small, armed schooners. Both sides settled down to a small-scale naval construction race. The British had the advantage because their fleet in the St. Lawrence had the equipment and the skilled manpower to build and man armed vessels more powerful than anything that could be built by Arnold, whose source of supplies and crews lay 250 miles away on the Atlantic coast. Nevertheless, Arnold accepted the challenge without hesitation.

At thirty-five, Arnold was at the height of his remarkable powers and still four years away from the treason that was to blacken his name. A member of a prominent Connecticut family, he had begun his career as a druggist and bookseller in New Haven. He became a successful merchant and sailed his own ships to the West Indies and Europe—experience that was to be invaluable on Lake Champlain. He is credited with both the design and construction of the Champlain fleet. The capital ships of his battle line were four 2-masted row galleys carrying varying numbers of guns and fitted with high-pointed lateen sails, a type of craft he had probably seen in the Mediterranean. Nine gondolas, armed with three guns each and propelled by two square sails set on a single mast, as well as by oarsmen, and four small schooners and sloops constituted the remainder of his fleet. For these hastily built vessels, he used the oak and pine growing beside the lake. Officers were recruited from the army or from along the seaboard, while the crews consisted of about 750 soldiers attracted by a bonus of eight shillings a month. Described by Arnold as "a wretched motley crew," these landlubbers were sorted into sailors, marines, and gunners.

As soon as General Sir Guy Carleton, the British commander, realized that it would be necessary to fight for control of the lake, he set about building a fleet that would overwhelm anything that the Yankees could put in the water. The mainstays of his force were the 18-gun sloop of war *Inflexible*, which had been built at Quebec, knocked down into sections, and hauled overland to the lake where she was reassembled, and a two-masted, scow-like floating battery, built on the lake, that mounted enough firepower to deal with Arnold's entire fleet all by itself. Carleton also had several small sailing vessels and a score of gunboats, each mounting a single cannon in the bow.

Sails bellying in the chill autumn wind, the British fleet began its move southward on October 11, 1776. Undaunted by the superior enemy force, Arnold anchored his ships in a narrow bay between Valcour Island and the New York shore. As he expected, the British sailed by without seeing his fleet and, when they did, had difficulty beating back against the wind to give battle. While they struggled to bring their guns to bear, Arnold's fleet poured a heavy fire into them. Flying his flag in the galley *Congress*, Arnold moved from gun to gun, training, elevating, and firing most of her cannon. But when the British eventually got into position, the results were devastating. The light wooden sides of the American vessels were shattered, their guns dismounted, and their crews cut up.

By nightfall all the American ships had been battered and some were sinking. The British, convinced that Arnold was trapped, expected to finish off the remnants of his fleet the next morning. But Arnold was at his best in adversity. Fog settled in, and with the *Congress* acting as a rear guard, the American vessels escaped through the British line and headed south. The British did not discover until morning that the Yankees had slipped through their fingers. In the desperate chase that followed, some of the American craft were captured and the remainder destroyed to prevent their falling into enemy hands. Arnold and his surviving crewmen escaped overland.

The British now controlled Lake Champlain and the invasion route to the south. But building a fleet to overwhelm Arnold's squadron and waiting for logistic support of their army advancing on Fort Ticonderoga, their next objective, delayed them so long that they had to postpone their attack until the following year because of the approach of the severe northern winter. In mid-1777 General John Burgoyne launched a fresh invasion. This time the Americans were ready and Burgoyne was eventually forced to surrender at Saratoga. The victory brought France into the war. "That the Americans were strong enough to impose the capitulation of Saratoga," notes Admiral Alfred Thayer Mahan, the great historian of sea power, "was due to the invaluable year of delay secured to them by their little navy on Lake Champlain. . . ."

"Let Old England See how they like to have an active Enemy at their door, they have sent Fire and Sword to Ours."[18] With this exhortation, Congress dispatched Captain Lambert Wickes and the 18-gun sloop of war *Reprisal* on one of the most momentous missions of the war. Wickes, a native of the eastern shore of Maryland, was ordered to carry Benjamin Franklin to France, where he was to serve as one of the new nation's diplomatic representatives. As soon as the old man had been safely deposited ashore, Wickes was to launch a raid on enemy commerce in the seas around Britain. It was thought that an attack upon British shipping mounted from French ports would tumble the two nations into war with each other—to the benefit of the United States.

Thirsting for revenge against Britain for the loss of her North American empire, France had been sympathetic to the American cause since the start of the Revolution. Yet the French were cautious. The Comte de Vergennes, foreign minister to young King Louis XVI, was pro-American but had no desire to provoke a war with Britain until France was ready and he was certain that the colonists were capable of putting up a sustained fight for their independence. To keep the flame of rebellion burning, large quantities of arms and other supplies were taken from French arsenals and funneled to the Americans through a dummy trading company. Thus, if the British complained, Vergennes could answer that his government had nothing to do with the transatlantic gun-running.

Shortly after the beginning of 1777, Wickes put to sea from Nantes and soon captured five prizes, including the Falmouth-Lisbon packet.[19] This cruise, which was climaxed by Wickes' return to a French port with the captive vessels, created considerable friction between Britain and France. The British demanded that the *Reprisal* be expelled from her haven, but Vergennes resisted with diplomatic subterfuges. On May 28, 1777, Wickes was at sea again, this time in command of a little squadron that consisted of the *Reprisal*, the 14-gun brigantine *Lexington*, and the cutter *Dolphin*, armed with several 3-pounders. Sailing into the Irish Sea, Wickes captured eighteen ships in a month, creating frantic demands from British merchants that the Royal Navy escort their ships in home waters. Elated by his success but running low on supplies, Wickes set a course for the French coast. Before he could make port, however, his squadron was pursued for a full day by the *Burford*, a 74-gun British ship of the line. The Americans escaped only after a desperate chase in the course of which Wickes ordered the *Reprisal*'s guns heaved over the side in order to lighten her.

Once back in port, the *Reprisal* became the focus of a lengthy diplomatic contest that was ended by a British ultimatum that the French expel the American vessels without delay. Unable to resist the pressure, Vergennes complied, and that autumn the *Reprisal* and *Lexington* sailed for home. The *Dolphin*, considered too unseaworthy to make the voyage, was left behind. The *Lexington* was captured off the French coast, and months later, it was learned that the *Reprisal* had foundered in a storm off Newfoundland, taking with her Wickes and all but one of his crew of 130. The survivor was picked up by a passing ship. "This loss is to be extremely lamented," mourned Benjamin Franklin, as Lambert Wickes "was a gallant officer and a worthy man."

In the meantime, Gustavus Conyngham, a Philadelphia shipmaster who was stranded in Europe at the outbreak of the war, had been given a captain's commission in the Continental Navy and command of a lugger, a type of small vessel much favored by the French for privateering.[20] On May 1, 1777, Conyngham took his ship, named the *Surprise*, out of Dunkirk and captured a British mail packet carrying important dispatches, which were turned over to Franklin. The British outcry against the "Dunkirk pirate" was so violent that Vergennes felt it necessary to appease it by seizing the lugger and arresting Conyngham. He refused, however, to turn Conyngham over to the British for trial.

A few months later, another vessel, a 14-gun cutter named *Revenge*, was procured for Conyngham. Ranging off the coasts of England, France, and Spain, the *Revenge* took nearly sixty prizes over a period of eighteen months, striking terror into the hearts of British merchants and shipowners. The psychological effect of Conyngham's and Wickes' raids exceeded the damage they did to British commerce and helped significantly to upset the balance that kept France and Britain at peace.

At the same time, American agents in France were trying to find a ship for John Paul Jones, another Yankee skipper ready to carry the war home to Britain. "I wish to have no Connection with any Ship that does not sail *fast*, for I intend *to go in harm's way*," Jones told them—and that was the guiding principle of his naval career. Born John Paul, Jr., the son of a gardener on an estate on the shores of Solway Firth, a deep inlet on the western border between Scotland and England, he went to sea in 1761 as a lad of thirteen.[21] There followed long years of voyaging to the West Indies and the American colonies, notably to Fredericksburg, Virginia, where his older brother, William, had become a tailor. At the age of twenty-one, he was a captain, no small accomplishment for a young man without influence.

In 1773 the whole course of the youthful Captain Paul's life was altered. According to his own account, a mutinous seaman attacked him while his ship lay in port in Tobago, and in self-defense, he killed the man. For some unexplained reason, friends urged him to flee, and what he did for the next twenty months remains a mystery. When he reappeared in Fredericksburg, he called himself John Paul Jones. Under this name, he secured a commission in the Continental Navy as first lieutenant of the *Alfred* and served in her during the New Providence expedition. As a reward for his accomplishments in the *Providence* and the *Alfred*, he was given command of the 18-gun sloop of war *Ranger*.

In this ship he sailed across the Atlantic at the end of 1777 to raise the curtain on a new era in American naval operations in European waters. News of the American victory at Saratoga preceded the arrival of the *Ranger* in Europe and was followed by a treaty of alliance between France and the United States. French ports, which at least officially had been closed to Yankee commerce-raiders, now welcomed them. The way was clear for Jones to win the fame that had been denied his predecessors because their exploits might have embarrassed the French.

Although he was burdened with jealous officers and a crew restive under his strict discipline, Jones resolved to make a hit-and-run raid on an unsuspecting enemy port so that the English might feel the effects of war. Before departing from the French coast, however, he sailed the *Ranger* into Quiberon Bay, where a French fleet lay at anchor. Jones had been the first to unfurl the Grand Union flag over Esek Hopkins' fleet in the Delaware in 1775, and he wanted to take advantage of the opportunity to be the first Continental officer to exchange salutes with a French admiral. Late on the afternoon of February 14, 1778, a thirteen-gun salute boomed out from the *Ranger* as she sailed past the French flagship. The latter answered with nine guns—the first salute to the Stars and Stripes by a foreign warship.

Unable to persuade the French to join him in a raid, Jones set sail on April 10 for the Irish Sea, en route to the northwest coast of England, where the port of Whitehaven was his first objective. Lambert Wickes and Gustavus Conyngham had sailed around Britain into these waters during the previous year and taken many prizes, but they had made no attempt to raid a British seaport—something no one had done since the Dutch had burned Sheerness in 1667. Although Jones had first sailed from Whitehaven as a youthful apprentice, he did not choose it as a target out of any animosity but because he knew its harbor and realized that it would be full of shipping. Late on the evening of April 22, 1778, he led two boatloads of volunteers into the port. An attempt was made to set fire to a large number of ships, but his men were so careless that the inhabitants, aided by a rainstorm, were able to put out the blazes before serious damage was done.

The next day the *Ranger* crossed Solway Firth to St. Mary's Isle, the home of the earl of Selkirk. Jones planned to seize Selkirk, with the hope of exchanging him for some of the American seamen being held in English prisons. Learning that the earl was not at home, he wanted to abandon the expedition, but his officers and men insisted on taking the Selkirk family silver. Although appalled at the suggestion, Jones thought it prudent to give in to the demands of his unruly men. Later, to satisfy his honor, he purchased the silver from his crew and returned it to the Selkirk family.

With the alarm being sounded up and down the coast and British cruisers searching for the *Ranger*, Jones had reason enough to return to the safety of France. Instead, he crossed the Irish Sea to deal with the *Drake*, a 20-gun sloop of war, which had been sighted earlier at anchor at Carrickfergus in Belfast

Lough. Shortly before sunset on April 24, the two ships closed for action. Although they were almost equal in firepower, the *Drake* was manned by raw volunteers and was short several officers.

"The action was warm, close and obstinate," reported Jones. The *Ranger* stood off with the intention of crippling the *Drake* so that she could be taken as a prize rather than of sinking her. With her masts splintered, some of her yards carried away, and her sails hanging in tatters, the British vessel soon became unmanageable. Little more than an hour after the first broadsides had been exchanged, her sailing master, the senior surviving officer, cried: "Quarter! Quarter!"

Jones returned to France with the captured *Drake* and the expectation that a cruise that had included a raid on an English seaport and the capture of the first British man-of-war taken in European waters would be amply rewarded. Instead, the next period of his life was one of bitter frustration that brought out all the worst aspects of his character—oversensitivity, vanity, and unpredictable outbursts of bad temper. Although Jones gave up command of the *Ranger* in August 1778, after being promised a more powerful ship, he did not get a vessel until the end of the year. And she was a far cry from what he had expected.

His new command was the *Duc de Duras*, a tired old East Indiaman of some 900 tons armed with a mixed bag of forty-two guns, some of questionable value. To compliment his patron, Benjamin Franklin, whose almanacs, translated into French as *Les Maximes du Bonhomme Richard*, were popular in Paris, Jones rechristened the vessel the *Bonhomme Richard*. Accounts vary as to the exact makeup of the complement of 380 officers and men who shipped on board the *Richard*. Samuel Eliot Morison states that 17 of the 20 officers were Americans and were handpicked by Jones. The three marine officers were Irishmen serving with the French. There were 43 petty officers, more than half of them British deserters or prisoners of war, while the remainder were Americans. There were 144 seamen and boys, of whom 46 were American, 54 British, and the rest from seven different countries. The complement included 137 French marines and 36 French "landsmen," most of whom were peasants and fishermen from Brittany. Many of the Americans, including Richard Dale, a twenty-two-year-old Virginian appointed first lieutenant of the *Richard*, had escaped from British prisons, while others had been released from captivity primarily through exchange for enemy seamen captured by Jones. "Revenge sometimes is quite pleasing to man," noted John Kilby, one of the former prisoners. "We believed . . . Jones would not disappoint us in our great wish and desire."[22]

Accompanied by a fine new American frigate, the *Alliance*, of 32 guns, under the command of a strange and erratic Frenchman named Pierre Landais, three ships belonging to the French navy, and two French privateers, which soon disappeared, Jones put to sea on August 14, 1779.[23] None of Jones' fellow captains took his authority as commodore very seriously—least of all Landais. Having been made an honorary citizen of Massachusetts, Landais told Jones that he was "the only American [captain] in the squadron and was determined to follow his own opinion in chasing where and when he thought proper." Writing of the voyage, which took him around Ireland and Scotland, Jones said, "I did not sleep three hours in the twenty four from Lorient to the Texel." While his captains' lack of discipline prevented him from putting some of his boldest plans into action, several rich prizes were taken and British trade was disrupted.

Her hold crammed with about 200 prisoners, the *Richard* and her consorts were off Flamborough Head, a rocky promontory on the east coast of England, on the evening of September 23, when they fell in with a large convoy southbound from the Baltic and shepherded by the powerful new frigate *Serapis*, 44 guns, and the sloop of war *Countess of Scarborough*, 20. Although night was falling, Jones ordered an immediate attack on the enemy men-of-war that had interposed themselves between his squadron and the merchantmen. Much to Jones' chagrin, his consorts swung away, leaving him to fight the *Serapis* alone. Later, however, one of the French ships, the frigate *Pallas*, joined him and, after a sharp fight, took the *Countess of Scarborough*.

Broadsides erupted from the *Richard* and the *Serapis*. "The battle being thus begun, was continued with unremitting fury," Jones reported. "Every method was practised on both sides to gain an advantage and rake each other." At the first or second broadside, there was a burst of flame on the lower gun deck of the *Richard* and she shuddered from stem to stern. Agonized screams and the smell of burnt flesh filled the night. Two of the old 18-pounders that were the mainstay of the *Richard*'s armament had exploded, wiping out their crews and blowing a gaping hole in the deck above. In an instant, the weight of her broadside had been reduced to 195 pounds as compared to 300 for her opponent.

Jones realized that his clumsy vessel was no match for the *Serapis*. His only hope was to lay her alongside his opponent and carry her by boarding. But all attempts to accomplish this were thwarted by the speed and maneuverability of the British frigate and the skill of her captain, Richard Pearson. At one point, Jones had the sickening experience of seeing the bow of his ship jammed into the stern of the *Serapis*. In this position, he was unable to bring a single gun to bear in answer to the murderous British fire. Having clearly demonstrated his ship's superior firepower and handling, Captain Pearson called out: "Has your ship struck?" Answered the indomitable Jones, "I have not yet begun to fight!"[24]

The *Richard* sheered off and took the wind from the *Serapis*, passing ahead of her. Jones then put his ship across the bow of the enemy vessel to rake her, but the *Serapis* was too fast for him. In the confusion, her bowsprit rode up on the *Richard*'s poop deck and hopelessly fouled the mizzen rigging. "Well done, my brave lads!" shouted Jones, who had desperately sought such an embrace. "We've got her now!" To seal the *Richard*'s grip upon her adversary, Jones seized one of the British vessel's forestays that had been parted by a random shot and fallen across his quarterdeck and made it fast to the *Richard*'s mizzenmast. For the rest of the battle, the two ships were locked together, their guns pressing against each other's sides.

Fires broke out on board both ships, and it was necessary periodically to break off combat to subdue them. According to Lieutenant Dale, flames licked to "within a few inches of the magazine" before they were extinguished. The *Serapis'* overwhelming power began to tell. Within two hours of the start of the battle, all the *Richard*'s broadside, with the exception of two 9-pounders on her quarterdeck, had been knocked out of commission and her gun crews decimated. Jones helped haul a third 9-pounder from his ship's unengaged port side and concentrated on bringing down the enemy's mainmast. "My prospects became gloomy indeed," he said with understatement, and the *Richard* was "mangled beyond my power of description."

Unexpectedly, the *Alliance* loomed out of the darkness. The ragged cheer from the *Richard* that greeted her appearance was drowned out by the roar of the frigate's guns. "To my utter astonishment, he discharged a broadside full into the stern of the *Bonhomme Richard*," Jones reported. "Every tongue cried out that he was firing into the wrong ship." But Landais put about and unleashed another broadside into Jones' stricken vessel. Although it may have been difficult to distinguish the ships from each other in the moonlight and although Landais did cease firing after Jones hoisted recognition signals, Jones regarded Landais' action as deliberate—apparently inspired by a desire to sink the *Richard* and take credit for the victory. It is difficult to believe, however, that the *Alliance*'s crew would have deliberately fired into the *Richard* even if Landais had ordered it. Later, Jones brought charges against Landais, who was ultimately dismissed from the navy.

When the rapidly rising water in the *Richard*'s hold began sloshing about the feet of the prisoners confined below, a master-at-arms released them. Expertly led, the prisoners might have seized the ship, but they were frightened and were quickly shoved and prodded to the pumps at sword's point. One of them managed to escape through a gunport to the *Serapis*. He told Captain Pearson that the *Richard* was sinking fast and Jones would soon have to surrender or go down with his ship.

But the British were having troubles of their own. The French marines and the sailors stationed in the *Richard*'s tops had swept the enemy vessel's spar deck clean of men, and sharpshooters stationed below had been picking off the British gunners through shot holes and gunports. The gun crews were so reduced by this steady fire that the powder monkeys were bringing up cartridges from the magazines faster than they could be used. The frightened boys simply dropped them on the deck near the guns and raced below for more. Carrying a basket of hand grenades, one of Jones' sailors crawled out to the end of a yard that hung directly over the decks of the *Serapis*. One of the grenades caromed off a hatch coaming and rolled onto the gun deck. It exploded among a pile of loose cartridges, which went up in a searing flash, killing at least twenty British seamen and horribly burning others. Some, their clothing afire, jumped screaming into the sea. "Many stood with only the collars of their shirts upon their bodies," reported Dale.

Unnerved by the explosion and the sight of his mainmast beginning to totter, and fearing that he might be attacked by the *Alliance*, Pearson hauled down his colors three-and-a-half hours after the battle had begun. Casualties were heavy on both sides; one of Jones' officers described the blood as being "over one's shoes." The *Richard* was so badly battered that, despite efforts to save her, she sank two days later. From the deck of the *Serapis*, Jones saw "with inexpressible grief, the last glimpse of the *Bonhomme Richard*," as she plunged below the bubbling waters of the North Sea. Later, he was to command the *Alliance*, the *Ariel*, and briefly, the 74-gun *America*, as well as to serve as an admiral in the Russian navy, but his name is linked forever with the lumbering old Indiaman. On her decks he spoke the words that won him undying fame.

France's entry into the conflict lifted American hopes of victory and independence. Shortly after the signing of the Treaty of Alliance between France and the United States, 4,000 French soldiers and a fleet commanded by the Comte d'Estaing were dispatched to America. The high hopes raised by this expedition were soon dashed, for d'Estaing was not aggressive, and on several occasions he ignored opportunities to deal smashing blows to weaker British forces, blows that might have ended the war.

For the Continental Navy, this was a period of mixed blessings. Early in 1778 Captain John P. Rathbun seized New Providence—this time with but a single ship and a handful of marines and sailors. Several valuable prizes were taken, fortifications were dismantled, and some American prisoners were released. This success was marred, however, by the loss within a ninety-day period of the new frigates *Randolph* and *Virginia*, as well as the *Alfred* and the *Columbus*, and the brig *Independence*.

The loss of the *Randolph*, commanded by Nicholas Biddle, was especially tragic. Having achieved some success as a commerce-raider, Biddle was sailing off Barbados on March 17, 1778, when he sighted a large British vessel. He unhesitatingly gave battle, even though the enemy vessel proved to be the *Yarmouth*, which carried 64 guns, double the number mounted by the *Randolph*. The American frigate held her own, and an eyewitness reported that she "appeared to fire four or five broadsides to the *Yarmouth*'s one." Suddenly, there was an explosion and the *Randolph* vanished in a tower of flame. Nicholas Biddle and all but four of his crew of 305 were lost.[25]

Two weeks later, on the night of March 31, Captain James Nicholson, the Continental Navy's senior officer since the dismissal of Esek Hopkins, tried to run the 28-gun frigate *Virginia* through the British blockade, which had kept her bottled up in the Chesapeake. Unhappily, a pilot ran her fast aground on a shoal off the Virginia Capes under the guns of the British. When daylight came,

Nicholson had himself rowed ashore, leaving the *Virginia* and her crew to be captured without a fight. Some of the men broke into the frigate's rum stores and were soon roaring drunk. It was "All Fool's Day," Joshua Barney, the frigate's first lieutenant, noted bitterly.[26]

The few remaining ships of the little Continental Navy were captured at sea, blockaded by the British, or could not sail because they were short of seamen and supplies. Two of the largest naval expeditions launched by the Americans during the war also ended in disaster. The first, mounted in July 1779, was aimed at driving the British from a base they had established on the Penobscot River in Maine. The Massachusetts authorities recruited a force of perhaps a thousand men who were transported to the Penobscot by a sizeable flotilla of ships, some of which belonged to the Continental Navy and others to the state. Captain Dudley Saltonstall, skipper of the 32-gun frigate *Warren*, was made commodore of the naval force, which included the old sloop *Providence*, the only survivor of Esek Hopkins' original fleet. Unfortunately, cooperation between the naval and land forces soon broke down and an operation that should have moved with lightning rapidity settled into a wearying siege of the British outpost.

As the Yankee commanders squabbled over tactics, a British relief force hurried to the Penobscot, arriving on August 12. Panic seized the Americans. Instead of attempting to make a stand, they made a mad rush for safety, with every man for himself. Ships were run aground and set on fire, and terrified soldiers and sailors fled into the woods. Nearly 500 men were killed or captured, nineteen armed vessels were lost, and about $7 million were wasted.

Nine months later, a second disaster struck the Continental Navy. At the beginning of 1780 the British, under the command of General Sir Henry Clinton, taking advantage of the mobility provided by British control of the sea, moved south to attack Charleston, South Carolina. The frigates *Boston*, *Providence*, and *Queen of France*, as well as the *Ranger*, Jones' old ship, were sent to help in the defense of the city. Four years before, Charleston had withstood an attack by a British fleet, but its defenses had been allowed to deteriorate. Following a month-long siege in which British land and naval artillery pounded it to pieces, the city surrendered on May 12, 1780. An estimated 5,000 prisoners were taken, as was the Continental Navy's last squadron. For all practical purposes, that navy had been eliminated as an effective fighting force.

Nevertheless, the overwhelming victory of the British at Charleston resulted in their undoing. Fearing an attack on New York by the French and Americans, Clinton returned to the north, leaving Lord Cornwallis in command. Restless and ambitious, Cornwallis disregarded his instructions to exercise caution, and set off on a march through the South aimed at rallying Tory support and destroying the remnants of the American army. In the bloody campaign that followed, Cornwallis' tattered army of some 7,000 men finally staggered into Yorktown, a sleepy village on the York River, Virginia, on August 1, 1781. There he hoped that the Royal Navy would come to his aid. Reporting to General Washington on the arrival of the British, the Marquis de Lafayette, who had been shadowing the enemy, said: "If we should have a great fleet arrive at this moment, our affairs would take a happy turn."

Just such a fleet was then on the way. The Comte de Grasse, the French naval commander in the Caribbean, had agreed in mid-July 1781 to sail north to the Chesapeake at the suggestion of the Comte de Rochambeau, commander of the French troops in America. Revelling in the naval superiority that had eluded him for so long, Washington abandoned a planned attack on New York and ordered a quick march to the south. Dismissing the movements of the American and French armies as a feint, Clinton remained in New York and ignored the trap that was closing about Cornwallis.[27]

In the meantime, the British had divided their West Indies fleet. With the hurricane season approaching, Admiral Sir George Rodney took some of his ships home to England while the remainder, under Admiral Sir Samuel Hood, were sent to the American coast in pursuit of de Grasse. There was a significant difference between the French and British fleets. Instead of detaching some of his ships to escort merchantmen home, as the British had done, de Grasse took a bold gamble. He brought his entire fleet of twenty-eight ships of the line, most of them in good condition, with him to the Chesapeake. Hood had but fourteen and many of them were almost worn out by long service in the tropics.

The two fleets missed each other on the way north and Hood reached the mouth of the Chesapeake first. He looked into the bay and, not seeing the French, sailed on to New York where he joined a small fleet commanded by Admiral Thomas Graves, his senior officer. Graves had been blockading some French ships at Newport, Rhode Island, and had not been paying much attention to the worsening plight of Cornwallis. The aggressive Hood implored Graves to put to sea at once—either to capture the French squadron that had escaped from Newport with Rochambeau's siege artillery on board or to sail to the Chesapeake to relieve Cornwallis.

Graves finally acceded to Hood's plea, and the British fleet, shorthanded and in poor repair, arrived off the Virginia Capes on the morning of September 5, 1781, to find de Grasse's vessels at anchor and Cornwallis under siege. Although he was outnumbered by twenty-four ships of the line to nineteen, Graves had the advantage of surprise and the French faced contrary winds and tides. But the cautious Graves did not fall upon the French ships and destroy them, one by one, as they struggled out of their anchorage in great confusion. Instead, following the rigidly formal tactics of the day, he allowed de Grasse to form a line of battle.

For about two hours, the two fleets fought an indecisive battle in conventional parallel lines. Formed in single columns, the British and French ships of the leading and center divisions placed themselves against their opposite numbers in the enemy line and pounded each other at close range. Confusion and mis-understood signals prevented Graves' ships in the rear, which were under Hood's command, from getting into action. When darkness came, the guns fell silent. Neither side had lost a ship, although the British had taken more of a battering than had the French. For the next several days, the opponents maneuvered within sight of each other but did not renew the battle. On September 10, the French returned to the Chesapeake to find the Newport squadron safely at anchor. Unable to face such a massive concentration of enemy ships, Graves' fleet returned to New York. The British made halfhearted plans to rescue Cornwallis, but his fate was sealed. French sea power had not only reversed for a moment the verdict of 1763, but had also handed Washington his irreversible victory. Shortly before 2:00 P.M. on October 19, 1781, Cornwallis surrendered to the French and American armies.

The war had sputtered to an end on land, yet it did not end at sea for another eighteen months. Rumors of impending peace had been circulating for some time when Captain John Barry sailed from Havana in the *Alliance* early in March 1783. In company with the smaller *Duc de Lauzun*, the frigate bowled along at top speed, for the *Lauzun* carried valuable cargo—a chest containing 100,000 Spanish-milled dollars, a fortune in Continental currency. Under Barry's com-mand, the *Alliance* had become a lucky ship. In May 1781, he had captured the British sloops of war *Atlanta*, 16, and *Trepassy*, 14, after a four-hour battle off Cape Sable. The frigate was becalmed and the lighter British vessels used their sweeps, or long oars, to gain a position from which they could knock the Yankee vessel to pieces without fear of her heavier guns. Only after the *Alliance* had suffered considerable damage did the wind spring up. Hands leaped to the braces and the frigate's broadsides crashed into her tormentors, soon bringing the action to a victorious close.

A few days out of Havana, on March 10, 1783, the *Alliance* and her consort made out three sails bearing down on them. They were the British frigates *Alarm*, 32, and *Sybil*, 28, and the sloop of war *Tobago*, 18. The newcomers tried to cut the *Lauzun* off from the *Alliance*, but Barry interposed the frigate between her and the *Sybil*, the fastest of the enemy vessels. The distance between the ships began to shorten, and although the *Alliance* was struck by a British shot, Barry ordered his gunners to hold their fire while the range closed. At pistol-shot distance, the *Alliance*'s broadside crashed into the *Sybil* and she sheered off to limp back to her companions. The American vessels pressed on to Newport, anchoring on March 20, 1783. Three days later, it was learned that the war was over. John Barry and the *Alliance* had fought the Continental Navy's last battle. The Treaty of Paris, although agreed to much earlier, was finally signed on September 3, 1783.

During nearly eight years of war, about sixty naval ships of various types and sizes saw service, capturing as many as 200 enemy vessels. But with war's end, the new republic could not afford a navy. Except for the *Alliance*, the few remaining ships were sold. Some members of Congress wanted to keep her "for the honor of the flag of the United States and the protection of its trade and coasts from the insults of pirates," but the expense was too much for such a gesture. On August 1, 1785, the frigate was auctioned off for $26,000—and the Continental Navy had sailed into history. Born in adversity and nurtured in hardship, it had never been a threat to Britain's command of the sea. But together with the privateers and the state navies, it had helped to keep the Revolution alive, and it provided our nation with some of its most gallant traditions.

2

IN PURSUIT OF PRIVATEERS AND PIRATES

It is difficult to conceive that there ever was a time when the United States paid a money tribute to anybody. It is even more difficult to imagine the United States paying blackmail to a set of small piratical tribes on the coast of Africa. Yet this is precisely what we once did with the Barbary powers. . . . The only excuse to be made for such action was that we merely followed the example of Christendom.

—Henry Cabot Lodge, 1895

On the morning of September 20, 1797, a large and boisterous crowd gathered at Edmund Hartt's shipyard in Boston where the trim, black hull of the frigate *Constitution* towered over them. Festooned with bunting, her copper-sheathed undersides glistening in the sunlight, she was ready for launching. Shortly after noon, the tide reached the flood, and Colonel George Claghorne, who had supervised construction of the vessel, gave the signal for her shoring timbers to be knocked out. A ragged cheer died on the lips of the onlookers. Instead of gliding gracefully into the water, the frigate hung motionless on the ways. Flustered by this mishap, Colonel Claghorne ordered screw jacks and other mechanical devices applied to force the ship to move, but she slid only a few feet before coming to a dead stop. Two days later another attempt was made to launch her, and this, too, ended in failure.[1] Not until a month later, on October 21, 1797, did the *Constitution* finally slip into the waters of Boston Harbor. A similar pattern of agonizingly fitful starts and stops marked the early years of the navy in which she served.

From the end of the Revolution until the inauguration of George Washington as president in 1789, the United States was not so much governed as maintained in a caretaker status under the feeble Articles of Confederation. Congress functioned as little more than a council of ambassadors of an uneasy league of thirteen more or less sovereign republics. Funds were short, there was only a shadow of an army, and there was no longer an American navy at all.

The seizure of American shipping in the Mediterranean by the Barbary pirates provided the impulse for the creation of another navy. Freed by independence from the restrictions of the British Navigation Acts and by peace from the danger of capture by British warships and privateers, Yankee trading vessels carried the Stars and Stripes around the globe. As soon as they returned to the Mediterranean, they fell prey to corsairs sailing from the Barbary states of Morocco, Algiers, Tunis, and Tripoli. For centuries these seagoing brigands had levied tribute upon the commerce of all nations. Unless they were paid bribes, they seized passing ships and held seamen and passengers for ransom. Britain, Spain, and France had the maritime might to put an end to these depredations, but they allowed the pirates to operate so that the trade of their rivals would be disrupted while their navies protected their own vessels. Until the American colonies won their independence, Yankee ships had been protected by the British flag. Now, the corsairs regarded them as fair game because the new nation neither paid tribute nor possessed a navy to protect its ships.[2]

In 1785, the same year in which the *Alliance*, the last ship of the Continental Navy, was sold, Algerian corsairs captured two American ships and held their crews for ransom. Thomas Jefferson and John Adams, the American ministers to Paris and London, who had been given the task of negotiating treaties with the Barbary States, agreed that in the long run it would be cheaper to organize a navy to protect American shipping than to pay tribute. Such a move would provide the government "with the safest of all the instruments of coercion," said Jefferson. But, as Adams pointed out, prospects were not bright, owing to lack of funds and sectional rivalries similar to those that had delayed formation of the Continental Navy—consequently, nothing was done to resist the demands of the Barbary pirates.[3]

The Constitution, which went into effect in 1789, authorized the Congress "to provide and maintain a navy," but during Washington's first term there was only peripheral discussion of the issue. In 1790 General Henry Knox, who, as secretary of war, was handling such naval affairs as there were, secured estimates for the cost of building several frigates. The following year Jefferson, then secretary of state, recommended that a naval force be fitted out to deal with the Barbary pirates, but the only thing that came of his recommendation and of Knox's estimates was a Senate report suggesting that a navy be organized "as soon as the state of our public finances will admit."[4]

The outbreak of a new conflict between Britain and France in 1793—the wars of the French Revolution, which were to last more than two decades—brought matters to a head. A truce between Portugal and the Algerians, negotiated with British help, ended Portugal's blockade of the Strait of Gibraltar, which had kept the corsairs bottled up in the Mediterranean. The pirates suddenly swarmed out into the Atlantic, taking eleven American ships and more than a hundred American seamen in two months.[5] While the British claimed that the blockade had been lifted so that their Portuguese ally could use its ships for other purposes, many Americans were convinced that the truce was part of a British plot to destroy American commerce in the Mediterranean.

Reacting to the seizure of the American vessels, the House of Representatives on January 2, 1794, approved by two votes a resolution that "a naval force adequate to the protection of the commerce of the United States ought to be provided." This resolution was referred to a committee dominated by pro-navy congressmen. Eighteen days later, the committee recommended the construction of four frigates of 44 guns and two vessels of 20 guns at a total cost of $600,000. Debate on the recommendation followed sectional lines. Northerners and tidewater representatives supported the creation of a navy; and inland and southern members, except for a few South Carolinians who represented mercantile interests, opposed it.[6]

Opponents of the measure charged that a navy would embroil the new nation in foreign adventures, be a drain on its finances, and saddle the country with an ever-expanding naval establishment and bureaucracy that would endanger the liberties of the people. Supporters argued, on the other hand, that a navy would result in savings in ransom payments and insurance, and that inasmuch as it operated offshore, it could scarcely be an instrument of domestic tyranny. A navy, they said, would not only protect American commerce but would force the British and French to respect the country's rights as a neutral. The struggle over the navy was one of the first of the running series of battles between the emerging political parties that was to mark the early years of the republic. The Republicans, ancestors of today's Democrats, opposed the formation of a navy, while the Federalists generally supported it.[7]

As finally approved on March 27, 1794, the Navy Act authorized the procurement of six frigates—four of 44 guns and two of 36 guns. But in order to ensure the bill's passage, its supporters had accepted an amendment providing that work on the ships would be summarily halted if peace terms were concluded between the United States and the dey of Algiers. Shortly after the bill passed, as if to emphasize the deep divisions over the navy, Congress authorized the expenditure of $800,000 to obtain a treaty with the Algerians and to ransom the American captives.

President Washington and General Knox decided to provide the navy with newly built ships rather than convert existing merchantmen into men-of-war. Writing to Joshua Humphreys, a prominent Philadelphia shipbuilder who had a hand in the design of the Continental Navy's first frigates, Knox suggested that "the vessels should combine such qualities of strength, durability, swiftness of sailing, and force, as to render them superior to any frigate belonging to the

European powers.'' Several other men were called in to work on the project and, as Howard Chapelle, the noted writer on naval architecture, has emphasized, the final design of the frigates was not Humphreys' alone, as is usually stated, but "represented the joint ideas of many individuals.''

Longer, wider in beam, and endowed with stouter sides and finer lines than any existing frigate, these vessels were designed to outrun any ship that they could not outfight. Although the larger vessels were rated at 44 guns, they sometimes carried as many as 56. Instead of the usual 18-pound long guns mounted by frigates, they carried 24-pounders as well as short-barreled carronades. Developed by the British in the closing years of the Revolution, carronades were particularly effective at close range. Some officers were wary of the new frigates because they considered them too large and clumsy to handle easily, but the vessels proved themselves so effective in battle that European navies copied them.[8]

To distribute the financial benefits of the construction program and to encourage popular support for the navy, the work of building and equipping the ships was spread up and down the Atlantic coast—setting the pattern of distributing defense contracts for political reasons that has endured to this day. The *Congress*, 36 guns, was to be built at Portsmouth, New Hampshire; the *Constitution*, 44, at Boston; the *President*, 44, at New York; the *United States*, 44, at Philadelphia; the *Constellation*, 36, at Baltimore; and the *Chesapeake*, 44, at Norfolk. Instead of awarding the contracts to private shipbuilders, the government itself rented yards and appointed captains, constructors, and naval agents to oversee the building of the vessels. This was thought to be cheaper than allocating the work to private contractors.[9]

Knox stipulated that the frigates were to be built of live oak and red cedar, which were supposed to be five times as durable as the white oak in common use. Work on the ships proceeded slowly because seasoned timber had not been stockpiled and because of the difficulty in obtaining cannon and other equipment. The shortage of cannon was particularly galling. American artisans were not experienced in casting such weapons and succeeded only after much trial and error. Moreover, American-made guns had a reputation for unreliability. Sometimes they burst, so that crews naturally distrusted the weapons remaining. Furthermore, American shot was lighter in weight by as much as 10 per cent than that fired by the English and French.

Unfortunately for the navy's advocates, a treaty was signed with the dey of Algiers in September 1795, and in compliance with the terms of the Navy Act of 1794, all work on the frigates was to be suspended immediately. President Washington strongly opposed this step on the grounds that it would be wasteful. True, the cost of finishing them would be higher than the original estimates, but the price of peace was also high. It cost almost $1 million, including $525,000 in bribes and ransom, the gift to the dey of Algiers of a newly built 36-gun frigate, and an annual present to him of $21,000 worth of naval stores. After considerable debate Congress allowed the completion of two 44-gun frigates and one of 36 guns—the *Constitution, United States*, and *Constellation*.[10]

In the meantime, relations with France were becoming strained. Under the terms of the Treaty of Alliance of 1778, which had brought the French into the American War of Independence, the United States had agreed to help defend the French West Indian islands and to throw open her ports to French privateers in case of war between France and Britain. But with the Royal Navy dominating the sea lanes, and British troops, in defiance of the Treaty of Paris, occupying a line of forts on the western frontier, the new nation was in no position to risk a war with Britain by implementing those terms. Besides, American sympathies were divided. Most ordinary citizens favored France because of their admiration for the French Revolution, while the more prosperous, fearing the excesses of the revolutionary regime, sided with the British.

But no matter where their sympathies lay, the majority of Americans wanted to stay out of war. Neutrality had proven to be extremely profitable. Yankee farmers prospered as France and Britain bid up the price of foodstuffs and other commodities. Shipowners reaped large profits by carrying American goods to Europe and secured a foothold in the trade with the French West Indian colonies, which had been restricted to French ships before the outbreak of war between Britain and France. President Washington, who sympathized with the British, and Secretary of State Jefferson, who favored France, agreed that the Franco-American alliance of 1778 had outlived its usefulness and that neutrality was the best policy for the United States.

The French were further angered in 1794 when John Jay, the chief justice who was serving as a special envoy to Britain, negotiated with the British a treaty aimed at settling the problems left over from the Revolution. Britain had flatly refused to accept the American argument that neutral ships could trade with all belligerents. Contending that trade which was restricted in peacetime could not be opened in time of war, the British seized as contraband of war all goods carried in American ships from the French West Indies to France. In addition, Royal Navy captains, whose ships were usually shorthanded because of desertion or disease, used the right of search to halt American ships and to impress likely hands into the king's service.

Under the terms of Jay's Treaty, the British relinquished their frontier forts and the United States softened its demands for the freedom of neutral trade. Because of the concession it made to the British, the treaty was unpopular in the United States. Nevertheless, for a while the British interfered less with American trade, and the possibility that the two nations might blunder into another war decreased.[11]

But the French, who claimed that the treaty was detrimental to their interests, stepped up their harassment of American shipping. Between October 1796 and the following June, they seized 316 American vessels.[12] As soon as the naval-minded John Adams became president, on March 4, 1797, he called Congress into special session to deal with the mounting crisis. ''A Naval power, next to the militia, is the natural defense of the United States,'' he declared as he sought authority to complete the *Constitution, United States,* and *Constellation* and to procure smaller vessels to help protect America's seaborne trade. The Republicans, led by Vice President Jefferson, suspecting that Adams' request for the naval legislation was but a step toward a declaration of war against France, opposed the president's program. With pro-navy Federalist majorities in control of Congress, a Navy Act was passed after acrimonious debate on July 1, 1797, enabling Adams to rush the three frigates to completion and to get them to sea.[13]

The *United States* had slid into the Delaware River on May 10, 1797. Work was speeded up on the other two frigates, and the *Constellation* went down the ways on September 7. After the two failures to get her into the water, the *Constitution* joined them six weeks later. Captains John Barry, Thomas Truxtun, and Samuel Nicholson, all veterans of the Continental Navy or successful privateersmen during the Revolution, had already been named to command the ships and had been helping to supervise their construction. Nicholson was the brother of James Nicholson, who had been senior captain of the Continental Navy. Officers were commissioned and crews were recruited. The rules and regulations written by Adams in 1775 for the Continental Navy were again put in effect. Building, arming, and maintaining the frigates from 1794 to 1798 cost the government about $2,510,730—a substantial amount at the time—but the savings in insurance charges paid by American shipowners during 1798 alone were estimated at $8,655,566.[14]

In an attempt to head off a full-scale clash with France, Adams dispatched a three-man commission to Paris to negotiate an agreement similar to the treaty Jay had reached with the British. Soon after they arrived in France in October 1797, the commissioners were approached by three agents of the French foreign minister, the devious Charles Maurice de Talleyrand-Périgord, with a demand for a $250,000 bribe for the minister and a large loan to the French government. The American envoys angrily rejected the proposal. One of them, Charles C. Pinckney, a South Carolina Federalist, is supposed to have declared, ''No! No! Not a sixpence!'' Legend transformed his retort into, ''Millions for defense, but not one cent for tribute!''

When Adams made public a report in which the French agents were identified only as ''X,'' ''Y,'' and ''Z,'' war fever swept the country. Throughout the early months of 1798 there followed in quick succession the measures that permitted the United States to conduct what, in all but name, was open war with France: new funds were appropriated for the seemingly endless task of outfitting the three frigates that had been launched the previous year; work was resumed on the three that had been left unfinished since the end of the Algerian crisis; and the president was empowered to purchase an additional two dozen ships, to be armed with from eighteen to thirty-two guns. Eight small cutters belonging to the Treasury Department's Revenue Marine—the forerunner of the Coast Guard—were added to the navy, and patriotic citizens in several seaports raised subscriptions for the building and outfitting of warships to be presented to the government. The best of these was the 32-gun frigate *Essex*, which was donated by the residents of Salem, in Essex County, Massachusetts. Logically, a declaration of a state of hostilities should have followed all these measures, but neither the United States nor France observed that formality. Thus, the two-and-a-half-year conflict that ensued is known as the Quasi-War with France.[15]

Mobilization of the navy for a war that was to be fought entirely at sea focused attention on the serious inadequacies in the administration of naval affairs. For some time, criticism of the inefficiency of the War Department— and particularly of its current secretary, James McHenry, a military surgeon who had once served as George Washington's secretary—had been mounting. As one congressional observer noted, cost overruns in ship construction were due to "the want of some regular establishment to overlook the business." McHenry, in effect, agreed and suggested that the administration of the navy be transferred to some other agency. Legislation authorizing the establishment of a Department of the Navy passed the Senate easily, but only got through the House by a 47-to-41 vote. On April 30, 1798, President Adams signed the bill into law.[16]

Adams' first choice for secretary of the navy was George Cabot, a prominent Massachusetts shipowner, but Cabot declined to serve. Benjamin Stoddert, a wealthy merchant and loyal Federalist living in Georgetown, then part of Maryland, was next offered the post, and he accepted it with some misgivings.[17] The appointment was a good one. Stoddert had served in the army during the Revolution and later became secretary to the Continental Board of War, predecessor of the War Department. Thus, he was familiar with the problems of military logistics and of ship design and construction, and he had a smattering of knowledge of other matters connected with the management of a fleet. Charles W. Goldsborough, the Navy Department's chief clerk for almost the entire first half-century of its existence, said Stoddert brought to his position "an inflexible integrity, a discriminating mind, a great capacity for business and the most persevering industry."[18]

To speed up the work of getting the ships to sea, Stoddert decentralized the administration of his department's affairs. While he kept final control in his own hands, he appointed naval agents in all the important ports and made them responsible for obtaining ships, men, and material. Under Stoddert's stewardship, the navy grew to a peak strength of fifty-four vessels, some of them newly built, some converted merchantmen, some gifts from the citizens of various seaports, and some captured from the French. There were about 750 officers and 5,000 or 6,000 men, plus another 1,100 officers and men in the Marine Corps, which had been established in July 1798. There was no great difficulty in recruiting seamen, as there had been in the Revolution, primarily because now few privateers competed for their services. It usually took about a week to man the largest frigates. Able seamen signed on for one year's service and were paid $17 a month.[19]

In his first report to Congress, on December 29, 1798, Stoddert unveiled a far-ranging program for expanding the navy. "The protection of our Coast, the security of our extensive Country from invasion . . . the safety of our important Commerce, and our future peace when the Maritime Nations of Europe war with each other, all seem to demand that our Naval force be augmented," the secretary declared. He recommended the building of a dozen two-decker, 74-gun ships of the line, an equal number of frigates, and from twenty to thirty smaller vessels: "It would not perhaps be hazarding too much to say that had we possessed this force a few years ago, we should not have lost, by depredations on our Trade, four times the sum necessary to have created & maintained it during the whole time the War has existed in Europe." Stoddert also suggested that timber and naval stores be stockpiled for future construction and that navy yards and dry docks be established along the coast. As one analyst has said, the report was "surprisingly complete and comprehensive."[20]

On votes in which Federalists and Republicans split along party lines, Congress approved several laws fleshing out Stoddert's recommendations. Construction of six of the ships of the line was authorized, timber was stockpiled, and two dry docks were approved but not opened. Although he was not authorized to establish navy yards, Stoddert, contending that existing yards were too small for the building of two-deckers, stretched his authority and opened facilities at Portsmouth, New Hampshire; Boston; New York; Philadelphia; Washington; and Norfolk. He laid so strong a foundation for the navy that even though it was reduced in size and effectiveness following the termination of the Quasi-War, it was not completely dismantled.

Blockaded by what Admiral Mahan later described as the "far-distant, storm-beaten ships" of the Royal Navy, the French sent few large warships across the Atlantic. They relied instead upon a handful of frigates and smaller vessels—and a swarm of privateers. Commerce-raiders darted out of the Caribbean and plundered American shipping almost at will. Stoddert, therefore, concentrated his ships in coastal waters where they escorted merchantmen, beat off privateers, and recaptured vessels that had been taken by the French.[21] French privateer skippers were so brazen that they sailed within sight of the American coast, and the first prize taken by America's new navy was captured just outside Egg Harbor, New Jersey. She was a 12-gun schooner, *La Croyable*, which had taken several American vessels before being captured on July 7, 1798, by the 20-gun sloop of war *Delaware*. The *Delaware* was a converted merchantman commanded by Captain Stephen Decatur, Sr., an old privateersman whose soon-to-be-famous son was then a midshipman in the frigate *United States*. Taken into the navy as the *Retaliation*, the schooner was recaptured four months later by the French, and then again by the Americans.

By the end of 1798 the American navy had become so strong that the French retreated to the Caribbean. Stoddert assigned twenty-one ships, including the *United States, Constitution,* and *Constellation,* to the West Indies with orders "to rid those seas . . . of French commissioned armed vessels as of the pirates which infest them. . . . We have nothing to fear but inactivity." Convinced that concerted action against the enemy by strong squadrons would be more effective than would random patrols by one or two ships, Stoddert organized the American vessels into four squadrons. Varying in size from three to ten ships, the units, which operated from British bases in the Caribbean, were commanded by Captains John Barry, Thomas Truxtun, Stephen Decatur, Sr., and Thomas Tingey.

No man better personified the increasing professionalism and aggressive spirit of the fledging navy than did Thomas Truxtun, the captain of the *Constellation.* Born on Long Island in 1755, he went to sea at the age of twelve. Three years later, he was snatched from the deck of a merchantman and impressed on board a British man-of-war. The young sailor's abilities attracted the attention of his captain, who offered Truxtun the promise of advancement if he would remain in the Royal Navy. Truxtun obtained his release, however, and by the time he was twenty had become a captain in the merchant service. During the Revolution, he commanded several successful privateers and emerged from the war with a respectable fortune, which he invested with excellent results in the newly opened China trade. Truxtun was not only a capable seaman but something of a scholar, too. In 1794, the same year in which he was commissioned a captain in the navy, he published a treatise on navigation and wind currents. This was followed by books on signalling and on naval tactics.

Truxtun was a strict disciplinarian and under his command the *Constellation* was a taut ship. Invited to dine one evening with the captain, Midshipman David Porter made the mistake of complaining about the harsh treatment meted out by John Rodgers, the first lieutenant, and remarked that he was considering resigning from the service.

"Why you young dog!" Truxtun shouted. "If I can help it you shall never leave the navy! Swear at you? Damn it, sir—every time I do that you go a round on the ladder of promotion! As for the first lieutenant's blowing you up every day, why sir, 'tis because he loves you and would not have you grow up a conceited young coxcomb. Go . . . and let us have no more whining."[22]

Cruising alone off the island of Nevis, in the West Indies, about noon on February 9, 1799, the *Constellation* fell in with a large vessel that hoisted American colors as the Yankee frigate sailed up to inspect her. When the stranger failed to respond to either American or British recognition signals, Truxtun was convinced that she was a French man-of-war. As if to confirm his suspicions, she broke out the French tricolor. The rolling of drums beating to quarters resounded throughout the *Constellation* as she cleared for action. Galley fires were extinguished, cabin bulkheads were dismantled to clear the gun deck into one great platform, the midshipmen's quarters were rigged as a casualty station, marines were drawn up on the quarter deck to repel boarders, topmen were sent aloft armed with muskets, and cartridges and round shot were brought up from the magazines. Tubs of water for drinking and extinguishing fires were placed between the guns, and the decks were wetted down and sanded. Finally, there was an ominous rumble like thunder as the loaded guns were run out.

The enemy vessel was *L'Insurgente*, a 40-gun frigate reputed to be the fastest ship in the French navy. Although *L'Insurgente* carried four more guns than the *Constellation*, the weight of her broadside was lighter. As the two vessels maneuvered for position, a sudden squall carried away the French ship's maintopmast.[23]

As soon as the *Constellation's* starboard guns began to bear on the enemy vessel, Truxtun unleashed a broadside into her. The French ship returned the fire with spirit and swerved toward the *Constellation*. "Stand by to board!" the French captain cried to his men. But Truxtun was alert to the danger and his handier ship swept ahead of *L'Insurgente* and across her bow, pouring a murderous fire into her opponent's hull at close range. The battle raged for about an hour-and-a-half, until the French vessel was a battered wreck. The *Constellation* had just crossed her stern to rake her again when the French hauled down their colors. A boarding party reported that *L'Insurgente* "resembled a slaughter house," with seventy of her crew either dead or wounded. Although the *Constellation* was cut up aloft, only one of her men was killed and two were wounded. In his account of the action, Truxtun said the French captain had charged that "I have caused a War with France," and added, "If so I am glad of it, for I detest Things being done by Halves."

Just about a year after the capture of *L'Insurgente*, the *Constellation* engaged in another memorable battle.[24] She was sailing off Guadeloupe on February 1, 1800, when a lookout spotted a large ship on the horizon. Truxtun surmised that she was *La Vengeance*, a 54-gun French frigate, which he had been warned was in the area. Although the French vessel's broadside outweighed that of the *Constellation*, the enemy declined to give battle and clapped on all sail. Only after a day-long chase did the *Constellation* draw close to her. Night had fallen, and in the eerie light cast by the dim battle lanterns, the men stood to their guns, as the distance between the two vessels narrowed to little more than a pistol shot.

The French fired without waiting to be hailed and the *Constellation*'s guns, double-shotted at Truxtun's command, immediately replied with a broadside that slammed into her opponent's hull. Orders were passed to the American gun crews to "load and fire as fast as possible, when it could be done with certain effect." For the next five hours, the two ships traded broadsides and both suffered severe damage. The battle was "as close and obstinate an action as was ever fought between two ships of war," said an American officer. Shortly before 1:00 A.M., Truxtun reported, "the Enemy's fire was completely silenced." Believing that *La Vengeance* had struck, he ordered the *Constellation* laid alongside her, only to discover that his own mainmast was "totally unsupported by rigging." Truxtun broke off the action. A desperate attempt was made to rig preventer stays, but it was too late. The mast toppled into the sea, taking with it a midshipman and three topmen.

In the confusion, the shattered French frigate limped off into the darkness. Before arriving at Curaçao, she lost her mainmast and fore- and mizzen-topmasts. An American prisoner on board reported that she had been hit nearly two hundred times, several of the shot ploughing through both sides of her hull. French casualties were twenty-eight men killed and forty wounded; American losses were fourteen killed and twenty-five wounded. In his report, the French captain described the *Constellation* as a two-deck ship of the line—quite a compliment to the fighting qualities of the Yankee frigate and her officers and men.

Before the Quasi-War petered out, several other American naval vessels gave good accounts of themselves, especially the 12-gun schooners *Enterprise* and *Experiment*. In a single cruise in 1800, the *Enterprise* captured seven French armed vessels, including the large 14-gun privateer *Flambeau*. Later that year, she bagged thirteen more enemy vessels and took 300 prisoners. The *Experiment* was almost as lucky, taking the privateers *Deux Amis*, 8 guns, and the *Diane*, 14, as well as recapturing several American merchantmen that had fallen into French hands. The frigate *Boston*, 28, pounded the French corvette *Le Berceau*, 24, into submission in a vigorous five-hour fight on October 13, 1800, in which both vessels were repeatedly forced to draw off for repairs. All together, about eighty French ships, mostly privateers, were captured during the Quasi-War.[25]

In the meantime, negotiations were under way with France for an end to hostilities. Although most leaders of the Federalist party, particularly Alexander Hamilton, wanted an all-out war with France so that New Orleans and Florida might be taken from France's ally, Spain, President Adams courageously put the welfare of the nation above that of his party. Even though he fully realized that peace would bring about the collapse of the Federalists' popularity and probably cost him reelection, he pressed ahead with the negotiations. The arrogant and corrupt Directory, which had provided the excuse for war, had been ousted by Napoleon Bonaparte, who, as first consul, did not want to continue a conflict that could only drive the United States into the arms of Britain. Seven months of negotiation ended when the French gave up their insistence that the Treaty of Alliance of 1778 was still in force and the United States dropped its claim for $20 million in reimbursement for damages inflicted on American commerce. The settlement was highly unpopular in America. As Adams had foreseen, he was defeated by Jefferson in the presidential election of 1800, and the Republicans were swept into control of Congress.[26]

Before the Federalists relinquished control of the government, they took steps to protect the navy from the budgetary ax certain to be swung by the incoming administration. On March 3, 1801, the day before the new president was inaugurated, an act providing for a peacetime naval establishment was approved by Congress. Based upon Secretary Stoddert's suggestions, it authorized the president to dispose of the fleet, but ordered that the frigates be retained: the *United States, Constitution, President, Chesapeake, Philadelphia, Constellation, Congress, New York, Boston, Adams, Essex, John Adams*, and *General Greene*. Six of the ships to be retained would be kept in commission, while the remainder were to be laid up. With the exception of 9 captains, 36 lieutenants, and 150 midshipmen, all officers were dismissed from the service with four months' pay, although Stoddert, following the practice of the Royal Navy, had recommended the formation of a reserve of officers on half-pay. Frigates on active duty were to be allowed only two-thirds of their usual complements. The reductions were drastic, but as Charles Goldsborough noted, "the existence of the [naval] establishment could be preserved by no other means than by reducing it to its lowest possible scale."[27]

Personally a spendthrift but publicly frugal, Jefferson came to power espousing a policy of economy in government and reduction of the national debt. His major ally in this objective was the Swiss-born Secretary of the Treasury, Albert Gallatin. Looking about them for areas in which spending could be pared, their eyes naturally fell upon the navy. During Adams' administration, governmental expenditures had averaged about $11 million a year, $2.5 million of which was earmarked for the navy—a service that Gallatin, as a member of Congress from Pennsylvania, had rigidly opposed on the grounds that it was wasteful and superfluous. Jefferson's attitude toward the navy was more ambiguous. He had advocated a navy to chastise, rather than bribe, the Barbary pirates, and he was an early supporter of the measures that eventually led to the organization of such a service. But by the time of his election as president, he had adopted the anti-navy ideology of most of his supporters. Outlining the principles that he wanted the government to follow, Jefferson said he would rely for defense upon "such a naval force only as may protect our coasts and harbors" and not upon a seagoing fleet "which, by its own expenses and the eternal wars in which it will implicate us, grind us with public burthens, & sink us under them."[28]

So dim were the navy's prospects under the Republicans that the first four men to whom Jefferson offered the post of secretary of the navy refused it. "I believe I shall have to advertise for a Secretary of the Navy," he declared at one point, possibly more in desperation than in jest. The man who finally accepted the appointment was Robert Smith, an admiralty lawyer from Baltimore and member of a family prominent in Republican politics. Henry Adams has described him as "easy and cordial, glad to oblige and fond of power and show, popular in the Navy, yielding in the Cabinet, but as little fitted as Jefferson himself for . . . administering with severe economy an unpopular service."[29]

Reductions in the size of the navy began even before Smith assumed the duties of his office in July 1801. Except for the thirteen frigates that the government was required by law to keep and the schooner *Enterprise*, all the remaining ships were stripped of their gear and sold. Sixteen ships brought in $276,000, an amount that might barely pay for a single frigate. Work ceased on the only 74-gun ship of the line laid down by Stoddert, and timber acquired for the construction of others was placed in storage, where some of it rotted. Naval constructors and agents were dismissed. Jefferson and Gallatin gave serious consideration to closing some of the yards established by the Federalists and to consolidating most shore operations at the Washington Navy Yard. Indulging his passion for tinkering, the president designed a huge, covered, dry dock for storage of the seven frigates that were to be laid up. Referring to the corruption said to prevail in the dockyards, he said that there "they would be under the immediate eye of the department, and would require but one set of plunderers to take care of them."[30]

Once again, however, the navy was saved by the insolence of the Barbary corsairs, whose activities had led to its organization in the first place. In September 1800, the frigate *George Washington*, 24, arrived at Algiers with an installment of tribute sent by the Adams administration. The dey, who had angered his nominal sovereign, the Ottoman sultan, ordered Captain William Bainbridge, the commanding officer, to carry an ambassador and a sizeable tribute to Constantinople. When Bainbridge refused, he was told: "You pay me tribute, by which you become my slaves. I have a right to order you as I may think proper." With Algerian guns trained on his ship, the chagrined Bainbridge had no choice but to hoist Algerian colors and carry out this distasteful mission.[31]

News of the incident preceded the return of the *Washington* to America and created a popular demand that Algiers be punished for its insult to the American flag. At about the same time, the American consuls at Tripoli and Tunis reported that these states were showing signs of increasing belligerence. Yusuf Karamanli, the pasha of Tripoli, was jealous because the United States was paying higher tribute to Algiers than to him, while the bey of Tunis was restive because no bribes had come his way in three years. On May 10, 1801, the Tripolitans declared war on the United States in their own picturesque fashion—by chopping down the flagstaff in front of the American consulate.

Jefferson, a long-time advocate of force in dealing with the Barbary pirates, decided early in May 1801 to send a squadron to the Mediterranean to protect American commerce. Bribing the corsairs was "money thrown away," he declared. Although the Tripolitan declaration of war still lay in the offing, a squadron consisting of the frigates *President, Philadelphia*, and *Essex* and the schooner *Enterprise* was readied for sea, and Thomas Truxtun was offered its command. Truxtun, whose head may have been turned by the adulation he had received during the Quasi-War, would not accept the appointment unless offensive action were contemplated. Informed that the squadron would see action only if war had been declared by the Tripolitans, he declined the appointment.

It was offered instead to Richard Dale, who had been John Paul Jones' first lieutenant in the *Bonhomme Richard*.

Dale sailed on June 1, 1801, flying his broad pennant in the *President*, with James Barron as his flag captain. He was directed to proceed first to Gibraltar to ascertain the state of affairs in the Mediterranean. If all were tranquil, he was to show the flag and return home at the end of the year, when the enlistments of most of the crews would be up. But if any of the Barbary powers had declared war on the United States, he was to "protect our commerce and chastise their insolence—by sinking, burning or destroying their ships & Vessels wherever you shall find them."[32] Arriving at Gibraltar a month later, Dale learned of the Tripolitan declaration of war against the United States and discovered two Tripolitan vessels awaiting the opportunity to slip out into the Atlantic, where they would be able to inflict severe losses on American commerce. He left the *Philadelphia* to keep a watchful eye on the corsairs and pressed on into the Mediterranean.

Although the sudden appearance of Dale's ships evoked expressions of devoted friendship from Algiers and Tunis, the ruler of Tripoli remained undisturbed behind his stout fortifications that had been built by generations of Christian prisoners. A sporadic blockade of Tripoli was established, but little was accomplished by Dale's squadron except for the capture, after a spirited three-hour battle, of a 14-gun Tripolitan cruiser by the lucky little *Enterprise*, commanded by Lieutenant Andrew Sterrett. With the enlistments of his crews running out, Dale headed for home near the end of the year but was delayed when a pilot ran his flagship aground and seriously damaged her. It was an ignominious ending to the first appearance of an American naval squadron in the Mediterranean.

Drawn into a conflict with the Barbary pirates, Jefferson abandoned his efforts to liquidate the navy and, early in 1802, dispatched a slightly more powerful squadron to the Mediterranean. Once again, command was offered to Truxtun who requested that a captain be appointed to handle the *Chesapeake*, which was to be his flagship, while he dealt with the squadron. He pointed out that Dale had received such assistance, and inasmuch as the squadron offered him contained many young and inexperienced officers, he would be even more in need of help. When the Navy Department turned down his request on the grounds that no captain could be spared because of the scarcity of officers, Truxtun declined the command. He was succeeded by Captain Richard V. Morris—an unhappy choice because Morris lacked the professional ability required of a fleet commander.[33]

Besides the *Chesapeake*, the flotilla that Morris took to the Mediterranean consisted of the frigates *Constellation, Adams, New York*, and *John Adams* and the schooner *Enterprise*. The crews of these ships had signed on for two years, double the customary enlistment, which meant they could remain on station for a longer period of time. Everyone was convinced that the Tripolitans would collapse under the first determined assault launched by the squadron. These expectations, however, failed to take into account the prevailing strategic and tactical realities.

Tripoli was far less vulnerable to attack than it appeared. The city was protected by walls that bristled with cannon and were impervious to most of the guns mounted by the American squadron. Further, the attackers had no small, shallow-draft craft that could operate among the reefs off the African coast to make their blockade effective. Since the theater of operations was more than 3,000 miles from home, the squadron depended upon the good will of various European powers for repair facilities and supplies, especially when merchant vessels sent out from the United States to replenish its provisions refused to venture past Gibraltar for fear of being captured by Barbary pirates. Moreover, the officers of the squadron were contentious and at least one fatal duel was fought. Faced with these difficulties, only a commodore with imagination and independent judgment stood a chance of succeeding—and these were qualities that Morris sadly lacked.

Wearying of the squadron's inaction, which was proving an embarrassment for his administration, in June 1803 Jefferson ordered Morris relieved. "From his inactivity hitherto I have no expectation that anything will be done against Tripoli by the frigates in the Mediterranean under his command," declared the exasperated president. Upon his return, Morris faced a court of inquiry, which found that he "did not conduct himself, in his command of the Mediterranean squadron, with the diligence or activity necessary to execute the important duties of his station. . . ." Dismissal from the navy followed—harsh treatment for a man who, as Goldsborough states, "might have acquitted himself well in the command of a single ship, under the orders of a superior, but . . . was not competent to the command of a squadron."[34]

Casting about for a replacement, the eye of Robert Smith, the secretary of the navy, fortunately fell upon Edward Preble.[35] Born in Maine, Preble served as a youth in a privateer during the Revolution and later became a midshipman in the Massachusetts State Navy. After the war, he sailed for fifteen years in various merchantmen before joining the newly organized navy in 1798 as a lieutenant. When the Quasi-War broke out, Preble was promoted to captain and given command of the *Essex*. Unlike most naval officers, he did not serve in the Caribbean during that conflict but was ordered to escort Yankee trading vessels around the Cape of Good Hope to the East Indies and back. During this long and lonely voyage, he contracted a sickness that prevented him from taking an active role in the opening stages of the war with the Barbary corsairs, and from which he never fully recovered.

Preble had considerable difficulty getting to sea with his new command. For one thing, the *Constitution*, which was assigned as his flagship, had been laid up since the end of the war with France and required extensive repair. For another, Albert Gallatin's economy measures made it difficult to recruit crews for the squadron because the monthly pay of able seamen had been slashed to $10. In order to obtain seamen, Preble offered volunteers four months' pay in advance instead of the usual two. International events also conspired against him. In 1802, after nearly a decade of war, France and Britain had negotiated the Peace of Amiens. This truce already showed signs of breaking down, and with the resumption of war seemingly imminent, the demand for America's produce soared—as did the wages of merchant seamen, making it even more difficult to recruit men for the navy. To man his ships, Preble fell back on foreign seamen trying to avoid impressment by roving British cruisers. Speaking of the first 165 men recruited for his flagship, the commodore remarked: "I do not believe that I have twenty native Americans aboard." Similar conditions prevailed throughout the squadron, about three-quarters of the *Philadelphia*'s crew being listed as British subjects.[36]

Putting to sea as each completed fitting out, rather than as a unit, the last of Preble's ships did not reach Gibraltar until November 1803. His squadron had only two frigates, but it included several small ships capable of operating close inshore—the 16-gun brigs *Argus* and *Siren* and the 12-gun schooners *Vixen* and *Nautilus*. At the same time as it authorized procurement of these ships, Congress approved the building of fifteen gunboats intended for harbor defense and gave Preble permission to purchase similar craft in the Mediterranean.

During the passage across the Atlantic, the commodore and his officers had the first opportunity to examine each other closely—and neither side liked what it saw. Preble was given to sudden gusts of temper, was often sick, and soon showed himself a strict disciplinarian. Sectional prejudices may also have been a factor in his unpopularity: he was a New Englander and most of his officers were from the middle and southern states. Youthful, high-spirited, and dreaming of glory, they contrasted markedly with their commander. The commodore, then forty-two years old, noted unhappily that most of his officers were half his age. "They have given me nothing but a pack of boys!" he exploded. Within a short time, however, Preble and his "boys" revised their opinions of each other.

Sailing off the coast of Spain in the failing light of evening on September 10, 1803, Preble sighted a strange vessel that he took to be a ship-of-war. He ordered the *Constitution*'s crew to quarters and her guns run out. After hailing the stranger several times and receiving unsatisfactory answers, Preble, operating as always on a short fuse, seized a speaking trumpet and shouted: "I am now going to hail you for the last time. If a proper answer is not returned, I will fire a shot into you!"

"If you fire a shot, I will return a broadside!" replied the stranger.

"What ship is that?" demanded Preble.

"This is His Britannic Majesty's ship *Donegal*, 84 guns, Sir Richard Strachan, an English commodore. Send a boat on board!"

Leaping atop the hammock nettings and steadying himself against the shrouds, Preble cried: "This is the United States ship *Constitution*, 44 guns, Edward Preble, an American commodore, who will be damned before he sends his boat on board of any vessel! Blow [on] your matches, boys!"

The creak of yards and the squeak of ropes in their blocks sounded louder than usual as the ships ran side by side. After a few minutes, the sound of an approaching boat was heard. A British lieutenant came on board to explain apologetically that he was not from the *Donegal*, a ship of the line, but only from the *Maidstone*, a 32-gun frigate. His captain had delayed answering Preble's challenge because he was certain that the larger ship was an enemy vessel and he needed time to get his crew to quarters. The incident delighted Preble's "boys" and helped to create a kind of bond between them and their commander.[37]

Arriving at Gibraltar a few days after the encounter with the *Maidstone*, Preble discovered that Morocco had evidently decided to disregard the treaty made with the United States in 1786 and was seizing Yankee trading vessels. The commodore took steps to put an end to it. He sent the *Philadelphia* and *Vixen* to blockade Tripoli, while he took the *Constitution*, two frigates diverted from the squadron that was returning home, and several smaller vessels across to Tangier. Overwhelmed by this show of power, the emperor of Morocco immediately pledged eternal peace with the United States.

This excellent beginning to Preble's tour of command was suddenly clouded by the sickening news that the *Philadelphia* had run aground off Tripoli and been captured by the enemy. Pursuing a small Tripolitan vessel inshore on October 31, 1803, the frigate had struck an uncharted reef. The unlucky William Bainbridge, her captain, tried to push her over the shoal by crowding on sail but only succeeded in making her fast. In attempts to lighten her, he ordered her fresh water pumped out, her guns thrown overboard except for a few aft, and, finally, her foremast cut away. It was all to no avail. With Tripolitan gunboats circling about and a pronounced list preventing him from bringing the *Philadelphia*'s guns to bear, Bainbridge destroyed his signal books, ordered holes chopped in the frigate's bottom, and surrendered.

Unfortunately, the work of scuttling the vessel was bungled. Two days after her capture a storm blew up, and the Tripolitans were able to free her from the reef. They towed her into the harbor for refitting under the guns of the citadel and in full view of her 307 former crewmen, who were to remain captive for nineteen months. For the most part, the officers were well treated by the pasha, who even allowed Bainbridge and David Porter, the frigate's first lieutenant, to conduct a school where the junior officers were taught navigation, tactics, and languages. But the men, regarded by the Tripolitans as slaves, were put to work on the fortifications and were beaten and mistreated. Even so, only five men defected to the enemy.[38]

The capture of the *Philadelphia* struck a severe blow at Preble's plans for offensive action. His force of frigates, already inadequate to the task at hand, had been halved and the enemy had added a powerful ship to their fleet. The prisoners also gave the Tripolitans an important bargaining chip in future negotiations. Worst of all, the blow to the prestige of the United States might cause the other Barbary states to declare war. Preble said nothing critical of Bainbridge in public, although he was less reserved in private. "Would to God that the officers and crew of the *Philadelphia* had, one and all, determined to prefer death to slavery!" he wrote the secretary of the navy. "It is possible such a determination might save them from either."[39]

The commodore's dilemma was resolved by Stephen Decatur, Jr. Packing a recently captured ketch that had been renamed the *Intrepid* with about seventy volunteers and a load of combustibles, the youthful lieutenant sailed her into the harbor of Tripoli on the night of February 16, 1804. The *Intrepid* crept up to the anchored frigate, which had her guns run out in readiness for a surprise attack. The ketch's Sicilian pilot, Salvatore Catalano, hailed the *Philadelphia* in Arabic and asked permission to tie up to her for the night because his vessel had lost her anchors. The request was granted, but as lines were being passed, someone cried out "Americanos! Americanos!"

"In a moment we were near enough, and the order 'Board!' was given," reported Midshipman Charles Morris. "With this cry our men were soon on the decks of the frigate." Wielding cutlasses and pikes and with Decatur in the lead, the Americans swarmed over the deck. No firearms were used, but Decatur estimated that about twenty Tripolitans were killed. The rest escaped in boats or jumped overboard. Within twenty minutes, the Americans were back in the *Intrepid* and flames were licking at the mastheads of the *Philadelphia*. The heat soon set off the ship's loaded guns, and her shot, as well as that of the shore batteries, splashed about the *Intrepid* as she made her escape. Only one American was wounded. When news of the exploit reached the United States, there was a tremendous outpouring of popular support for the navy, and Decatur was hailed as a hero. Admiral Lord Nelson, commanding a fleet blockading Toulon, called the exploit "the most bold and daring act of the age." The twenty-five-year-old Decatur was promoted to captain, the youngest man ever to hold that rank in the U. S. Navy, and Congress awarded the *Intrepid*'s crew two months' extra pay.[40]

Even though the specter of the *Philadelphia* ceased to haunt Preble, he still faced the problem of dealing with Tripoli. With the few ships under his command, it was obvious he could not mount an effective blockade, so the commodore decided to batter the Tripolitans into making peace. Gunboats were required to carry out this task and he obtained some from the Kingdom of the Two Sicilies. Six shallow-draft gunboats, each mounting a single 24-pounder, and two bomb ketches, each carrying a powerful 13-inch mortar, were towed across the Mediterranean to join the American squadron off Tripoli in the summer of 1804. Before unleashing his attack, Preble attempted to secure the release of the *Phil-*

adelphia's crew by peaceful means, but the pasha flatly rejected the offer. The commodore concluded that he would have to "endeavor to beat & distress his serene highness" into a more reasonable attitude.[41]

The prospects for achieving that end were not bright. In addition to the two mortars, the squadron carried only 42 guns that were capable of breaching the Tripolitan fortifications, while against it were ranged the 115 guns of the shore batteries and a flotilla of armed vessels and gunboats. Preble's bombardment began on the afternoon of August 3, 1804, and was promptly answered by brisk fire from both ashore and afloat. Decatur, in command of a division of gunboats, laid his craft alongside one of the Tripolitan vessels and led his men in boarding her. Slashing about with cutlasses, axes, and pikes, the Americans drove the enemy from the deck.

As Decatur was towing his prize out of the harbor, he learned that his younger brother, James, who was in charge of another gunboat, had been killed as a result of Tripolitan treachery. The younger Decatur's boat had engaged a more powerful opponent and he had been mortally wounded by a shot fired after the enemy was thought to have surrendered. Sighting the fleeing Tripolitan gunboat, Stephen Decatur boarded her and killed her captain in a hand-to-hand fight.[42] A third gunboat was captured at sword's point by Lieutenant John Trippe. Followed by ten men, he leaped on board the vessel only to see his own boat drift away before reinforcements could join him. Facing thirty-six Tripolitans, he was, as Preble reported, "compelled to conquer or perish." Trippe and his little band killed fourteen and captured twenty-two of the enemy.

Four days later, on August 7, a second attack was launched against Tripoli. Just as it was ending, the *John Adams* arrived from home with orders relieving Preble of command of the Mediterranean squadron. The loss of the *Philadelphia* had no doubt raised questions about Preble's competence, and President Jefferson had decided to dispatch "a force which would be able, beyond the possibility of a doubt, to coerce the enemy to a peace upon terms compatible with our honor and our interest." Five frigates, three brigs, and three schooners, as well as smaller vessels, were gathered, and Captain Samuel Barron was appointed commodore. Before the squadron sailed, however, news was received of the prompt action taken by Preble to deny the captured frigate to the Tripolitans, but it was too late to countermand Barron's orders. The secretary of the navy could only try to placate Preble by assuring him that his replacement by Barron reflected no dissatisfaction with his conduct of the squadron's operations. The official explanation was that there were not enough captains junior to Preble available for the commands in the reinforcing squadron—hence the need to relieve Preble with the senior Barron.[43]

"I cannot but regret that our naval establishment is so limited as to deprive me of the means and glory of completely subduing the haughty tyrant of Tripoli," declared Preble somewhat bitterly, upon learning that he was to be replaced. While awaiting Barron, he bombarded Tripoli three more times with the hope of forcing the pasha into making peace, but the attacks were in vain. Everything else having failed, the commodore decided to transform the *Intrepid* into a floating bomb and send her into the harbor to destroy the Tripolitan flotilla and damage the city's defenses. About 100 barrels of powder and 150 mortar shells were loaded into the ketch, which was placed under the command of Lieutenant Richard Somers and manned by a dozen volunteers. Once in position, they were to light the fuses and make their escape in a small boat.

On the night of September 4, 1804, the *Intrepid* disappeared into the darkness. Nothing more was heard from her until shortly before 10:00 P.M., when the harbor was suddenly rocked by a tremendous explosion that momentarily transformed night into day. Throughout the rest of the night the squadron nervously awaited some sign of Somers and his crew, but nothing was heard of them. It was presumed that either the vessel had exploded prematurely by accident or Somers had blown her up with all hands to prevent her capture. Six days later, Samuel Barron arrived to assume his new command.[44]

Barron's squadron consisted of the frigates *President, Constitution, Congress, Constellation*, and *Essex*, and several smaller vessels, but it accomplished little. Barron was stricken with a near-fatal liver ailment and spent most of his tour of duty ashore in Sicily, while the squadron maintained a desultory blockade of Tripoli. The focus of action had, in the meantime, switched to the land. William Eaton, the swashbuckling former American consul at Tunis, had persuaded Jefferson to support a bold scheme for replacing Yusuf Karamanli Pasha with his older brother, Hamet, who had been ousted from the throne a few years before. Early in 1805, Eaton led Hamet and an army of some 400 adventurers, including Marine Lieutenant Presley N. O'Bannon, a sergeant, and six marine privates from the *Argus*, across nearly 600 miles of Libyan desert to attack Derna, a port second only to Tripoli itself. Supported by the guns of three of Barron's ships, the *Argus, Nautilus*, and *Hornet*, Eaton's army captured the town on April 27, 1805, and held it against several counterattacks.[45]

Before further operations could commence, a peace treaty was negotiated with Tripoli by Tobias Lear, who had been dispatched to the Mediterranean by Jefferson for that purpose. Faced with the twin threats of Eaton's army and Barron's ships, the pasha had dropped his demand for the payment of American tribute and accepted $60,000—about half what he had previously demanded—as a ransom for the crew of the *Philadelphia*. Lear's peace at a price received a mixed reception in the United States. Critics charged that the treaty was ill timed because resumption of the naval bombardment, combined with an attack by Eaton's force, would have brought the war to an end without the payment of ransom. Others argued that this was the best treaty ever extracted from the Tripolitans, and as long as the *Philadelphia*'s crew remained in enemy hands, no better one could have been obtained without endangering their lives.[46]

One by one, the vessels kept in the Mediterranean to protect American commerce were withdrawn until only a skeleton force remained. The Barbary corsairs were more aware of American sea power than they had been, but they were not completely humbled until 1815. Nevertheless, the seven years of maritime struggle—first with France and then with the Barbary States—had positive results. They led to the establishment of the navy as a permanent force with its own traditions and standards of professionalism. The young officers who had learned their trade under Truxtun and Preble provided the navy and the nation with leadership that was to prove invaluable in trying years to come.

3

"A HANDFUL OF FIR-BUILT FRIGATES"

A crash as when some swollen cloud
Cracks o'er the tangled trees!
With side to side, and spar to spar,
Whose smoking decks are these?
I know St. George's blood-red cross,
Thou mistress of the seas,
But what is she whose streaming bars
Roll out before the breeze?

Ah, well her iron ribs are knit,
Whose thunders strive to quell
The bellowing throats, the blazing lips,
That pealed the Armada's knell!
The mist was cleared,—a wreath of stars
Rose o'er the crimsoned swell,
And, wavering from its haughty peak,
The cross of England fell!
　　　　　　　　　—Oliver Wendell Holmes

Outward-bound for the Mediterranean with the broad pennant of Commodore James Barron snapping at her masthead, the frigate *Chesapeake* slipped past Cape Henry, at the mouth of the Chesapeake Bay, on the morning of June 22, 1807, and headed for the open sea. Signal flags fluttered from a cluster of British men-of-war that lay off in the distance as she passed. The 50-gun *Leopard* immediately weighed anchor and began shadowing the Yankee frigate. Although the dozen years of more-or-less-peaceful coexistence between Britain and America that had followed the signing of Jay's Treaty was breaking up under the pressures of global war, Barron saw nothing suspicious in the movements of the British vessels.

At thirty-nine years of age, the commodore, younger brother of Samuel Barron, was regarded as an able officer. Only a year after being commissioned a lieutenant in 1798, he had been promoted to captain and was credited with having worked out the signal system used by the navy.[1] Now, he had been given command of what was left of the American force in the Mediterranean. As Barron glanced about the deck of his flagship, he must have been grateful that a long voyage lay ahead because it would provide time to whip his vessel and crew into shape. The *Chesapeake* was a shambles of unstowed gear and supplies. Some of her forty cannon were not properly mounted, oversize sponges and wads had been issued, and most of the crew were green hands who did not know where their battle stations were.

Shortly after 3:00 P.M., when the *Chesapeake* was about ten miles south of Cape Henry Light, the *Leopard* bore down with a request to send dispatches aboard.[2] Such a procedure was not unusual because, in this period, British and American warships often carried dispatches to foreign stations for each other. Upon being ushered into Barron's cabin, a British lieutenant gave the commodore two communications. One was a copy of an order from Vice Admiral George Cranfield Berkeley, commander of the North American Station, requiring that captains of all British ships meeting the *Chesapeake* search her for deserters from the Royal Navy. The other, from the *Leopard*'s captain, expressed the hope that the matter could be "adjusted" without disturbing "the harmony subsisting between the two countries."

Surprised, but mindful of his own navy's standing instruction not to allow such a search, Barron flatly refused. As the lieutenant was being rowed back to his ship, Barron noted that the *Leopard*'s gunports had been triced up and her guns run out. He immediately ordered the *Chesapeake*'s captain, Master Commandant Charles Gordon, to clear for action and, in an attempt at secrecy, to omit the customary drumbeat. Unfortunately, through some mistake, the drummer sounded his urgent beat long enough for it to be heard on the British vessel, a cable's length away. A shot was fired across the *Chesapeake*'s bow, and when this was disregarded, three broadsides were poured into the defenseless vessel. As British shot smashed into her and tore her sails and rigging to tatters, some men ran below and others huddled at the guns, cursing the fact that they had no matches to fire them.

Throughout the carnage, the anguished Barron tried to get his ship into action. "For God's sake, gentlemen," he cried to his officers, "will nobody do their duty?" Finally, after about fifteen minutes of pounding, in which the *Chesapeake* did not fire a single shot and he was wounded, the commodore ordered her colors struck, but not before imploring his crew "to fire one gun for the honor of the flag!" Plucking a hot coal from the galley, an officer juggled it in his bare hand and touched off a gun just as the Stars and Stripes was hauled down. Three Americans had been killed and eighteen were wounded.

A boarding party from the *Leopard* rounded up the *Chesapeake*'s crew and arrested three Americans—two of them free blacks—identified as deserters from one of the British ships lying off the Virginia coast. A British deserter who had enlisted in the U.S. Navy under a false name was discovered cowering below decks. The shattered *Chesapeake* was then left to limp homeward with her tidings of humiliation and defeat. The British deserter was hanged from the yardarm of his ship, and the Americans were each sentenced to 500 lashes. That sentence, which meant death, was not carried out; and, after four years of diplomatic protestation during which time one of the three died, the two surviving seamen were returned to the *Chesapeake*. Barron was made the scapegoat of the affair. Tried on several charges by a court-martial in which two of his judges, John Rodgers and Stephen Decatur, were admittedly hostile owing to private conflicts, he was found guilty of "neglecting on the probability of an engagement to clear his ship for action," and was suspended from the navy for five years without pay.

An unprecedented wave of anger swept the United States in the wake of this unprovoked attack on an American man-of-war. British officers ashore fled to the safety of their ships; infuriated mobs destroyed water casks belonging to British men-of-war; the governor of Virginia called out the militia to repel a British invasion. From all sections of the country came demands for war with Britain to avenge the insult to American honor and neutrality. "Never since the battle of Lexington have I seen this country in such a state of exasperation as at present," observed President Jefferson, "and even that did not produce such unanimity."[3]

Tension between Britain and the United States had been mounting since the renewal of hostilities between Britain and France in 1803. British traders had jealously watched the growth of Yankee commerce as it more than doubled from 1795 to 1806 to $60 million annually.[4] The British were further angered by the realization that while they were engaged in a life-and-death struggle with Napoleon, the Americans were getting rich by supplying their enemy. Nelson's smashing victory over the combined fleets of France and Spain off Trafalgar on October 21, 1805, made Britain secure at last from the threat of invasion, but Napoleon remained master of Europe. The belligerents now sought victory by cutting off each other's commerce with the rest of the world. The United States, as the only neutral with a significant carrying trade, was trapped between them.

The British issued a series of Orders in Council that established a blockade of European ports under French control. Neutral vessels were prohibited from entering unless they had first stopped at a British port and paid duty on their cargoes. Napoleon responded in kind with the Berlin and Milan decrees, which declared that Britain was also under blockade and warned that any neutral vessel that visited a British port, submitted to search by a British warship, or paid British duties would henceforth be considered British—and subject to capture and confiscation.

Inasmuch as France could not enforce its decrees because its navy had been all but driven from the seas while British cruisers had established a virtual blockade of the American coast, Britain bore the brunt of American anger. Using the right of a belligerent to inspect neutral vessels for the purpose of establishing their identities and the nature of their cargoes, British men-of-war often seized ships merely suspected of irregularities and sent them off for adjudication by the admiralty court at Halifax. In some cases, that was the last an owner saw of his vessel. As Basil Hall, then a midshipman in the *Leander*, a frigate on patrol off New York, recalled:

> Every morning at daybreak during our stay off New York we set about arresting the progress of all vessels we saw, firing off guns to the right and left, to make every ship that was running in heave to, or wait until we had leisure to send a boat on board "to see" in our lingo, "what she was made of." I have frequently known a dozen, and sometimes a couple of dozen ships lying a league or two off the port, losing their fair wind, their tide, and worse than all, their market for many hours, sometimes the whole day, before our search was completed.[5]

Sometimes, the British were none too careful in laying warning shots across the bows of Yankee vessels. On one occasion, reported Hall, "a casual shot from the *Leander* hit an unfortunate ship's main boom; and the broken spar, striking the mate, John Pierce by name, killed him instantly."

Relations between Britain and the United States were further embittered by continued impressment of Americans into the Royal Navy to replace British seamen who had deserted. Nelson estimated that between 1793 and 1801 at least 42,000 men fled the service. The British claimed that only Britons were impressed, but a boarding officer in need of an experienced topman was not likely to inquire too deeply into a man's background. If there were no British seamen to hand, as often as not native-born Americans were pressed into the king's navy. If a man looked like an Englishman and sounded like an Englishman, he was fair game.

Naturalization papers were of little value because Britain did not recognize the right of expatriation. "Once an Englishman, always an Englishman," was the simple doctrine of the quarterdeck. Some seamen carried "protections" identifying them as native Americans, but when they presented them press gangs laughed in their faces. It was claimed such documents could be obtained overnight for a dollar or so. If a man resisted, he would be knocked unconscious and dragged on board a man-of-war, where death or the end of hostilities was the only release. Up to 10,000 American sailors may have been forced into this type of slavery between 1799 and 1812.[6]

* * *

To placate an outraged citizenry, Jefferson ordered all British vessels to leave American waters and summoned Congress into special session. But he had no intention of acceding to the popular demand for war. He sought to capitalize on British errors not only by obtaining reparations, but also by wringing long-sought concessions from the British regarding the rights of neutrals and an end to impressment of Americans. "They have touched a chord which vibrates in every heart," Jefferson told James Monroe, his envoy to London. "Now . . . is the time to settle the old and the new."

It was just as well that Jefferson meant to avoid war with Britain, because the nation was completely unprepared. Most of the navy had been laid up after the winding down of hostilities in the Mediterranean, and only two frigates, the *Constitution* and the unlucky *Chesapeake*, were in service. The rest were in varying states of disrepair. The bulk of the nation's active naval strength consisted of some sixty small gunboats stationed along the coast.[7] Ranging in size from about 50 feet to 70 feet in length, propelled by oars and sails, and armed with one or two guns, these craft epitomized the Jeffersonian ideal of a purely defensive navy. They were cheap to build and operate and could not become "an excitement to engage in offensive maritime war." Eventually, nearly 200 of these craft were built, and almost every river and harbor from Maine to Louisiana had its squadron. Although gunboats were not generally regarded as seagoing vessels, nine of them, with their guns stowed, set sail to serve under Samuel Barron in the Mediterranean. One disappeared with all hands and the others, like most of Barron's squadron, saw little action.[8]

But for all its appeal to logic and economy, Jefferson's gunboat policy was a failure. Gunboats could not convoy merchant shipping on the high seas, could not prevent a blockade from being imposed on the coast of the United States, and could not ward off an invasion. They drained the treasury of some $1.85 million that could have been used for building frigates, and even worse, critics charged, they were "subversive to good morals, discipline and subordination" by confining officers and men to harbor duty. In almost all respects, the gunboat policy ignored the hard-bought naval lessons of the Revolution. As Admiral Mahan later pointed out, a "true defense consists in imposing upon the enemy a wholesome fear of yourself."[9]

The British eventually provided reparations for the attack on the *Chesapeake*—not even they claimed the right to search the men-of-war of another nation in time of peace—but Jefferson's demands for an end to impressment and harassment of American trade were ignored. Economic coercion was tried next; Congress declared an embargo on overseas trade with the belligerents, hoping to bring them to a more reasonable attitude, but the results of Jefferson's alternative to war were not what he had anticipated. Commerce stagnated, vessels rotted at their piers, jobless sailors thronged the streets, and cargo piled high on the wharves. Widespread evasion was resorted to and smuggling became big business, especially along the Canadian border. Exasperated New England merchants and shipowners likened the embargo to "cutting one's throat to cure the nosebleed."[10]

After a year of attempted economic coercion, Jefferson and Albert Gallatin were forced to recognize the bankruptcy of their policy. Gallatin reported that revenues from customs duties had shrunk from $16 million to $8 million a year—a disaster equal to war, as far as that thrifty gentleman was concerned. On March 1, 1809, three days before James Madison was inaugurated as president, Congress repealed the embargo and replaced it with the Non-Intercourse Act. Trade was restored with all nations except Britain and France, and Madison was empowered to reopen it with either of those powers if they agreed to cease harassing American commerce. Non-intercourse proved as complete a failure as the embargo, however. Both Britain and France toyed with the United States, now one and then the other raising false hopes that the galling restrictions on Yankee trade would be removed. Impressment also continued to be an irritant, as the Royal Navy persisted in stopping American ships and taking off crew members almost within sight of land.

Matters reached the flash point in April 1811, when the British frigate *Guerrière*, 38, halted an American merchantman off New York and impressed a seaman who claimed to be a native of Maine. John Rodgers was sent to sea in the 44-gun *President* to protect American shipping. On the evening of May 16, off the Chesapeake Capes, just as darkness was falling, the *President* fell in with a strange ship that refused to identify herself. Later, the question of who fired first was hotly debated, but be that as it may, in the ensuing engagement the *President* poured broadside into her adversary. The stranger's guns were quickly silenced and she drifted off into the night. When dawn came, Rodgers sighted her lying a short distance away in great distress. The vessel, the British sloop of war *Little Belt*, 18, limped off to Halifax with thirty-two of her crew either dead or wounded. Rodgers was hailed as a hero for having avenged the *Chesapeake*.[11]

New England, which had suffered most from the depredations of the Royal Navy, stoutly resisted the drift toward war. In spite of all the harassment of their seaborne commerce, the Yankees were making money. If one cargo in three reached its destination safely, they could still show a profit—and that was of more concern than idle talk of preserving the national honor. Paradoxically, the loudest demands for a war to protect sailors' rights came from the landlocked West. Led by a group of hot-blooded young congressmen known as "war hawks," the westerners blamed British trade restrictions for a depression in the South and West and held the British responsible for a series of Indian uprisings that set the frontier ablaze. They saw war as a golden opportunity to wrest Canada from Britain and Florida from Spain. With the cry of "On to Canada!" on their lips, they predicted an easy victory because most of Britain's naval and military strength would be engaged in the struggle with France on the other side of the Atlantic.

Under the inexorable pressure of the West, the nation was borne along to war. On June 1, 1812, Madison sent a message to Congress asking for a declaration of war against Britain. Impressment, interference with neutral trade, and British intrigues with the Indians were cited as the causes of the conflict. War was declared on June 18—but only on a 79-to-49 vote in the House and by the closer margin of 19-to-13 in the Senate. New England and the Middle Atlantic states were strongly opposed to the war, even though it had been declared supposedly to protect the maritime commerce on which they depended for their livelihoods, while the agrarian western and southern states were wholeheartedly for it. A Boston newspaper noted bitterly that "we . . . whose ships were the nursery of Sailors, are insulted with the hypocrisy of a devotedness to Sailors' rights . . . by those whose country furnishes no navigation beyond the size of a ferryboat or an Indian canoe." Ironically, Britain had five days before suspended the obnoxious Orders in Council, which were alleged to be a major cause of the conflict.[12]

"An infant Hercules, destined by the presage of early prowess to extirpate the race of pirates and free-booters." So went the toast to the U.S. Navy at a Fourth of July dinner in Washington attended by the president and most of the cabinet shortly after the declaration of war. Old John Adams took a different view. Writing to his grandson, he said: "Our Navy is so lilliputian that . . . Gulliver might bury it in the deep by making water on it."[13] Of the two appraisals, that of the former president was closer to reality.

The American navy consisted of sixteen ships, seven of them frigates. Many were in need of extensive repair and all were shorthanded. The Washington Navy Yard, which was poorly located, was the only functioning base, and stocks of timber, naval stores, and munitions were depleted. Only seven months before the outbreak of war, Congress had balked at a plan to build a dozen 74s and twenty frigates, most westerners, who were vociferously demanding war, having voted against the proposal. The prospects of the navy had fallen so low since the Tripolitan war that some officers—William Bainbridge, for one—thought about taking leave and joining the merchant service.

Britain, on the other hand, had more than 600 men-of-war, among them some 250 ships of the line and frigates. In fact, it was said, the Royal Navy had more fighting ships than the Americans had guns. Most of this enormous fleet was in European waters serving as "the knife at the throat of Napoleon," in the words of Theodore Roosevelt, but it was thought that no more than a few two-deckers and a handful of frigates would be needed to deal with the upstart Yankees. At the outbreak of war, the squadron on the North American Station consisted of only the *Africa*, 64, seven frigates, and some smaller vessels, but 100 more ships were within easy call, off Newfoundland and in the West Indies.[14]

Many American leaders were convinced that it would be useless to try to oppose such force. For example, Paul Hamilton, the heavy-drinking politician from South Carolina who had been appointed secretary of the navy by Madison in 1809, thought that the larger ships ought to be laid up in various ports, where they could serve as floating batteries and as receiving ships for crews recruited to man the gunboats. Irving Brant, Madison's most recent biographer, states that it was the president himself who decreed that the navy should be employed at sea.[15] Even so, Hamilton did not make any plans for the use of the navy until a few days before the actual declaration of war. The basic strategy was clear— to protect the nation's maritime frontiers and to disrupt British naval and commercial operations—but how was the meager force available best to be used to accomplish these ends?

Hamilton put this question to his ranking captains. Decatur replied that the "best use of the Navy would be to send single ships out . . . no more than 2 frigates together." Bainbridge supported his position. John Rodgers, however, argued that the navy should operate in squadrons built around heavy frigates, while lighter vessels could harass British commerce in the Caribbean. It should be noted that although they differed in approach, all the officers favored offensive action at sea.[16]

Supporting Rodgers' proposal, the secretary ordered him, on June 22, 1812, to divide the naval force at New York into two squadrons, one under his own command and the other under Decatur. One was to cruise off New York and the other off the Chesapeake Capes for the purpose of protecting the large number of merchant vessels that had rushed off to Europe in anticipation of the declaration of war and were now homeward bound with rich cargoes. An hour after learning of the declaration of hostilities and a day before he received his orders, Rodgers put to sea. Flying his flag in the *President*, 44, and accompanied by the *United States*, 44, and *Congress*, 38, the sloop of war *Hornet* and the brig *Argus*, both of 16 guns, he sailed southeastward in search of a rich convoy from Jamaica, which was reported to be at sea on its way home. Two days out, Rodgers sighted the 36-gun British frigate *Belvidera* and, forgetting about the convoy, gave chase. The *President* fired several ranging shots, one of which struck the *Belvidera* and killed or wounded nine men. It looked as if the enemy frigate would soon be bagged, but one of the *President*'s bow-chasers exploded, wounding sixteen men, including Rodgers, whose leg was broken. In the confusion, the *Belvidera* escaped.

The Yankee squadron pressed on with its search for the convoy, which it sighted and shadowed almost into the mouth of the English Channel, but it did not take a single prize from it. Rodgers returned to port after capturing seven merchantmen off Madeira. He claimed that because his squadron was at sea, the British had been forced to divert a significant force to searching for it. As a result, he contended, the enemy had not been able to establish a blockade of the American coast and most of the returning merchant vessels arrived safely. In the meantime, the *Essex*, 32, under the command of David Porter, carried off a troop-laden British transport from a convoy bound for Quebec, as well as nine other vessels, including the 16-gun sloop of war *Alert*.[17]

When war came, the *Constitution* was lying at Annapolis, taking on a crew and supplies. Captain Isaac Hull, fearing that his ship might be trapped in the Chesapeake, put to sea as soon as he had filled out her complement. Several of his men were free blacks, although Negroes were supposed to be barred from service in the navy. Most of the crew were green hands who signed on for two years and were paid $12 a month. "The crew are as yet unacquainted with a ship of war, as many have but lately joined, and have never been on an armed vessel before. . . ." Hull wrote the secretary of the navy. "We are doing all we can to make them acquainted with their duties, and in a few days we shall have nothing to fear from any single-decked ship."[18]

As the *Constitution* sailed up the coast, life aboard settled down into the daily routine of a ship-of-war at sea. The crew was divided into two watches, one being on duty on deck at all times. The day began at 4:00 A.M. when, as the boatswain's mates piped the shrill call "All Hands!" the watch below tumbled out of their hammocks. They were given twelve minutes to lash their hammocks and carry them on deck, where they were stowed in the nettings along the top of the bulwarks. The men were then mustered and sent to their duties. Laggards were enlivened by knotted rope ends wielded by the boatswain's mates. The lookouts and helmsmen were relieved, the log was heaved, and the speed of the ship recorded. The watch that had been on deck since midnight was allowed to go below.

Rolling up their wide trousers, the men rigged the pumps, got out swabs and buckets, and began to scrub the decks. Twice a week clothes were washed. The deck was dried, brightwork polished, and lines coiled in place. At seven o'clock the men were piped to breakfast, which was usually eaten on a tarpaulin spread between the guns, eight men to a mess. Most mornings were taken up by gunnery drills or in practicing evolutions under sail. There was a constant round of painting and polishing to be done. When the weather was good, the sailmaker, carpenter, and cooper worked on the spar deck. Sailors who were not on duty could chat with their mates, mend their clothes, or sleep, if they could find a bit of unoccupied space between the guns.

At eleven o'clock, the captain, who had breakfasted alone in his cabin, scanned the accounts of the various departments of the ship, and conferred with his first lieutenant, sometimes appeared on deck with the list of men awaiting punishment. Naval regulations provided that no captain could order more than a dozen lashes without a court-martial, but many captains circumvented that prohibition by awarding twelve lashes for each violation contained in a single crime. The amount of flogging on any ship depended almost entirely on her captain. In some vessels, punishment was administered almost daily; in others, it was rare. Hull, for example, rarely resorted to the lash, while Rodgers was considered more harsh. Most floggings were for drunkenness or the myriad crimes covered by the term "neglect of duty."

"All hands witness punishment!" bawled the boatswain's mates, and the master-at-arms, the ship's policeman, brought up the prisoners who were to be punished. The captain and his officers took their places on the quarterdeck; the marines, with loaded muskets, fell in on the poop; and the crew gathered where they could in the waist. Upon being given the order to rig the gratings, the carpenter and his mates laid one of the wooden gratings that covered the hatches flat upon the deck and placed another upright against the bulwarks. The offender, having been ordered to strip to the waist, was tied to the upright grating. Taking the cat-o'-nine-tails from the red baize bag where traditionally it was kept, a boatswain's mate laid the whip on the victim's bare back with all his strength. The impact was enough to knock a man down, were he not supported by the grating. One blow produced a welt, and twelve lashes—the usual punishment —was enough to turn the victim's back into a raw, bloody mess.

Sextants were broken out and the ship's position was fixed at noon. Dinner was piped and it was followed a half-hour later by the day's first issue of grog. Fifers tootled a merry tune; the men went to the tubs, where a mixture of whiskey and water had been prepared. Rum was served until 1806, when whiskey was substituted on the ground that it was healthier. At one o'clock the men returned to their duties, which lasted until four, at which time routine ship's work was secured for the day. With supper a second allowance of grog was served.

Just before sunset, the drummer beat to quarters and the seamen scampered to their battle stations. The guns were cast loose and the officers inspected the ship, keeping an eye out to see if any of the men were drunk. When the guns had been secured, the hammocks were piped down from the nettings and slung into place. The first night watch was set, and the watch below and "idlers" were permitted to crawl into their hammocks. "By ten o'clock, the tread of the officers of the watch, is the only sound heard," recalled one old salt, "except . . . at every half hour, the striking of the ship's time, answered by sentries above with 'all's—well,' 'all's—well.' "[19]

The *Constitution* was patrolling off the Jersey coast on July 17, 1812, when she was sighted by four British frigates, which had just snapped up the 14-gun brig *Nautilus*. They immediately gave chase to the Yankee man-of-war. A towering cloud of canvas billowed on the *Constitution's* tall masts, marking the beginning of one of the most exciting chases in the age of fighting sail. The winds were so light that both sides were forced to bend every effort to coax a few more knots from their vessels. Each captain wetted down his sails in the hope of catching a breeze. They also resorted to a backbreaking task called kedging. Boats were put into the water to carry anchors ahead of the ship and drop them. Men hove in the cables and picked up the anchors, which were again carried forward to repeat the process. After three days of this, Hull took advantage of a sudden squall, and the *Constitution* made her getaway. She ran in to Boston, where, despite the unpopularity of "Mr. Madison's war," a warm welcome awaited her.[20]

Putting back to sea, the *Constitution* was off Cape Race, athwart the main lane of transatlantic traffic on the afternoon of August 19, when Captain Hull sighted the *Guerrière*. The British frigate took in sail and waited for the Americans to draw closer. Just a few days before, her captain, James R. Dacres, had sent a challenge to Rodgers in New York daring the *President* "or any other American frigate of equal force" to come out and meet his vessel "for the purpose of having a few minutes tête-à-tête." Although the *Constitution* was a much more powerful ship, mounting thirty 24-pound long guns and twenty-four 32-pound carronades to the *Guerrière*'s thirty 18-pounders, two 12-pounders, and eighteen 32-pound carronades, Dacres unhesitatingly offered battle. For nearly two decades, the Royal Navy had emerged victorious from almost every ship-to-ship encounter, and he had no fear of what *The Times* of London had called "a handful of fir-built frigates under a bit of striped bunting."

For the next three-quarters of an hour the ships maneuvered for position, the *Guerrière* firing her starboard broadside at long range, then wearing or zigzagging downwind and firing her portside guns. Shortly before 6:00 P.M., Hull gave the order to fire. "Now, boys, pour it into them!" he shouted. A line of flame spread along the side of the *Constitution*, as her double-shotted cannon poured death and destruction into her lighter opponent. Within fifteen minutes, the *Guerrière*'s mizzenmast had been shot away, her sides riddled, and her sails and rigging reduced to a tangle of wreckage. "We've made a brig out of her," cried Hull. Drawing ahead of the wallowing British vessel, the *Constitution* raked her with a port and then a starboard broadside. A fluke of the wind caused the *Guerrière*'s bowsprit to catch in the Yankee vessel's mizzen rigging, and for a few moments, the ships clung together. Boarding parties gathered on the decks of both vessels but were dispersed by heavy small-arms fire.

As suddenly as they had come together, the ships drifted apart. The *Guerrière*'s foremast toppled over the side, taking her mainmast with it. The British frigate was now a mastless hulk, nearly rolling the muzzles of her main-deck guns into the sea. Dacres surrendered at about 7:00 P.M., little more than an hour after the engagement had begun. An American boarding party found their prize a shambles, with fifteen of her crew dead and sixty-three wounded. The *Constitution* suffered only fourteen casualties, half of whom were killed. The *Guerrière*, damaged beyond salvaging, was set afire. In his official report, Hull paid special tribute to the courage of his black seamen. "I never had any better fighters than those niggers—they stripped to the waist, & fought like devils, sir . . . utterly insensible to danger & . . . possessed with a determination to outfight white sailors."[21]

The *Constitution* returned to Boston and to a celebration made even more enthusiastic by the fact that her victory had come amid a rising tide of disasters in the war on land. The conquest of Canada, which Jefferson had considered "a mere matter of marching," had gone awry as a result of poor planning and leadership. Fort Dearborn (now Chicago) had been captured by the Indians, who promptly proceeded to massacre the entire garrison. And only a few hours before Hull's arrival, word had been received that his uncle, General William Hull, had surrendered Detroit to the British, after only a token defense. Consequently, the most was made of the occasion for a celebration offered by the defeat of the *Guerrière*. Salutes were fired, fetes were held, and Congress awarded Captain Hull and his crew $50,000 in lieu of prize money. The victory did more than lift American spirits; it also provided popular support for an expansion of the navy. In January 1813, Congress authorized four 74-gun ships of the line and six heavy frigates of 44 guns, as well as several smaller vessels. The ineffectual Hamilton, who was said to have been drunk in public on several occasions and to have been "incapable of working in the second half of the day," was dropped as secretary of the navy. He was replaced by an abler man, William Jones, a Philadelphia merchant with considerable experience at sea.[22]

To the British, the loss of the *Guerrière* came as a profound shock. *The Times* said it "spread a degree of gloom through the town, which it was painful to observe." But there was worse to come. While the *Constitution* owed her victory to superior strength, it was superior gunnery and seamanship that gave victory to the next American vessel to encounter a British man-of-war. The 18-gun sloop of war *Wasp*, commanded by Captain Jacob Jones, met the brig *Frolic*, 18, in the West Indies on October 18, 1812, and the *Wasp*'s gunnery was so accurate despite a boisterous sea that in less than an hour the enemy vessel was easily captured by an American boarding party. Later in the day, however, the *Wasp*, slowed by the damage she had suffered in the fight, was taken by a British two-decker.[23]

With the intention of inflicting the severest possible damage on British seaborne commerce, the Navy Department, following Rodgers' early suggestion, divided its ships into three squadrons under the command of Rodgers, Decatur, and Bainbridge. On October 25, the *United States*, commanded by Decatur, sighted the British frigate *Macedonian* off the Canary Islands. Although the flamboyant Decatur had put to sea in company with the brig *Argus*, he preferred cruising alone and had parted company with his consort.

Even without her, the *United States* was more than a match for the *Macedonian*. Rated at 44 guns, she actually carried 54 guns, including twenty-two 42-pound carronades, rather than the usual 32s. The *Macedonian* was rated at 38, as was the *Guerrière*, but she mounted 11 more guns and was newly refitted. The *Macedonian* was considered a crack ship, and her captain, John S. Carden, had laid particular emphasis on gunnery at a time when such training was neglected in the Royal Navy. She was anything but a happy ship, however. Samuel

Leech, one of the few sailors of the era to write his memoirs, described her skipper as "a heartless, unfeeling lover of whip discipline." Ignoring the pleas of several impressed American seamen that they not be forced to fight against their countrymen, Carden ordered them to their battle stations under pain of death. Some were killed in action.

Instead of closing with the *United States*, Carden made the fatal mistake of standing off and trying to engage her at long range. The 24-pound long guns on the *United States*' gun deck were more than a match for the *Macedonian*'s 18s, and by the time Carden tried to repair his mistake and close the range, his ship's mainmast had been shot away and many of her guns had been dismounted.

"The whole scene grew indescribably confused and horrible," wrote Sam Leech. "It was like some awfully tremendous thunder-storm whose deafening roar is attended by incessant streaks of lightning, carrying death in every flash . . . the scene was rendered more horrible . . . by the presence of torrents of blood which dyed our decks." Throughout the hour-long battle, the normally daring and impetuous Decatur handled his ship with prudent calculation because he wanted to take the *Macedonian* as a prize rather than to shoot her to pieces. Except for some damage to sails and rigging, the *United States* emerged from the battle unscathed. A prize crew was placed aboard the *Macedonian*, and under escort by the *United States*, she was sailed to New London and taken into the U.S. Navy. Leech was among the British sailors who shifted allegiance and enlisted in the American service.[24]

On December 29, 1812, the *Constitution*, under William Bainbridge's command, scored another momentous victory. Cruising off the coast of Brazil in company with the sloop of war *Hornet*, Bainbridge sighted a large British frigate, which turned out to be the *Java*. As usual, the American vessel was more powerful than her adversary, but this time the ratio of firepower was about 6 to 5, rather than 7 to 5, as in the two previous frigate actions. At 2:00 P.M. the *Constitution* fired the first broadside of the engagement, but, Bainbridge reported, "the enemy [was] keeping at a much greater distance than I wished." In the forty minutes of complicated maneuvering that followed, the *Java* vainly tried to use her greater speed to rake the *Constitution*.

A lucky shot carried away the *Constitution*'s wheel, but superior American shiphandling and firepower soon began to take their toll. The British fired faster, but the American gunners were more accurate, and within two hours the *Java* was a wreck. Twenty-two of her crew were killed and another 102 wounded, including her captain, who later died. American casualties totalled twelve killed and twenty-two wounded. The *Java* was so battered that she had to be scuttled. Bainbridge had at last redeemed himself for the loss of the *Philadelphia*.

The last in the series of stunning American victories occurred about two months later, on February 24, 1813, when the *Hornet*, commanded by James Lawrence, captured the brig *Peacock* off the coast of what is now Guyana. Both vessels were rated at 18 guns, but the *Hornet* had heavier carronades than the

Peacock, and she made short work of her opponent. Within fifteen minutes, the *Peacock*'s crew was decimated and the ship began to sink. William James, the contemporary British naval historian, attributed her loss to "neglect to exercise the ship's company at the guns." Similar conditions "prevailed . . . over two thirds of the British navy," he added, "to which the Admiralty, by their sparing allowance of powder and shot for practice, were in some degree instrumental."[25]

During the opening months of the war at sea, the Americans had been successful far beyond their wildest expectations—giving rise to the legend that the United States won the War of 1812. Not only had three frigates and several smaller men-of-war been taken, but Lloyd's reported that upward of 500 merchant vessels had been bagged by Yankee privateers and commerce-raiders. *The Pilot*, bible of Britain's maritime community, said that "any one who had predicted such a result of an American war this time last year would have been treated as a madman or traitor." Nevertheless, despite the alarm generated among Britain's commercial interests, the American victories at sea had little effect on the course of the war.

In 1813, the British began to make full use of their overwhelming strength at sea. They increased the number of ships deployed along the American coast and the American frigates were bottled up in port after their return from victorious cruises—some not getting to sea again for the remainder of the war. The *Constellation*, for example, was moored at Norfolk throughout the entire war, while a vigilant blockading squadron lay in wait for her. The *United States* and captured *Macedonian* were blockaded in New London. Napoleon's defeat in Russia, and then his abdication, compounded the difficulties of the Americans. They had expected that most of the Royal Navy would be tied up in European waters, but with the French no longer threatening Britain's lifelines, the British were free to reinforce their squadrons on this side of the Atlantic. Convoys were established to protect merchantmen from the slashing attacks of Yankee commerce-raiders, and the captains of solitary British frigates were ordered to avoid engaging the heavier American ships.[26]

The British soon got their turn to cheer. As a reward for his services in the *Hornet*, James Lawrence was given command of the *Chesapeake*, fitting out in Boston. Just a few weeks before, when a blockading force commanded by Captain Philip Bowes Vere Broke of HMS *Shannon* was blown offshore by a storm, John Rodgers had escaped from Boston with the *President* and *Congress*. He captured a dozen ships in a voyage that took him into British waters, and Broke resolved that the *Chesapeake* would not be allowed to escape. He sent Lawrence a message saying that he was sending away a supporting vessel and suggesting an encounter "ship to ship, to try the fortune of our respective flags." Lawrence put to sea on June 1, 1813, before he could receive the challenge, but he made no effort to elude the *Shannon*.

He had experienced considerable difficulty in manning his vessel, not only because she was considered an unlucky ship, but also because many seamen had succumbed to the lures of privateering. A large number of those who did sign on were green hands and foreigners. In contrast, Broke, the most efficient and innovative gunnery enthusiast in the Royal Navy, had been in command of the *Shannon* for seven years. Unlike many British captains, he drilled his men at the guns twice a day and sighted-in each piece. An officer of Lawrence's energy and skill would probably have had his ship in fighting trim after a few weeks at sea, but when he saw a single enemy ship cruising off Boston Light, he elected to fight then and there. Considering the limits of American naval power, he would have been wiser had he reined in his enthusiasm, awaited some dark and stormy night to run the blockade, and then terrorized British commerce.

Undoubtedly because he realized his crew was unskilled, Lawrence simply sailed the *Chesapeake* to within fifty yards of the *Shannon* without intricate maneuvering, and both vessels unleashed broadsides at point-blank range. Although the two ships were about equal in firepower, the training that Broke had given his men soon paid off. The British fired faster and more accurately than the Americans. British shot shrieked across the quarterdeck of the *Chesapeake*, and early in the battle Lawrence and several of his officers were mortally wounded. Badly damaged, her headsails shot away and her stern swinging to the wind, the *Chesapeake* fouled the *Shannon* and the two ships were lashed together. "Boarders away!" cried Broke, as he led about fifty men onto the deck of the shattered American frigate. With most of their officers shot down, the terror-stricken polyglot crew of the *Chesapeake* fled below deck and only her forty-four marines made a stand. Gathered around the mainmast, they fought with bayonet and clubbed musket until but ten of their number were still on their feet. "The enemy fought desperately, but in disorder," reported Broke, who was among the wounded. Nevertheless, within fifteen minutes of the firing of the first broadsides, the *Chesapeake* was in British hands. Below, the dying Lawrence implored: "Don't give up the ship!"[27]

The sight of the *Shannon* shepherding the *Chesapeake* into the harbor of Halifax sent British spirits soaring and the Royal Navy regained some of the luster it had lost. The City of London presented Broke with a sword, and the guns of the Tower of London boomed out Britain's jubilation.

Little more than two months later, the brig *Argus*, which had captured twenty British merchantmen in the waters about Britain, was at last brought to bay by the brig *Pelican*, off Cornwall on August 14, 1813. The night before, the *Argus* had captured a wine-laden vessel bound from Oporto. The ship was burned, but not before some of the Americans had gotten drunk, which may have influenced their performance in action. Although the *Argus* easily could have shown her heels to the slower British vessel, her captain, William H. Allen, chose to give battle. The vessels were almost equal in force but the British fire was brisk and, in short order, the *Argus* struck her flag. The entire action reflected little credit upon the judgment of Allen, who lost a leg and died of his wounds.

Like James Lawrence, he displayed a certain romantic élan but showed no understanding of strategic reality. To have continued the *Argus'* successful career as a commerce-raider would have been far more damaging to Britain than would have been the capture of an insignificant brig—and even that was bungled.[28]

In vivid contrast, early in 1813, David Porter took the stoutly built *Essex* around Cape Horn into the Pacific on what became a classic raiding voyage. Porter's objective was to destroy the British whaling fleet off the Galápagos Islands and, at the same time, to protect American ships engaged in that trade. Within six months he captured a dozen whalers as well as several other vessels whose value he estimated at $2.5 million. All this he accomplished without a base from which to operate and while living off captured supplies and gear. Prizes were so plentiful that even twelve-year-old Midshipman David Glasgow Farragut, the captain's ward, was detailed to one of them. When the *Essex* needed a refit, Porter sailed her 3,000 miles across the Pacific to the Marquesas Islands, where his crew had a taste of life in the South Seas while they overhauled their vessel.

Early in 1814, the *Essex* put in to Valparaiso, Chile, where two British vessels, the frigate *Phoebe* and the sloop of war *Cherub*, which had been sent in search of the raider, found her. Although the *Essex* was rated at 32 guns, she actually mounted 46. The *Phoebe* carried the same number, and the *Cherub* mounted 26 guns. The American frigate could have dealt with either of the enemy ships alone, but as a team they were more than a match for her. The main battery of the *Essex* consisted of carronades, which were effective only at close quarters, while the *Phoebe* carried long 18s, which meant that she could stand off and demolish the *Essex* at long range without danger to herself. Lying in sight of each other in neutral waters for the better part of a month, the vessels waged a war of propaganda. The *Essex* hoisted a white flag with the motto "Free Trade and Sailors' Rights," and the British countered with "God and country; British sailors' best rights."

On March 28, 1814, the wind blew up and the *Essex* slipped her cable and headed for the open sea. Escape seemed possible until a sudden squall struck her, sending the frigate's main-topmast by the board. The *Phoebe* and *Cherub* bore down upon the disabled vessel as she lay in a small cove, about three miles from Valparaiso. Ignoring Chilean neutrality, the British captains launched an attack. Porter made such excellent use of his few long 12s that he forced his opponents to draw off momentarily to make repairs. But after taking up a position where the guns of the *Essex* could not bear, they began systematically to knock her to pieces. Midshipman Farragut later recalled that one gun was manned three times, one crew after another having been wiped out. As he helped work another gun, a single round shot killed four of the gunners. Unable to close with the enemy, Porter tried to run the *Essex* ashore and put the torch to her, but there was no escape. The odyssey of the Salem frigate was over and more than half her crew had been either killed or wounded.[29]

* * *

Although some warships managed to elude the tightening blockade—including the *Enterprise*, which captured the *Boxer* in September 1813 in a bitter battle in which both captains were killed—the task of twisting the lion's tail fell increasingly to the privateers. Shrewdly mixing patriotism with a lust for profit, Yankee sailors in fast and handy vessels had fanned out across the sea lanes at the beginning of hostilities. One authority estimates that in all at least 515 privateers were commissioned, most of them from Massachusetts, New York, and Maryland. They were credited with capturing 1,345 vessels, and probably took others that were not reported. Many of the captures took place off the coast of Spain and Portugal, where the victims were carrying supplies to the Duke of Wellington's army. The navy's ships captured another 165 prizes.[30]

To meet the needs of the privateersmen, as well as those of slavers and smugglers, ship designers had developed the swift-sailing Baltimore clipper, a topsail schooner with a slim hull crowned by two tall masts with an immense spread of canvas. Usually armed with one heavy "Long Tom" and several smaller guns, they were among the most graceful ships ever built, leading even a landsman such as Henry Adams to rhapsodize:

> Beautiful beyond anything then known in naval construction . . . the schooner was a wonderful invention. Not her battles, but her escapes won for her the open-mouthed admiration of the British captains who saw their prize double like a hare and slip through their fingers at the moment when capture was sure. Under any ordinary conditions of wind and weather, with an open sea, the schooner, if only she could get to windward, laughed at a frigate.

Privateer skippers often matched their ships in dash and daring. Captain Thomas Boyle, of Baltimore, raised havoc in the waters around Britain, first in the *Comet* and then in the *Chasseur*. The profits from one cruise alone were $400,000. Taking a leaf from the British book, Boyle, in the summer of 1814, published a mock proclamation "blockading" the British Isles. Within two months he captured eighteen ships, burning them after removing their cargoes, which were valued at more than $100,000. The Baltimore schooner *Kemp* snatched five of seven merchant vessels in a convoy from under the nose of their escort and made it back into port—all within eight days. The prizes were sold for $500,000, making this probably the shortest and most successful cruise of the war.

Privateers generally avoided engaging men-of-war, but in February 1815, after the war had ended but before news of peace had reached him, Boyle captured the Royal Navy schooner *St. Lawrence* after a brisk fight. Explaining that he had been under the impression that his opponent was a merchantman until it was too late to do anything but fight, he apologized to the *Chasseur*'s owners for having risked their ship: "I should not willingly perhaps have sought a contest with a king's vessel knowing it was not our object, but my expectations were at first a valuable vessel and a valuable cargo. When I found myself deceived, the honor of the flag left with me was not to be disgraced by flight.''[31]

Yet, for all the enthusiasm with which Americans embraced privateering, it was not an effective weapon of war. Privateers damaged British commerce and sometimes captured valuable cargoes, but they were no substitute for a navy. They did nothing to weaken the stranglehold of British sea power on the American coast, and possibly one-half of the prizes they captured ended up in British hands when they tried to make port. Throttled by the blockade and by British privateers, American trade sank to disastrous levels. Exports, which had been valued at $108.3 million in 1807, were only $7 million in 1814. Coastal shipping was also almost completely disrupted. A Boston newspaper printed a gloomy picture of conditions: "Our harbors blockaded; our shipping destroyed or rotting at the docks; silence and stillness in our cities; the grass growing upon the public wharves." The American merchant marine paid a stiff price for the belief of the Jeffersonians that because no enemy would be able to detach enough ships to blockade the entire coast, it was not necessary to have a seagoing navy to protect shipping.[32]

With nothing to oppose them, the British were able to put ashore landing parties at almost any point to disrupt trade and to try to prevent American naval vessels and privateers from getting to sea. The Chesapeake Bay was a major theater for such operations, which were climaxed by an amphibious assault on Washington and Baltimore in the late summer of 1814. A flotilla of gunboats tried to intervene in the attack on Washington, but these craft were brushed aside and finally destroyed to prevent their falling into enemy hands. The militiamen defending Washington were soon scattered and the capital fell to the British almost without a fight. Public buildings were put to the torch by the invaders, and several ships on the stocks at the navy yard, including the 44-gun frigate *Columbia*, were destroyed by the retreating American forces.

The British next turned their attention to Baltimore, which, as the home port of 126 privateers, they regarded as "a nest of pirates." Stalled by the city's hastily erected defenses, a British army of nearly 5,000 men waited for a fleet of frigates and bomb vessels to silence Fort McHenry, at the entrance of the harbor. The night-long bombardment on September 14 inspired Francis Scott Key to write the words of "The Star-Spangled Banner." The British guns outranged those of the fort, but the ships were prevented from running past it by a line of sunken hulks that blocked the channel, and the attack failed. A few days later, the army was reembarked, neither side having done much damage to the other.[33]

With the war at sea going against the Americans, attention was increasingly focused on the Great Lakes. The defeat of General William Hull on the northern frontier during the opening months of hostilities convinced President Madison and his advisers that control of the lakes was essential to successful operations against Canada. Few roads existed in the wilderness, and the chain of lakes provided the only satisfactory means of moving large military forces. Captain Isaac Chauncey was given command of the American naval forces on the lakes and the task of overcoming Britain's naval supremacy. He made his headquarters on Lake Ontario, where the most powerful forces on both sides were deployed and which should have been the scene of the most important actions. But this did not prove to be the case.

Chauncey turned out to be a conservative and methodical officer. Except for a few indecisive skirmishes, he and his British opposite number, Captain Sir James Yeo, conducted a "warfare of Dockyards and Arsenals," in which first one side and then the other secured temporary supremacy on the lake. By the time the war ended, the British had completed building a 102-gun ship of the line, while the Americans had two three-deckers of 120 guns each on the stocks.[34]

Master Commandant Oliver Hazard Perry, directing the American naval effort on Lake Erie, was more vigorous than Chauncey. The twenty-seven-year-old Perry had been in command of a gunboat flotilla at Newport and had sought more active service. When he realized the magnitude of the task given him, he may well have wondered at the wisdom of his request, for his new mission was nothing less than to build a fleet in the wilderness and use it to wrest control of the lake from a superior British force. Perry established his base at Presque Isle (now Erie, Pennsylvania), at the eastern end of the lake, early in 1813, and there, with the assistance of two remarkable craftsmen, Adam and Noah Brown, he set about building a fleet.

Originally, the Browns were carpenters and house-builders rather than shipwrights, but they had turned to shipbuilding in the years before the war. With the outbreak of hostilities, they designed and built at New York several privateers that were notable for their clean lines and speed. Using the green timber that grew beside the lake, Noah Brown, who was in charge of construction, built Perry two 20-gun brigs, the *Lawrence* and the *Niagara*, and a flotilla of smaller craft. Iron, cordage, canvas, oakum—almost everything needed for the building of the ships—as well as guns and munitions had to be hauled overland from Pittsburgh or sailed from Buffalo, and the construction of the fleet assumed epic proportions. "The amount of work that Brown accomplished with about 200 men, without power tools, and in a wilderness during the worst winter months, makes some of the modern wartime production feats something less than impressive," Howard Chapelle has observed. "The man was tireless and ingenious."[35]

Although Perry had brought the nucleus of his crews with him from Newport, his ships were still shorthanded. Most seamen in the coastal ports avoided service on the lakes, if they could, even though a bonus of 25 per cent was paid. For one thing, there was little prospect of prize money in this frontier region. William Jones, the secretary of the navy, observed that such service was regarded as "one of peculiar privation, destitute of pecuniary stimulus . . . unpopular both with the Officers and Men." Perry pleaded for men from Chauncey's comparatively inactive force, but only a handful was sent. Relations between the two officers became so strained that Perry submitted his resignation, but the Navy Department refused to accept it. To fill out his crews, Perry recruited untrained militiamen, Indians, and even one Russian "who couldn't speak a word of English." Fully one-quarter of the men signed on and given hasty training as sailors and marines were black.

While Perry's fleet was being built, it had been protected from British attack by a sandbar at the mouth of the harbor. Now Perry faced the problem of getting the *Lawrence* and *Niagara* over the shoal in the face of the British blockade. Fortunately for the Americans, the British force under Commander Robert H. Barclay, a one-armed veteran of Trafalgar, left its station for a few days early in August. Seizing the opportunity, Perry lightened his heaviest ships by removing their guns, and using "camels," or pontoons, floated them over the bar. Suddenly faced with this powerful force, Barclay wanted to avoid giving battle until he had strengthened his flotilla, but he was so short of provisions that he could not afford to delay very long.

The two fleets met about twenty miles northwest of Put-in-Bay, at the western end of the lake, on September 10, 1813. Perry's squadron consisted of nine vessels firing a broadside of 896 pounds, to Barclay's six, with a broadside of 459 pounds. The Americans also carried more long guns than the British, even though the *Lawrence* and *Niagara* were armed primarily with carronades. Flying a blue banner emblazoned with James Lawrence's dying words, "Don't Give Up The Ship," Perry led his fleet into battle in the *Lawrence*. The *Niagara* was commanded by Jesse D. Elliott, who had been senior officer on the lake before Perry's arrival. Four years older than Perry, he was junior to him on the Navy List and was not happy with his subordinate position.

Perry bore down on the British line in a single column, so the *Lawrence*, which was in the van, absorbed the bulk of the British fire. Shortly before noon, the band on board Barclay's flagship, the *Detroit*, struck up "Rule Britannia!" as her long 24s pounded the slowly approaching Yankee flagship. Perry could not reply effectively because the range was too long for his carronades. Shot thudded into the *Lawrence*'s hull and severed lines and blocks trailed from aloft. The *Lawrence* closed with the *Detroit* and the ships engaged at pistol range. Almost all the British fire was soon trained on Perry's vessel. Some of his smaller ships and gunboats came to his aid, but for some still unexplained reason, Elliott, in the *Niagara*, stood off, taking little part in the action.

The battle was fought at such close range that it was difficult for the gunners to miss. Both the *Detroit* and the *Lawrence* suffered terribly. Barclay was badly wounded, as were many of his officers. The *Lawrence* went into action with a crew of 103 men; all but 20 were killed or wounded. Many of the wounded were maimed again or killed while they were being treated by the surgeons, because the cockpit, where they were taken, was above the waterline. Within two hours, almost every gun had been dismounted and there were not enough men to fire those that remained. Undaunted, Perry summoned the surgeon's assistants to lend a hand at the guns and, when no one else was left, called down into the cockpit, "Can any of the wounded pull a rope?" Several pitiful men limped up on deck to help aim and fire the few remaining cannon.

Finally, at about 2:30 P.M., when the *Lawrence*'s last gun had fallen silent, Perry decided to transfer to the *Niagara*. Taking his twelve-year-old brother James, who was serving in the squadron as a midshipman, four seamen, his broad pennant, and the blue flag bearing Lawrence's words, he had himself rowed a half-mile through a hail of shot to Elliott's undamaged vessel. The *Lawrence*, an unmanageable wreck, surrendered, but the otherwise-engaged British did not take possession of her.

Wasting no time on recriminations, Perry ordered Elliott to take the boat and bring up the remaining vessels of his fleet, while the *Niagara*'s sails caught a breeze that had sprung up. To the cheers of the rest of the squadron, Perry signalled close action and drove the brig, her guns pouring smoke and flame, into the enemy line. The British were in no condition to resist this fresh onslaught, and their battered vessels struck their colors. As soon as the surrendered ships had been secured, Perry quickly penned on the back of an old letter a dispatch to General William Henry Harrison, the military commander in the northwest:

> We have met the enemy; and they are ours. Two ships, two Brigs, one schooner, and one Sloop.

Perry's victory gave the Americans complete command of Lake Erie and allowed them to regain control of the northwest, which had been lost by William Hull's blunders. A year later, however, the British, reinforced by veterans of the Duke of Wellington's army, launched an invasion of the United States along the route that General John Burgoyne had followed nearly a half-century before. Preparations were also made for an attack on New Orleans. The major objective of these offensives was to win pawns that could be used at the peace conference, which was already under way in Ghent, Belgium. In August 1814, Sir George Prevost, the governor general of Canada, halted at Plattsburg, on the western shore of Lake Champlain, and waited for the British naval commander, Captain George Downie, to deal with a small American squadron under Master Commandant Thomas Macdonough. Prevost, with upwards of 12,000 men under his command, could have easily brushed aside the 1,500 Americans under the command of Brigadier General Alexander Macomb who were defending Plattsburg, but he insisted that so long as the Yankees controlled the lake, his flank and supply lines were endangered.

With the aid of Noah Brown, the thirty-one-year-old Macdonough, who had been with Decatur in the burning of the *Philadelphia*, built his fleet on the shores of the lake. They worked with such speed that the largest ship, the 26-gun corvette *Saratoga*, was completed in little more than a month. She was joined by the *Eagle*, a 20-gun brig delivered just five days before the fleet went into action, two other sailing vessels, and ten oar-propelled gunboats carrying one or two cannon. The British flotilla consisted of the powerful frigate *Confiance*, 36, one brig, two sloops, and twelve gunboats manned mostly by soldiers and a handful of seamen. Although Downie wanted to delay action until he had had time to shake down his vessels and train his crews, which included a sizeable number of Canadian militiamen, he was prodded into action by Prevost, and the *Confiance* went into battle with fitters still on board. The two fleets were about equal in number of guns and the weight of their broadsides. Some of Macdonough's vessels were armed with 18-pound shell guns that were created by boring out carronades to fire spherical explosive shells rather than solid shot.

Macdonough realized that to deny control of the lake he had only to maintain what Mahan later called "a fleet in being," whereas Downie, to gain control, had to win a decisive victory. Accordingly, he decided to anchor his ships in Plattsburg Bay, a deep inlet on the western side of the lake, and await a British attack, as Benedict Arnold had done at Valcour during the Revolution. He ordered his ships drawn up in a line from Cumberland Head to the shallows off Crab Island, close to the shore so his line could not be turned. As an added precaution, Macdonough had spring lines run out of the sterns of his ships and attached to their anchor cables, allowing them to be swung so their guns could be brought to bear on the approaching enemy.[36]

The British sailed southward on September 11, propelled along the reed-lined shore by a light breeze. When he sighted them rounding Cumberland Head, Macdonough, a devout man, called his officers and crew to prayer—and then to quarters. Most of the ranging shots that the British ships fired at the *Saratoga* fell short, but one of them splintered a coop that housed a pet gamecock. Unharmed, the bird flew to a gun where it crowed and flapped its wings defiantly. To Macdonough's anxious crews, this seemed a good omen and they cheered lustily. The commodore himself laid one of the first 24-pounders that bore on the approaching British flagship and the shot struck home.

Sailing into the bay in line abreast, the British came under heavy fire from the American vessels. Downie tried to pass down the American line, but under the lee of Cumberland Head, the wind fell and he was forced to anchor his flagship only 300 yards from the *Saratoga*. A broadside erupted from the *Confiance* and smashed into Macdonough's ship. The *Saratoga*'s deck ran red with blood and some forty of her men were killed or wounded, but she briskly returned the enemy fire. Fifteen minutes later, one of the *Confiance*'s guns, dismounted by a shot, fell upon Downie, killing him instantly. The death of their commander so early in the engagement had a serious effect on British morale. Macdonough himself had several narrow escapes. As he was aiming a gun, a spar fell on him, knocking him unconscious. Later, a round shot tore off the head of one of the gun's crew and drove it into Macdonough's face with such force that it sent him sprawling.

Fighting spread up and down the line and the two British sloops and a small American vessel were knocked out of action. The *Saratoga* and the *Confiance* suffered the most, however. Both were taking on water and the *Saratoga* was twice set afire by hot shot from the British flagship. The *Saratoga* was hulled 55 times and the *Confiance*, 105 times, Macdonough reported. Within two hours of the start of the action, every starboard gun on the *Saratoga* had been disabled. Heaving in on his spring, Macdonough pulled his ship around so that her un-damaged port battery faced the *Confiance*. The British tried the same trick but failed—and were caught by the *Saratoga*'s merciless fire. Soon it was all over, and one by one the British vessels surrendered. Both sides had suffered severely. American casualties totalled more than a hundred killed and wounded, while Macdonough estimated that the British had lost double that number.

Macdonough's victory forced Prevost, whose simultaneous assault had been repulsed by Macomb, to call off the invasion and its effects reverberated far beyond the lake frontier. The peace talks at Ghent had been stalled over British insistence on retaining all the land that had been captured during the war, with a view to creating an Indian "buffer state" in the Northwest Territory. But the Duke of Wellington, who had been offered command of the British forces in America, said that unless Britain regained "a naval superiority on the Lakes" peace should be made at once—and without territorial demands. On Christmas Eve 1814, a peace treaty was signed, a treaty that made no mention of impress-ment or of the protection of neutral rights, the reasons given by Madison for declaring war. Repeal of the Orders in Council and the end of the war in Europe had rendered these issues moot.

Although the war was officially over, the fighting was not. News travelled slowly in those days, so the British continued their preparations for the descent on New Orleans. The expedition appeared off the mouth of the Mississippi on December 8, 1814, but before an advance on the city could begin, the British had to deal with a handful of small sailing vessels and gunboats under the command of Master Commandant Daniel T. Patterson. The shortest route to the city led through Lake Borgne, a shallow bayou that opened to the sea. Patterson stationed his five gunboats there under Lieutenant Thomas ap Catesby Jones. Forty-two British launches, each armed with a carronade and carrying a total of 1,000 men, captured all of Jones' boats in a short, bloody battle on December 14, but at the cost of about 100 men killed and wounded—and valuable time, which Andrew Jackson put to good use in preparing his defense of New Orleans.

By December 23, the British had pushed to within nine miles of the city but were thrown into confusion when the schooner *Carolina*, 14, bombarded their encampment and Jackson launched a supporting attack. The Americans were driven off, but the final assault on the city was delayed until heavy guns were brought up from the fleet to deal with the schooner. The *Carolina* was eventually destroyed, but the *Louisiana*, 16, sole survivor of Patterson's squadron, took part in repulsing the British attack on New Orleans on January 8, 1815. Recognizing the important role that the navy had played in the fight, a grateful Jackson told Patterson: "To your well directed exertions must be ascribed in a great degree that embarrassment of the enemy which led to his ignominious flight."[37]

Throughout the closing months of the war, American naval captains impatiently awaited opportunities to escape the vigilant British blockading squadrons that lay offshore. The *Constitution* managed to escape from Boston in December 1814, and the *President*, under the command of Stephen Decatur, slipped to sea from New York in January 1815 during a blinding snowstorm. Decatur's fabled luck soon ran out, however. His frigate was severely damaged when the pilot who was taking her to sea ran her aground. Decatur later said he would have returned to port had not the severity of the storm prevented him. The British blockading squadron, consisting of the *Majestic*, 56, and three frigates, sighted the limping *President* the next day and captured her after a half-day chase in which one of the pursuing vessels was badly knocked about by the Yankee frigate's guns. The *President* also suffered in the exchanges. "With about one-fifth of my crew killed and wounded, my ship crippled, and a more than four-fold force opposed to me, without a chance of escape left, I deemed it my duty to surrender," Decatur declared.[38]

A month later the *Constitution*, sought by every available ship of the Royal Navy, was cruising off Madeira when she encountered two British vessels, the light frigate *Cyane*, 22, and the sloop of war *Levant*, 20. The British captains gallantly if unwisely chose to fight, and within forty minutes, their vessels had been battered into submission. The *Constitution*'s captain, Charles Stewart, put on one of the most brilliant demonstrations of shiphandling witnessed during the war. He attacked the *Cyane*, backed down to engage the *Levant*, then sailed ahead to re-engage the *Cyane*, and finally wore around to knock out the *Levant*.[39] The American sloops of war *Hornet* and *Peacock* were also at sea, and they took the last prizes of the war. The *Hornet*, under Captain James Biddle, captured the brig *Penguin*, 18, after a twenty-minute fight in which the British vessel was transformed into little more than kindling. The *Peacock* sailed into the Indian Ocean where she captured four large Indiamen. On June 30, 1815, in the Sunda Strait, she sighted a 14-gun brig belonging to the East India Company. The merchantman's captain informed the *Peacock*'s commander, Lewis Warrington, that the war was over. Believing this a ruse designed to permit his prey to escape, Warrington ordered the brig's skipper to strike his flag and send a boat. When this was refused, however, he poured a broadside into the vessel, causing fifteen casualties. The name of the brig was *Nautilus*—the same as that of the first

American vessel that had been captured by the British at the outbreak of the war three years before.[40]

In years to come, Americans would forget the humiliations of the War of 1812—the military defeats, the burning of the capital, the raids on the defenseless coast, and the blockade. With pride, they recalled the exploits of Hull, Decatur, Perry, and Macdonough that had preserved the national honor and established a tradition of victory. By providing such a heritage, the navy not only fostered a spirit of nationalism that helped put an end to the narrow sectionalism that threatened to tear the nation apart—it also gained popularity and acceptance for itself.

4

DISTANT STATIONS

Log book United States Ship John Adams, *Thomas W. Wyman, Esq., Commander.*

Zanzibar 12 September 1838.

From 8 to meridian. Light breezes and pleasant. At 9 saluted the Grand Sultan's flag with 21 guns which was returned with 20 guns. Sent on board the flagship to know the reason why it was not returned gun for gun. The commanding officer said he had fired 21 guns.

Zanzibar 13 September 1838.

Commences with light breezes and pleasant. At 2 P.M. *a gun was fired from His Highness' Flag Ship to make up the deficient gun in return for our salute to the Sultan. Received a present of four buffaloes from His Highness.*

—The American Neptune, *October, 1963*

With the unruffled majesty of a flock of swans, the most powerful fleet yet assembled by the United States put to sea on May 20, 1815. The pennant of Commodore Stephen Decatur flew from the main truck of the graceful new 44-gun frigate *Guerriére*, whose name was a proud reminder of one of the navy's great victories in the recently ended war. The frigates *Constellation* and *Macedonian* and a total of seven sloops of war, brigs, and schooners followed in her wake as Sandy Hook dropped below the pitching horizon. The squadron was bound for the Mediterranean to settle unfinished business with the Barbary corsairs that had been dangling since 1807.

Shortly after the ratification of the Peace of Ghent in February 1815, President Madison had asked Congress to declare war upon the Algerians. While the nation was at war with Britain, the dey of Algiers had seized American ships and crews, claiming that the United States had reneged on its promises to pay tribute. Relations between the countries had been broken off in 1812, but the

Yankees had not been in a position to exact retribution until the end of the war with England.

Having fought its way into public favor, the navy was in 1815 at the height of its prestige and popularity. Buoyed by the spirit of exuberant nationalism spreading across the country, it escaped, at least temporarily, the crippling cutbacks that had plagued it after previous conflicts. "The importance of a permanent naval establishment appears to be sanctioned by the voice of the nation, and . . . the means of its gradual increase are completely within the reach of our national resources," said Benjamin W. Crowninshield, the secretary of the navy, as he raised the curtain on a period of naval expansion and reform.[1]

The navy had never been stronger. Three 74-gun ships of the line, the *Washington, Franklin,* and *Independence,* the heavy frigates *Guerriére* and *Java,* both named for defeated British vessels, and several smaller ships had all been recently commissioned and manned with well-trained officers and crews. Two powerful squadrons were dispatched to the Mediterranean, one under Decatur and the other under William Bainbridge. A month after sailing, Decatur's squadron arrived off Gibraltar, where the commodore learned that an Algerian flotilla that had been cruising in the Atlantic had recently passed through the strait on its way home.

Decatur pressed into the Mediterranean in the hope of intercepting the enemy ships before they reached a safe harbor. A strange sail sighted off Cabo de Gata on the morning of June 17 proved to be the Algerian flagship *Mashuda,* a 46-gun frigate. She tried to escape but was soon pounded into submission. One of the ships in company with her, a small brig, was also captured, but most of the Algerian ships scattered to neutral ports. Decatur stood in to the harbor of Algiers and presented the dey with terms dictated, as Decatur said, "at the mouth of our cannon." Faced with this threat, the dey agreed to a treaty that granted the United States most-favored-nation status, ended the payment of tribute, and freed all American prisoners without ransom.

The American squadron next visited Tunis and Tripoli, which had also violated treaties with the United States by seizing prizes taken by American privateers during the War of 1812. Bainbridge's squadron, consisting of the two-decker *Independence,* the frigates *United States* and *Congress,* and six smaller vessels, also arrived on the scene, further impressing the Barbary chieftains with the growing naval power of the United States. Reflecting upon the rows of cannon frowning from the black sides of the American ships, the rulers of these two states readily agreed to pay indemnities.

The two squadrons cruised the Mediterranean independently, showing the flag at various ports, until early October 1815, when they met at Gibraltar for the voyage home. Decatur, who had little faith in the good intentions of the rulers of the Barbary States once the fleet had gone, wrote Secretary of State James Monroe that "the only secure guarantee we can have for the maintenance of the peace just concluded with those people is the presence in the Mediterranean of a respectable naval force." In keeping with his suggestion, two frigates and several smaller vessels were left behind to form the nucleus of a Mediterranean Squadron, which was given the task of protecting American commerce in those waters.[2]

Pointing to the devastating effects of the British blockade upon the American war effort and maritime commerce. Crowninshield convinced the president and Congress of the need for a long-range building program to augment the navy's strength at a steady rate. Nine additional 74s and twelve 44-gun frigates were to be laid down over a six-year period at an annual cost of $1 million. Three experimental "steam batteries" were also authorized. Not all these ships were completed, but this construction program had an important impact on naval policy because it committed the United States to building a navy in the mold of those of the European powers.

Following the standard practice, the new ships of the line greatly exceeded their rated gun power. For example, the *Ohio*, nominally a 74 and considered one of the finest ships of her size in the world, carried anywhere from 86 to 102 guns, depending on the wishes of her various captains. The 120-gun *Pennsylvania* was the largest sailing ship ever to serve in the navy. John Quincy Adams, on a visit to this mammoth, with her huge crew and seemingly endless expanse of scrubbed deck, said that she looked "like a city."[3]

Although the individual captains had behaved with gallantry, the War of 1812 had laid bare the administrative weakness of the Navy Department, and Crowninshield moved to institute sweeping reforms. Neither of his wartime predecessors, Paul Hamilton and William Jones, had been able to exercise strategic control of naval operations because they had only a limited knowledge of the art of strategy and no staff of professional advisers. Most of their time was spent on the provisioning, arming, and manning of naval forces, and they were completely caught up in bureaucratic routine.

The chain of command was also inadequate and administrative procedures were primitive. Since most of the navy's senior officers were men of considerable independence and strong character, such a loose arrangement sometimes resulted in professional rivalries and personality clashes. Although the highest rank was that of captain, when two or more ships operated together, the senior officer took the courtesy title of commodore. Yet his fellow officers sometimes considered themselves independent of his command. Despite repeated recommendations, Congress balked at creating the rank of admiral, for fear of founding a naval aristocracy.

Building on a detailed plan for the reorganization of the Navy Department proposed by Jones and modified by the suggestions of ranking officers and by Crowninshield, Congress created a Board of Navy Commissioners in February 1815. Composed of three captains appointed by the president and confirmed by the Senate, the board was placed under the "superintendence" of the secretary of the navy and was to "discharge all the ministerial duties of said office, relative to the procurement of naval stores and materials, and the construction, armament, equipment, and employment of vessels of war." The selection of personnel and control of operations remained in the hands of the secretary of the navy, however, Captains John Rodgers, Isaac Hull, and David Porter were chosen to be the first commissioners. Rodgers was named the board's president, and from 1815 to 1837, with the exception of a three-year period when he was at sea, his was the dominant voice in the conduct of naval affairs. Twice he was offered the post of secretary of the navy but was never appointed because he declined to give up his commission.

Within weeks of the establishment of the board, the commissioners were involved in a dispute with the secretary of the navy over their respective jurisdictions. They tried to assume control of naval operations and of personnel and to bypass the secretary and deal directly with the chief executive. Crowninshield argued that while the commissioners could advise him, they could not infringe upon his "direction of naval forces." The matter was finally resolved by President Madison, who agreed with the secretary. Rodgers and Porter accepted the decision, but Hull declined to do so and resigned to become commander of the Boston Navy Yard. Stephen Decatur was appointed his successor.

While there were some failures in the board's operations—particularly in its ability to take advantage of the vast technological changes ushered in by the industrial revolution—it provided an important service to the navy. The commissioners relieved the secretary of much of the burden of routine administration and provided him with professional advice. Improvements were made in the administration of navy yards and naval hospitals, and a naval gun factory and ordnance department were established. The navy's first dry docks were opened at Boston and Norfolk—more than a third of a century after Benjamin Stoddert had first suggested the construction of such facilities. Surveying the accomplishments of the commissioners, a visiting British officer said "the organization of the American naval department . . . [seems] to be the best system extant."[4]

The commissioners were particularly effective in dealing with Congress, which was showing an increasing interest in naval affairs. In 1816 the Senate Naval Affairs Committee was established, and six years later the House created its counterpart. These were the first standing committees of Congress to be concerned exclusively with naval matters, and for more than 125 years they exerted a profound influence on almost every aspect of the navy, afloat and ashore. As popular heroes, Rodgers, Porter, and Decatur cut a wide swath on the Washington social scene and used their prestige to cultivate a favorable opinion of the navy among the congressmen upon whose votes the future of the service rested.[5]

With the return of peace, merchantmen rushed to sea, and the navy's major mission in the years between the end of the War of 1812 and the beginning of the Civil War was to further maritime commerce. Yankee merchant vessels carried cotton, flour, tobacco, rice, and lumber around the world and returned with manufactures from Europe and silks, sandalwood, porcelains, tea, and pepper from East Asia and the Indies. Imports almost quintupled from $74.5 million in 1820 to $353.6 million in 1860; exports rose by almost the same rate, from $70.7 million to $333.6 million. In 1841 Abel P. Upshur, then secretary of the navy, best described the link between naval policy and commercial activity. "Wars often arise from the rivalry in trade, and from the conflicts and interests which belong to it," he said. "The presence of an adequate naval force to protect commerce, by promptly redressing the injuries which are done to it, is one of the best means of preventing those disputes and collisions."[6] The navy showed the flag, opened new markets, and defended American shipping against discrimination by foreign traders and against attack by pirates. Such tasks were usually assigned to single ships, but the need for a naval presence around the globe required squadrons, similar to the one in the Mediterranean; and soon they were sent to the coasts of South America, the Far East, and West Africa.[7]

The dispersal of most of the navy to "distant stations" coincided with the end of the honeymoon that the service had enjoyed since the end of the War of 1812. Postwar recession, the shift of public attention to the expanding West, and the sectional rivalries created by the struggle over slavery left people indifferent to the navy. Work was suspended on the ships of the line and the heavy frigates authorized a few years before, and what funds were available were earmarked for the construction of smaller craft manned by fewer officers and men. The largest vessels were laid up; no provision was made for the scattered squadrons to join together for fleet maneuvers; and such technological advances as steam propulsion and the shell gun, which had been pioneered by Americans, were for the most part ignored.

Although steamships were still a novelty, Robert Fulton's *Clermont* had begun regular service on the Hudson River as early as 1807. Seven years later, he built the *Demologos*, the first steam-powered warship, for the defense of New York Harbor. By placing the vessel's thirty 32-pounders behind wooden sides nearly five feet thick and her huge paddle wheel between massive twin hulls, he anticipated armored warships. Although the *Demologos* was fitted with a pair of masts and lateen sails at the suggestion of David Porter, her first captain, she never ventured out to sea. The War of 1812 ended before she was finished, and renamed the *Fulton* in honor of her designer who died in 1815, she was shunted aside to serve as a receiving ship at the Brooklyn Navy Yard. Legislation providing for the construction of "steam batteries" was approved in 1816, but nothing came of it. In 1829 the *Fulton* was destroyed and twenty-four of her crew were killed when a few barrels of defective powder kept on board for firing salutes exploded.[8]

The shell gun, an innovation that sounded the death knell of the wooden warship, was also ignored by the unimaginative authorities. Explosive shells had been in use in the world's navies for some time, but they were usually fired in an arching trajectory from mortars rather than directly at a target. In 1814 Colonel John Stevens, of Hoboken, New Jersey, and his sons, Edwin and Robert, prolific inventors in the field of locomotives and steamships, produced the prototype of a shell gun that they hoped would free the American coast from the grip of the British blockade. But with the war ended, government interest in the project sagged.

The ideas advanced by the Stevens family and others were refined by Henri Joseph Paixhans, a French artillery general, who produced a practical shell gun for naval use in 1824. Paixhans' gun upset the balance between offense and defense that had prevailed in naval warfare for centuries, but conservative officers were reluctant to adopt it. There were claims that shells were unsafe, particularly on wooden ships, and had a tendency to explode prematurely. It was agreed that they were certainly more destructive than solid shot, but critics pointed out that shell guns did not have the range of those that fired solid shot.[9]

The navy was further handicapped by the fact that American military thinking during the first half of the nineteenth century was dominated by army engineers who put their faith in an elaborate and costly system of coastal fortifications. Ignoring the hard lessons of the Revolution and the War of 1812 that only a strong navy could prevent a European naval power from imposing a stringent blockade on the American coast, strategic planners assigned the navy to its familiar mission of commerce-raiding on the high seas in case of war—a mission that had proven glamorous and profitable but ineffective as a weapon of war.[10]

Just as the challenge of the Barbary corsairs in 1798 had led to the establishment of the navy, so an outbreak of piracy in the Caribbean and Gulf of Mexico resulted in its rescue from the doldrums. The struggle for independence of Spain's colonies in Central and South America in the wake of the Napoleonic Wars led to their unleashing hordes of privateers that soon passed over the thin line separating privateering from piracy. Lurking among the passages of the West Indies and at the mouth of the Mississippi, off New Orleans, the pirates preyed upon any merchantman unlucky enough to pass their way. It was estimated that between 1815 and 1822 as many as 3,000 ships were attacked by these freebooters, with American commerce bearing the brunt of the depredations. Newspapers made much of the atrocities alleged to have been committed by the pirates. For example, *Niles Weekly Register*, published in Baltimore, reported that a gang of cutthroats had captured "a small vessel with a man and his wife on board; the first was exceedingly abused and at last in mercy shot through the head and thrown overboard—the latter violated in the most beastly manner."

Merchants, shipowners, and insurance companies demanded an end to these outrages. On March 3, 1819, Congress authorized President James Monroe to launch a campaign against the pirates.[11] Wishing to cultivate friendly relations with the new Latin-American republics, which had awarded privateering commissions to many of the pirates, Monroe began with peaceful overtures that were backed up by the navy's guns. As a first step, Oliver Hazard Perry, the victor of Lake Erie, was given the task of persuading the government of Venezuela to restrict raiders flying its flag and to pay an indemnity for American ships and cargoes that had been illegally seized. Perry accomplished his mission but at the cost of his life. He died of yellow fever off the coast of South America on August 23, 1819, just a few days after his thirty-fourth birthday.

Despite the agreement with Venezuela, piracy continued to flourish. Twenty-seven Yankee vessels were reported seized in 1820, or about one every other week. Within two years, the damage to American trade in the Caribbean had become so great that the United States decided to suppress the pirates once and for all. In 1822 Commodore James Biddle was appointed to command the West India Squadron, which had been set up the year before and included the frigates *Macedonian* and *Congress*, as well as several smaller craft. Although Biddle captured or destroyed about thirty pirate vessels in less than a year, his squadron failed to live up to the high hopes that had sailed with it. Most of his ships were too large to operate close inshore where the pirates lurked, and Spanish officials in Cuba and Puerto Rico, resenting the help that the United States had given the Latin-American revolutionaries, refused him permission to pursue pirates who beached their vessels and escaped ashore. Yellow fever decimated his crews and he suffered a humiliating loss of prestige when a boatload of pirates attacked one of his schooners and killed a lieutenant and four seamen.

Late in 1822 David Porter, who had resigned from the Board of Navy Commissioners because his financial reverses made it too expensive for him to live in always costly Washington, was ordered to the West India Station to take over the campaign against piracy. Learning from Biddle's experience, he gathered a squadron that consisted primarily of small vessels, gunboats, and barges. Deeply impressed by the steam-powered *Fulton* when she was under his command, Porter added the steamer *Sea Gull* to his force. The 100-ton former Hudson River ferryboat was armed with three guns, making her the first steam-powered vessel to take part in wartime operations. Propelled by two paddle wheels and belching smoke from a pair of funnels, she pursued pirates when even the lightest sailing craft in Porter's fleet lay becalmed.

For two years Porter's squadron hunted pirates among the islands and reefs of the Caribbean. His large vessels escorted merchant ships through danger areas, while his light craft poked into hundreds of coves and inlets and worked their way into shoal water and mangrove swamps. "A large portion of the officers and men were employed in the small schooners and in open boats—in a severe climate—exposed to the heat of the tropical sun by day and to the not less dangerous dews and exhalations at night," reported one officer. Yellow fever, malaria, and other sicknesses carried off many of the men. Naval officers also complained they were being undercut by the civilians at home. Captured pirates were often pardoned or given surprisingly light sentences by American courts.

As a result, the navy contrived to let captives fall into the hands of the British and Spanish authorities, who wasted no time in hanging them.[12]

Although Porter was an able commander, he was no diplomat. In 1825, in the wake of an international row created by his landing a force of 200 sailors and marines at Fajardo, Puerto Rico, and demanding—and receiving—an apology from the local authorities for a supposed insult to one of his officers, he was recalled and court-martialed on charges of insubordination and violation of Spanish sovereignty. Found guilty, he was suspended from active duty for six months; the sentence created a public outcry that he had been made a scapegoat by his political and professional enemies. Ending a quarter-century of valiant service, the angry Porter resigned his commission and accepted an offer to become commander in chief of the newly organized Mexican navy.[13]

Command of the campaign against the pirates then passed to Captain Lewis Warrington, who not only had the experience of two predecessors on which to build but also enjoyed more favorable conditions. Having achieved their independence from Spain, the revolutionary governments ceased issuing privateering commissions to all comers, and the Spanish authorities in Cuba and Puerto Rico were more cooperative in dealing with pirates operating from their islands. By mid-1826 Warrington reported that "depredations on our commerce are fortunately unheard of where they were formerly so frequent." Although isolated attacks continued for some years, the navy played a major role in clearing the Caribbean of the scourge of piracy. For the first time in three centuries, the ships of all nations could sail those waters without fear of being plundered.[14]

Revolutionary unrest on the Pacific coast of South America also threatened the safety of American trading and whaling vessels, so, once again, commercial interests called upon the navy to cast a protective net over their ships. In 1818 the sloop of war *Ontario*, 22, following in the wake of the *Essex*, which had made the voyage five years earlier, became the second ship of the U. S. Navy to sail around Cape Horn and into the Pacific. Her captain, James Biddle, had orders to proclaim American sovereignty over the land on both sides of the Columbia River in the Oregon territory. But as he proceeded along the west coast of South America, Biddle received numerous pleas from American merchants and seamen for protection from the Spaniards and Latin-American rebels.

Captain Biddle provided what assistance he could, but the task was too much for one ship. Consequently, the Pacific Squadron was established in 1821, when the *Franklin* and the schooner *Dolphin* were sent to those waters. Five years later, during a war between Brazil and Argentina, a similar force, known as the Brazil Squadron, was established in the South Atlantic to protect American commerce on the east coast of South America.[15]

The East India Squadron evolved more slowly. Yankee vessels had been trading with China ever since the end of the American Revolution. In 1801 alone thirty-four ships flying the Stars and Stripes called at Canton, the only port open to the "barbarians." This trade not only benefited American commerce but also contributed to American expansion in two ways: Chinese demands for sea-otter pelts reinforced American claims to Oregon; and the use of Hawaii as a way station for the fur trade and as a source of sandalwood, which was much prized in China, gave the Americans a foothold in those islands.

Beginning in 1819, American warships made sporadic appearances in eastern waters to protect Yankee merchantmen from pirates and to impress local officials with the necessity of fair dealing. In 1831, the frigate *Potomac*, 44, Captain John Downes, was dispatched to Quallah Battoo, on the west coast of Sumatra, "to obtain redress" for the murder of several members of the crew of the Salem trader *Friendship*. Disguising his ship as a Danish merchantman, Captain Downes landed 282 seamen and marines near Quallah Battoo on February 6, 1832, and stormed the three forts guarding the town. The chief responsible for the attack on the *Friendship* and 150 of his followers were killed. His successors soon promised to respect American ships, and the *Potomac* returned home after showing the flag in eastern waters.[16]

The East India Squadron was established three years later and its commanders faced everything from clashes with pirates to conducting the most delicate diplomatic negotiations. The sloop of war *Peacock* and the schooner *Enterprise* were the first ships sent to this station, but by 1842, when Commodore Lawrence Kearny hoisted his flag, the squadron included the frigates *Constellation* and *Boston*. Arriving on station at the close of the Opium War in which Britain forced the opium trade on China, Kearny created a favorable impression among the hard-pressed Chinese by announcing that the United States "does not sanction the smuggling of opium on this coast under the American flag, in violation of the laws of China." When Kearny learned that the British had extracted from the Chinese a treaty that opened five ports to British merchants, he seized the opportunity to win a similar concession for American traders. Through his bold initiative, the United States was granted the status of most favored nation in China and the way was paved for a treaty between the two countries that was ratified in 1845. Kearny's diplomacy was the beginning of a century-long Open Door policy, which had as its aim equal trading opportunities for all foreign nations in China.[17]

The African Squadron, established about 1820 for the suppression of the slave trade and to aid in the settlement of Liberia by free blacks from the United States, was regarded as something of a stepchild by both Congress and the Navy Department. It had its roots in the decision of Congress in 1807 to end the importation of slaves and to bar the participation of American citizens and American-flag vessels in the slave trade. Unfortunately, this humanitarian gesture was a dead letter because few efforts were made to enforce it. In the meantime, the British, whose own colonial slaves had been freed, were making gallant attempts to stamp out the slave trade on the coast of West Africa. They negotiated treaties with Portugal, Spain, Holland, and France, which allowed the Royal Navy to search vessels flying their flags that were suspected of engaging in slaving. The touchy United States—fresh from a war caused in part by Britain's insistence on the right of search—flatly refused to enter such an agreement. Taking advantage of this, slavers of many nations often broke out the Stars and Stripes when they sighted ships of the Royal Navy—and sailed away with impunity.

The British complained bitterly to Washington. John Quincy Adams, the secretary of state, was asked at one point if he knew of any more atrocious evil than the slave trade. "Yes," replied the stiff-backed Adams, expressing the viewpoint of many Americans, "admitting the right of search by foreign officers of our vessels upon the seas in time of peace, for that would be making slaves of ourselves."[18]

Even so, conditions on the Middle Passage—the voyage from West Africa to the chief slave markets in Cuba and Brazil—were so horrible that, in 1820, Congress declared the slave trade to be on a par with piracy. A few small ships were dispatched to the West African coast to aid in suppressing the trade. The frigate *Cyane*, which had been captured from the British by the *Constitution*, was the first U. S. ship to arrive there. She was probably chosen, it has been suggested, for the purpose of "rubbing it into the English."[19] Sailing under the *Cyane*'s wing was the merchant brig *Elizabeth*, carrying eighty-six free blacks to Africa for resettlement—a voyage that marked the beginning of the navy's efforts to nurse the African nation of Liberia during its infancy.

Captain Edward Trenchard, the *Cyane*'s commanding officer, estimated that some 300 American ships were involved in the West African slave trade, of which he captured five. Nevertheless, one of his officers claimed that he could not find any American slavers and added, rather implausibly, "I am fully impressed with the belief that there is not one at present afloat."[20] On one occasion an American cruiser halted a slaver that proved to have French papers, and a Yankee officer wrote a vivid account of conditions on board:

The overpowering smell and the sight presented by her slave-deck, can never be obliterated from the memory. In a space of about 15 by 40 feet, and four feet high, between decks, 163 negroes, men, women and children, were promiscuously confined. In sleeping they were made to dovetail, each drawn up to the shortest span, and the children were obliged to lie upon the full grown. They were all naked, and to protect from vermin not a hair was permitted to grow upon their persons. Their bodies were so emaciated, and their black skins were so shrunk upon their facial bones that in their torpor, they resembled so many Egyptian mummies half-awakened into life. A pint of water and a half pint of rice each was their daily allowance, which is reduced if the passage be prolonged. The passage is performed in from sixty to seventy days.[21]

In 1823 the handful of ships on the African Station was withdrawn, ostensibly because small vessels were needed to combat the West Indian pirates. The unpopularity of the antislavery patrol undoubtedly had something to do with it. As soon as the ships had gone, the slavers again took cover under the protection of the American flag, much to the frustration of the Royal Navy. Over the next two decades, a few vessels were dispatched to the West African coast to lend assistance to the settlers of Liberia, but it was not until the signing of the Webster-Ashburton Treaty with Britain in 1842 that another American squadron was sent out.

This treaty required the United States to maintain off the African coast a force mounting at least eighty guns; it constituted the greatest commitment to the suppression of the slave trade yet made by the United States. But even this modest requirement was seldom met. Perhaps influenced by the pro-slavery forces in Congress, and as if to show its own lack of interest, the Navy Department sometimes sent out heavy frigates, which were useless for operating close inshore. They were based at Madeira or in the Cape Verde Islands, a thousand miles from the slave coast. Commander Andrew H. Foote, at one time in charge of the patrol, complained that his base was so far from the scene of action that his ship "could hardly reach the southern point of the slave station before she was compelled, for want of provisions, to return and replenish."[22] Between 1845 and 1850, the U. S. Navy captured only ten slavers carrying perhaps a thousand captives, while the British took 423 prizes with 27,000 blacks. Both the Americans and the British returned the captured slaves to Africa, where they were freed.[23]

Many American naval officers on the African coast considered the slave trade a devilish business and wanted to stamp it out, but they were handicapped by lack of support from the government and by the difficulty of getting American juries to convict captured slavers. When Flag Officer William Inman was given proper support in the years immediately preceding the outbreak of the Civil War, he showed what the navy could accomplish. Maintaining a ceaseless vigil off the African coast, his ships captured 25 slavers and freed 4,800 blacks within a short period.[24] When war came, Inman's squadron was withdrawn, but that conflict itself brought the African slave trade to an end.

The navy was also called upon to lend a hand closer to home. Naval forces assisted the army in its efforts forcibly to move the Seminole Indians from their home in Florida to a reservation west of the Mississippi. The struggle erupted in December 1835, when an army detachment was massacred near Tampa. Marines and sailors from the West India Squadron were immediately put ashore to help relieve the pressure on the army. Although they numbered no more than 5,000 souls, the formidable Seminoles bitterly resisted for more than six years.[25]

Operating from the malaria-ridden Everglades, they would raid lonely outposts and settlements and then evaporate before the bewildered troops could attack them. A "mosquito fleet" consisting of a few schooners and a flotilla of flat-bottomed barges and canoes manned by a motley collection of sailors, marines, and soldiers was pressed into service to pursue the Seminoles into the Everglades. Under the command of Lieutenant John T. McLaughlin, the fleet penetrated the cypress swamps to attack and destroy Seminole strongholds. The saw grass was often so thick, McLaughlin reported, that his men were forced to pull their boats more than they rode in them. On many nights they dozed at their oars because there was no dry land on which to camp. Food and water were in meager supply and temperatures sometimes reached 120 degrees.

Eventually, significant numbers of Seminoles were either captured or agreed to move, and the government decided to leave the hard-core resisters in possession of the Everglades and the area around Lake Okeechobee. This limited victory cost the lives of 1,500 soldiers. From the navy's professional standpoint, the Seminole War provided training in riverine tactics that was to be of use in the Mexican War—and was a forerunner of naval operations on the inland waters of Vietnam a century and a quarter later.[26]

Life in the Old Navy was not all hazardous duty and unpleasant stations. During the forty years preceding the Civil War, officers and men alike prized service in the Mediterranean Squadron. With no other task than to show the flag and to protect American commerce during the minor crises that periodically flared about the rim of these waters, the stately ships cruised from Gibraltar to the Levant, touching at such romantic ports as Naples, Constantinople, and Alexandria, while establishing their base at Port Mahon, on the island of Minorca. The officers found opportunities to inspect the relics of vanished civilizations and to attend balls and parties given by hospitable local aristocrats. Sailors found their way to harborside taverns where there was no lack of feminine companionship.[27]

Constantly under the critical eye of European naval officers, the Yankee ships became models of spit and polish. Decks were holystoned to a creamy whiteness, canvas was kept spotless, brightwork was polished to a glittering sheen, and the guns were not fired except in salute. Catching his first sight of his new ship, the frigate *Brandywine*, an officer with a poetic turn of mind wrote:

> The *Brandywine* rose before me, nice in every proportion, her spars delicately tapered, and all above like a thing of fancy and taste while all below looked proud defiance . . . I thought of her . . . as rushing out on the broad deep ocean; receiving homage from man and elements; giving protection to the feeble, and putting the mighty to flight; carrying her banner into every port, and making the name of American feared and respected.[28]

Yet, for all the glamour and romance surrounding these majestic ships, the navy was becalmed in a sea of inertia and conservatism. The Navy List was barnacled with aging men who had won fame in the wars against the Barbary pirates and the British. For decades, they clung to the exalted rank of commodore, blocking younger men from climbing the ladder of promotion. Graying, middle-aged lieutenants were not uncommon; morale and discipline were poor. Some officers resigned in disgust while others resorted to political influence to obtain advancement. It was often said that "a cruise in Washington was worth two around Cape Horn," according to one historian. James Fenimore Cooper, who had served as an officer in the navy, observed in 1839 that "when young men . . . are condemned to pass fifteen or twenty years in the same rank, the spirit grows weary, the character loses its elasticity . . . [and] ambition is deadened."[29]

Jealousy, insubordination, and factionalism were the harvest of this hap-hazard establishment. These factors, combined with the tensions that resulted from being pent up in men-of-war on long cruises and the exaggerated sense of personal honor that prevailed among naval officers, produced a significant number of duels. In fact, two-thirds as many naval officers met their deaths on the "field of honor" as were killed in all the naval battles that took place from the Quasi-War to the Civil War.

The most notorious of the duels between naval officers was the encounter in 1820 between Commodores Stephen Decatur and James Barron. Decatur was a member of the court-martial that had ordered Barron suspended from the navy for five years as a result of the *Chesapeake* affair in 1807. When the period of suspension expired during the War of 1812, Barron, who was in Europe, wrote the Navy Department seeking reinstatement. Receiving no answer and too pov-erty-stricken to pay his own passage home, he let the matter drop until he returned to the United States in 1818. He reported to Washington and requested active duty, but Decatur, an influential member of the Board of Naval Commissioners, resisted any move to restore Barron to the active list. He maintained that Barron had proved himself a coward by not coming to his country's assistance during the war.

The two men had once been friends. Barron, eleven years older than De-catur, was a lieutenant in the *United States* when Decatur reported for duty as a midshipman in 1798. They served together against the French and the Barbary pirates, and their professional relationship had deepened into friendship. Now, Decatur accepted all the slurs he heard against Barron's character and repeated them before others. Talebearers—particularly Captain Jesse D. Elliott, who had his own ax to grind—lost no time in carrying Decatur's insults to Barron. Elliott, a midshipman in the *Chesapeake* under Barron, had been engaged in a running battle with Oliver Hazard Perry over Elliott's conduct at the Battle of Lake Erie. With Perry dead, Elliott seems to have transferred his hatred to Decatur, Perry's closest friend, and decided to strike at him through the hapless Barron.

Goaded by Elliott's reports—which the recklessly arrogant Decatur refused to retract—Barron issued a challenge and chose Elliott as his second. Decatur asked his fellow naval commissioners, John Rodgers and David Porter, to serve in the same capacity for him. When they refused, he turned to William Bainbridge. Unknown to Decatur, Bainbridge harbored a grudge and was deeply jealous of him. Thus, the seconds on both sides, who under the code of honor were supposed to try to bring about a reconciliation of the parties, had a vested interest in seeing the duel proceed to a fatal conclusion. As if to make certain of their objectives, they agreed that it should be fought at eight paces rather than the usual ten—a distance at which neither man could miss.

Early on the morning of March 22, 1820, the parties met at the duelling ground at Bladensburg, just over the Maryland line from the District of Columbia. As the final preparations were being made, Barron took the unusual step of addressing his antagonist.

"Now, Decatur," he said in a calm voice, "if we meet in another world, let us hope that we may be better friends."

"I was never your enemy," Decatur instantly replied.

This was the moment when the seconds should have taken steps to halt the encounter. Instead, Elliott ordered Barron and Decatur to their places. Facing each other with long-barreled pistols at their sides, the two men awaited Bainbridge's signal to take aim and fire. Tall and slim, Decatur looked younger than his forty years, while the graying Barron was careworn by adversity. Both pistols came up at the command, "Take aim!"

"Fire!"

When the smoke cleared, both antagonists lay crumpled on the grass. Barron had been hit in the groin and Decatur in the abdomen. Appalled at what had happened and apparently fearful of the consequences, Elliott abandoned Barron and fled the scene. David Porter, who had arrived just as the shots were fired, pursued Elliott's coach on horseback and forced him to return to care for Barron. Decatur was taken to his home on Lafayette Square, in Washington, where he lingered throughout the day in intense agony. "I did not know that any man could suffer such pain!" he cried, before death released him later that evening. Barron recovered from his wound and was eventually restored to active duty, but he never received another seagoing command.

The public outcry that followed Decatur's death put an end to duelling among high-ranking officers, but a great number of duels took place between midshipmen. Little effort seems to have been made by their seniors to curb the slaughter. "Midshipmen, on the slightest provocation, would go out and have a crack at each other," said one officer. William O. Stevens, a historian of duelling, reports that a duel resulted when one midshipman sprinkled water over a letter being written by a messmate. Another midshipman gave offense, he says, by entering the cockpit of his ship wearing his hat. And two touchy young gentlemen quarrelled over whether a bottle—"which they had no doubt emptied together"—was black or dark green.

Such encounters were no laughing matters. In 1811 two youngsters killed each other in a duel fought at such close range that the antagonists' pistols almost touched. And in 1825 *Niles Weekly Register* caustically reported: "Two boys, midshipmen attached to the *Constellation* frigate, amused themselves by shooting one another on the 22nd ult., at Fort Nelson, by which one of them was killed, and the other had the pleasure of saying that he has slain his brother." In 1857 duelling was made punishable by dismissal from the navy.[30]

The world of the enlisted man was circumscribed by hard labor, hard treatment, hard biscuit, and little hard cash. Discipline rested on fear—and fear was instilled by the threat of the lash. Although some youths attracted by the prospect of adventure or the romance of the sea joined the navy, most native-born Americans avoided the service, and warships were usually manned almost entirely by foreigners and social outcasts. One officer described his crew as "persons who are disqualified by their vices from employment on shore—thieves, gamblers, drunkards, play actors, circus riders. Many of them escaped civil punishment by enlisting." In 1835, 3,000 merchant seamen sailed out of Boston, but the navy could enlist only 90 men at that port, even though conditions were often as harsh in the merchant marine as in the navy. On warships the shortage of hands was sometimes so acute that, in violation of the law, black slaves were hired and their masters pocketed their pay. In 1842, there were as many as forty free blacks serving in the *Brandywine*, and according to the vessel's first lieutenant, they received "exactly the same bounty, the same wages, and the same privileges as the whites. . . . No distinction was made between black & white, but each were mingled indiscriminately, and classed only by their relative degrees of seamanship."[31]

Recalling his service as a youth in the pre-Civil War navy, Charles Nordhoff, a prominent journalist, wrote:

> I had always fancied that the stories of worm-eaten bread, and water, the smell of which could cause violent nausea, were a little more than apocryphal; but . . . we experienced both. I have seen drinking water pumped out of our tanks, into a butt on deck, which smelt so abominably as to make any approach to it utterly impossible, ere it had stood in the open air an hour or two. . . . And I have seen a biscuit literally crawl off the mess cloth. . . .[32]

The navy did not furnish uniforms and a man had to purchase his clothing from the purser—usually at a considerable markup. Supplied by grasping contractors, these garments were often of poor quality and quickly wore out under the rigors of shipboard life. When that happened, the sailor was forced to buy a new outfit, which might cost several months' pay. Twenty cents a month was deducted from his already inadequate wages for the support of naval hospitals. Until 1841, when the first regulations concerning the clothing of enlisted men were issued, they wore whatever the purser carried in stock, although some captains ordered their crews to be dressed according to their personal whims.[33]

The uniform prescribed by the regulations consisted of "blue woolen frocks, with white linen or duck collars and cuffs, or blue cloth jacket and trousers, blue vests when vests were worn, black hat, black handkerchief, and shoes." In warm weather or on tropic stations, the uniform was "white frock and trousers, and blue or white hats . . . black handkerchiefs and shoes." The frock, forerunner of the middy blouse, was a long-skirted shirt that was worn tucked into the trousers. Its collar and "breast" were "lined or faced with blue cotton cloth stitched with white thread." Originally, the white uniforms were made of linen, which was easy to keep clean, but southern lawmakers persuaded the navy to switch to cotton duck. Most sailors were skilled with needle and thread and turned these rather plain garments into dashing uniforms worn with a swagger.[34]

The backbone of the navy then—as now—were the experienced petty officers who remained in the service despite harsh conditions. Herman Melville, who served fourteen months as an ordinary seaman in the *United States* from 1843 to 1844, described them in *White-Jacket* as "the fellows who spin interminable yarns about Decatur, Hull, and Bainbridge; and carry about their persons bits of 'Old Ironsides,' as Catholics do the wood of the true cross. These are the fellows that some officers never pretend to damn, however much they may anathematize others. . . . These are the fellows whose society some of the younger midshipmen must affect; from whom they learn their best seamanship; and to whom they look up as veterans. . . ." Melville's own hero was Jack Chase, the captain of the maintop, to whom he later dedicated *Billy Budd*:

> He was a Briton, and a true-blue; tall and well-knit, with a clear open eye, a fine broad brow, and an abounding nut-brown beard. No man had a better heart or a bolder. He was loved by the seamen, and admired by the officers; and even when the captain spoke to him, it was with a slight air of respect. . . . He had a high conceit of his profession as a seaman; and being deeply versed in all things pertaining to a man of war, was universally regarded as an oracle. . . .[35]

Flogging and drunkenness were the twin banes of the navy, and critics professed to see a cause-and-effect relationship, saying the cruelty of the sailors' lives stimulated their thirst for drink. "The ingenuity they shew in procuring grog is often surprising," said an officer serving in the Mediterranean Squadron. Bumboats would come alongside and "a man goes over and barters for a string of sausages; he comes up; his sausages are examined, and turn out to be full of rum, instead of meat. Another buys eggs . . . they are looked to, and a puncture is found at one end, through which the original matter has been let out, and its place supplied with the more beloved fluid." Such efforts to obtain drink led to more flogging, and reformers and humanitarians contended that if the grog ration were eliminated, better health and discipline would naturally follow. The navy could recruit men of higher character who would require less harsh treatment.

The struggle for reform was a long one, because some officers feared that without the threat of the lash naval discipline would collapse. But the reformers and more humane officers such as Commodore Uriah P. Levy, aided by the powerful denunciation of flogging in *White-Jacket* and the need for better personnel to operate steamships, eventually succeeded in having corporal punishment abolished by Congress in 1850. The spirits ration was ended twelve years later, during the Civil War, and the men were given an additional five cents a day in lieu of grog. Another of the major reforms of the period was the introduction of the "continuous service" system under which reenlistment with automatic retention of rating first became possible.[36]

Abroad Britain and France were turning increasingly to steam-powered warships, despite some foot-dragging—one British admiral said he could not look at steamers without revulsion because their decks were filthy with coal dust and their captains looked like chimney sweeps. But the U. S. Navy lagged in accommodating itself to the technological revolution. Captain Matthew Calbraith Perry, a younger brother of Oliver Hazard Perry, noted in January 1837 that the navy ranked eighth among the fleets of the world, behind even Sweden and Egypt. The Royal Navy had twenty-one steamships in commission and the French had twenty-three, Perry observed, while the United States, which had produced the first steam-powered warship, could not boast a single such vessel. Later that year, this gap was filled when a new steam frigate, the *Fulton*, named after her predecessor, which had been destroyed by an explosion in 1829, was commissioned and the younger Perry appointed her captain. Overcoming the prejudice against "tea kettles," Mahlon Dickerson, secretary of the navy in Andrew Jackson's cabinet, had ordered her construction in 1835. Lacking money, he inventively fell back on the law providing for the building of "steam-batteries" that had been passed in 1816 but not implemented, then went back, hand extended, to Congress.

The *Fulton*, which had four funnels and three masts, was a strange-looking and cumbersome craft, but in Perry she had an ideal captain. Convinced that steam was the wave of the future, he used his new command and his considerable family influence to stimulate public interest in a steam navy. Since the navy commissioners had taken no steps to provide men capable of operating the *Fulton*'s engines, Perry drafted the regulations establishing the rank, pay, and duties of the engineers whom the navy was going to need. In effect, he created the engineer corps. Charles H. Haswell, who had designed the *Fulton*'s engines, was an excellent chief engineer, and four assistant engineers, six firemen, and four coal-passers were recruited to help him. The chief engineer was entitled to use the wardroom, but the assistants had to mess with the warrant officers. The engineer corps was not absorbed into the line until 1899.

On her trials in New York Harbor, the *Fulton* made the phenomenal speed of ten knots, and during a shakedown cruise on Long Island Sound, she covered twenty-eight miles in less than two hours. Perry, also a crusader for the shell gun, used his new craft as a test bed for experiments with various types of cannon and projectiles, determining that shells could be fired with nearly as much precision and safety as could old-fashioned solid shot. Designed for harbor defense, the *Fulton* was not intended as a seagoing vessel, but in mid-1838 Perry sailed her from New York to Washington. There she was inspected by President Martin Van Buren and by congressional leaders, who were deeply impressed with both the vessel's potential and her captain's zeal for a steam navy.[37]

Although James K. Paulding, then the secretary of the navy, had vowed that he would "never consent to let our old ships perish, and transform our navy into a fleet of sea monsters," Congress in 1839 authorized the construction of two seagoing steam men-of-war, the side-wheel frigates *Missouri* and *Mississippi*, which were completed in 1842. Displacing 3,220 tons each, they were regarded as the equals of any vessel in service in the European navies and mounted the heaviest weapons yet carried by an American warship—two 10-inch and eight 8-inch shell guns that could be pivoted from side to side. The *Missouri* and *Mississippi* were built of wood, but a year after they were commissioned, the iron-hulled steamer *Michigan* was launched on Lake Erie; she served on the Great Lakes until 1923.

The shift from sail to steam was stimulated by a war scare with Britain over the boundary between Maine and New Brunswick, which also inspired the creation in 1841 of the Home Squadron to protect the American coast against surprise attack. Fearing that the British would use their fast new Cunard passenger ships as troop transports, Abel P. Upshur, who became secretary of the navy that same year, assigned the *Missouri* and *Mississippi* to this force. The Home Squadron absorbed the West India Squadron and the combination formed the nucleus of what later became the Atlantic Fleet.

Despite the movement toward steam, it was basically regarded as an auxiliary to sail, because the primitive engines consumed large amounts of coal and bulky boilers and machinery reduced the room for stores and other equipment required for long cruises. The cumbersome paddle wheels and machinery projecting above the waterline reduced the number of guns and were easy targets for enemy gunners. This defect was remedied when the screw propeller was introduced, because paddle wheels were no longer needed and the engines could be placed below the waterline.[38]

The screw propeller has many fathers, but John Ericsson, a Swedish engineer living in England, was among the first to make practical use of it. His experiments attracted the attention of Captain Robert F. Stockton, an American naval officer with an innovative turn of mind, who suggested he come to America and assist in the construction of the world's first screw-propelled warship, the sloop of war *Princeton*. Ready for sea in January 1844, the 672-ton vessel, named for Stockton's home town, embodied several concepts new to marine engineering. She was the first man-of-war to burn anthracite coal, thereby reducing the cloud of black smoke that usually betrayed the presence of a steamer to the enemy, had steam-driven fans, or "blowers," to force air to the fires and produce better combustion, and a funnel that could be lowered when she was in action or when her engines were not in use. The *Princeton* carried twelve 42-pound carronades and a pair of 12-inch wrought-iron guns, each capable of firing shot weighing 225 pounds, which in tests had penetrated 57 inches of oak timber and 4 inches of wrought iron.[39]

The United States was in a bellicose mood when Stockton brought the *Princeton* to Washington to show her off. A bitter dispute with Britain over the Oregon boundary was threatening to develop into war, and mounting popular pressure for the annexation of Texas seemed almost certain to create a conflict with Mexico. The public was fascinated by the revolutionary warship. One of her 12-inchers, which had been brought from England by Ericsson, was dubbed the "Oregon," while the other, a copy forged under the direction of Stockton, who had only a limited knowledge of metallurgy, was known as the "Peacemaker." On February 28, 1844, Stockton invited President John Tyler, his cabinet, ranking members of Congress, and the capital's social elite for an excursion down the Potomac during which the huge cannon were to be demonstrated.

In the course of the trip the guns were fired several times, and as the *Princeton* was returning home late in the day, the proud and pleased Stockton was persuaded to fire the "Peacemaker" once more. With a tremendous roar, the cannon's breech exploded, hurling sharp pieces of hot metal into the multitude. Eight persons were killed, including Abel Upshur, who had recently become secretary of state, Thomas W. Gilmer, who had held the post of secretary of the navy for only ten days, and Senator David Gardiner of New York. President Tyler, who was on his way to the deck when the explosion occurred, was saved from death or injury because he stopped to talk to pretty Julia Gardiner, the senator's daughter, who was soon thereafter to become his wife. Nine men were injured, Stockton among them.[40]

The expansion of maritime commerce and the presence of American warships in every quarter of the globe created a need to chart the seas and to explore unknown coasts. In the quarter-century preceding the Civil War, the navy organized eleven such expeditions, which took its men and ships from Antarctica and the Amazon, and from the Dead Sea to Central America.[41] The best-known of these scientific forays was the U.S. Exploring Expedition, which was dispatched in 1838 to chart the Antarctic, the Pacific, and the coast of Oregon. Under the command of Lieutenant Charles Wilkes, chief of the navy's Depot of Charts and Instruments, the expedition consisted of the small sloops of war *Vincennes* and *Peacock*, two schooners, a storeship, and a small steamer. A few scientists, who were to make observations and gather specimens, were invited to participate.

Leaving from Norfolk on August 19, 1838, seventy years to the week after Captain James Cook had departed from England on his first voyage to the Pacific, the expedition headed south to the polar region. Yankee whalers and sealers had frequently penetrated into those seas. In 1820 Captain Nathaniel B. Palmer, on a search for new seal rookeries, had sighted an archipelago of barren, snow-covered islands, some 700 miles southwest of Cape Horn, just above the Antarctic Circle. The area was called Palmer Land in honor of its discoverer and it was Wilkes' first destination. "I have rarely seen a finer sight," he wrote as he coasted along the eastern shore of Palmer Land amid drifting icebergs. "The sea was literally studded with these beautiful masses, some of them pure white, and others showing shades of opal, others emerald green, and occasionally here and there some would be black, a strong contrast to the pure white."[42]

Conditions on board Wilkes' vessels were harsh. Ice coated the decks and rigging of the ships, and in the constant fog and mist there was always the danger of collision with an iceberg. The men endured gales, wet, unheated quarters, and inadequate supplies. Breaking out of the ice, Wilkes turned northward into the South Pacific, but not before the steamer that was accompanying him disappeared with all hands.

After surveying the Society Islands, the Fijis, the New Hebrides, and New Caledonia, the expedition called at Sydney, Australia, to take on fresh supplies before again venturing into the Antarctic. Familiar with the rigors of polar exploration, the Australians thought the Americans poorly equipped for the task ahead. "They inquired whether we had compartments in our ships to prevent them from sinking?" Wilkes reported, "How we intended to keep ourselves warm? What kind of anti-scorbutic we were to use? And where were our great ice-saws?"[43] The expedition left Sydney on Christmas Day, 1839, but its ships were soon scattered by a storm. Wilkes, in the *Vincennes*, sighted the ice barrier shortly after the turn of the year. Maneuvering carefully past floating icebergs and avoiding pack ice, he skirted the shore of what he was convinced was Antarctica. Sighting a range of snow-covered mountains from the masthead of his ship on February 12, 1840, Wilkes wrote: "The . . . land clearly determines or settles the question of our having discovered the Antarctic Continent."[44]

Bad weather, the poor condition of his ship, and rampant sickness among his crew eventually forced Wilkes to return to Sydney. Luckily, the rest of his ships had made rendezvous there, after having undergone adventures of their own. Further surveys were made of the Pacific islands and along the northwest coast of North America, including Puget Sound and the mouth of the Columbia River, where the *Peacock* ran aground in a fog and was lost. After that disaster, Wilkes dropped his plan to visit Japan and returned home via the Cape of Good Hope, arriving at New York on June 10, 1842. Summarizing the achievements of the expedition, one historian estimates that it sailed about 85,000 miles and surveyed 280 islands, 800 miles of Oregon coastline and rivers, and 1,500 miles of Antarctic shore.[45]

Not all the great maritime discoveries were made at sea. Lieutenant Matthew Fontaine Maury evolved the revolutionary theories of wind and ocean currents that made him known as the "Pathfinder of the Seas" in a Washington office. As a midshipman, Maury had become interested in the science of navigation and in 1836, at the age of thirty, he produced a popular textbook on the subject, *A New Theoretical and Practical Treatise on Navigation*. Three years later he was severely injured in a stagecoach accident that left him lame and ended his career as a seagoing officer. Appointed to head the Depot of Charts and Instruments, a billet that included the superintendency of the newly established Naval Observatory, Maury began a close study of the dusty ships' logs piled up at his headquarters.

In 1847 he published the results of his research in the *Wind and Current Chart of the North Atlantic*, a book that created controversy among mariners because it contended that if the winds and currents plotted by Maury were followed, the time required for ocean passages could be significantly reduced. When a ship following Maury's suggestions cut ten days from the voyage to Rio de Janeiro, his theories gained wide acceptance. This work was followed in 1855 by his pioneering work on oceanography, *The Physical Geography of the Sea and Its Meteorology*, which begins with the poetic evocation: "One planet is invested with two great oceans; one visible, the other invisible; one underfoot, the other overhead; one entirely envelopes it, the other covers about two-thirds of its surface."

Maury's was the guiding hand behind an international congress on oceanography held in Brussels in 1853, at which a uniform system for recording oceanographic and meteorological data was established. With such information pouring in, he was able to draft wind and current charts for all the major trade routes of the world. His renown grew so great that when a special navy board ordered him retired because of physical disability, pressure from maritime interests caused the order to be rescinded and he was promoted to commander. Before the Civil War brought an end to his career in the U.S. Navy—as a Virginian, Maury elected to go with his state into the Confederacy—he suggested the practicality of a transatlantic telegraph cable, which became a reality in 1866, and he plotted steamer lanes in the North Atlantic, which were adopted almost twenty years after his death in 1873.[46]

A period of wide-ranging scientific and technological change, the 1840s were also a time of sweeping reform in the navy's administrative operations and methods of recruiting and training officers and enlisted men. Over the years, there had been mounting criticism of the inherent conservatism of the Board of Navy Commissioners and the reluctance of its aging members to come to terms with the naval revolution under way. Critics charged that "administrative rigor mortis" had set in. While the members shared collective responsibility for the details of shipbuilding, maintenance, and procurement, no one was individually responsible for seeing that these tasks were carried out in an efficient manner. "When criticism arose concerning sailing qualities or guns or equipment for vessels," states Robert G. Albion in his history of naval administration, "it was almost impossible to place the responsibility on any one member of the Board."[47]

In 1842, Congress abolished the old board and "compartmentalized" the navy's administrative functions into five bureaus: the Bureau of Navy-Yards and Docks; the Bureau of Construction, Equipment and Repairs; the Bureau of Provisions and Clothing; the Bureau of Ordnance and Hydrography; and the Bureau of Medicine and Surgery. There was little coordination among the bureaus and operational control remained in the hands of the politically appointed, often inexperienced, secretary of the navy, who, according to Albion, "might turn for advice to any one of the several bureau chiefs, or even to some glib 'palace favorite.' " Except for an increase in the number of bureaus, no major change was made in the navy's administrative system until 1915, when the post of Chief of Naval Operations was established.[48]

At the same time, naval reformers led by Matthew C. Perry persuaded Congress to approve an apprentice system designed to enlist better recruits and to end the reliance on foreign sailors. Under the terms of Perry's plan, boys of fourteen and upward were recruited for training, to serve in the navy until they reached the age of twenty-one. "In this way our Navy would soon be manned entirely by Americans, among whom it is not now popular, owing to the existence of a harsh system which has grown out of the unlimited introduction of foreigners," Perry said. The brig *Somers* was designated as the first school ship for naval apprentices, and with Commander Alexander Slidell Mackenzie, Perry's brother-in-law, as her skipper, she put to sea in September 1842 with a complement that included seventy-four youthful apprentices.[49]

The voyage ended in tragedy. The *Somers* was homeward bound from the West African coast on November 26, 1842, when James W. Wales, the purser's steward, came to the first lieutenant, Guert Gansevoort, with a bizarre tale. The night before, Wales claimed, Acting Midshipman Philip Spencer had tried to persuade him to join a plot to seize the ship, murder her officers, and turn pirate. Thoroughly shaken, Gansevoort passed this tale on to Captain Mackenzie. At first Mackenzie was skeptical but had Spencer placed under surveillance. Amid reports of suspicious conduct on the part of Spencer and some of the crew, Mackenzie, now gripped by unreasoning panic, ordered the midshipman's arrest. Protesting that he had only been joking with Wales, Spencer was chained to an arms chest on the quarterdeck. A search of his locker produced a list of names of some of the ship's company written in Greek letters under such headings as "certain" and "doubtful." To the aroused Mackenzie, this was irrefutable proof that mutiny and murder were being plotted in his ship.

Spencer, the nineteen-year-old black-sheep son of John C. Spencer, the secretary of war, had been expelled from two colleges and had drunk his way off two ships before being sent to the *Somers*. When Mackenzie saw Spencer's record, he refused to accept him but was overruled by the Navy Department. During the voyage, Spencer performed his duties in a lackluster manner, often talked of piracy in conversations with his fellow officers, and tried to curry favor with the enlisted men. He was frequently seen talking secretively with Boatswain's Mate Samuel Cromwell and a seaman named Elisha Small. They too were arrested and joined Spencer in chains on the quarterdeck, although Cromwell's name was not on Spencer's list. Mackenzie said he kept the prisoners there because the crowded vessel had no secure place of confinement.

Mackenzie assured the prisoners that they would be taken to New York for trial before a court-martial, but on November 30, he convened a board of inquiry to determine what should be done with them. He claimed that the presence of the prisoners on the quarterdeck interfered with the efficient working of the ship and was a constant temptation for fellow plotters to rescue them. Without taking any formal testimony from the accused, the board—made up primarily of young officers who were related to Mackenzie or dependent upon him for patronage —recommended on December 1, 1842, that the prisoners be hanged immediately. Mackenzie concurred in the decision, which he had apparently expected and sought. "In the necessities of my position, I found my law and in them also I must trust to find my justification," he declared.

Coming on deck in his full-dress uniform, Mackenzie told the condemned men they were to be hanged in ten minutes. Three nooses were dangled from the main yard-arm—two on the starboard side for Cromwell and Small and one to port for Spencer. Shortly after midday, a gun boomed out. Three hooded and manacled figures were jerked smartly aloft, where they swung in unison with the gentle motion of the brig. The Stars and Stripes was broken at the gaff and Mackenzie ordered three cheers.

When the *Somers* reached New York, controversy raged over whether Mackenzie was justified in having executed the three men on the basis of the evidence that was available, or whether he was guilty of murder. He was cleared of misconduct by both a court of inquiry and a court-martial, although the verdict of the latter was not unanimous. The *Somers* affair ended Perry's attempt to establish school ships for seamen, but it played a vital role in the creation of the U. S. Naval Academy for the training of officers.[50]

Public uproar over the case focused attention on the haphazard, politically influenced manner in which midshipmen were appointed. Their warrants had become part of the spoils system, presidential appointments were made without regard to age, education, or fitness, and there was no standardized system of training for these "young gentlemen." Sent to sea immediately upon appointment, midshipmen picked up only such learning as their superiors were able to impart. Later, schools were established at some of the navy yards where senior midshipmen could prepare for promotion to lieutenant. Demands for a better system were as old as the navy itself. As early as 1777, John Paul Jones had suggested the establishment of a naval academy to train young naval officers. Although the U. S. Military Academy was founded in 1802, every one of the twenty attempts made between 1800 and 1845 to persuade Congress to approve a similar institution for the navy was flatly rejected.

Lord Nelson did not attend a naval school, nor did any of the American captains who had served so brilliantly in the War of 1812, opponents claimed, so where was the need for such an institution? Senator William Smith, of South Carolina, said that brave American sailors "would look with contempt upon [the] trifling or effeminate leaders" produced by a naval academy. Others charged that the school would embroil the nation in future wars because its graduates "must have fighting to do, to keep them out of mischief."[51]

George Bancroft, the distinguished historian who was appointed secretary of the navy by President James K. Polk in 1845, realized the futility of trying to obtain congressional approval for the opening of a naval academy. Without seeking an authorization or an appropriation, he acted on his own. He asked a council of officers that included Commodore Perry to prepare a plan for "a more efficient system of instruction for the young naval officers," and persuaded the War Department to turn old Fort Severn at Annapolis over to the navy. With a plan of studies and a table of organization produced by the council of officers, the school opened on October 10, 1845, with Commander Franklin Buchanan, a strict disciplinarian, as superintendent and some forty midshipmen already serving in the navy as its first students. Three years after the founding of the institution, the course was prescribed as one year at Annapolis, three years at sea, and a final year at the school. In 1851 the present four-year course with practice cruises in the summer was established and the school was officially designated as the U. S. Naval Academy.[52]

War with Mexico, brewing for some time, finally broke out in 1846. The annexation of Texas, which had won its independence from Mexico a decade before, led directly to the declaration of war, but the underlying cause of the conflict was the conviction of the American people that it was the manifest destiny of the United States to extend its boundaries to the shores of the Pacific. In fact, the first Yankee effort to grab California was made as early as 1842. Receiving information, which later turned out to be false, that the United States and Mexico were at war and fearful of British and French designs on California, Commodore Thomas ap Catesby Jones, commander of the Pacific Squadron, decided to seize the territory.

The impetuous Jones, who as a young lieutenant commanded the gunboats that tried to block the British attack on New Orleans three decades before, slipped out of Callao, Peru, and sailed northward to Monterey with his flagship, the frigate *United States*, and several smaller vessels. On October 19, 1842, he seized the town from the astonished Mexican authorities. Two days later, having received assurances that Mexico and the United States were indeed still at peace, Jones returned Monterey to the Mexicans with profuse apologies. The affair led to his dismissal, but it clearly demonstrated the weakness of Mexico's grip on California.[53]

The U.S. Navy has rarely been summoned to conduct naval operations under less favorable conditions than in the war with Mexico. There was a shortage of light craft that could operate in the shallow waters of the Gulf coast. The crews of what vessels there were suffered the ravages of malaria and yellow fever in the summer and were hampered in winter by violent storms, called "northers." Moreover, the Navy Department's newly organized bureaus were extremely lax and inefficient in providing stores and ammunition for Commodore David Conner, commander of the Home Squadron, who was conducting operations in the gulf. As Dudley W. Knox wrote in his history of the navy:

> The only base was at Pensacola, nearly nine hundred miles from Vera Cruz [where Conner maintained a blockade], and it was very poorly equipped with facilities and supplies. For example, thirty days were required to bake enough bread there to last the flagship three months, and even fresh water was difficult to obtain in sufficient quantities. There was no coal, and more than two months elapsed after the first three small steamers arrived, nearly three months after war began, before a cargo of coal reached Pensacola. Obviously, the Department was poorly organized for conducting a war which it had fully expected for nearly two years. . . .[54]

Luckily, the Mexicans were even less prepared and failed to prevent Conner from fulfilling his tasks of keeping the sea lanes open for the passage of American troops and supplies, maintaining a tight blockade of the Mexican coast, and supporting an advance across the Rio Grande into Mexico by General Zachary Taylor's army. There was not much glory in blockade duty. Except when a raid was launched with the intent of capturing vessels from the Mexicans, the ships cruised slowly offshore with nothing to break the routine. "During the parching heats of summer, and the long boisterous nights of winter, our vigilance was expected to be, and was, unremitting," wrote Raphael Semmes, Conner's flag lieutenant.[55]

Living conditions on board the blockading ships were poor. The ships were crowded with large wartime complements and provisions were often short. Rations consisted almost entirely of salt pork or beef and hardtack, washed down with boiling-hot tea. The crews sometimes went for months without fresh vegetables, so scurvy was rampant. It was not surprising, then, that although volunteers flocked to the army, the navy was unable to attract adequate manpower. Soon after the declaration of war, the navy's authorized strength was increased from 7,500 men and boys to 10,000, but it never actually rose above 8,100 men, despite the offer of a fifteen-dollar bounty to those who enlisted. One of the few successful recruiting officers was Lieutenant David Dixon Porter, son of Commodore David Porter, who established a rendezvous at New Orleans. Paradoxically, Porter's naval career began in the Mexican navy when his father was in command of that service.[56]

While Conner's squadron was engaged in the wearying task of blockading Veracruz and launching raids on smaller ports, the Pacific Squadron, under Commodore John D. Sloat, began the long-awaited conquest of California. Almost a year before the outbreak of war, Secretary of the Navy Bancroft had told Sloat that in case of war, "you will at once . . . possess yourself of the port of San Francisco, and blockade or occupy . . . other ports." In readiness to comply with these orders, Sloat deployed his handful of ships at strategic points up and down the coast of California while he remained with his flagship, the frigate *Savannah*, at Mazatlán, Mexico, regarded as an excellent listening post. He received news of the fighting between Mexican and American troops on the Rio Grande in mid-May 1846, but overly cautious and in poor health, he did not sail for Monterey until June 8.

The *Savannah* arrived on July 1 at Monterey, where two other vessels awaited her, but Sloat, apparently influenced by the consequences of Jones' premature action four years before, dallied until July 7 before seizing the town. The next day, Commander John B. Montgomery of the sloop *Portsmouth* took possession of San Francisco. Army Captain John C. Frémont, leading a band of irregulars, had already captured the city from the Mexicans and proclaimed the independent Bear Flag Republic, which was now brought to an end. Both Monterey and San Francisco were taken without bloodshed.

On July 29 Sloat relinquished command of the squadron to Commodore Stockton, by this time recovered from the injuries he received in the explosion on board the *Princeton*. Using the 200 or so marines attached to the squadron as a striking force, the commodore began a vigorous campaign to conquer all of California. The mobility provided by sea transport allowed Stockton to move his forces, which included those of Frémont and General Stephen W. Kearny, to meet the various challenges mounted by the Mexicans. By the beginning of 1847, the Americans had gained complete control of California.[57]

In the meantime, President Polk and his advisers studied with increasing dissatisfaction the dispatches from northern Mexico. Despite several victories, Zachary Taylor's army had bogged down. To speed the campaign Polk decided to strike into the enemy's heartland from the sea and to capture Mexico City. Late in 1846 Veracruz was chosen as the target for a landing. Once that city was theirs, the invaders would be able to advance on the Mexican capital. General Winfield Scott was chosen to command the invasion force of some 12,000 men, while Commodore Conner was given the task of getting the troops safely ashore.

By March 9, 1847, all was ready for the largest amphibious assault American forces had ever attempted. Conner selected for the landing a lonely beach about three miles south of Veracruz, but no one knew what the invaders would find there. As the first wave of assault troops crowded into a flotilla of specially built surfboats, a line of small naval vessels took station inshore for a close-range bombardment in case the enemy should resist the landing. It took several hours to load the boats, each manned by eight sailors, and to form them up in a single line parallel to the beach. While these preparations were under way, Mexican cavalrymen were spotted among the dunes and the inshore squadron fired several shots at the horsemen.

At 5:30 P.M., a gun was fired from the army steamer *Massachusetts*, General Scott's command ship, and the signal for the landing was broken at her masthead. Everyone expected the dunes to erupt into a fury of musket balls and shot, but there was only a brooding stillness as the surfboats moved in. About a hundred yards from the beach, the boats grounded and the soldiers, holding their arms and cartridge belts above their heads, waded ashore unopposed. Almost as if at some prearranged signal, a dozen army bands simultaneously crashed into "The Star-Spangled Banner."

As the first wave dashed up the beach and raised the American flag, the surfboats put about and returned to the transports for another load of men. In five hours, some 8,600 troops were landed on the beachhead without the loss of a man. K. Jack Bauer, the historian of the naval side of the Mexican War, terms this a "considerable achievement" even by today's standards, and "unprecedented" in 1847. Conner and Scott "truly deserve that laconic but meaningful accolade, 'well done,' " he adds.

The fleet, now under Matthew C. Perry's command, the ailing Conner having received orders to return home, played an important role in the capture of Veracruz. Several seaborne attacks were made on its fortifications, regarded as among the strongest in North America, and a naval battery armed with the most powerful guns possessed by the Americans was landed and helped batter the defenders into submission. The Mexicans surrendered on March 29, 1847, seven days after the shelling began. A few weeks later, Scott's army, including 300 marines, marched off to Mexico City over the same route taken by Cortez three centuries before.

Perry launched several attacks on some of the smaller ports on the gulf coast, but the Veracruz expedition was the high point of the navy's participation in the Mexican War. As Scott said in a general order issued the day after the fall of the city: "Thanks higher than those of the general-in-chief have . . . been earned by the entire Home Squadron, under the successive orders of Commodores Conner and Perry, for prompt, cheerful, and able assistance from the arrival of this army off this coast."[58]

The discovery of gold in newly conquered California focused the attention of Americans upon the Pacific world that lay at their doorstep. China and the

East Indies had been opened to American trade, but Japan remained a challenge. Holding themselves aloof from the Western "barbarians," the Japanese had closed their islands to the outside world two centuries before. Except for those Dutchmen involved in a tightly restricted trade with the Japanese at Nagasaki, no foreigner was allowed to enter the country and any Japanese who left was put to death if he returned. Japan was still a feudal state without steam engines, factories, or telegraphs. In 1846, Commodore James Biddle in the ship of the line *Columbus*, with the sloop of war *Vincennes* in company, was sent knocking on the Japanese door, but the authorities treated him in an insulting manner and refused to negotiate. Two years later, Commander James Glynn went to Nagasaki in the small sloop of war *Preble* to pick up fifteen shipwrecked American whalers. Finding the Japanese still elated by their "victory" over Biddle, Glynn decided not to tolerate any delay. He threatened to open fire upon Nagasaki if the whalers were not delivered within two days. When they were handed over, the *Preble* sailed away.[59]

The lure of the Japanese market, the need for a coaling station for ships crossing the Pacific to China, and demands for the protection of castaways ultimately led to the organization of a naval expedition to open up Japan. Matthew Perry was selected for the assignment. He was to present a letter from President Millard Fillmore to the emperor of Japan and to conclude a treaty which covered the above-mentioned matters. Although Perry would have preferred command of the prestigious Mediterranean Squadron, he was ideally suited for the task he was given. As Samuel Eliot Morison said, "if a computer system had been invented by 1851, and officers' records kept on I.B.M. cards, a query as to what naval officer was best qualified to negotiate with Japan would have elicited a punched pattern spelling out 'Matthew Calbraith Perry.' " The commodore had more diplomatic experience than any other American officer, and his dignified, if somewhat pompous, manner was to serve him well in his negotiations with the Japanese.[60]

Perry's four "black ships"—the side-wheelers *Mississippi* and *Susquehanna* with the sloops of war *Saratoga* and *Plymouth* in tow—appeared off Uraga, at the entrance to Tokyo Bay, shortly after dawn on July 8, 1853. Gradually, the sun burned away the early-morning mist, revealing a scene from a delicate Japanese painting. The smooth sea was dotted with fishing boats and lumbering junks, and in the distance the snow-covered cone of Mount Fuji brooded in lonely majesty. As the ships glided along at eight knots with guns loaded and run out, thousands of Japanese who had never before seen a steamer lined the shore and gazed with amazement at the "burning ships." At about 5:00 P.M., Perry's squadron anchored in line of battle in Tokyo Bay, within thirty miles of the capital.[61]

Rejecting overtures from inferior officials, Perry made it clear that he would not entrust President Fillmore's letter to the emperor to anyone who was not of imperial rank. For a week, the commodore held himself aloof, while the Japanese authorities desperately debated what was to be done. Finally satisfied by the appearance of the Prince of Izu, one of the emperor's counselors, Perry, with the full panoply of his rank, went ashore on July 14 for the ceremony of handing over the president's letter. He realized the importance of pageantry and "face" in the conduct of affairs with the Japanese.[62]

A thirteen-gun salute echoed over the anchorage as he stepped into his barge. Fifteen boatloads of marines, sailors, and two bands were landed as a guard of honor. Perry was flanked by two huge Negro seamen who served as bodyguards—the first blacks the Japanese had seen—as he marched the short distance from the beach at Kurihama to a hastily constructed pavilion. Once the letter had been delivered to the prince, Perry announced that the squadron would depart within a few days for China but would return with more vessels in the following spring for a reply to Fillmore's letter.

Perry returned to his Japanese anchorage sooner than he had expected. Fearing that a Russian squadron then in the area might force the Japanese to sign a treaty while he was still wintering on the China coast, he hurried back to Tokyo Bay in February 1854 with a much larger squadron. Undoubtedly it was this incident that caused him to predict two years later that the Americans and Russians—or "the Saxon and the Cossack," as he put it—would become rivals in the Far East.[64]

The Japanese had already agreed to yield to Perry's demands, but as masters of the arts of evasion and procrastination, they delayed as long as they could in coming to terms. But in Perry they met their match in diplomatic skill and steadfastness. As his ships lay close inshore, he endured day after wearying day of negotiations in a treaty house set up near the village of Yokohama. The Japanese offered to open Nagasaki as a port of entry, but Perry insisted it was unsuitable and held out for the use of other ports.

Midway in the negotiations, there was an exchange of gifts that seemed to symbolize the cultural differences between the two nations. The Japanese gave the Americans gold-lacquered furniture and boxes, bronze ornaments, delicate porcelain goblets, and a collection of seashells. The American gifts consisted of firearms, one hundred gallons of whiskey, farm implements, clocks, stoves, a telegraph, and a quarter-sized locomotive, complete with tender, coach, and track. The track was quickly laid, and the onlookers were treated to the spectacle of "a dignified mandarin whirling about the circular road at a rate of 20 miles an hour, with his loose robe flying in the wind."[65]

Finally, on March 31, 1854, the Treaty of Kanagawa was signed amid elaborate ceremonies. It provided for the opening of Shimoda and Hakodate to American shipping, the protection of shipwrecked American seamen, and the granting of most-favored-nation status to the United States. Trade was not mentioned, but the United States was given the right to establish a consulate at Shimoda. This was the entering wedge for the agreement signed two years later that completed the opening of Japan to commerce with foreign nations.

Plaudits were showered upon Perry when he returned home, but no one summed up his accomplishments better than Washington Irving. "You have gained yourself a lasting name, and have won it without shedding a drop of blood or inflicting misery on a human being," he wrote the commodore "What naval commander ever won laurels at such a rate?"[66]

5

DIVIDED WATERS

The transcending facts of the American Civil War are the military genius of Robert E. Lee and the naval superiority of the North. Behind all the blood and sacrifice, behind the movements of armies and the pronouncements of political leaders, the war was essentially a contest between these two strategic forces. Lee's tactical opponent was the Army of the Potomac, but his strategic rival was the Union Navy.
—Rear Admiral John D. Hayes:
Sea Power in the Civil War

The Norfolk Navy Yard was burning. Pulsing and wavering in the sky, the flames turned the black night to amber red. Flames licked up the masts of nearly a dozen ships that had been scuttled and set ablaze. The machine shop was burning. The sail loft was burning. The ordnance building was burning. Flaming debris swirled through the choking smoke, touching off caches of powder and flammable stores. It was April 21, 1861, just six years after Commodore Matthew C. Perry had returned in triumph from opening up Japan, and the navy in which he had served was being split in two. Fort Sumter had fallen the week before, and wrecking crews were working frantically to destroy the yard before it fell into secessionist hands. When the last straggler had rowed out to the Federal steam sloop *Pawnee*, she slipped away to safety. Grim-faced men huddled on her deck or climbed into her lower shrouds for a better view of the inferno they had left behind them.

The hasty—almost panic-stricken—abandonment of the navy's largest and best-equipped base typified the confusion and turmoil that marked the opening of the Civil War. Treachery and disloyalty were in the air. Naval stations at Pensacola and Charleston and other vital facilities in the Southern states had been handed over to the rebels without a fight. Blundering and mismanagement by President Abraham Lincoln's new cabinet had thwarted plans for the relief of Fort Sumter. Washington was in danger of being captured by rebel mobs and the Naval Academy at nearby Annapolis was moved to Newport, Rhode Island, for safety. Every ship brought letters of resignation from Southern-born officers. No one could tell friend from foe. Lincoln's call for 75,000 volunteers to put down the rebellion swelled the flow of resignations from a trickle to a torrent. Nearly a quarter of the navy's 1,457 commissioned officers, most of them able men with service in important posts, eventually "went South."[1]

There were many similarities between the position of the Union at the beginning of the Civil War and that of Britain in the American Revolution. Like the British, the North had to suppress a wide-scale rebellion, while the Confederacy had but to maintain its existence long enough to wear down the will of the Yankees to persist in a costly and bloody struggle. Like the rebellious Americans of a century before, the South depended upon foreign support because it did not have the capacity to produce the arms and munitions needed to wage war. Thus, the primary task of the U.S. Navy, which had command of the sea, was to prevent the Confederacy from exchanging its cotton for the tools of war. While the army tried to crush the Confederacy on land, the navy blockaded the Southern coast, captured or closed Southern ports, and eventually cut the South in two by winning control of the Mississippi River. This strategy became known as the "Anaconda Plan" because it called for the Confederacy to be slowly constricted in the same way the South American reptile finishes off its victims.[2]

The South had no navy at all; but for Stephen R. Mallory, the Confederate secretary of the navy, necessity was the mother of invention. No one understood better than did the energetic and experienced Mallory that the Confederacy had to break the Union blockade if it were to win its independence. As senator from Florida before the war, he had served as chairman of the Senate Naval Affairs Committee. He had observed the technological progress made by the European navies and now decided to make use of these developments. Mallory's task was not an easy one. The South had no maritime tradition, no reserve of trained seamen, no large shipyards, and no shops capable of turning out marine engines. Nevertheless, the Confederacy built several powerful ironclads, secured commerce-raiders abroad, and improvised such revolutionary weapons as electrically exploded mines, torpedo boats, and the first submarine to sink an enemy warship.

The Norfolk Navy Yard was a tempting target for the rebels. Stretching for three-quarters of a mile along the Elizabeth River, across from the City of Norfolk, it contained all the resources required to maintain a fleet: a dry dock capable of handling any ship in the world, a pair of covered ways, a foundry, machine shop, boiler shop, rope walk, and mountains of supplies and foodstuffs. Tons of powder, thousands of shells, and some 1,200 cannon of all types were stored at the yard or in nearby magazines. The most important of the vessels berthed at Norfolk was the large screw frigate *Merrimack*, which was undergoing badly needed repairs. The rest were decaying sailing vessels, among them the old *United States*, one of the navy's first frigates.

During the month following Lincoln's inauguration on March 4, 1861, nothing had been done to protect the navy yard or to prepare the *Merrimack* for sea, should Virginia join the Confederacy. The administration's attention was fixed on Charleston Harbor and the unfolding crisis at Fort Sumter. Gideon Welles, the Connecticut politician and editor who had been appointed secretary of the navy, pleaded with the president to send reinforcements to Norfolk, but Lincoln contended that such a step might create unrest in Virginia, already trembling on the brink of secession, and push her into the arms of the rebels. In the meantime, the sixty-eight-year-old commandant of the Norfolk yard, Commodore Charles S. McCauley, who was under the influence of a staff weighted with Southern officers, tried to conduct business as usual.[3]

On the eve of the attack on Fort Sumter, Secretary Welles ordered the *Merrimack* readied for sea. Working around the clock with double crews for four days, Benjamin F. Isherwood, the navy's engineer in chief, had the frigate's engines in working order by April 17. That same day, Virginia seceded from the Union. Even so, the doddering McCauley refused permission for the *Merrimack* to sail, saying he wanted to avoid alarming the local populace. The next day, with steam up, Isherwood again sought permission for her to cast off. "To my great surprise and dissatisfaction," he later reported, the commandant denied the request.

Welles stripped the Washington Navy Yard of available marines and sent Commodore Hiram Paulding to Norfolk in the *Pawnee* to replace McCauley. "On no account should the arms and munitions be permitted to fall into the hands of the insurrectionists," he told Paulding. "Should it finally become necessary, you will, in order to prevent that result, destroy the property." Paulding arrived at Norfolk on the evening of April 20 to find that McCauley, convinced that the Virginia militia was about to storm the base, had ordered the *Merrimack* and several other vessels scuttled at their berths.

Unable to bring the ships out, Paulding decided to destroy the navy yard, although he had 1,000 well-armed sailors and marines and probably could have defended it against an assault by poorly disciplined militia. Paulding's decision was a blunder, and he compounded it by bungling the way in which it was carried out. A demolitions expert who had been brought along to blow up the dry dock was ordered first to fire the sinking ships and the dock was not mined until the last moment. Valuable time was also wasted in setting fire to the easily replaceable covered ways, while there was no systematic plan for burning more valuable facilities.

At 4:20 A.M. a signal rocket blazed into the sky, and in the words of a *New York Times* correspondent in the *Pawnee*, a "great conflagration . . . burst, like the day of judgement, on the startled citizens of Norfolk and Portsmouth and all the surrounding country. . . ."[4]

As soon as the last Yankees had abandoned the base, the Confederates raced into the yard and extinguished the flames. The dry dock was flooded before the mine exploded and most of the vital shops were saved from the blaze. Although the *Merrimack* burned to her waterline, her lower hull and engines were only slightly damaged. The essential shore installations were working again within a few weeks and the rich haul of cannon provided the Confederacy with weapons that it could not have produced. Many of them were eventually used to protect major ports against assault by the Federal navy.

To blockade the 3,500-odd miles of coastline running from the Potomac River to the Rio Grande, a coastline punctuated by 189 rivers and countless inlets and estuaries, the navy had ninety vessels listed as available for service. In the mid-1850s thirty steamers, including six powerful screw frigates of the *Merrimack* class and twelve sizeable sloops of war, of which the *Hartford* was typical, had been added to the navy's strength. They were armed with the newly developed Dahlgren gun, an invention of Commander John A. Dahlgren. Shaped like soda bottles because the thickness of the barrel followed the curve of internal pressures, Dahlgren guns could fire both solid shot and shells and were available in calibres up to eleven inches. But over the years, these ships had been allowed to fall into disrepair and only forty-two vessels of various types were in commission at the outbreak of war. Many of them were scattered about the globe on distant stations and some did not get home until two years later. With only 7,600 men on active duty and 207 in all receiving ships on the Atlantic coast, there was also a shortage of crews.[5]

The responsibility for making the Union blockade work rested upon Gideon Welles. With his full white beard and flowing wig, the secretary of the navy was an eccentric-looking figure, but he had a talent for organization. Although Welles had been appointed to the cabinet primarily for political and geographic reasons—he was an ex-Democrat and a New Englander—he had been chief of the Bureau of Provisions and Clothing during the Mexican War and, unlike most of his predecessors, was familiar with the administrative side of the navy. "In spite of his peculiarities, I think Mr. Welles a very wise, strong man," said Charles A. Dana, a War Department official and later the influential editor of the *New York Sun*: "He understood his duty, and did it efficiently, continually and unvaryingly." No one realized this more than Abraham Lincoln, who relied upon Welles for counsel throughout the war.

To assist him in the technical details of the operation of the navy, Welles was fortunate in having the services of Gustavus V. Fox, a former naval officer. So stagnant was promotion that in eighteen long years he had risen only to lieutenant; in 1856 he had resigned to manage a textile mill in Massachusetts. During the Sumter crisis, he presented Lincoln with a plan for the relief of the besieged outpost which so impressed the president that he appointed Fox chief clerk of the Navy Department. On July 31, 1861, he was named to the newly created post of assistant secretary of the navy. Although some people contended that Welles was merely a figurehead and that Fox ran the Navy Department, in fact the two men complemented each other and acted as a team, Welles having the final say in most matters.[6]

Their first job was to plug the holes in the blockade through which blockade-runners were sailing with impunity. Having received full authority from Lincoln to build, purchase, and charter as many vessels as required, Welles commissioned every type of craft he could lay his hands on. Excursion boats, ferryboats, freighters, yachts, passenger vessels, and tugboats driven by propellers, paddle wheels, or sails—anything, it was said, from "Captain Noah to Captain Cook" that floated and could carry a gun was sent South to join the blockading fleet. The smaller craft manned the "inshore line" covering harbor entrances and estuaries, while the larger vessels maintained the offshore line (100 miles out) with lots of sea room for pursuit. Loose and hurried procurement on such a scale made for corruption, and George D. Morgan, Welles' brother-in-law, pocketed $90,000 through dealings that congressional investigators later branded as "unwise and pernicious."[7] By July 1861 at least one Union vessel was on station off each of the nine major ports between the Chesapeake and the Mississippi connected by railroad to the interior of the Confederacy. Welles reported 82 vessels in commission two months later; 264 in December 1861; 427 in December 1862; 588 in December 1863; and 671 in December 1864. In the words of J. Thomas Scharf, who served in the Confederate navy and became its historian, the blockade "shut the Confederacy out from the world, deprived it of supplies, weakened its military and naval strength, and compelled exhaustion. . . ."[8]

To man these ships, on July 24, 1861, Congress passed an "Act to Provide for the Temporary Increase of the Navy," which authorized the enrollment of additional officers and men. About 7,500 volunteer officers were added to the navy, and by war's end, four out of every five officers on active duty were volunteers who had come from the merchant marine or from other areas of civilian life. Courses intended to give these officers at least a smattering of the skills required in their new profession were offered at the navy yards, but they were so hurried that it was not uncommon for a man to arrive on board his new ship wearing only part of his uniform—much to the disgust of veterans of the "Old Navy."

Enlisted volunteers also flooded into the navy to accept a bounty of $20, and at its greatest strength, in 1864, the navy numbered 51,500 men. As in the past, citizens of other lands made up a large proportion of the crews. In March 1863 the 324-man crew of the *Hartford* included 216 aliens, of whom 84 were Irish. Half the crew of the frigate *Wabash* were foreigners and on some of the smaller vessels the proportion was even higher. Captains were also authorized to enlist blacks who had fled from slavery and sought sanctuary in their ships.[9]

Welles and Fox modernized the navy's administration. Saddled with a Navy List dominated by superannuated officers, they obtained passage of the service's first retirement law, which allowed them to trim off the deadwood. Younger and more imaginative officers were appointed to high posts. Perhaps the best measure of their success is that, unlike the army, the navy did not require years of trial and error to find able commanders. Officers of distinction were found almost immediately and placed in positions of command. To reward them, Congress was at last persuaded to abandon its prejudice against high naval rank, and the grades of rear admiral and commodore were established in 1862. That same year the number of bureaus in the Navy Department was increased from five to eight so that the department's tasks would be more efficiently distributed: the Bureau of Construction, Equipment, and Repairs was divided into three new bureaus—the Bureau of Equipment and Recruiting, the Bureau of Construction and Repair, and the Bureau of Steam Engineering; and the Bureau of Ordnance and Hydrography was divided and designated the Bureau of Navigation and the Bureau of Ordnance.[10]

Soon Welles could proudly report that the navy had gone about its grim business so efficiently that "four powerful squadrons have been collected, organized, and stationed for duty on our maritime frontier with a rapidity and suddenness which finds no approach to a parallel in previous naval history and which it is believed no other country but our own could have achieved."[11]

Early on the morning of September 1, 1861, President Lincoln was awakened by a White House watchman who informed him that important visitors wished to see him. Without waiting to don a robe, Lincoln dashed downstairs in his nightshirt to find Gustavus Fox and Benjamin F. Butler, a cross-eyed Massachusetts politician turned general. An amphibious force led by Butler had captured the two Confederate forts guarding Hatteras Inlet, on the low-lying coast of North Carolina, thereby putting a stopper in a passage much favored by blockade-runners. "Fox communicated the news, and then he and Lincoln fell into each other's arms," said Butler. The diminutive assistant secretary, "about five feet nothing," embraced the gaunt Lincoln "as high as the hips, and Lincoln reached down over him so that his arms were pretty near the floor, and thus holding each other they flew about the room." As the president and Fox danced their jig, Butler sprawled on a sofa and laughed.[12]

Lincoln had good reason to be jubilant. A Union defeat at Bull Run in mid-July had cast a pall over the nation, and Butler's victory—even though it proved to be only a minor one—lifted spirits and temporarily cooled criticism of the conduct of the war. The attack had been suggested by a four-member Blockade Board, headed by Captain Samuel F. Du Pont, that had been convened by Welles to plot the navy's wartime strategy. It had soon become apparent that ships on blockade duty needed a Southern base so that they would not have to sail all the way back to Hampton Roads for coal and supplies, and Port Royal Sound, between Charleston and Savannah, and Hatteras Inlet were pinpointed for attack.

Crowded with a hastily assembled force of about 900 soldiers under Ben Butler's command, seven warships and two transports dropped anchor off Hatteras Inlet on August 27, 1861. Flag Officer Silas H. Stringham, commander of the Atlantic Blockading Squadron, surveyed the scene and, in preparation for a landing the next day, ordered the surfboats hoisted out. The inlet was defended by a pair of poorly armed sand-and-log forts, the larger called Fort Hatteras and the smaller, Fort Clark. Early the next morning with the screw frigate *Minnesota*, Stringham's flagship, in the van, the squadron moved inshore and opened fire on Fort Clark, which was nearer the beach than Fort Hatteras. The old Confederate 32-pounders were outranged by the 9- and 10-inch naval guns, which methodically pumped shells into the rebel works.

Some 300 men were loaded into the boats, several of which capsized in the rough surf before they got to the beach. With arms and ammunition soaked, the soldiers straggled ashore to find that further landing operations had been suspended. Luckily, the Confederates had abandoned Fort Clark and fled to Fort Hatteras. Next morning, Stringham rained a hail of shells down on that fort, compelling it to surrender. A shifting channel made Hatteras Inlet unsatisfactory as a base, but the expedition demonstrated that the rebel coastal defenses were vulnerable to amphibious attack.[13]

Samuel Du Pont was given the task of capturing Port Royal Sound. Unlike Hatteras, Port Royal was a tough nut to crack. Two stout batteries guarded the 2.2-mile-wide entrance to the sound, Fort Walker on Hilton Head Island to the south and Fort Beauregard on St. Helena Island to the north, both armed with long-range guns. The conventional wisdom of the day held that wooden ships could not successfully engage fortifications unless they had overwhelming superiority in firepower. Du Pont had made a study of such operations in the Crimean War and reached the conclusion that steamships might give a seaborne attacking force an advantage, because such ships could always keep moving, whatever the wind and tide.[14]

It took two months for Du Pont to gather a fleet that he considered equal to the task assigned it. At the end of October 1861, some 13,000 troops under the command of General Thomas W. Sherman were shepherded to the coast of South Carolina by about thirty warships. A raging storm struck the invasion fleet off Cape Hatteras, scattering the ships and driving two supply vessels aground. An old side-wheeler carrying a battalion of marines foundered, but only six men were lost. While awaiting the arrival of all his ships, Du Pont surveyed the scene and discovered that Fort Walker was not as impregnable as had been feared because only a few guns were mounted on the northern wall facing the sound.[15]

Shortly after 9:00 A.M. on November 7, the *Wabash*, Du Pont's flagship, led two columns of ships up the channel between the forts—one a squadron of nine heavy vessels and the other a flanking squadron of five shallow-draft gunboats that were to fend off any rebel craft that might try to interfere. As they passed up the channel close to Fort Beauregard, the ships poured shells into the forts "as fast as a horse's feet beat the ground in a gallop." They received a brisk fire in return and several were hit but not seriously damaged. When the ships had run the gauntlet between the forts and were two miles into the sound, Du Pont ordered his largest ships to put about. The *Wabash* and two other heavy vessels turned to port and sailed past the batteries again, this time within close range of Fort Walker, while those that remained behind with the gunboats pounded the fort's weakest side. The three big ships steamed back and forth between the batteries twice more before Fort Walker was abandoned by its defenders early in the afternoon. By nightfall Fort Beauregard had also fallen to the navy's guns, with not a single soldier having been landed. For the rest of the war, Port Royal served as an important base for the conduct of the Union's naval operations.[16]

Du Pont's victory buoyed morale in the North, but in the South it created panic and demands that the defenses of the Atlantic coast be reinforced. General Robert E. Lee, sent to strengthen the defenses of the Carolina coast, was deeply impressed by the long arm of the Union navy. He suggested that vulnerable outlying positions be abandoned and a defense line established inland. "Wher.-ever [the enemy's] fleet can be brought, no opposition to his landing car be made," said Lee. "We have nothing to oppose to its heavy guns, which sweep over the low banks of this country with irresistible force."[17]

The British consul in Charleston reported early in 1862 that the blockade-runners were doing a great business. "Everything is brought in in abundance . . . and no one seems to think that there is the slightest risk."[18] There were risks—but there were also enormous profits to be reaped from running the blockade. Although the first blockade-runners were regular merchantmen, a distinct type soon developed. Long, low, and painted the color of an Atlantic fog, these silent ghosts picked up cargoes of arms, munitions, medical supplies, and luxury goods at St. George, Bermuda, or Nassau, in the Bahamas, and raced into Southern ports under cover of darkness. Then, after loading bales of cotton for the hungry mills of the British midlands, they tried to slip past the Federal patrols to safety. An estimated 1,500 blockade-runners were captured or wrecked during the war, but with profits ranging upward of fifteen times costs, it took only one or two successful trips to pay for a vessel and her cargo. Speculators were eager to get into the trade, and for a successful voyage a captain might receive as much as $5,000 in gold, and an ordinary seaman, $250—clear evidence of the risks involved.

For the men who manned the vessels on blockade duty, life dragged on monotonously through sweltering summer and stormy winter. "Day after day, day after day, we lay inactive," Admiral Mahan recalled of his time on blockade duty. Every suspicious ship had to be inspected. Often the men would no sooner tumble into their hammocks after a long chase than they would be turned out to repeat the same exhausting routine. Officers and men usually slept half-dressed, so as to be ready should a strange sail or plume of smoke be sighted.[19]

Charles A. Post, a young volunteer officer on blockade duty off Wilmington, wrote disgustedly:

> I told her [his mother] she could get a fair idea of our "adventures" if she would go the roof of the house on a hot summer day, and talk to a half a dozen hotel hallboys, who are generally far more intelligent and agreeable than the average "acting officer." Then descend to the attic and drink some tepid water, full of iron-rust. Then go on to the roof again and repeat this "adventurous process" at intervals, until she has tired out, and go to bed, with everything shut down tight, so as not to show a light. Adventure! Bah![20]

And then when Congress abolished the enlisted men's grog ration in 1862, that was the last straw. As soon as the unhappy news reached the South Atlantic Blockading Squadron, a petition for repeal was submitted to Du Pont. Some sailors resorted to home-brew secretly made aboard ship or bought whiskey from smugglers who demanded $10 a bottle. Sympathizing with his men, one commander obtained six barrels of whiskey, which he planned to dole out "under medical direction." When the temperance-minded Welles learned of this, he irately suggested "oatmeal mixed with water" as a substitute.[21]

In their zeal to close Southern ports. Yankee naval officers adopted many of the practices used by the British in the Napoleonic period—practices the United States had bitterly opposed and which had helped bring about the War of 1812. It was a further irony that the British, in turn, resorted to all the old arguments in defense of neutral shipping that the Americans had vainly espoused a half-century before. At times relations between Britain and the United States were severely strained, particularly by the so-called *Trent* affair.

In November 1861 Captain Charles Wilkes, who had gained fame as an Antarctic explorer and was now in command of the screw sloop *San Jacinto*, seized James M. Mason and John Slidell, two Confederate diplomatic agents, from the English mail steamer *Trent*, which was en route from Havana to England. Although Wilkes' action was wildly cheered in the North, the British regarded it as a serious breach of neutrality. They reinforced their garrisons in Canada and threatened an embargo on the export of saltpeter to the North. Only Lincoln's cool-headed decision to tell the British that Wilkes had acted on his own initiative, and his freeing of Mason and Slidell, avoided a confrontation that might have led to war.[22]

Frequent storms made life miserable for the sailors on blockade duty at Hampton Roads, so when March 8, 1862, turned sunny and clear, the crew of the sailing frigate *Congress* did their wash. It fluttered in the rigging, whites on the starboard side and blues on the port. About 12:45 P.M. a quartermaster, surveying the glistening water through a spyglass, spotted a pillar of heavy black smoke approaching from the direction of Norfolk. "I wish you would take the glass and have a look over there, sir," he said to a nearby officer. "I believe that thing is a-comin' down at last."[23]

"That thing" was the Confederacy's answer to the blockade—an ironclad floating citadel, bristling with heavy cannon. She was the brainchild of Confederate Navy Secretary Mallory. Realizing that the Confederacy. with its limited industrial capacity, would never be able to build enough ships to outmatch the North, he saw in the ironclad—already in use in Europe—a means of consigning the Federal fleet to obsolescence in one fell swoop. "I regard the possession of an iron-armored ship as a matter of the first necessity," he declared less than a month after the fall of Fort Sumter. "Such a vessel . . . could traverse the entire coast of the United States, prevent all blockades, and encounter, with a fair prospect of success, their entire Navy."[24]

Mallory secured an appropriation of $2 million for the purchase of armored warships in England or France, but a vessel was found closer to home. Lieutenant John M. Brooke, Naval Constructor John L. Porter, and Chief Engineer William P. Williamson jointly produced plans for a ship with a slant-sided iron casemate and suggested she be built on the lower hull of the *Merrimack*, which had been salvaged from the mud of the Elizabeth River. The charred hulk was placed in dry dock, where she was razed to her berth deck, and the casemate, which consisted of a double layer of two-inch iron plates bolted to an oak and pine backing two-feet thick, slowly took shape upon it. Six 9-inch Dahlgrens and a pair of 6.4-inch rifled guns lined her sides, while a 7-inch rifle poked from the forward and after ends of her casemate. A 1,500-pound cast-iron ram was fitted to her bow below the waterline. Captain Franklin Buchanan, who had been the first superintendent of the U. S. Naval Academy and had commanded one of the ships on Perry's expedition to Japan, was placed in charge of the ironclad, which had been renamed the *Virginia*. Because the South did not have a seafaring tradition, finding a crew was more difficult than finding a commander. Three hundred volunteers were recruited from the army.[25]

Propelled by cranky engines and only clumsily answering her helm, the *Virginia* combined her shakedown cruise with her first foray against the Federal ships in Hampton Roads. The major elements of the blockading squadron were the sailing frigate *Congress*, the sailing sloop *Cumberland*, and the steam frigates *Minnesota* and *Roanoke*. Having followed reports of the conversion of the *Merrimack* with close attention, their captains had been expecting her appearance for some time, and as soon as the strange vessel was sighted, they cleared for action. The *Congress* was the first ship in the *Virginia*'s path, but Buchanan pressed implacably on toward the *Cumberland*, which he believed was armed with new rifled cannon. The sloop's twenty-four guns fired broadside after broadside at the iron monster, but to the consternation of the Union gunners, their shot glanced off her greased sides. The *Virginia*'s cast-iron beak smashed into the *Cumberland*'s starboard bow. "The crash below the water was distinctly heard, and she commenced sinking, gallantly fighting her guns as long as they were above water," Buchanan reported. "She went down with her colors flying."[26]

The *Virginia*, which had lost her ram in pulling away from the stricken *Cumberland*, then turned her attention to the *Congress*, in which Buchanan's brother was serving as an officer. The frigate had sought protection in shoal water near some Union batteries and had run aground. Standing off to rake, the *Virginia* pounded away at her. Only two of the *Congress'* fifty guns could be brought to bear on the ironclad, and they were soon knocked out of action. "The men were swept away from [the guns] with great rapidity and slaughtered by the terrible fire of the enemy," said her senior surviving officer. Within an hour the disabled *Congress* struck her flag. Boarding parties were sent to take charge of her, but the Union batteries, ignoring the white flag flying from the mainmast of the frigate, opened up a brisk fire on the rebels. Angered by this "vile treachery," Buchanan ordered hot shot poured into the *Congress*. The excited Confederate commander climbed to the top of the casemate, the better to direct operations, and was wounded in the leg. With her captain wounded and with darkness falling, the victorious ironclad left the destruction of the remaining ships for the next day. Behind her, the burning *Congress*, lit up the night sky.[27]

The sun rose "red and angry" over Hampton Roads on March 9, 1862— a Sunday—and by seven o'clock the *Virginia* was ready to complete her work of destruction. In Washington, President Lincoln's cabinet was meeting in a hastily called session at the White House. "The *Merrimack* will destroy every vessel in the service," declared Edwin M. Stanton, the secretary of war, according to Welles' account. The blockade would be broken and Washington, New York, and Boston would be shelled or forced to pay ransom. Periodically, the president gazed thoughtfully out of the window, as if he expected the rebel monster to appear momentarily in the Potomac and blow the unfinished dome off the Capitol.[28] Lincoln and his ministers did not know that because of her unreliable engines, deep draft, and general lack of seaworthiness the *Virginia* was no threat to the cities of the North.

While Lincoln was trying to assess the situation, Lieutenant Catesby ap Roger Jones, a nephew of Commodore Thomas ap Catesby Jones and Buchanan's successor in command of the *Virginia*, was setting course for the *Minnesota*, which had run aground the previous day in her efforts to escape destruction. Suddenly Jones noticed that the helpless frigate was not alone. "There was an iron battery near her," he reported. Peering through a gunport, another officer saw "the strangest looking craft we had ever seen before." The vessel appeared to be "an immense shingle floating in the water with a gigantic cheese box rising from its center; no sails, no wheels, no smokestack, no guns."[29]

The *Monitor*, a revolutionary new vessel that had sprung from the fertile brain of John Ericsson, had arrived on the scene, and not a minute too early. As soon as rumors of the *Merrimack*'s conversion to an ironclad had reached Washington the previous summer, Welles had convened an Ironclad Board to consider proposals for three ships to be built for a total of $1.5 million. Two of the designs selected, the gunboat *Galena* and the larger *New Ironsides*, which had a broadside belt of armor similar to the ironclads already in use in Europe, were conventional designs; but Ericsson's *Monitor* was radically different. Her most distinctive feature was a revolving turret mounted on a low-lying iron deck that covered and projected beyond a submerged hull containing the engines and the crew's quarters. Upon viewing a model of the *Monitor*, President Lincoln remarked: "All I have to say is what the girl said when she stuck her foot into the stocking. It strikes me there's something in it."

The keel of "Ericsson's Folly," as the *Monitor* was derisively called, was laid at Greenpoint, Long Island, on October 25, 1861, and she was launched on January 30, 1862. Her turret, nine feet high and twenty feet wide, was constructed of eight 1-inch layers of iron plates. Mounted in it were two 11-inch Dahlgrens, but because they had not been fully tested, the gunners were forbidden to use powder charges of more than fifteen pounds, half the strength, it was later determined, that could have been used with safety. Lieutenant John L. Worden was appointed her captain and a crew of fifty-seven volunteers was recruited from the receiving ships at New York. Trials completed, the *Monitor* put to sea under tow by a steam tug on March 6, bound for Hampton Roads.

Fair weather gave way to a storm after the first day and the *Monitor*'s seakeeping inadequacies quickly became apparent. Because of her low freeboard, heavy seas rolled over her, washed out turret caulking, and poured into her berth deck like a waterfall. Sea water also entered her air-inlet pipes and disabled her blowers, nearly putting out her boiler fires. Paymaster William F. Keeler described the nighmarish scene within the *Monitor*'s iron hull:

> Turning to go down from the turret I met one of our engineers coming up the steps, pale, black, wet & staggering along gasping for breath. He asked me for brandy & I turned to go down & get him some & met the Sailors dragging up the fireman & other engineers apparent[ly] lifeless. I got down as soon as possible & found the whole between decks filled with steam & gas & Smoke, the Sailors were rushing up stifled with the gas. I found when I reached the berth deck that it came from the engine room, the door of which was open. As I went to shut it one of our Sailors said he believed that one of the engineers was still in there—no time was to be lost, though by this time almost suffocated myself I rushed in over heaps of coal & ashes & fortunately found the man lying insensible. One of the Sailors who had followed me helped pull him out & close the door.[30]

Along toward evening the storm abated and the *Monitor*'s engines and blowers were started up again. She arrived at the entrance to Chesapeake Bay late on the afternoon of March 8 to hear the sound of gunfire coming from Hampton Roads. "As the darkness increased," wrote Keeler, "the flashes of guns lit up the distant horizon & bursting shells flashed in the air."[31] With the light of the burning *Congress* to guide her, the *Monitor* took up a position near the *Minnesota* and awaited the dawn.

The first battle ever fought between ironclads began when a ball of smoke puffed at the bow of the *Virginia* and a rebel shell screamed over the *Monitor* to strike the *Minnesota*. In the *Monitor*'s turret, Worden stopped to watch a 168-pound solid shot being loaded into one of her guns before proceeding forward to the pilot house. "Send them that with our compliments, my lads," he said.[32] The shot shook the *Virginia*'s iron plates but did not penetrate them. Ignoring the *Monitor*, Jones pressed on toward the *Minnesota*, firing as he went. Shoal water prevented the ungainly Confederate ironclad from getting within a mile of the frigate, so she stood off and traded shots with the *Minnesota* and *Monitor*. At about 8:45 A.M., Jones turned his attention completely to the Yankee ironclad, and the two strange-looking craft engaged in a ponderous and deadly ballet.

Opening and closing the range, they fought from fifty to one hundred yards apart. Sometimes they were so close that they almost scraped against each other. The *Monitor*, with her shallow draft and better engines, was more maneuverable, but she could only get off a shot every seven or eight minutes. The *Virginia*, on the other hand, fired faster, but she was so clumsy that her gunners had difficulty in keeping their cannon on her agile opponent. Both vessels were repeatedly hit without being seriously damaged, although Worden was temporarily blinded by a shot that struck the *Monitor*'s pilot house. At the height of the battle, her turret seemed like an inferno, according to Paymaster Keeler:

> The sounds of the conflict at this time were terrible. The rapid firing of our own guns amid the clouds of smoke, the howling of the *Minnesota*'s shells, which was firing whole broadsides at a time just over our heads (two of her shot struck us), mingled with the crash of solid shot against our sides & the bursting of shells all around us. Two men . . . were knocked senseless by balls striking the outside of the turret while they happened to be in contact with the inside.[33]

After four hours, neither vessel having gained a significant advantage, combat was broken off. The *Virginia* limped back to Norfolk, while the *Monitor* remained in possession of Hampton Roads. Both sides claimed victory, but they had fought to a draw. The outcome might have been more decisive if the *Monitor* had used more powerful charges in her guns, or if the *Virginia*—which had come out expecting to deal only with wooden ships—had fired solid shot as well as shells at her adversary. They did not meet again, but the *Virginia*, by her mere existence, played a strategic role in the Peninsula Campaign, which unfolded immediately after the encounter at Hampton Roads. Because her presence prevented the Union army from making a quick offensive up the James River to Richmond, the Confederates gained time to prepare the defenses of the capital.[34]

Neither ironclad survived the year. The *Virginia* was blown up in May 1862 when the rebels abandoned Norfolk in the face of a Union advance. She drew too much water to go up the James to Richmond and was too unseaworthy to break out into open water. As soon as the *Virginia* had been scuttled, the *Monitor* joined the ironclad gunboat *Galena* and several other vessels in a thrust up the James to breach the back door to Richmond's defenses. The naval force was to destroy the river batteries and shell the city to force its surrender while the bulk of its garrison was twenty miles away to the eastward, facing General George B. McClellan's ponderous and wary advance. Eight miles below the Confederate capital, at Drewry's Bluff, the raiders, halted by elaborate obstructions, were battered by plunging fire from rebel fortifications on the hills above. The *Monitor* was unscathed but the thinly armored *Galena* was severely damaged, and the raiding force retreated downriver. Later the ironclads played an important role in defending the Union army when it reeled back from Richmond in retreat after the Seven Days' Battles in mid-1862. Drewry's Bluff was the *Monitor*'s last battle, however. She went down in a storm off Cape Hatteras at the end of the year, while on her way to take part in an attack on Charleston.

In the meantime a bitter struggle was under way for control of the Mississippi River, which General William T. Sherman described as "the spinal column of America." The river and its network of tributaries carried a substantial part of the nation's internal commerce, even though the railroads had been steadily encroaching upon this traffic before the war. New Orleans was the port through which most of the crops of the Middle West had proceeded to market before the war disrupted this traffic. Thus, the North had both a military and an economic stake in reopening the waterway and recapturing that city. If the Union won control of the river, the Confederacy would be split in two, supplies and reinforcements from Texas, Louisiana, and Arkansas would be unable to reach Confederate armies in the east, and Middle Western commerce would again be able to follow its traditional route to market.[35]

The "fresh-water fleet" had its beginnings in May 1861, when Commander John Rodgers, son of the long-time head of the old Board of Navy Commissioners, purchased three wooden river steamers and converted them into gunboats. Although naval officers commanded these vessels, the *Tyler*, *Lexington*, and *Conestoga*, Welles placed them under the control of the local army commanders. Operating from Cairo, where the tip of Illinois points like a dagger toward the heart of the South, the gunboats protected the strategic junction of the Ohio and Mississippi rivers and harassed Confederate positions. They also helped keep the border states of Kentucky and Missouri in the Union.

The War Department also ordered seven new ironclad gunboats. Designed by Samuel Pook, a naval constructor, and built at St. Louis by James B. Eads, a civil engineer, these craft were called "Pook's Turtles." Hundreds of men worked around the clock, seven days a week, and the first of these flat-bottomed stern-wheelers, the *St. Louis*, was launched in forty-five days. The six others, the *Cairo, Carondelet, Cincinnati, Mound City, Louisville*, and *Pittsburg*, were completed by November 1861. With slope-sided casemates resembling that of the *Virginia*, the gunboats had most of their armor mounted forward because it was thought they would do their fighting bow-on. As a result, their sides and sterns were vulnerable to enemy fire. They carried a mixture of old 32- and 42-pounders and 8-inch Dahlgrens. Eads also converted two river steamers into gunboats, the *Benton*, which with 16 guns was the most powerful craft to appear on the Mississippi, and the more lightly armed *Essex*.[36]

Flag Officer Andrew H. Foote, who had displayed considerable energy while on antislavery patrol off the west coast of Africa, was placed in command of this Western Flotilla. Early in 1862, all was also deemed ready for a move to the South; but the way was barred by Confederate strongholds at Columbus, Kentucky, on the Mississippi; Fort Henry, on the Tennessee River; and Fort Donelson, on the Cumberland River. The military district commander, General Ulysses S. Grant, decided that Columbus was so strongly defended that it would be inadvisable to attack it before the two forts had been taken. Working well together without the friction and jealousy that existed between some army and naval officers, Grant and Foote produced a plan for a joint land-water attack on Fort Henry. As soon as that fort had been reduced, the troops were to be hurried overland to Fort Donelson.

Seventeen thousand men were crammed into every river steamer that Grant could lay his hands on, and escorted by four of Foote's ironclads and three wooden gunboats, the flotilla moved up the Ohio River and turned into the muddy Tennessee. The plan called for the army to attack the rebel emplacements from the rear, while the gunboats took them under fire from the river. The troops disembarked about two miles below Fort Henry, but a recent storm had flooded the ground and they bogged down in the mud. Observing what was going on, Foote told Grant: "General, I shall have the fort in my possession before you get into position."

With Foote's warning that "every charge you fire from one of these guns costs the government about $8," the four "turtles" advanced on Fort Henry on February 6, opening fire at 1,700 yards. The Confederates replied with a fast and accurate fire, as Foote steadily closed the range to 600 yards. Neither side could miss at that distance and the gunboats were hit repeatedly. The *Essex* took a shot in one of her boilers, which exploded, scalding a number of men and forcing her to drop out of the fight. Foote's gunners kept up their fire, however, and in little more than an hour, Fort Henry hoisted the white flag, and the ironclads went back to Cairo for refitting. Andrew Foote had lived up to his boast that he would capture the fort without the army's help.[37]

Foote found Fort Donelson a more formidable objective than Fort Henry. Built on a bluff about 150 feet above the Cumberland River, it commanded a long stretch of the river. Foote had intended to bring his entire flotilla in for this attack, but he sailed into the Cumberland on February 14 with only four ironclads—all he had been able to man. While Grant's army besieged Fort Donelson, the gunboats advanced and opened fire on it at a range of about a mile, which was speedily reduced to 400 yards. The Confederate guns poured down a heavy fire into the attacking vessels, causing heavy casualties. One by one, the badly battered gunboats dropped out of action and limped away to nurse their injuries. Foote's flagship, the *St. Louis*, was among the most roughly handled and the flag officer himself was wounded. Encouraged by their repulse of the Yankee gunboats, the Confederates tried to break out of the iron grip that the Union army had imposed on the fort, but when this failed, they gave in to Grant's demand for "unconditional surrender."[38]

With the fall of Forts Henry and Donelson the Confederates hastily abandoned Columbus, Kentucky, and fell downriver to a strongpoint at Island No. 10, where the states of Kentucky, Tennessee, and Missouri come together. Nestled in a lazy S curve of the Mississippi, the island was so named because it was the tenth one in the river below Cairo. Numerous batteries along the nearby shoreline, swamps, and high water made it difficult to approach this heavily defended place. A Union force under the command of General John Pope managed to bypass the island, but rebel batteries dominating the river prevented any Federal troops from crossing from the western to the eastern bank of the Mississippi to cut Confederate communications with the island's garrison. Pope demanded that the Western Flotilla immediately come downriver to cover his attempt to cross. Having learned the shortcomings of his gunboats, Foote refused to risk them in what he considered the suicidal venture of trying to run past Island No. 10.

Pope kept up his appeals for an ironclad to come to his assistance, and towards the end of the month, Commander Henry Walke volunteered to run the *Carondelet* through the rebel gauntlet. With a barge laden with coal and hay lashed to her port side and heavy cable wrapped about her pilot house, the gunboat sped past Island No. 10 on the night of April 4. The enemy gunners aimed too high and she passed unscathed. "The passage of the *Carondelet* was not only one of the most daring and dramatic events of the war," wrote Mahan, "it was also the death blow to the Confederate defense of this position."[39] Two nights later the *Pittsburg* followed, and covered by the gunboats, Pope crossed the Mississippi and cut off the escape route of the Confederates on Island No. 10, who quickly surrendered.

At the same time, Grant, escorted by gunboats, was advancing down the Tennessee River into the heart of the South. At Shiloh on April 6, the guns of two of the wooden steamers, the *Tyler* and *Lexington*, helped turn back a surprise Confederate attack that was driving Grant's troops into the river. Following the capture of Island No. 10, the "fresh-water navy," now under the command of Flag Officer Charles H. Davis, moved down the Mississippi on June 6, 1862, to capture Memphis, the hub of a Southern rail network and a center of river traffic. In the nearest thing to a fleet action during the entire war, two opposing flotillas of gunboats, the Union's Western Flotilla and the Confederate River Defense Fleet, fought a short and savage battle off the town, in full view of thousands of spectators. While the gunboats duelled, the Union army's Colonel Charles Ellet, commanding a pair of fast rams, smashed into the enemy line, destroying two of the rebel vessels. Meanwhile the fire of the Union gunboats scattered the remainder, and all except one were either sunk or captured during a wild pursuit down the river. Working together like the blades of a pair of shears—to use Foote's analogy—the army and navy had opened up the Mississippi as far south as the fortress city of Vicksburg.[40]

Plans were also being made to launch an attack up the Mississippi from the Gulf of Mexico. The primary objectives of the expedition were the capture of New Orleans, the South's largest city and major cotton port, and the reduction of Vicksburg. When those objectives had been achieved, the Confederacy would be cut in two, but an attack on New Orleans was not an operation to be undertaken lightly. The approaches to the city were guarded by Forts St. Philip and Jackson, a pair of formidable works mounting 100 guns, by a flotilla of rebel gunboats, and by fire rafts, as well as by obstructions designed to hold attacking ships under the fire of the forts. Although there were some misgivings about the ability of wooden ships to deal with shore batteries, Gustavus Fox, pointing to Samuel Du Pont's success at Port Royal, urged the attack. His arguments were skillfully supported by his long-time friend, Commander David Dixon Porter, who, despite his comparatively junior rank, longed to lend a hand in running the navy.

Flag Officer David Glasgow Farragut was given command of the West Gulf Squadron, which was to make the attack. Because Farragut had a Southern wife and had made his home in the South before the war, he had been shunted into a desk job, which he had held until he had proved his loyalty to the satisfaction of Gideon Welles. A half-century before, Farragut had gone to sea in the *Essex* as a midshipman with his guardian, Commodore David Porter, and over the years he had proved to be a competent, if not brilliant, officer with a special interest in gunnery. Perhaps his most important accomplishment had been the establishment of the navy yard at Mare Island, California. Unlike most naval officers of the period, he was something of a linguist, having a command of French, Italian, Spanish, and Arabic. Although past sixty, Farragut received the news of his appointment in December 1861 with the breathless excitement of a midshipman. "Keep your lips closed, and burn my letters; for perfect silence is to be observed," he wrote his wife. "I am to have a flag in the Gulf, and the rest depends upon myself. Keep calm and silent. I shall sail in three weeks."[41]

The attacking forces were made up of three parts: a flotilla of twenty-one schooners converted into mortar boats and led by Porter; a squadron of warships and gunboats led by Farragut in the steam sloop *Hartford*; and a fleet of transports led by General Ben Butler and carrying 13,000 soldiers who were to occupy New Orleans. On April 18, 1862, with treetops tied to their mastheads as camouflage, Porter's mortar boats were towed into position behind a screen of trees, just below Forts St. Philip and Jackson, from where they rained a barrage of 13-inch shells on the rebel strongholds. "The enemy's fire was excellent," said a Confederate officer, and considerable damage was done to Fort Jackson, the closer of the two forts. But in spite of Porter's promise to reduce them within forty-eight hours, the forts held out for five days. Farragut resolved to wait no longer. "Conquer or . . . be conquered," he told his officers.[42] With anchor chains hung over the sides of his ships to protect their engines and hammocks and sacks of sand, coal, and ashes packed around their vulnerable machinery, he decided to try to run past the batteries.

With a pair of red lanterns showing at her mizzen peak, the *Hartford* got under way at two o'clock on the morning of April 24 and led a fleet of seventeen vessels through a gap, made some nights before, in a boom that the rebels had laid across the river. To cover the ships advancing upriver, the mortar boats kept a steady stream of shells pouring into the forts, "each following the other through [the] heavens like large stars," said Bartholomew Diggins, a sailor in the *Hartford*. The first of Farragut's ships, the gunboat *Cayuga*, took about a half-hour to run past the rebel batteries. She was hit forty-two times, but with her crew lying flat on the deck, only six men were slightly wounded. The *Hartford* grounded on a shoal under the guns of Fort St. Philip and a fire raft set her port side ablaze. Diggins painted a vivid picture of the scene on the flagship:

> Misfortunes seemed to crowd the old ship and it looked that only a miracle could save her. We were hard aground, the engines backing with all their power, and could not relieve her, in flames from water to masthead from the fire raft, the cabin ablaze from an exploded shell, and the ship the center of a terrible storm of shot and shell, the crew in a death struggle with the flames, heat and smoke, the latter at times so thick that we were compelled to grope our way while connecting the hose. . . .[43]

Firing broadsides all the while, the flagship's crew eventually beat out the flames and freed the ship from the mud without her suffering serious damage. "The passing of the forts . . . was one of the most awful sights and events I ever saw or expect to experience," Farragut later reported. "The smoke was so dense that it was only now and then you could see anything but the flash of the cannon and the fireships." The *Mississippi*, third in the battle line, came close to being rammed by the Confederate ironclad *Manassas*, a turtle-backed converted tugboat. Thanks to the skillful maneuvering of her executive officer, Lieutenant George Dewey, the old side-wheeler escaped serious damage. Looking like a sieve, the *Manassas* was finally beached and abandoned by her crew.

Once above the forts, Farragut's ships had little trouble with the converted river craft they encountered there. Stopping just long enough to make hasty repairs and leaving Porter to secure the surrender of the now useless forts, Farragut steamed the remaining thirty-five miles upstream to New Orleans. He dropped anchor off the city on the morning of April 25, 1862, to find the levee a "scene of desolation; ships, steamers, cotton, coal, etc., were all one common blaze, and our ingenuity was much taxed to avoid the floating conflagration." The North was jubilant at the capture of the busiest port in the South, and when Congress established the grade of rear admiral three months later, Farragut was the first to receive it.[44]

As soon as New Orleans had been secured, Farragut wanted to attack Mobile, but he was ordered to clear the Mississippi instead. Privately, he had strong misgivings about the feasibility of thrusting his big ships into those treacherous waters, but he sailed part of his squadron some 400 miles up the river to Vicksburg, taking Baton Rouge and Natchez along the way. He led his ships round hairpin bends, past rebel batteries, over shoals and sandbars, and through shifting currents and snags that reached out to rip open the bottoms of his ships. "The elements of destruction . . . in this river are beyond anything I have encountered," he reported.[45]

Farragut arrived off Vicksburg late in May 1862 to raise the curtain on a bitterly fought amphibious campaign. Perched high on the eastern bank of the Mississippi overlooking a horseshoe bend, Vicksburg was being transformed by the Confederates into "a little Gibraltar." Unable to attack the town because there were not enough troops, the squadron ran past it on June 28 and joined forces with the "fresh-water fleet," which had recently taken Memphis. "I passed up the river this morning to no purpose," said Farragut, "I am satisfied that it is not possible for us to take Vicksburg without an army force of 12 to 15 thousand men." David Porter agreed. "Ships . . . cannot crawl up hills 300 feet high, and it is that part of Vicksburg which must be taken by the army," he declared.[46]

While the combined squadrons of Farragut and Davis lay at anchor above Vicksburg, they suddenly found themselves in peril from an unexpected quarter. On July 15 the ironclad *Arkansas*, built at Memphis out of railroad iron and boiler plate, dashed out of the Yazoo River just above Farragut's anchorage. Slugging her way through the surprised Yankee squadron, she disabled the *Carondelet* and *Tyler* and made for Vicksburg, leaving in her wake heavy casualties, anger, and frustration. Worried that the ironclad might cut him off from his base at New Orleans, Farragut decided to drop below Vicksburg that night. His ships fired broadside after broadside at the *Arkansas* as she lay moored under the protection of the batteries, but they did little damage to her.[47] With the river falling every day, Farragut took his big ships down to New Orleans and Davis moved his gunboats up the river to Helena, Arkansas, leaving the rebels in control of a long stretch of the lower Mississippi. Close coordination between land and naval forces is a keystone of amphibious operations, and the repeated failure of the army to provide sufficient troops to attack Vicksburg when its defenses were weak doomed the Yankees to another year of bloody fighting and wearying siege before they won control of the Mississippi.

While an army was being gathered for a campaign against Vicksburg, the naval force on the Mississippi underwent a drastic shakeup. On October 1, 1862, the Western Flotilla was transferred from the jurisdiction of the War Department to that of the navy and renamed the Mississippi Squadron. The transfer put an end to interservice squabbling. Davis was relieved of command and replaced by David D. Porter, who, in one of the most unusual promotions in the history of the navy, was designated an acting rear admiral. Porter, who was jumped over the heads of eighty commodores and captains, had been a mere lieutenant only two years before. In that time, he had shown audacity and resourcefulness and, even more important, had made skillful use of friends in high places, particularly Gustavus Fox.[48]

Porter immediately threw himself into reorganizing and strengthening his new command. He showered the Navy Department with demands for more ships, more men, more guns—more of everything. By late 1862 Grant, who had taken command of all Union troops in the West, and Porter had worked out a pincers movement against Vicksburg. The plan called for Grant to attack the town from the rear while Sherman, transported by Porter's vessels, launched an attack from above it, at the junction of the Mississippi and Yazoo rivers. If the rebels attacked Sherman, Grant would take Vicksburg. If they concentrated on Grant, Sherman would take it.

Alas for clever schemes: Confederate cavalry infiltrated Grant's rear and destroyed his supplies, forcing him to make a hasty retreat. But Sherman and Porter, unaware of what had happened, continued their part of the operation. On December 12, 1862, the gunboat *Cairo* nosed her way into the Yazoo River in support of the operation. Suddenly she was torn by an explosion and sank within ten minutes—the victim of a torpedo, as mines were then called. About forty Yankee vessels met a similar fate during the war. Watching from shore, the officer who had set the mine, a whiskey demijohn filled with powder and fired by a trip wire, said he felt "much as a schoolboy might whose practical joke has taken a more serious shape than he expected." Porter and Sherman were undeterred, however, and the troops were landed. But without Grant's force to relieve the pressure on them, they were soon forced to abandon their positions with heavy losses. The second phase of the Union campaign against Vicksburg had ended on a dismal note.[49]

In early February 1863 Porter launched the Yazoo Pass Expedition, which was designed to make use of the numerous but barely navigable bayous and creeks that crisscrossed the area between the Yazoo and the Mississippi so that a small squadron of gunboats could approach Vicksburg from the rear. Caught in a tangle of trees, swamps, and bogs, the expedition lost all chance for surprise and, checked by rebel batteries, was forced to give up the attempt. Other routes

were also explored in an attempt to outflank the Confederate defenses, but these
expeditions failed, too.

With the coming of spring, Admiral Farragut decided to take four of his
large ships and three gunboats up the Mississippi, run past Port Hudson, about
175 miles south of Vicksburg, cut off enemy supplies flowing down the Red
River, and join the forces at Vicksburg. His gunboats were lashed to the sides
of the heavy vessels, and on the night of March 14, 1863, the squadron was
ready to run the Confederate batteries at Port Hudson. "The best protection
against the enemy's fire, is a well directed fire from our own guns," the admiral
told his captains. As soon as the rebels sighted the squadron, they lit bonfires
along the river banks and opened fire on the silhouetted ships.

The *Hartford*, with her pilot in the mizzen top, hugged the battery-
crowned bluffs to get below the enemy's line of fire. Smoke settled over the
river and blinded the squadron, except for the flagship at the head of the line.
Even so, the *Hartford* grounded under the batteries. She was backed clear and
continued upriver with only one man killed and two wounded. The *Richmond*,
following her leader, was hit in the boiler room and, losing steam, was dragged
downriver by the gunboat lashed to her side. The *Monongahela*, next astern,
grounded at the river bend but backed off only to disable her engines in the
effort, and she, too, drifted downstream. The gallant old *Mississippi*, last in
line, ran aground under enemy fire and her crew set her ablaze to prevent her
from falling into rebel hands. Leaving the *Richmond* and *Monongahela* behind
to lick their wounds—and to join in a siege of Port Hudson—Farragut steamed
up to Vicksburg, where he found that the climactic campaign was about to be
launched.[50]

Following a plan similar to that used by Foote and Pope against Island No.
10 the previous year, Grant took his army well south along the undefended
western side of the Mississippi, intending to cross back over the river with the
aid of Porter's gunboats and then come up behind Vicksburg. To confuse the
enemy, Sherman made a landing up the Yazoo, where his attack in December
had failed. On the night of April 16, nine of Porter's gunboats ran downriver
past Vicksburg. The flotilla joined Grant at Grand Gulf, about seventy miles
below the city, where the crossing was to be made, and the gunboats fought a
nearly six-hour duel with rebel batteries without succeeding in silencing them.
Impatient with the delay, Grant moved farther south to an undefended area and
his men were ferried across the river without opposition. Grand Gulf was abandoned by the Confederates, and the armies of Grant and Sherman converged on
Vicksburg from the south and north. Two direct assaults on the fortifications,
combined with naval bombardments, failed, and the town was placed under
siege.[51]

For forty days and nights, Porter's mortar boats rained death and destruction
upon Vicksburg, while the army tightened its noose. Cut off from outside help

and with their homes pulverized, Vicksburg's defenders took shelter in caves and lived on horse meat and rats. One citizen wondered that with so much destruction, hunger, exposure, and death about them, "many did not become insane." With all hope gone, Vicksburg and more than 30,000 troops surrendered on July 4, 1863, the day after the Union victory at Gettysburg. Four days later Port Hudson capitulated, and as Abraham Lincoln said, "The Father of Waters goes again unvexed to the sea." The twin defeats of Vicksburg and Gettysburg sounded the death knell of the Confederacy.

As the "cradle of secession," Charleston was a special target, second only to Richmond, in the eyes of Northern strategists. It was as much a political and psychological objective as a military one, and Welles and Fox, eager for the navy to outshine the army, were obsessed with the idea of capturing it. Had the city been attacked immediately after Samuel Du Pont had seized Port Royal in November 1861, when it was unprepared, it might have been easily taken, but a lack of coordination between Union land and sea forces had prevented such action. The delay had given the Confederates time to erect the strongest defenses against seaborne attack of any Southern port.

Du Pont, now a rear admiral, was appointed to command the assault, but while he was awaiting the arrival of promised reinforcements, two Confederate ironclads, the *Palmetto State* and the *Chicora*, attacked the blockaders lying off Charleston on January 31, 1863. They rammed the converted merchantman *Mercedita*, forcing her to surrender, and crippled the *Keystone State*, another ex-cargo-carrier, which had to be towed to safety. The Confederates claimed that they had raised the blockade of Charleston, but one by one, nine ironclads joined Du Pont's squadron—the belted warship *New Ironsides*, which became his flagship, the twin-casemated *Keokuk*, and seven monitors.[52]

Battle experience had resulted in several improvements in the design of monitors since Hampton Roads. The pilot house had been moved from the foredeck, where it impeded the fire of the guns, and placed atop the turret; and a 15-inch Dahlgren had been substituted for one of the two 11-inch guns carried by the original *Monitor*, but little could be done to improve the seaworthiness of these craft or their notoriously slow rate of fire.

Du Pont reluctantly launched his attack against Charleston on April 7, 1863.[53] Shortly after noon, the monitor *Weehawken*, pushing a cumbersome, sledlike raft that was supposed to detonate underwater mines, led a line of ironclads into a narrow channel between Forts Sumter and Moultrie, at the harbor's mouth. From its beginning, the day went badly. Because of their erratic handling qualities it took the ships more than two hours to get into position. In fact, the *New Ironsides* was so unmanageable that she almost collided with several of the monitors, and Du Pont had to hoist an embarrassing signal reading, "Disregard the movements of the flagship."

Alvah F. Hunter, a fifteen-year-old boy who served in the monitor *Nahant*, described the start of the battle:

> "Four bells" sounding on the gong in the engine room which ordered the engineer to go ahead at full speed, was distinctly heard by us on the berth deck, and in a few minutes cannon shot began to strike the *Nahant*; at first the hits were few and scattered, but as we drew nearer to Sumter, they were more frequent . . . the shots came down upon us in an irregular staccato. There was twenty five minutes' time when we were struck on an average about once a minute.[54]

Beset by mines and other obstructions and unable to silence the forts, the ironclads were subjected to intense crossfire. Some of them almost disappeared amid bursting shells and huge waterspouts. Turrets jammed, gunports stuck, steering gears were disabled, and armor was loosened by the accurate enemy fire. The lightly armored *Keokuk*, hit several times below the waterline, limped out of action and sank the next day. The *Nahant* was badly damaged. Broken bolts flew about her pilot house and turret like bullets, killing one man and injuring two others, including her captain.

As darkness fell, Du Pont signalled his ships to withdraw. The abortive action had proved his worst fears about the ironclads. Whereas the forts fired some 2,200 shots during the battle, the squadron got off only 139—and these did no more than superficial damage. Du Pont planned to attack again the next day, but when he received the reports of his captains, he called off the assault, "fearing that any attempt to renew it would convert failure into disaster." The failure of this attack on Charleston was the Union navy's greatest defeat of the war, a defeat that George E. Belknap, executive officer of the *New Ironsides*, blamed on Du Pont's decision to slug it out with the forts rather than run in past them, as Farragut had done at New Orleans. Other officers pointed out, however, that the entrance to the harbor was blocked by obstructions. The monitors did score one victory, however. The *Weehawken* and *Nahant* battered the rebel ironclad *Atlanta* into submission near Savannah on June 17, 1863, two months after the abortive attack on Charleston.

The hapless Du Pont was replaced by Rear Admiral John A. Dahlgren, the ordnance expert who had served as Lincoln's unofficial naval adviser since the beginning of the war. After testing the city's defense, Dahlgren also was convinced that the city could not be taken by naval attack. Consequently, he conducted a campaign of attrition. In cooperation with the army, he seized batteries and redoubts on the outlying islands, battered Fort Sumter to rubble, and sealed off the harbor. Through summer and winter the ironclads maintained their positions offshore. Winter storms were bad, but summer was even worse. Rocking in the greasy swells, the vessels were like giant pressure cookers. Temperatures of 150 degrees were recorded in their engine rooms and the men were unable to touch the machinery unless they wore heavy canvas gloves. "I will never go to sea again in a monitor," said one officer. "I have suffered more in mind and body since this affair commenced than I will suffer again if I can help it. No glory, no promotion, can ever pay for it."[55]

The Union blockaders had to contend not only with the enemy batteries and adverse weather conditions, but also with ingenious secret weapons devised by the rebels. The first to appear were low-lying torpedo boats called "Davids" because they were intended to destroy the Goliaths of the Union navy. These craft ran submerged except for a short stack and had at their bows a long spar, at the end of which was a sixty-pound charge that exploded on contact. One of them slipped out of Charleston on the night of October 5, 1863, and made for the *New Ironsides*. Although she was detected, her commander, Lieutenant William T. Glassell, jammed his torpedo into the ironclad's stern just below the waterline, badly damaging her. The huge geyser of water thrown up by the explosion swamped the "David" and her crew abandoned her. Glassell and one of his men were captured and the two others escaped.[56]

The Confederates next resorted to a submarine to harass the blockading fleet. The *H. L. Hunley*, as the cigar-shaped craft was called, was powered by eight men who turned a crank that was attached to a propeller. She towed a powerful mine designed to be attached to the hull of an unsuspecting enemy ship and to be exploded by a trip wire. More than a dozen men, including Horace L. Hunley, her inventor, drowned or suffocated in three disastrous tests before she was deemed ready for service. Operating her as a semisubmerged torpedo boat with a spar torpedo, the Confederates launched her on the night of February 17, 1864, against the steam sloop *Housatonic*. Rammed amidships, the sloop sank in five minutes, taking the ill-fated *Hunley* and all her crew with her.[57]

Charleston held out until the approach of General Sherman's avenging army a year later forced the city's defenders to abandon it. Nevertheless, defiant Charleston had the distinction of being the only Southern seaport to withstand a furious Union attack until almost the end of the war.

A desperate game of hide and seek was under way on the high seas while the fate of the Confederacy was being decided on the inland waters and along the coasts of America. With the hope of forcing Gideon Welles to divert ships from the blockade, the rebels sent a dozen raiders to sea to prey on Yankee commerce, and five of them scored substantial success. Unlike the privateers of earlier wars, these vessels were commissioned in the Confederate Navy, commanded by regular officers, and destroyed most of their prizes because they had little expectation of being able to sail them into Southern ports. Few naval efforts have resulted in greater damage in proportion to investment than those of such raiders as the *Alabama, Florida*, and *Shenandoah*. But, because of Welles' single-minded determination not to weaken the blockade, they failed to accomplish their assigned objective. Ignoring the anguish and lamentations of Northern merchants and shipowners, Welles refused to divert more than a handful of ships to scouring the seas in search of the raiders.

Welles' policy was sound but it offered cold comfort to Yankee maritime interests. More than 200 vessels and cargoes valued at as much as $25 million were captured and destroyed by the commerce-raiders, and the *Shenandoah* dealt a death blow to the American whaling industry; but this was only a small part of the loss to the North. Fearing that their ships would be destroyed if they sailed under the Stars and Stripes, many owners sold them to foreigners or switched to foreign registry. The "flight from the flag" had begun before the Civil War, as shipowners sought to evade the rising cost of operating under the American flag, as they do to this day, and the rebel cruisers merely quickened the trend. By war's end, more than half the once-great American merchant fleet had vanished. The raiders burned or sank 110,000 tons of shipping, but another 800,000 tons were sold to foreigners or shifted registry—a blow from which the merchant marine did not recover for generations.[58]

The *Alabama*, commanded by hot-eyed Raphael Semmes, was the most successful of the rebel raiders. Semmes, a native of Maryland, began his career as a midshipman in the U.S. Navy in 1826 and had risen to the rank of commander by the outbreak of the war. When Alabama, his adopted home, left the Union, he resigned and offered his services to the Confederate navy. Late in June 1861 he went to sea in the Confederacy's first commerce-raider, a converted passenger steamer named the *Sumter*. Semmes captured or destroyed eighteen merchantmen in six months before he was trapped by three Union warships at Gibraltar, where he had put in for repairs. Facing hopeless odds, he sold the *Sumter* and went to England, where James D. Bulloch, a Confederate agent, was secretly having a powerful new steam raider built in the Laird shipyards near Liverpool.

Engaged in a duel of wits with Charles Francis Adams, the American minister to Britain, and fearing that an attempt might be made to seize the vessel, Bulloch decided to complete her fitting-out in the Azores. At the end of July 1862, the ship, bearing papers that identified her as the British merchantman *Enrica*, put to sea on what was billed as a trial run, but instead of returning to port she made for the Azores and a rendezvous with a supply ship carrying guns and other equipment. Most of the preliminary arrangements required to fit the vessel with her armament had already been made, so the work was finished within a few days. On August 24, 1862, Semmes raised the Confederate flag over his new command and placed her in commission as the *Alabama*.

Semmes was justifiably proud of the *Alabama*, saying "she sat upon the water with the lightness and grace of a swan." Because her bunkers carried only enough coal for eighteen days of steaming, the *Alabama* did most of her cruising under sail. With her propeller raised out of the water to reduce resistance, she could make ten knots in a good wind and under both sail and steam could do thirteen knots. The raider was armed with eight guns—six 32-pounders mounted in broadside and two pivot guns, one a 100-pound rifle and the other an 8-inch smoothbore. To permit her to remain at sea for long periods of time, the *Alabama* carried a machine shop and other facilities for making emergency repairs. Emblazoned in gilt on her stern was the motto that Semmes obviously intended to be his guide: *Aide-toi et Dieu t'aidera* (God helps those who help themselves.)[59]

For twenty-two months the *Alabama*, manned by Southern officers and hard-bitten English and Irish seamen, ranged over the high seas playing havoc with Yankee commerce. Ghostlike, she appeared off the Newfoundland Banks, in the Caribbean and the Gulf of Mexico, sailed around the Cape of Good Hope and across the Indian Ocean to Singapore, cruised off Indo-China and returned to the Atlantic by way of Cape Town. With an uncanny instinct of determining just how long his ship could remain in an area before news of her presence would bring down one of the Union cruisers assigned to search for her, Semmes covered some 75,000 miles, or the equivalent of three voyages around the globe.[60]

In the course of her rovings, the *Alabama* captured about sixty-five merchant vessels, valued at over $5 million, most of which were burned after officers, crew, passengers, and needed supplies and equipment had been taken on board the raider. When she became too crowded, Semmes would put his prisoners on a captured vessel and release her, after obtaining a pledge of future ransom payment. The *Alabama* received many courtesies and much help from friendly officials in English ports around the world—a fact that proved galling to Yankee skippers sent in pursuit of the raider and that stuck in the memory of the American people. After the war the British paid $15.5 million in an arbitration award to settle the claims arising from the damage done by the *Alabama* and the other British-built raiders.

With his crew restive and demanding immediate payment of overdue wages, Semmes cruised the Caribbean at the end of 1862 in search of a Panama-New York steamer carrying gold from California. On December 7 the paddle-wheeler *Ariel* was sighted and the crew of the *Alabama*, with visions of a million dollars in gold floating before their eyes, put their hearts into the chase. As it turned out, the steamer was outward bound to Panama and, instead of a cargo of gold, carried some 500 passengers, most of them women in a state of near hysteria. To put an end to the panic, Semmes summoned his best-looking lieutenant— "and I had some very handsome young fellows on board the *Alabama*"—and told him to put on his newest uniform and "go on board the *Ariel* and coax the ladies out of their hysterics." The dashing young officer assured the ladies that they had nothing to fear, and the sobs ceased. Soon, one of the prettiest girls asked him if she might have one of his glistening buttons as a memento of the adventure. This wish was granted and others also sought souvenirs. "When I got my handsome lieutenant back," said Semmes, "he was like a plucked peacock—he had scarcely a button to his coat!"[61]

The *Ariel* was released to continue her voyage and the *Alabama* returned to the grim business of war. Receiving news that a large Union force was planning to attack Galveston after a smaller force had been expelled with the embarrassing loss of several vessels, Semmes headed into the Gulf of Mexico with the intention of swooping down on the helpless troop transports. But when he arrived off Galveston on January 11, 1863, he found only five small Union warships off-shore. The hapless side-wheeler *Hatteras*, a lightly armed former excursion boat, put out to check on the stranger. The *Alabama* sank her in only thirteen minutes, adding to her laurels a victory over a Yankee naval vessel.[62]

After eighteen more months of cruising, Semmes put in at Cherbourg, France, on June 11, 1864, where he hoped to give his ship a complete overhaul. Emperor Napoleon III was regarded as friendly to the Confederacy because he wanted to keep the North busy while his troops occupied Mexico. News of the raider's arrival was telegraphed to Yankee cruisers lying in European harbors. Three days later, on June 14, the steam sloop *Kearsarge*, which had been vainly searching for the *Alabama*, arrived off the French port from nearby Flushing. The newly fitted vessel was under the command of Captain John A. Winslow, who had shared a cabin with Semmes in the *Raritan* during the Mexican War.

Because the French had delayed in giving Semmes permission to dock, he had no option but to fight. If he waited for repairs to be made, Yankee ships would concentrate offshore and he would not be able to escape. Although the *Kearsarge* was slightly stronger than his own vessel, the ships were almost evenly matched and there seemed to be a chance that the *Alabama* could score a victory under European eyes, something that would brighten a period of un-remitted disaster for the Confederate cause. Waiting only long enough to refill his bunkers, Semmes sent Winslow a note informing him that the *Alabama* would be coming out within a few days.

Shortly before ten o'clock on the morning of June 19, 1864, the *Alabama* put to sea under the eye of a French ironclad that took up station at the three-mile limit. Spectators gathered on the rooftops or put out in small boats to watch the expected battle. The usual Sunday-morning routine was being observed on board the *Kearsarge*. Captain Winslow, a devout man, was standing with Bible in hand to begin church services when a lookout cried: "The *Alabama*!" Calmly taking up his speaking trumpet, Winslow ordered his men to quarters. Stripped to the waist, they trained their guns on the raider as the *Kearsarge* steamed down on her at full speed. About seven miles from shore, the two ships turned, their starboard batteries facing each other. The *Alabama* fired first, at a range of a mile, but the broadside whistled over the *Kearsarge*. Two more broadsides, also wide of the mark, were fired before the Union gunners replied with a steady and deliberate fire aimed at the raider's waterline.

For the next hour the ships fought in circles of about 900 yards in diameter that looped to the westward as each captain tried to prevent his opponent from getting into a position to rake. Practice improved the marksmanship of the *Alabama*'s gunners, but Semmes was surprised to see his shells explode without penetrating the sides of the *Kearsarge*. Winslow had taken the precaution of armoring his ship by draping her with 120 fathoms of chain that had been covered with boards. Also, in the twenty-two months the *Alabama* had been at sea, her powder had deteriorated and an 8-inch shell that penetrated the *Kearsarge*'s sternpost, where there were no chains, failed to explode. Had it gone off, the battle might have ended differently.

By the time the adversaries had completed their seventh circle, Semmes reported, the *Alabama* was "in a sinking condition, the enemy's shell having exploded in our side and between decks, opening large apertures through which the water rushed with great rapidity." He tried to break off the action and race for the French coast. "The ship filled so rapidly, however, that before we had made much progress, the fires were extinguished in the furnaces, and we were evidently on the point of sinking." The *Alabama*'s colors were struck, but Winslow, momentarily confused, did not cease firing until she had been hit several more times. As the *Alabama*'s crew abandoned ship, the *Kearsarge* sent out her only undamaged boat and asked the *Deerhound*, a yacht belonging to a wealthy Englishman who had come out to see the battle, to pick up survivors. Seventy men were rescued by the *Kearsarge* and forty, including Semmes, were pulled on board the yacht. Much to Winslow's anger and surprise, the *Deerhound* sped away to the safety of the English coast, rescuing the "rebel pirate" from expected captivity. Despite this clouded end to his victory, Winslow won a deserved "well done." "I would sooner have fought that fight than any ever fought on the ocean," Admiral Farragut declared.[63]

Farragut had problems of his own. Following his victory at New Orleans, he had wanted to attack Mobile, and if he had been permitted to do so, the city probably would have fallen easily into Union hands. Now it was the last major port on the Gulf of Mexico left to the Confederacy and the delay had given the rebels time to improve significantly the defenses of Mobile Bay. Like New Orleans, it was defended by a pair of heavily armed fortifications—Forts Morgan and Gaines—which guarded the main ship channel. Pilings sunk at the entrance to the bay, thirty miles south of the city, forced approaching ships close under the guns of Fort Morgan, the stronger of the works, and the narrow channel between them had been liberally planted with torpedoes, or mines.

Other projects such as the assault against Charleston and an abortive raid up the Red River into Louisiana, in which the gunboat fleet was almost lost, had higher priority in 1863. Not until early in 1864 was serious consideration again. given to an attack on Mobile. Word was received in Washington that Franklin Buchanan, the *Virginia*'s former commander and the Confederacy's first admiral, was planning to smash the blockade of Mobile with the *Tennessee*, a formidable ironclad that had been built at Selma, on the Alabama River, and floated downstream on pontoons to Mobile Bay. From her armored casemate—six inches of iron on the front and five inches along the sides—peered a pair of 7-inch and four 6-inch rifles. Although it was soon evident that the *Tennessee*, like the previous rebel ironclads, was unseaworthy, underpowered, and poorly designed, Farragut was worried about her. He poured demands for monitors upon the Navy Department and in the late summer of 1864, the seagoing monitors *Tecumseh* and *Manhattan*, and the *Winnebago* and *Chickasaw*, twin-turreted craft designed for river use, were sent to join his squadron. Additional pressure for an attack came from General Sherman, who was nearing Atlanta, principal center of Confederate resistance in Georgia. He said an amphibious assault on the defenses of Mobile Bay would serve as an effective diversionary operation that would secure his right flank.

Following the plan that had proved successful at Port Hudson the previous year, Farragut tied his fourteen wooden ships together in pairs, the larger ships being to starboard, to shield the smaller ones from the guns of Fort Morgan. The monitors formed a column to the starboard of the main battle line, and after running past the forts, they were to engage the *Tennessee* while the rest of the ships disposed of a trio of wooden gunboats that supported her. Farragut planned to lead his squadron in the *Hartford*, but his officers persuaded him to let the steam sloop *Brooklyn* have the van because she was fitted with four bow-chasers and a device designed to sweep torpedoes from her path. Chains were draped around wooden hulls and bags of sand and ashes piled about boilers and engines.

The admiral himself mounted into the lower main rigging of the flagship so that he would be able to see above the smoke of battle and was tied in place for safety. He gave the order to get under way at 5:30 A.M. on August 5. Shortly before seven o'clock the monitor *Tecumseh* opened the battle by firing a 15-inch shell at Fort Morgan. The rebel batteries replied with blistering fire. The monitor, spotting the *Tennessee* in the bay ahead and eager to close with her, took a short cut that led her across the edge of the minefield. Suddenly she was rocked by a terrific explosion, capsized and sank within minutes, her propeller racing in the air. As the stricken monitor's crew scrambled to the few hatches leading to safety, her captain, Commander T.A.M. Craven, and her pilot, John Collins, arrived at the foot of a ladder at the same time. "After you, pilot," said Craven, waving Collins ahead. As he escaped through a turret gunport, Collins felt the *Tecumseh* lurch beneath him. Twenty-two men were saved; Craven and ninety-one others went down with their ship.

Just after the *Tecumseh* struck the mine, the captain of the *Brooklyn* spotted some buoys dead ahead, which he took to mark the limits of the minefield. Instead of trying to clear them, as might have been expected, he reversed engines. The rest of the ships began to bunch up behind him and came under the guns of Fort Morgan. Hailing the *Brooklyn*, Farragut demanded to know the cause of the delay and was told that there were torpedoes ahead. "Damn the torpedoes," he called out from his perch in the rigging, "Full speed ahead!"

The *Hartford*, with the gunboat *Metacomet* lashed to her side, surged ahead of the *Brooklyn* and "between the buoys where the torpedoes were supposed to have been sunk," the admiral later reported. "Believing that from their having been some time in the water, they were probably innocuous, I determined to take the chance of their explosion." The ominous sound of mines bumping against the flagship's wooden hull was heard as she steamed past Fort Morgan, but Farragut's guess seemed to have been correct, for none went off.

Under cover of their own steady fire and the clouds of heavy smoke that drifted down on the rebel gunners, the ships ran past Fort Morgan and into the bay. The smaller craft were cast loose and soon took care of the three Confederate gunboats that had been pouring a raking fire into Farragut's advancing line. The *Tennessee* fought on alone. Belching black smoke, the gallant ironclad lumbered down on the entire Union squadron as fast as her creaky engines would permit. Buchanan could have chosen to fight at long range or to remain under the protection of the guns of Fort Morgan, but that was not his style.

And so began what Farragut called "one of the fiercest naval combats on record." The *Monongahela* and *Lackawanna*, fitted with iron prows, tried to ram the *Tennessee* but only stove in their own bows. Next came the *Hartford*, but she struck only a glancing blow, while pouring in a full broadside at a distance of only ten feet. Amid the smoke and flames, the *Lackawanna* collided with the flagship and an angry Farragut ordered her skipper to anchor where he could do no more damage. Only the 15-inch solid shot of the monitor *Manhattan* appeared to have any effect on the rebel ironclad. One of the *Tennessee*'s officers reported:

> The *Monongahela* was hardly clear of us when a hideous-looking monster came creeping up on our Port side, whose slowly revolving turret revealed the cavernous depths of a mammoth gun. "Stand clear of the Port side!" I shouted. A moment after, a thunderous report shook us all, while a blast of dense, sulphurous smoke covered our port-holes, and 440 pounds of iron, impelled by sixty pounds of powder, admitted daylight through our side, where before it struck us, there had been over two feet of solid wood, covered with five inches of solid iron. This was the only 15-inch shot that hit us fair. It did not come through . . . [but] I was glad to find myself alive after that shot.

The unequal battle raged for the better part of an hour. Finally, the battered *Tennessee*, surrounded by enemy vessels and with her gunports jammed, her exposed steering gear shot away, and Buchanan seriously wounded, hoisted the white flag. The forts surrendered later on, but Mobile itself held out until the end of the war. Farragut's victory, however, ended the city's importance as a center for blockade-running. One by one, the South's most important ports— Beaufort, New Bern, Charleston, Savannah, Pensacola, Mobile, New Orleans, and Galveston—had been either captured or effectively sealed. Now, Wilmington, North Carolina, was the only major port through which Lee's army in Virginia, under relentless attack by Grant, could be supplied from abroad.[64]

The Confederates had lavished considerable attention on the defenses of Wilmington. Its importance to the Confederate cause can be gauged by the fact that between late October 1864 and January 1865 blockade-runners brought in 4,300 tons of meat, 750 tons of lead, nearly 100 tons of saltpeter, 546,000 pairs of shoes, 69,000 muskets, and 43 cannon.[65] Lying nearly thirty miles up the Cape Fear River, the city was defended against attack from the sea by a series of log-and-sand fortifications armed with 169 guns known collectively as Fort Fisher. A minefield guarded the land approaches to the defenses and the Cape Fear River was too treacherous to permit the fleet to run past the fort, as Admiral Farragut had done at New Orleans and Mobile Bay.

Gideon Welles intended to offer command of the naval operations against Wilmington to Farragut, but the sixty-three-year-old admiral, suffering from vertigo and gout, asked to be relieved from duty, and the post went to David D. Porter. Anxious to restore his reputation after the Red River fiasco, Porter assumed command on October 12, 1864, and immediately set about gathering ironclads and wooden vessels to reinforce the existing blockaders. In the meantime he was worried about the Confederate ironclad *Albemarle*, which lay in the Roanoke River at Plymouth, North Carolina. She had already rammed and sunk one of the Union gunboats guarding Albemarle Sound and no Federal vessel could get across the bar at Hatteras Inlet to support them. Porter also feared that she might break the blockade. Lieutenant William B. Cushing, a young daredevil, volunteered to try to sink her. On the night of October 27, 1864, using a steam launch with a spar torpedo, he attacked the heavily guarded *Albemarle* and sank her in one of the most daring exploits of the war. Cushing's own boat was sunk and two men were lost, but he managed to swim ashore, escape capture, and make a heroic return to a Federal ship.

Porter was greatly elated by the removal of this threat to his force, but the attack of Fort Fisher fell further and further behind schedule. Ben Butler, the overall military commander in the area, suggested that if a shipload of explosives were detonated close to the ocean face of the fort, the defenders might be stunned and terrorized long enough to allow him to get troops ashore to capture the fortifications. Porter reluctantly agreed, and an ex-blockade-runner, the *Louisiana*, was converted into a floating bomb, carrying 215 tons of gunpowder.

From this point, however, cooperation between the army and navy began to collapse. Porter and Butler had been barely on speaking terms since the attack on New Orleans, and with the commanders working at cross-purposes, the expedition bogged down in a welter of petty jealousies. The *Louisiana* was towed under the guns of Fort Fisher and exploded at 1:40 A.M. on December 24, 1864, but the explosion had little effect on the rebels. And, although the blast was supposed to be coordinated with an immediate attack, ten hours passed before the fleet began to shell the fortifications. To conserve ammunition, the rebels held their fire, convincing Porter that their guns had been silenced. On Christmas morning, some 2,100 of Butler's troops were put ashore—only to be evacuated almost immediately as the weather deteriorated, and it was discovered that Fort Fisher had suffered little damage.[66]

Butler blamed Porter for the fiasco and Porter blamed Butler, but General Grant, as general in chief, had the final say. Angry with Butler for failing to hold his beachhead, he appointed Major General Alfred H. Terry in his place and brought the landing force up to 8,000 men. When a fresh assault was launched on Fort Fisher on January 13, 1865, cooperation between the army and the navy improved. Porter's ironclads kept up a steady fire, sometimes pouring as many as 100 shots a minute on the enemy positions. Two days later, a naval brigade of 1,600 sailors and 400 marines was landed and attacked the fort's sea face while Terry's men concentrated on the land side. With no concern whatever for the realities of land warfare, the brigade was armed with cutlasses, revolvers, and a few rifles—as if it were a boarding party.

Charging across an open beach toward the fort's parapet, the sailors and marines were met by a concentrated fire that ploughed wide lanes in their ranks. Ensign Robley D. Evans, wounded four times in the assault, recalled:

> About five hundred yards from the fort the head of the column suddenly stopped, and, as if by magic, the whole mass of men went down like a row of falling bricks. . . . The officers called on the men, and they responded instantly, starting forward as fast as they could go. At about three hundred yards they again went down, this time under the effect of canister added to rifle fire. Again we rallied them, and once more started to the front under a perfect hail of lead, with men dropping rapidly in every direction.

Lieutenant Commander Thomas O. Selfridge and about sixty men reached the parapet but they were swept away by heavy fire. The naval brigade suffered 350 casualties—80 killed and the rest wounded—but their effort was not in vain. While the Confederates were busy dealing with the attack, General Terry's troops were scrambling through a breach made by the naval bombardment in the fort's side face. The fort's gun bays and dugouts were then mopped up successively in a hand-to-hand fight that lasted for seven hours. With Fort Fisher in the hands of the Yankees, the South's last major port had been bolted shut. "The anaconda had, at last, wound his fatal folds around us," said Raphael Semmes.[67]

The capture of Wilmington ended the navy's role in the Civil War—a role which, if not decisive, was vital to the final Northern victory. Command of the sea and inland waters provided the Union armies with a mobility that overcame the Confederacy's interior lines of communication. It provided the Union with the tactical and strategic advantage of being able to shift its forces to apply pressure at almost any given point. At the same time, the blockade discouraged normal trade between the South and the outside world, while cutting the Confederacy off from the primary source of the tools of war. A strong and vigorous Union navy also served as a silent warning to foreign nations that might have been tempted to come to the aid of the South that, if they did, they would not escape unscathed. No one better summed up the navy's contribution to winning the war than Abraham Lincoln. "Nor must Uncle Sam's web-feet be forgotten," he said, in distributing the laurels of victory. "At all the watery margins they have been present. Not only on the deep sea, the broad bay, and the rapid river, but also up the narrow bayou, and wherever the ground was a little damp, they have been, and made their tracks. Thanks to all."[68]

6

A NAVAL RENAISSANCE

*An hour or two at Manila, an hour or two at Santiago, and
the maps of the world were changed.*
—Rear Admiral A. S. Barker, USN

B oilers wheezing asthmatically and engines clanking, the fleet groped out of Key West in the dawn's early light of February 3, 1874. Soon the mixture of stubby monitors and graceful steam frigates and sloops was spread out over the sea, plowing ahead at a barely perceptible 4.5 knots. The United States, teetering on the brink of war with Spain, had mobilized the largest display of naval power it had gathered in one place since the Civil War. But as this antiquated armada slowly maneuvered off the Florida coast, American naval officers were appalled at the sight that met their eyes. "It became painfully apparent to us that the vessels before us were in no respect worthy of a great nation like our own," declared Commodore Foxhall A. Parker. "What could be more lamentable—what more painful to one who loved his country and his profession?"[1]

In October 1873 a Spanish warship had seized the *Virginius*, a Cuban-owned vessel crammed with revolutionaries that was illegally flying the American flag, and taken her into Santiago, Cuba. Fifty-three passengers and crewmen, some of them Americans, were summarily court-martialed and shot, touching off a wave of indignation in the United States. Eventually the Spaniards released the *Virginius* and 102 survivors, proved conclusively that the vessel had been sailing under false colors, and paid an indemnity—thereby postponing war with the Americans for a quarter-century. The postponement was fortunate for the United States because the mobilization had provided bountiful evidence of the fleet's decrepit state. A future admiral, Robley D. Evans, observed, "two modern vessels of war would have done us up in thirty minutes" without serious danger to themselves. But the navy was not to blame, he added. "We did the best we could with what Congress gave us."[2]

The navy had emerged from the Civil War with nearly 700 ships in

143

commission—sixty-five of them ironclads—but once again a victorious United States began scrapping its fleet. Many of the ships disposed of were converted merchantmen or hastily built vessels of no great value. But powerful ironclads and fast cruisers, supposed essentials of a strategic reserve, were allowed to rot and rust. By 1880 the navy roster had shrunk to forty-eight outmoded vessels. Admiral David D. Porter, the navy's senior officer since the death of Admiral Farragut in 1870, compared them to "ancient Chinese forts on which dragons have been painted to frighten away the enemy." The United States ranked twelfth among the naval powers of the world—behind Denmark, China, and Chile.

Burdened with debt, weary of war, and eager to get on with political reconstruction and the exploitation of the nation's rich resources, the American people had turned their backs on the sea. There were no overseas colonies to defend, and the United States was insulated from Europe's rivalries by 3,000 miles of ocean. The international horizon seemed calm and peaceful. France's intervention in Mexico, U. S. claims against Britain arising from the depredations of the *Alabama* and her consorts, and tensions with Spain were all settled through diplomatic negotiation.

Frustrated American naval officers were chagrined to find their ships a source of amusement to foreigners. In one of Oscar Wilde's satirical stories, an American girl who said there were no ruins or curiosities in her country was told by the Canterville Ghost: "No ruins! No curiosities! You have your navy and your manners." While in command of the old steam sloop *Wachusett* on the Pacific Station in 1884, Alfred Thayer Mahan was visited by a French officer who gazed in wonderment upon one of her muzzle-loading pivot guns. "Where are the snows of yesteryear?" the Frenchman sighed, as he patted the antique on the breech. "Ah yes, the old system. We had it, too." Stung by these remarks, Mahan observed bitterly: "We 'had' things which other nations 'had had.' "[3]

Abroad, it was a time of technological progress—of self-propelled torpedoes, improved armor plate, large rifled guns, and compound engines. In 1873 the British launched the *Devastation*, which, with her heavy armor, powerful twin turrets, and solitary signal mast, was the prototype of the modern battleship. She could steam to North America and back to England without coaling. Such innovations had thrown naval design into turmoil, but many responsible naval and civilian leaders at home reasoned that the United States should not adopt any of them until the Europeans had tested them to find out which was best.

Although steam had proven its superiority over sail under wartime conditions, after the war the navy returned to sail. This move did not result solely from the inherent conservatism of such senior officers as Admiral Porter. It reflected the prevailing strategic reality that the United States did not have the coaling stations necessary to support a sizeable steam fleet in foreign waters and the political reality that the American people were not in an imperialist mood. Suggestions that the nation acquire the Hawaiian Islands, Samoa, Samanà Bay in the Dominican Republic, and a site on the Isthmus of Panama for naval stations fell on deaf ears.[4]

Sailing ships, after all, were ideally suited for long-range cruising because their self-sufficiency permitted them to remain at sea until their supplies ran out. A general order issued in 1869 required all naval vessels to have "full sail power." To improve the sailing qualities of steamships when under canvas, the number of their propeller blades was reduced from four to two, but there was a corresponding drop in the ships' efficiency under steam. Existing boilers and engines were replaced by smaller and less powerful ones and, in some cases, were completely removed. "To burn coal was so grievous an offense in the eyes of the authorities, that for years the captain was obliged to enter in the logbook in *red ink* his reasons for getting up steam," recalled Admiral Caspar F. Goodrich. Captains were warned that if excessive amounts of coal were consumed, they might have to pay the cost themselves.

Life under sail on distant stations was much the same as it had been in the prewar navy. Target practice was held only intermittently, and the ability to handle a ship under sail was considered the hallmark of a good officer. "Every morning in port, when the colors were hoisted at eight o'clock, there was an evolution of some sort, such as sending up topgallant masts, crossing topgallant and royal yards, and loosing sail to a bowline," recalled Admiral Goodrich. Many officers agreed with George M. Robeson, the secretary of the navy, when he said in 1869 that steam had led to a deterioration in the quality of American seamen. "Lounging through the watches of a steamer, or acting as firemen and coal heavers will not produce in a seaman that combination of boldness, strength, and skill which characterized the American sailor of the elder day," he observed.[5]

The subordination of steam to sail had a stultifying effect on technological progress after the Civil War. For example, the *Wampanoag*, a fast cruiser designed by Engineer-in-Chief Benjamin F. Isherwood, aroused the ire of conservative officers because Isherwood regarded sails as mere auxiliaries. The first ship to use superheated steam, the long and narrow *Wampanoag* reached the phenomenal speed of 17.7 knots during her trials in 1868 and averaged 16.6 knots over thirty-eight hours. But a special board dominated by line officers, who regarded themselves as the navy's aristocracy and feared that a steam navy would be controlled by engineers, ordered, with the announced intention of improving her sailing qualities under canvas, a number of her boilers removed. The *Wampanoag* never went to sea again. She rotted away at a pier. Eleven years elapsed before a commercial steamer equalled her speed, and it was another twenty-one years before an American war vessel matched it.[6]

Unable to persuade Congress to appropriate funds for new ships but with more than $6 million a year for repairs, Robeson had certain ships virtually rebuilt from the keel up. In some cases, the amount spent on repairing a ship was greater than her construction cost. Much of the money disappeared into the

pockets of contractors, and when Robeson left office in 1877, about all there
was to show for the expenditures was "an obsolete fleet in poor condition."
His successor, Richard W. Thompson, of Indiana, was said to be "so densely
ignorant of naval affairs as to have expressed surprise . . . on learning that ships
were hollow."[7]

Naval service in this era lacked attraction for either officers or men. As one
authority has said, it offered "all the dreary monotony and mechanical grind of
a socialistic regime without any of the latter's promised equity and elevation of
ideals." Promotion was by seniority, and the "hump" created by the large
number of officers commissioned during the Civil War made it so slow that men
who were lieutenants in 1869 were still lieutenants twelve years later. Politics
and favoritism often had as much to do with assignments as did skill and efficiency, and there was considerable squabbling between line and staff officers.
Upon graduation, students at the Naval Academy, whose designation had been
changed from "midshipman" to "cadet," were appointed midshipmen instead
of being commissioned as ensigns. One cadet estimated that it would take him
seven years from the time of his graduation to win a commission.[8]

In addition, the quality and quantity of enlisted men declined. By 1878
there were no more than 6,000 men in the navy, the smallest number since the
administration of Andrew Jackson. Most of them were foreigners who had been
picked up in various ports around the world. In 1876 an officer of the Asiatic
Squadron surveyed the 128 men on board his ship and found 47 Americans, 21
Chinese, 20 Irishmen, 9 Englishmen, and representatives of twenty-two other
nationalities. A few years later Commodore Stephen B. Luce recalled seeing a
sign that read *Ici on parle Anglais* posted by the gangway of a ship of the
European Squadron. Although the posting of the sign was a jest, Luce said it
was "a severe commentary on the character of the crews we have been for years
employing to maintain the honor and integrity of the American flag."

To provide trained seamen for both the navy and the merchant marine, Luce
recommended a system for training apprentices similar to the one Commodore
Perry had advocated thirty years before. On April 8, 1875, Congress authorized
the enlistment of 750 youths between the ages of sixteen and eighteen to serve
in the navy until they reached the age of twenty-one. Under Luce's plan, they
were given preliminary instruction on station ships and then transferred to training
vessels, where they were taught gunnery, seamanship, and other skills. Over
the years, this system was expanded, and although Luce, who favored training
men at sea under sail, objected when "boot" camps were established ashore, it
was the forerunner of the navy's modern training system for enlisted men.[9]

Even though the postwar navy was small and its ships decaying, it effectively
performed its tasks of showing the flag and protecting American commercial
interests in distant parts of the world. The most significant of these operations
was an attempt by John Rodgers, now a rear admiral and commander of the

Asiatic Squadron, to open Korea to Western trade. The "Hermit Kingdom" had kept itself secluded from the outside world until Rodgers, with five ships, arrived at the mouth of the Salee River, below Seoul, on May 30, 1871. Several American trading vessels had been wrecked off the coast of Korea and their crews murdered, and Rodgers' mission was to secure both satisfaction from the Koreans and a treaty to protect shipwrecked foreigners in the future. While awaiting the arrival of Korean officials of sufficient stature to begin negotiations, he sent out several small boats to make soundings in the river. They were fired upon from a Korean fort and two men were wounded.

When ten days had passed without an apology, Rodgers launched an amphibious assault on the five forts guarding the approaches to Seoul. On June 10 about 650 sailors and marines landed and attacked the forts under the supporting fire of the ships' guns. Although the Koreans were armed with outmoded weapons, they resisted fiercely and, despite many casualties, refused to negotiate before Rodgers was forced by the approach of the typhoon season to sail away. Although Rodgers' attempt to blow open the door to Korea failed, it prepared the way for Commodore Robert W. Shufeldt to negotiate a treaty between Korea and the United States in 1881—the first that Korea signed with a Western nation.[10]

The navy also showed renewed interest in the exploration of uncharted seas, particularly in the Arctic. Several expeditions had ventured into this area before the Civil War, including one led by Elisha Kent Kane, a surgeon in the navy, which, under conditions of considerable hardship, surveyed the northern reaches of Greenland and made other contributions to scientific knowledge. James Gordon Bennett, Jr., flamboyant publisher of the *New York Herald*, conceived the idea of sponsoring an expedition to discover the North Pole by following a route through the Bering Sea and persuaded the navy, which hoped to influence public opinion in its favor, to support it. The steamer *Jeannette*, purchased by Bennett and manned by a crew of volunteers led by Lieutenant George W. De Long, put to sea in 1879. Nothing was heard of her for two years.

Word eventually filtered through from Siberia that the *Jeannette*, trapped in the Arctic ice, had drifted helplessly toward the delta of the Lena River where in 1881 she was crushed by grinding floes. After De Long and his crew had spent about a month marching over the ice, the water opened up sufficiently for them to try to reach land in three ship's boats. They sailed some 500 miles, then became separated during a violent gale. George W. Melville, the *Jeannette*'s engineer, landed his boat safely on the coast of Siberia and sent out a search party to look for the others. De Long and two men were found dead of starvation and exposure in a makeshift camp, and three survivors were discovered in a nearby village. No trace of the third party was ever discovered.

In 1884 the indomitable Melville took part in an expedition fitted out by the navy to rescue Lieutenant A. W. Greely, an army officer and leader of a twenty-five-man party that was exploring Grinnell Land, to the west of Greenland. For two years supply vessels had tried without success to get through the ice to Greely, whose situation had become perilous. Three ships, including the steam bark *Bear*, an ex-sealer that had been purchased for this purpose and which later had a long and honorable career in patrolling Arctic waters as part of the Coast Guard, were sent to look for the missing men. After a lengthy search, the rescuers found Greely and seven starving survivors marooned on a bleak island in Baffin Bay.[11]

Naval officers did not remain silent about the lamentable state of their service. In October 1873 the U. S. Naval Institute was established to give voice to some of their criticism. Founded by a group of reform-minded officers who met regularly at the Naval Academy to advance professional and scientific knowledge, the institute soon became a major sounding board for ideas and proposals designed to improve the navy. Beginning in 1875, papers on technical subjects and on strategy that had been read and discussed at the meetings were published intermittently in a journal, the U. S. Naval Institute *Proceedings*, which became a quarterly four years later. In 1917 the publication began to appear monthly and has done so ever since.[12]

Following years of dogged criticism of the state of the fleet in the pages of the *Proceedings* and in other forums, the tide slowly began turning in favor of a new navy. Industry and agriculture had experienced tremendous growth since the end of the Civil War, and the American people were looking for new frontiers to conquer now that the West had been won. Foreign trade was increasing, and the merchant marine was beginning to stir again. Commercial expansion inspired fears that rivalries over access to foreign markets might precipitate a conflict with one or more of the European powers. Pro-navy spokesmen emphasized the need for a fleet to protect America's burgeoning interests abroad and pointed out that there was a sizeable surplus in the treasury to pay for it.

The transformation of the U. S. Navy into a modern fighting machine began a full decade before Admiral Mahan enunciated his doctrine of sea power. Some members of Congress were already calling for a big navy to project national power and prestige overseas. "What nation ever became a first-class power without a navy?" asked Senator Samuel B. Maxey, a Texas Democrat. Among those who suggested that the United States abandon its traditional maritime strategy was Senator Matthew C. Butler, of South Carolina, another Democrat, who described commerce-raiding as an "insignificant kind of guerrilla, bushwhacking warfare."[13]

The catalyst for change was William H. Hunt, secretary of the navy in the cabinet of President James A. Garfield. An experienced political hand, Hunt was convinced that the navy's senior officers were greatly to blame for the fact that the service did not receive a sympathetic ear when Congress was making appropriations. Instead of providing a coherent outline of the navy's requirements, they bickered among themselves over the relative merits of steam and sail and over technical details. With the intention of presenting to Congress a detailed and comprehensive program of naval development, Hunt convened a Naval Advisory Board and appointed John Rodgers to head it.

Typically, the board rarely showed unanimity. Beginning their meetings in July 1881, the fifteen members clashed over whether the new ships should be built of iron or steel, whether they should be fully rigged with sails, and whether cruising range should be sacrificed to heavy ordnance and capacious magazines. Factional differences were so great that, late in the year, the board submitted both a majority and a minority report. The majority report recommended an ambitious program calling for the construction of no less than sixty-eight vessels, including eighteen steel cruisers to be propelled by steam but fitted with auxiliary sails. Before Hunt could move to implement this report, however, President Garfield was assassinated and his successor, Chester A. Arthur, replaced Hunt with William E. Chandler, a machine politician who had played a leading role in the shady dealings that had given Rutherford B. Hayes the presidency after the disputed election of 1876.

Supporters of the new navy were heartened when Chandler called the fleet's existing ships "a subject of ridicule" and moved ahead with the modernization plan. On August 5, 1882, Congress, which had whittled away at the advisory board's recommendations, authorized two cruisers but provided no funds for construction. It did, however, take an important step toward revitalizing the navy by prohibiting repairs when the cost was 30 per cent of the estimated price of a new ship of the same size. Later the figure was reduced to 20 per cent— hastening the retirement of most of the seagoing antiques that dated from before the Civil War.[14]

But what sort of ships should be built? European navies had battleships and armored cruisers, the former averaging 9,000 tons and the latter 6,000 tons, with guns varying in size from eight to sixteen inches, and heavy belts of armor. The United States, it was argued, having no extensive commitments abroad, did not need a blue-water offensive navy. Its requirements would best be met by squadrons of fast, protected cruisers suitable for hit-and-run commerce-raiding. Protected cruisers were smaller than armored cruisers and derived their name from the thin armored deck built over their boilers, engines, and other vital machinery. They were the largest vessels that could then be built in domestic yards. American steelmakers, although leading every other nation in production after 1880, were not equipped for naval work, and there was some doubt as to whether the industry could produce armor plate and gun forgings of the size, strength, and quality required for even these ships.[15]

The steel navy was born on March 3, 1883, when Congress appropriated $1.3 million for the construction of what became known as the ABCD ships— the protected cruisers *Atlanta* and *Boston* of 3,000 tons each and the *Chicago*, 4,500 tons, and the 1,500-ton dispatch vessel *Dolphin*. Two events of the previous year may have speeded final approval of this important legislation. In July

1882 a British fleet had bombarded Alexandria, Egypt, pounding into rubble fortifications stronger than those that defended major American ports. Like a specter from another age, the Yankee steam sloop *Lancaster* was an interested witness to the power of the Royal Navy. At about the same time, the protected cruiser *Esmeralda* was laid down in a British yard for the Chilean navy. With her armored deck, battery of 10-inch breechloaders, and speed of eighteen knots, she was the prototype of the modern cruiser and completely outclassed anything in the U. S. Navy.[16]

The ABC cruisers were experimental, a curious mixture of the contemporary and the backward. The *Chicago*, for example, had twin propellers, but her outdated engines and boilers reminded one observer of a sawmill. All three vessels were fitted with full sail rigs, yet they were the first American warships to be completely electrified and equipped with double bottoms and watertight compartments. The *Chicago*'s four 8-inch breechloading rifles, eight 6-inchers, and two 5-inch guns were regarded as powerful armament for a vessel of her size. The *Atlanta* and *Boston* were each armed with two 8-inch and six 6-inch guns. A great improvement over previous American weapons, these cannon had great range and power, but the method of aiming them—as was the case with all naval ordnance of the time—was by looking along the barrel through open sights.[17]

The building of the ABCD ships did not go smoothly. Secretary Chandler was so anxious to get construction under way that the contracts were advertised even before detailed specifications and drawings for all the vessels had been completed. When the bids were opened, there was considerable controversy. John Roach, owner of a shipyard at Chester, Pennsylvania, and a pioneer steel-maker, had submitted the low bid on all four of the ships. Outraged rivals immediately charged fraud and collusion. They pointed out that Roach was a substantial contributor to Republican causes, that he and Chandler were old political cronies, and that Roach had reaped a golden harvest from the questionable repair contracts let by George Robeson a few years before.

Roach ran into trouble almost immediately. Procuring high-quality steel plate was a more difficult task than he had expected. A fire in the shipyard and the numerous changes that the Navy Department ordered in the *Dolphin*, the first of the vessels to be laid down, delayed her completion. Then she failed her sea trials. To complete Roach's woes, Grover Cleveland, a Democrat, was elected president in 1884. William C. Whitney, a prominent New York financier who was chosen to be secretary of the navy, leaped upon the *Dolphin*'s problems in order to settle old political scores, and Roach was forced into bankruptcy after completing the ships.[18]

Despite their experimental, indeed controversial, nature, the ABCD ships provided good service. In 1889 the *Dolphin* completed a 58,000-mile world cruise, during which her engines were shut down at sea for adjustment for only two hours. The three cruisers were organized into a Squadron of Evolution—

popularly known as the White Squadron because of the color of their hulls—
and provided valuable training for the new generation of officers and men. In
1885 two 4,000-ton protected cruisers were authorized—the *Charleston*, built
from British plans and the first American warship to better the old *Wampanoag*'s
speed of 17.7 knots, and the *Newark*, the last American cruiser to be fitted with
a full sail rig.[19]

The following year, the steel industry having developed the capacity to
produce armor in sufficient quantity and quality for large ships, the *Texas* and
Maine were authorized. Designated as second-class battleships, they were in
reality armored cruisers and were built from British designs. Secretary Whitney
stipulated that domestic steel and machinery had to be used in their construction,
and in order to ensure a continuous supply of domestic armor and forgings, he
pooled all the navy's requirements into one $4.4-million contract, wherein one
might perhaps espy an early manifestation of what has become known as the
military-industrial complex. The contract was awarded to the Bethlehem Iron
Company. At the same time, Whitney ordered the navy's first high-speed torpedo
boat and established the Naval Gun Factory in Washington, D.C. He also tried
to reform the creaky administration of the navy by requiring more cooperation
between the bureaus, which often acted as independent satrapies. However, a
plan to consolidate the bureaus into three principal branches dealing with personnel, construction, and finance failed to win congressional approval.[20]

The intellectual Commodore Luce, who had commanded a monitor in the
long and frustrating siege of Charleston, noted with fascination how quickly
the city fell after General Sherman's army had severed its line of communications with the interior. From observations such as this, he concluded that
there were "certain fundamental principles underlying a military operation which
it were well to look into; principles of general application whether the operations were conducted on land or sea." For the next two decades, he tried to
persuade successive secretaries of the navy to establish a senior school to
"teach officers the science of their own profession—the science of war."[21]

Luce's proposal met with skepticism and hostility. The prevailing opinion
of senior officers and civilians was that the great naval leaders of the past had
not studied "the science of war," so there was no need for such a thing now.
"*Teach* the art of war!" snorted one crusty admiral, "Well, I'll be damned!"
Nevertheless, Luce pressed ahead, pointing out that good seamanship was no
longer the sole mark of a successful naval officer. Naval warfare in the future
would not be limited to single-ship engagements, he argued, and there must be
a nucleus of officers trained in the broad principles of strategy. Finally, on
October 6, 1884, Secretary Chandler signed a general order establishing the
Naval War College in what had formerly been the city poorhouse on Coaster's
Harbor Island at Newport, Rhode Island, and Luce was named its first president.

"Poor little Poor House," Luce whimsically remarked at the opening of
the first school of its kind in the world. "I christen thee the United States Naval

War College.'' Tactics, strategy, international law, and naval history and policy were the subjects that he proposed for the curriculum, and he foresaw that the lecturer on naval history would be the key man on the staff. It would be this man's role to discover broad principles in the study of the past that could be applied to current and future naval strategy. Luce hoped to find a ''master mind'' who would do for naval strategy what Baron Antoine Henri Jomini had done for military science in the Napoleonic era. He found the man he was looking for on the Pacific Station in the person of Commander Alfred Thayer Mahan, the same who had suffered the pitying remarks of the visiting French officer and who was still captain of the *Wachusett*.

Tall, balding, and ascetic-looking, Mahan was not a typical naval officer.[22] Born at West Point, he was the son of Dennis Hart Mahan, a member of the faculty at the Military Academy and a pioneer in the teaching of strategy. Mahan obtained an appointment to the Naval Academy and because he had previously attended Columbia College for two years was allowed to enter the third class, the last man in the school's history to be permitted to skip plebe year. In the twenty-five years of service that followed his graduation in 1859, Mahan drifted along with the tide, accomplishing little except for writing a small book on naval operations in the Civil War, *The Gulf and Inland Waters*. Impressed with this work, Luce offered its author the post of lecturer in naval history. Mahan accepted with alacrity, but because an unsympathetic Navy Department ruled that he would have to complete his tour on the Pacific Station before reporting to Newport, he missed the school's first term.

Mahan's duties on the *Wachusett* were not onerous, and as she lay in the dreary Peruvian port of Callao, he spent most of his time at the local English Club devouring every history book he could find in order to prepare himself for his new assignment. Trying to find a way to ''make the experience of wooden sailing ships, with their pop-guns, useful in the naval present,'' he perceived in the long sweep of history a pattern that indicated that command of the sea had been a decisive factor in the rise and fall of empires. The idea came to him while he was reading Theodor Mommsen's *History of Rome*. ''It suddenly struck me,'' Mahan related, ''how different things might have been could Hannibal have invaded Italy by sea . . . instead of by the long land route, or could he after arrival, have been in free communication with Carthage by water.'' With every faculty ''alive and jumping,'' he saw that ''control of the sea was an historic factor which had never been systematically appreciated and expounded.''[23]

When Luce was ordered to sea duty in 1886, Mahan was appointed president of the college. This was something of an empty honor. Government financing for the institution was pitifully inadequate, and he had to lobby steadily for funds to keep its doors open. The president's quarters were in such deplorable condition that Mahan had to attach rubber tubing to a radiator to obtain bath water. He also had to fight off officers and civilians who wanted the course at Newport to devote less time to the study of strategy and more to the use of evolving technologies. Now a captain, he persevered in his efforts to keep the school open and found time to turn his lectures into a book that, after being rejected by several publishers, was published by Little, Brown and Company in 1890 as *The Influence of Sea Power Upon History, 1660–1783*.

Mahan argued that it was command of the sea that had enabled the British to create their colonial empire, reap the profits of maritime commerce, and defeat the land powers that tried to challenge their dominance of the trade routes of the world. Sea power depended upon more than naval strength, however. Geography, demography, character of the people, and the nature of a nation's government were factors to be considered. In summary, a seafaring nation that had good harbors and no frontier to be defended by a large land army could, if led by an enlightened and dynamic government, exploit the sea to its own advantage. For the United States the lesson was clear—national survival depended on control of the sea. Mahan's book was a brilliant exposition of maritime history and naval strategy and became the intellectual foundation for the proponents of a big navy.

Only a few years before his book was published, Mahan had been an anti-imperialist. Like many naval officers, he abhorred some of the practices of Yankee businessmen that he had observed in various foreign ports. Now he argued that foreign trade was essential to national prosperity. Commerce required a strong merchant marine, an effective navy for its protection, and overseas bases. Mahan urged the construction of a powerful fleet to prevent the American coast from being blockaded. Small coast-defense ships and commerce-raiders, the traditional American weapons of sea war, were useless for this mission. A fleet of battleships that could command the high seas was the best guarantee of continued access to American ports in time of war. Benjamin Stoddert had put forward this proposition almost a century before, and its validity had been demonstrated by the British blockade in the War of 1812.

Mahan's ideas and fame spread quickly around the globe. In 1893, shortly after he had finished another book, *The Influence of Sea Power Upon the French Revolution and Empire, 1793–1812*, he was ordered to sea as captain of the *Chicago*, flagship of the European Squadron. Although he fought tooth and nail to avoid a seagoing billet, the cruise had a happy outcome, for he discovered that his books had taken Britain by storm. As the admiring chronicler of Britain's naval greatness, he was entertained by Queen Victoria, lionized by statesmen and admirals, and given honorary degrees at both Oxford and Cambridge. The British were not alone in their adulation. Almost immediately after their publication, Mahan's books were translated into Japanese and adopted as texts in that nation's military and naval schools. A misreading of *The Influence of Sea Power Upon History* implanted in the mind of Kaiser Wilhelm II the idea that Germany's destiny lay on the ocean, and inspired a fateful challenge to Britain's dominion of the seas. "I am just now not reading but devouring Captain Mahan's book and am trying to learn it by heart," the kaiser wrote a friend. He ordered copies of the book placed on all ships of the German navy.[24]

At home, Mahan became the high priest of a rising imperialism. "Americans must now begin to look outward," he declared in one of the numerous articles he wrote to popularize his ideas. Businessmen and politicians echoed the statement, for in the closing years of the nineteenth century the spirit of manifest destiny, dormant since the Civil War, was again abroad in the land. Latin America and the Far East were eyed as areas where the great surpluses pouring from America's farms and factories could be disposed of at a profit. As Walter LaFeber points out in his study of the dynamics of American expansion, the new imperialists did not envision colonizing these areas but wanted to exploit them commercially and bring the benefits of American civilization to the benighted.[25] Mahan and his disciples emphasized the need for a large navy and overseas bases to protect trade and settle any conflicts that might grow out of it. Expansion across the Pacific, the annexation of Hawaii as a bridge to the East and as a first line of defense to ward off attacks on the mainland, and a canal across Nicaragua or Panama were cardinal principles in their thinking.

Mahan's doctrine on the need for capital ships was incorporated into the nation's naval policy by Benjamin F. Tracy, secretary of the navy under President Benjamin Harrison. The objective of the U. S. Navy "is not conquest but defense," Tracy said in his first annual report, issued in 1889, but he emphasized that "to carry on even a defensive war with any hope of success we must have armored battleships. . . . The capture or destruction of two or three dozen or two or three score of [enemy] merchant vessels is not going to prevent a fleet of ironclads from shelling our cities," Tracy warned. "The country needs a navy that will exempt it from war but the only navy that will accomplish this is a navy that can wage war." To underscore the naval weakness of the United States,[26] Tracy pointed to the loss of three old wooden cruisers—almost the entire Pacific Squadron—in a hurricane while they were trying to make a showing in defense of American interests in Samoa during the visit of a rival German squadron.

A Naval Policy Board appointed by Tracy proposed in January 1890 that the United States immediately embark on the construction of no less than 200 warships of all types, including a large number of battleships. Realizing that this was much too ambitious, Tracy reduced it to twenty battleships, but Congress flatly rejected both proposals. Instead, the Navy Act of 1890 provided funds for only three battleships, the *Indiana, Massachusetts,* and *Oregon,* each of 10,288 tons. These well-designed vessels, although smaller than some European battleships, compensated for lack of size by mounting four 13-inch, eight 8-inch, and four 6-inch guns protected by up to eighteen inches of nickel-steel armor. In 1892 they were followed by the *Iowa,* slightly larger than her consorts and embodying improvements in design and construction. To placate opponents of an offensive navy, these ships, particularly the *Indiana* class, had low freeboards and were referred to as "sea-going coast-line battleships." Nevertheless, the law passed in 1890 marked the beginning of a new era in American naval policy: a commitment had been made to the building of a blue-water navy similar to those of the European powers.[27]

Naval expansion was given a strong boost in 1891 when a liberty party from the cruiser *Baltimore* got into a brawl in the True Blue Saloon in Valparaiso and an anti-Yankee riot erupted in which two Americans were killed and eighteen injured. Relations between the United States and Chile grew tense and war feeling ran dangerously high in both countries. The Chileans, who had a strong fleet, openly boasted of what they would do to the vulnerable cities on the west coast of the United States if war should come. The incident was finally settled amicably, but it focused attention on the unprepared state of the navy and the possibility that the Chileans might have made good their threats.[28]

President Cleveland returned to office in 1893, and he and his secretary of the navy, Hilary A. Herbert, who was under Mahan's influence, veered away from the traditional Democratic opposition to a big navy. Financial panic and depression that year halted the build-up until 1895, however, when the battleships *Kentucky* and *Kearsarge* were authorized. (The latter is the only American battleship that was not named for a state.) Three more capital ships—the *Alabama*, *Illinois*, and *Wisconsin*—were ordered in 1896 during the crisis arising from an Anglo-Venezuelan boundary dispute in which the United States took the position that the British were violating the Monroe Doctrine. All five ships were of about 11,500 tons and carried four 13-inch guns and varying secondary batteries.[29]

In this manner, during the closing years of the nineteenth century, the U. S. Navy rose to fifth place among the world's navies, and as it increased in popular esteem, more young Americans were persuaded to enlist. The number of foreign seamen in the fleet was whittled down, until in 1896 there were more native-born sailors than foreign-born: 5,133 to 4,400. The increasing complexity of ships and weapons, which caused an English admiral to observe that "a seaman of today must know as much as a lieutenant of forty years ago," led to educational programs that fitted the men to handle sophisticated steam engines, electrical motors, high-powered guns, and other complicated machinery. In 1891 Congress appropriated funds to form state naval militia units that became the nucleus of the Naval Reserve. Composed of urban youths, yachtsmen, and ex-officers and men of the navy, these units were provided with outmoded ships and equipment for training purposes and were subject to call to active duty in an emergency.[30]

On the evening of February 15, 1898, Captain Charles D. Sigsbee, commanding officer of the battleship *Maine*, which was moored to a buoy in Havana Harbor, had just finished a letter to his wife. His ship had been sent to Cuba the previous month to protect American lives and property during one of the rebellions that periodically broke out against Spanish rule. At about 9:40 P.M., Sigsbee later recalled, a marine bugler sounded taps:

> I laid down my pen to listen to the notes of the bugle, which were singularly beautiful in the oppressive stillness of the night. . . . the echoes floated back to the ship repeating the strains of the bugle fully and exactly. . . . I was enclosing my letter in its envelope when the explosion came. . . . It was a bursting, rending, and crashing roar of immense volume. . . . there was a trembling and lurching motion . . . a list to port, and a movement of subsidence. The electric lights went out. Then there was intense blackness and smoke.[31]

Groping his way on deck, Sigsbee found the forward part of his ship shattered; she was rapidly sinking into the mud. Although nearby vessels sent boats to pick up survivors, casualties were heavy—266 of the 354 officers and men on board lost their lives. The jingoistic "yellow" press, spoiling for a war with Spain, immediately charged the Spaniards with having blown up the ship, but the cause of the blast has never been conclusively determined. In 1976 Admiral Hyman G. Rickover theorized, on the basis of modern technical studies, that a fire resulting from spontaneous combustion in a forward coal bunker—a common enough occurrence in that period—set off ammunition in an adjoining magazine.[32]

The United States had long looked upon Cuba with keen interest and had given much consideration to purchasing or annexing the island. The Cubans had revolted against Spain in 1895 and most Americans sympathized with them. Although Yankee investments on the island were significant, the major reason for intervention was not imperialistic greed, but a human, if misguided, desire to end the suffering of the Cuban people and to help them win their independence. Despite the efforts of the Spaniards to avert a conflict, American public opinion was whipped up to a frenzy. On April 19, 1898, Congress, with the clarion call "Remember the *Maine*! To hell with Spain!" ringing in its ears, approved a joint resolution that was tantamount to a declaration of war, but the formal declaration did not come until six days later.

European commentators, grossly overestimating the strength of the Spanish navy, forecast a long war, but Mahan, then retired from active service, predicted an American victory in "about three months." Command of the western Atlantic and the Caribbean was the key to victory, and the U. S. Navy mustered in that area three first-line battleships, the *Iowa*, *Massachusetts*, and *Indiana*, the smaller *Texas*, the armored cruisers *Brooklyn* and *New York*, and several lighter vessels. In March, the *Oregon*, fitting out on the West Coast, was ordered to join this force. She raced around Cape Horn to Key West, a distance of some 13,000 miles, in sixty-six days, a feat that dramatized the navy's need for a transisthmian canal connecting the Atlantic with the Pacific.

To protect Puerto Rico as well as Cuba, the Spaniards dispatched from Spain a fleet of four armored cruisers and several smaller ships under the command of Admiral Pascual Cervera y Topete. Although on paper these ships were the equal of their Yankee counterparts, they were in poor condition, and the *Cristóbal Colón*, Cervera's best ship, had to sail before her main battery of 10-inch guns had been installed. Perhaps the most significant difference between the Spanish and American naval forces, however, was in morale. While the Americans were supremely confident and anxious to meet the enemy, the Spaniards were gloomy about their prospects. The realistic Admiral Cervera had no hope of victory. "Nothing can be expected . . . except the total destruction of the fleet or its hasty and demoralized return," he declared after surveying his ships.[33]

American confidence stemmed from the high state of readiness of the navy. Convinced that war with Spain was inevitable, the ferociously dynamic assistant secretary of the navy, Theodore Roosevelt, had begun preparing for a conflict immediately after being appointed the year before. An ardent imperialist, he was the living embodiment of Mahan's doctrine of sea power and believed a big navy was vital to the design for national greatness that he had discerned in Mahan's teachings. Not content with operating behind a desk, Roosevelt frequently inspected the navy yards and took great delight in reviewing the navy's new ships at sea.[34]

Taking it upon himself to provide the aggressive leadership that he felt was lacking in the McKinley administration, Roosevelt often bypassed John D. Long, the secretary of the navy. Although most strategists envisioned a war with Spain as being limited to the Caribbean, Roosevelt laid plans not only to intervene in Cuba but to seize the Philippines. He was convinced that when war came, the Asiatic Squadron should immediately steam into Philippine waters, destroy the Spanish fleet based there, and take possession of the islands. He engineered the selection of Commodore George Dewey, whose temperament matched his own, to command the squadron.

Wearied by the series of emergency meetings that followed the sinking of the *Maine*, Secretary Long took a day off on February 25, 1898, leaving Roosevelt in charge of the Navy Department. The latter wasted no time in sending Dewey, who was at Hong Kong, a cablegram ordering him to concentrate his scattered ships:

> Keep full of coal. In the event of declaration of war Spain, your duty will be
> to see that the Spanish squadron does not leave the Asiatic coast and then
> offensive operations in Philippine Islands.

Dewey's reaction was to issue a flurry of orders to his captains to make their ships battle-ready. Bunkers were filled with coal, engines were repaired, magazines were restocked, and white hulls were painted slate gray. One ship was dry-docked, scraped, and painted within twenty-four hours. Besides his flagship, the cruiser *Olympia*, he had three other cruisers, the *Baltimore*, *Boston*, and *Raleigh*; two gunboats, the *Concord* and *Petrel*; and the revenue cutter *McCulloch*, all together mounting 33 guns of six inches or more and firing a broadside totalling 3,700 pounds. Intelligence reports from Manila indicated that the Spanish squadron there, under Admiral Patricio Montojo y Pasarón, appeared barely able to deal with a flotilla of Chinese junks. Montojo's flagship, the cruiser *Reina Cristina*, was the only modern ship he had, and she was not seaworthy because her hull leaked. Five other cruisers of about 1,100 tons each, a 3,300-ton wooden cruiser, the *Castilla*, and a trio of gunboats—all in poor condition—constituted the rest of the Spanish squadron. It carried one-third as many 6-inch guns as the American squadron and fired a broadside of only 1,273 pounds.

Having already moved into Chinese waters to avoid the problem of British neutrality, Dewey stood out for the South China Sea on April 27, 1898, bound for Manila Bay, some 600 miles away, with the *Olympia*'s band playing Sousa's march "El Capitán." In the squadron's wake, wooden chairs, tables, chests, waste, and paint cans—anything that might feed a fire—bobbed in the water. Early on the morning of Sunday, May 1, 1898, the squadron, the *Olympia* in the van, slipped into the passage separating the fortified islands of Corregidor and El Fraile and leading into Manila Bay.[35] Showing only carefully hooded stern lanterns that enabled each ship to follow her leader, half the vessels had passed the dark and silent batteries and entered the bay when soot from the *McCulloch*'s funnel caught fire. The ships were illuminated by rockets, and guns boomed out from the islands. Although shells splashed about the vessels still in the channel, they managed to pass safely into the bay.

Speed reduced to four knots, Dewey's ships covered the remaining twenty-two miles to Manila without incident. At about 5:00 A.M., as dawn was breaking, the enemy squadron was sighted off the naval station at Cavite, about ten miles from Manila; it lay anchored in an irregular east-west line. The morning was warm and misty, the water like glass. The Spanish ships and shore batteries opened fire at long range as the American vessels plowed silently toward them. The end of an era was at hand.

Dewey, wearing a golf cap in place of the uniform cap he had misplaced in the excitement, was on the *Olympia*'s open bridge, and he listened thoughtfully as an officer called out the diminishing range . . . 6,500 yards . . . 6,000 yards . . . 5,500 yards . . . 5,000 yards. . . . He ordered his column to starboard, putting it on a course roughly parallel to the anchored Spanish ships. At 5:41 A.M. he called down to Charles V. Gridley, captain of the ship, who was in the armored conning tower below him, "You may fire when you are ready, Gridley."

One of the flagship's forward 8-inch guns opened the battle and the rest of the ships joined in. The *Reina Cristina* and the *Castilla* were the primary targets of the American gunners. Soon such a thick pall of smoke settled over both squadrons that it was almost impossible for either to aim their guns with any precision, and the gunners were firing at muzzle flashes. Dewey ordered his force to pass back and forth in a series of ovals parallel to the enemy vessels, narrowing the range with each run until it was only 2,000 yards. By 7:30 A.M. the commodore was concerned because the Spanish ships were showing few signs of having been disabled. To add to his worries, he received a report—later proven false—that his squadron was running low on 5-inch ammunition for the secondary batteries. He decided to send the men to breakfast while the smoke cleared. "For God's sake, don't let us stop now!" cried one gun captain as the *Olympia* hauled off. "To hell with breakfast!"

When the smoke began to dissipate, it was apparent that except for a few gunboats the Spanish squadron had been annihilated. The *Reina Cristina* and *Castilla* had been sunk, and the rest of the ships lay twisted and burning in the shallows. Dewey returned to action shortly after eleven o'clock, and mopping-up operations were completed within an hour. The American ships had not been seriously damaged and only a handful of men had been wounded. When the news of Dewey's victory reached home, the nation went wild, even though many celebrants could have joined President McKinley in his confession that he "could not have told where those darned islands were within two thousand miles."

For several months Dewey sweltered in Manila Bay, awaiting the arrival of about 11,000 troops who were on their way from California to capture Manila and occupy the islands. He had less trouble with the Spaniards than he did with a powerful German squadron of five ships that arrived on the scene, apparently hoping to pick up a few scraps of the disintegrating Spanish empire. Vice Admiral Otto von Diederichs came and went as he pleased and practiced troop landings on the shores of Manila Bay. Dewey, who suspected that the Germans were trying to steal his prize, exploded when von Diederichs protested that an American vessel had improperly stopped one of his ships. "Why, I shall stop each vessel whatever may be her colors!" Dewey declared. "And if she does not stop, I shall fire at her. . . . If Germany wants a war, all right, we are ready." Dewey was supported by the British and Japanese, and the Germans sailed away. A year later, they purchased the Caroline, Marshall, Mariana, and Palau islands from the bankrupt Spanish government. The incident, which recalled to many Americans the friction at Samoa in 1889, helped fan anti-German prejudice.[36]

The American army finally arrived, and on August 13, 1898, Manila fell after only token resistance from the Spaniards, who apparently hoped the Americans would take the city before it was occupied by Filipino insurgents led by Emilio Aguinaldo. Later, the United States annexed the islands, thereby acquiring a long-sought foothold in the Far East—and with it a three-year guerrilla war with the Filipinos, who desired freedom from all foreign domination.

Dewey's victory at Manila Bay was complete, but where was the fleet under Admiral Cervera that had been sent out from Spain? Panic raced up and down the Atlantic coast like fire in a ship's rigging. Newspapers proclaimed, inaccurately, that the "galleons of Spain" were off Boston and New York, and demands for protection poured in upon the Navy Department. Long and Roosevelt wanted to concentrate the fleet at Key West ready for action against Cuba but were forced by public clamor to divide it into three squadrons. Most of the ships were sent to Key West under the command of Rear Admiral William T. Sampson. A "Flying Squadron" of fast ships under Commodore Winfield Scott Schley was based at Hampton Roads, where theoretically it could deal with a Spanish fleet in either the Atlantic or the Caribbean. A third squadron, consisting of the cruiser *San Francisco* and four commissioned, armed merchant ships, was assigned to patrol north of the Delaware Capes, primarily as a sop to public opinion.

Sampson immediately imposed a blockade on Havana, whose enforcement had overtones of a tropic cruise. "There were some exciting races after blockade runners, some heavy firing, some wonderful effects of land and sea and sky, some instances of coolness and courage," rhapsodized Richard Harding Davis, who was covering the war for the *New York Herald*. Sampson suggested a bombardment of Havana, but the Navy Department rejected the proposal; while an enemy naval force was unaccounted for, the fleet should not be risked against fortifications. This decision was reinforced by a Naval War Board composed of Mahan, who had been recalled to active duty, and two admirals appointed to provide Long with professional advice and to formulate strategy in the mold of the various boards organized by Gideon Welles during the Civil War.

Calculating that Cervera, who had left the Cape Verde Islands on April 29, would head for San Juan, Puerto Rico, to refuel, Sampson sent three auxiliary cruisers to the Windward Islands to watch for the Spanish and proceeded to San Juan with most of his squadron. He expected to be off San Juan on May 8, but two monitors accompanying him had to be towed and he did not arrive until four days later. Cervera was nowhere to be seen. Sampson bombarded the town for an hour, to little effect, then sailed back to Key West. That same day, the Navy Department received the momentous news that the Spanish squadron had been sighted at Martinique, some distance from San Juan. Suspecting that Sampson would think he was steaming for Puerto Rico, Cervera naturally avoided the island. Since he was believed to be carrying ammunition for the garrison at Havana, it was surmised that he would head for that port or for Cienfuegos, which is on the southern coast of Cuba and connected to the capital by railroad.

Schley's "Flying Squadron" was ordered from Hampton Roads to Key West, arriving there on May 18, the same day as Sampson, who had left his slow monitors behind. Sampson now transferred the *Iowa* to Schley's squadron and sent him to blockade Cienfuegos. At the same time, he strengthened the watch off Havana, but to no good purpose, for once again Cervera outsmarted the American commanders. Having been denied coal by the French at Martinique, he sailed to Curaçao, where the Dutch were willing to oblige. With their bunkers partially refilled, the Spanish steamed directly across the Caribbean to Santiago, near the southeastern tip of Cuba, and took shelter behind the batteries and minefields guarding the narrow passage into the harbor.

With an agonizing deliberation that made a mockery of the name "Flying Squadron," Schley, who said he was trying to conserve fuel, took his time in getting to Cienfuegos. Arriving offshore there on May 22, he was unable to ascertain whether Cervera's ships were inside the harbor. The next day he received word from Sampson that the Spaniards were believed to be at Santiago, but he did not sail until May 24 and took two days getting to that vicinity. Without waiting to determine whether Cervera was indeed there, Schley, reporting that his ships were low on coal and that the weather was too bad for him to refuel at sea from an accompanying collier, put about for Key West. As he was leaving, a dispatch vessel arrived with a message from the Navy Department ordering him to find out whether Cervera was actually at Santiago and, if he was, to take appropriate action.

"Much to be regretted, cannot obey orders," Schley replied, and steamed on toward Key West. Soon, however, a break in the weather enabled him to coal at sea, and he returned to Santiago on the evening of May 28. The next morning he spotted Cervera's ships inside the harbor, the *Cristóbal Colón* lying close to the entrance, and launched an ineffectual bombardment at long range. Sampson, his squadron augmented by the *Oregon*, arrived on the scene on June 1 to establish a close blockade. No recriminations were exchanged at the time, but Sampson later described Schley's conduct of the search for Cervera as "reprehensible," and a court of inquiry found that it had been characterized by "vacillation, dilatoriness, and lack of enterprise."[37]

Sampson placed his squadron, which consisted of the battleships *Oregon, Massachusetts, Indiana, Iowa,* and *Texas,* the armored cruisers *Brooklyn* and *New York,* and several smaller vessels, in a semicircle, about six miles from the entrance to Santiago Harbor. During the night, one of the battleships edged in closer and played her searchlights on the harbor mouth. Since they possessed only ancient guns and no searchlights, the Spanish forts were unable to reply effectively to the frequent bombardments ordered by Sampson. When it appeared that the blockade would last for some time, Sampson decided to put a battalion of marines ashore about forty miles to the east to seize Guantánamo Bay, where the ships would be able to take on coal and supplies in safety. The landing, which was made on June 10, led to the first fighting on Cuban soil.

Sampson had Cervera's squadron bottled up in Santiago, but he wanted to put a cork in the bottle in case a hurricane should force his ships to abandon the blockade. Lieutenant Richmond P. Hobson volunteered to sail the collier *Merrimac* into the winding channel and sink her at its narrowest point. Fitted with ten electrically fired explosive charges and manned by seven picked men, the *Merrimac* slipped up to the channel entrance on the night of June 3. She was about 500 yards from shore when the Spaniards opened up with every gun that would bear. Hobson stopped the vessel's engines and let her drift to the spot where she was to be turned and sunk:

> There was the position! "Hard aport!" "Hard aport, sir." No response of the ship! "Hard aport, I say!" "The helm is hard aport, sir, and lashed." . . . Oh, heaven! Our steering-gear was gone, shot away at the last moment, and we were charging forward straight down the channel!

Hobson ordered the charges detonated but only two of them exploded. As the *Merrimac* settled into the water, her crew took to a tiny raft. The heroism of Hobson and his crew was to no avail because the channel was not blocked. After floating in Santiago Harbor for several hours, the half-drowned men were pulled aboard a Spanish steam launch by no less a person than Admiral Cervera.[38]

Sampson called upon the army to capture the fortifications defending the harbor so that he could sweep the mines guarding the passage and go in after Cervera's fleet. Eager for a share of the glory that was being harvested by the navy, the War Department ordered some 16,000 men embarked from Tampa under the command of General William R. Shafter, a 300-pound veteran of the Civil War. Packed like sardines in thirty-two transports, the troops were convoyed by the navy to the southeastern coast of Cuba, where surfboats landed them at Daiquirí and Siboney, about twenty miles to the east of Santiago. Landing operations continued day and night for some four days. Looking down from a nearby hillside one evening, Richard Harding Davis described it as one of the most bizarre episodes in the history of warfare:

> An army was being landed on an enemy's coast at the dead of night, but with somewhat more of cheers and shrieks and laughter than rise from the bathers in the surf at Coney Island on a hot Sunday. It was a pandemonium of noises. The men still to be landed from the "prison hulks," as they called the transports, were singing in chorus, the men already on shore were dancing naked around the camp-fires on the beach, shouting with delight as they plunged into the first bath that had offered in seven days, and those in the launches, as soon as they were pitched headfirst at the soil of Cuba, signalized their arrival by howls of triumph.[39]

Luckily, the Spaniards chose not to resist the landing and retreated to the blockhouses and barbed wire that formed the outer-defense perimeter of Santiago. Sampson and Shafter met for the first time to discuss strategy on June 20, and the admiral came away from the conference under the impression that the army would attack the fortifications, as requested. Shafter was equally certain that Sampson realized that Santiago itself was the objective of the military campaign. On July 1 Shafter ordered an attack on the heavily defended Spanish positions at El Caney and San Juan Hill, which were the keys to Santiago. In the desperate fighting that followed, about 1,500 Americans—nearly 10 per cent of the attacking force—were killed or wounded.

Surveying the precarious toehold the troops had on the ridges overlooking Santiago, Theodore Roosevelt, who had abandoned the Navy Department to become lieutenant colonel of the Rough Riders, commented, "We are within measurable distance of a terrible military disaster." Shocked at the heavy casualties and sick with fever, Shafter considered retreating. He sent an urgent call for help to Sampson. "Terrible fight yesterday. . . . I urge that you make every effort immediately to force the entrance to avoid future losses among my men, which are already very heavy." Much to his surprise, Sampson was being asked to come to the rescue of the army, which had been summoned to Cuba to make the navy's task easier. Early the next morning he sailed eastward along the coast in his flagship *New York* to confer personally with Shafter about the realities of sweeping mines under enemy gunfire.[40]

By breakfast time the early morning mist had burned away and July 3, 1898, promised to be beautiful. It was a Sunday, so the routine of another day on the blockade would be broken by church services and the monthly reading of the Articles of War. In the *Iowa*, Captain Robley D. Evans was smoking a post-breakfast cigar and chatting with his son, a naval cadet:

> At thirty-one minutes after nine o'clock the general alarm for action rang all over the ship. My son jumped to his feet, exclaiming, "Papa, the enemy's ships are coming out!" and we both started as fast as we could for the bridge. Before I reached the spar-deck I heard a gun fired from the *Iowa*, and upon reaching the bridge found the signal flying [Signal 250: Enemy Ships Coming Out]. The engine gongs rang "Full speed ahead," and the *Iowa* closed in as she slowly gathered speed. At this moment the Spanish cruiser *Infanta Maria Teresa* was in plain view . . . her magnificent battleflag showing clear of the land.

The Spanish sortie took the Americans by surprise. Not only had Sampson gone in the *New York* to confer with Shafter, leaving command of the squadron to Schley, but the *Massachusetts* had been sent to Guantánamo to refuel, and several of the blockading ships did not have steam up. The decision to break out of Santiago was not made by Cervera. He was ordered by the authorities in Havana, who were convinced that Santiago was about to fall, to try to escape to Cienfuegos or Havana. Some analysts have suggested that he might have had better luck had he made his dash for freedom at night rather than in broad daylight, but Cervera feared that he would not be able to negotiate the narrow and treacherous channel in the dark and that the sunken *Merrimac* and the blinding searchlights of the Americans would compound his navigational difficulties. He and his captains were under no illusions about their chances of escape. The bottoms of their ships were foul, and some of their guns were defective, as was most of their ammunition. Even without the *New York* and *Massachusetts*, the American squadron mounted sixty guns of six inches or more and fired a broadside of 18,847 pounds, while the Spanish had only sixteen big guns and a total broadside of 6,014 pounds.

The *Texas, Brooklyn*, and *Iowa* steered straight for the enemy "with cascades of water pouring away from their bows" and guns firing, reported Captain John W. Philip, of the *Texas*. It was a simple "charge," with no thought of tactics. Farther east, the *Oregon* and *Indiana* were also steaming into the fray. Sampson, who had not yet reached his rendezvous with Shafter, heard the sound of gunfire and put about, but he got back too late to take part in the battle. The *Infanta Maria Teresa*, Cervera's flagship, was followed out of the harbor at tenminute intervals by his three other armored cruisers, the *Vizcaya, Almirante Oquendo*, and *Cristóbal Colón*, and two destroyers, the *Furor* and *Plutón*. Already on fire and almost hidden by smoke and by huge spouts of water caused by falling shells, the *Teresa* headed for Schley's flagship, the *Brooklyn*, apparently with the intent to ram. To avoid her, Schley ordered a turn to starboard, a maneuver that carried the *Brooklyn* across the bow of the *Texas* and almost into collision with her, and then to the east away from the fighting. Some time elapsed before the *Brooklyn* got back into action.

In the confusion, all the Spanish ships managed to get out of the channel and make a dash along the coast to the west, the American squadron in hot pursuit. The battered *Teresa*, her decks aflame and her captain fearing that her magazines would explode, was deliberately run aground about six miles from Santiago. The *Vizcaya*, also afire, with all her guns knocked out, was beached about ten miles farther up the coast, just before her magazines exploded. The *Oquendo* "rolled and staggered like a drunken thing," reported Captain Evans, as the *Iowa*'s shells poured into her. Burning fiercely, she was run aground not far from the *Teresa*. The *Colón*, fastest of Cervera's ships, rapidly widened the gap with the pursuing American vessels, making as much as eighteen knots during one stage of the pursuit. But with her stokers worn out by their superhuman efforts, she fell within range of the *Oregon*'s 13-inch guns. Shells dropping around his ship, the *Colón*'s captain ran her onto a beach about seventy miles west of Santiago. The destroyers *Furor* and *Plutón*, the last of the Spanish vessels to come out, were attacked and disposed of in short order.

The entire action took little more than three hours. One American was killed and another seriously wounded, while the Spanish ships looked like "slaughter pens." It was estimated that 323 Spaniards were killed and 151 wounded, out of a total of some 2,200 men. Despite the ease with which the victory had been achieved—in fact Mahan said the United States would never again fight so weak an adversary as Spain—the battle had some disquieting aspects. In all probability, some of the Spanish ships would have escaped had they been better prepared for action. Also, American marksmanship was surprisingly poor. More than 8,000 shells were fired at the fleeing ships, but an examination of the hulks of the four cruisers showed only 120 hits. The bitter dispute that erupted between Schley and Sampson over who deserved credit for the victory and over Schley's earlier operations poisoned the atmosphere for several years, causing a factional split in the navy. But that lay in the future—the navy had presented Cervera's entire squadron to the nation as a Fourth of July gift.[41]

The rest of the war was anticlimactic. Following a brief siege that was accompanied by long-range naval bombardment, Santiago surrendered on July 14. With the navy in firm control of the Caribbean, an expeditionary force that was sent to Puerto Rico mopped up the island's defenders with little difficulty, and hostilities ended on August 12, 1898, less than four months after war had been declared and one month over Mahan's estimate. In the peace treaty signed in Paris at the end of the year, Spain acknowledged the independence of Cuba and ceded Puerto Rico, the Philippines, and Guam to the United States in exchange for a payment of $20 million. Hawaii, Samoa, and Wake Island were annexed, and the American empire was born.

The conflict with Spain had indeed been, in John Hay's words, "a splendid little war." Bathed in the warm glow of the victories at Manila Bay and Santiago, the navy reached heights of popular acclaim not known since 1812. But over the next four decades, the acquisition of new territory in the Caribbean and the Pacific Ocean brought in its train far-reaching consequences for the navy as well as for the nation's foreign and domestic policies.[42]

7
A NAVY SECOND TO NONE

He who controls communications by sea controls his fate;
the master of the seas is master of the situation.
—Barbara W. Tuchman: The Guns of August

Plumes of smoke rising from tall funnels and hulls gleaming in the wintry sunshine, the sixteen battleships of the Great White Fleet steamed majestically out of Hampton Roads on December 16, 1907. Marine honor guards snapped to attention, salutes boomed out, and bands crashed into the national anthem as the ships passed in review before the presidential yacht *Mayflower*. "Did you ever see such a fleet and such a day?" cried Theodore Roosevelt, ebulliently acknowledging these honors with a flash of teeth and a wave of his top hat. "By George, isn't it magnificent!" Ready for "a feast, a frolic or a fight," in the words of Rear Admiral Robley D. Evans, its commander, this armada was off on an unprecedented voyage around the world.[1]

It was altogether fitting that the Great White Fleet should pay tribute to Teddy Roosevelt because no man had done more than he to create the modern American navy. Catapulted into the presidency by the assassination of William McKinley in 1901, Roosevelt brought to the White House a love of the sea and of the navy. Pugnacious, exuberant, and bubbling over with missionary zeal, he was the first American president eager to play an active role in international affairs—and the navy was the instrument through which he projected American power and prestige abroad.

Viewing the world in the perspective of his adviser and friend, Alfred Thayer Mahan, who was now a rear admiral on the retired list, Roosevelt believed that the United States should have an influence in the world commensurate with its wealth and strength. He was convinced that the nation should follow a policy of expansion. Trade with the Far East must be increased and the door to China kept open. The 13,000-mile dash of the *Oregon* around Cape Horn to join the fleet in the Caribbean in 1898 had emphasized the need for a canal through Central America to facilitate communications with the new American empire

166

and the fact that bases would have to be acquired to defend such a waterway. The capstone of this imperialist structure was to be a strong navy. Within a few months of taking office, Roosevelt threw down a challenge to Congress and the nation: "The American people must either build and maintain an adequate Navy or else make up their minds definitely to accept a secondary position in international affairs, not only in political, but in commercial matters."[2]

Colorful naval reviews, news stories, and ceremonies such as the interment of the body of John Paul Jones at the Naval Academy were all part of the president's plan to bring the public under the spell of the navy. The Navy League, a body organized by retired officers, patriotic citizens, and industrialists who hoped to profit from naval expansion, provided a drumfire of propaganda. The success of this campaign can best be measured by the growth of the battleship fleet. In every year of Roosevelt's administration, at least one battleship was authorized; in 1903 five were ordered laid down—the most in any single year. By 1907 the navy had twenty of them. The construction of a fleet in the mold proposed by Admiral Mahan marked the demise of the concepts of coastal defense and commerce-raiding that had been the staples of American naval doctrine for a century. Even the term *coast defense battleship* was stricken from the naval and congressional lexicon.[3]

In 1902 Roosevelt ordered all the battleships to the Caribbean, where large-scale maneuvers were held under the command of George Dewey, whose victory at Manila Bay had earned him the rank of admiral of the navy. At the end of that exercise, instead of dispersing the ships to the "distant stations" from which they had come, Roosevelt, following Mahan's advice that the fleet should be concentrated, organized them into two fleets, eight battleships being assigned to the Atlantic and three to the Pacific. Three years later the European and South Atlantic squadrons were abolished and their ships were incorporated into the newly established Atlantic Fleet. Except for the Asiatic Fleet, which was whittled down over the years to a handful of cruisers and a few shallow-draft gunboats serving on the rivers of China, the "distant stations" policy was abandoned— not to be revived until the advent of the Cold War, when the Sixth Fleet was sent to the Mediterranean and the wartime Seventh Fleet was kept in the Far East.[4]

The problem of manning all the new vessels was not easily resolved. Shortages of officers and men plagued the navy, and American battleships were undermanned compared with their European and Japanese counterparts. As ships grew in complexity, seamen ceased to be prized "more for strength than intelligence," but the low pay and poor living conditions made it difficult to attract and hold skilled technicians. No one understood this better than Roosevelt. "It is important to have our Navy of adequate size, but it is even more important that ship for ship, it should equal in efficiency any navy in the world," he declared. "This is possible only with highly drilled crews and officers."

With his encouragement, life was made more agreeable for the bluejacket.

Fresh meat, vegetables, milk, fruit, and eggs replaced the traditional ration of salt meat and hardtack, more liberty was allowed, and opportunities for recreation were provided. To broaden the base from which volunteers might be drawn, recruiting stations were opened inland, and "Join the Navy and See the World" became the navy's slogan. Unable to compete with industry for skilled craftsmen, the navy created its own training establishment, beginning with an artificers' school, which opened at Norfolk in 1903. Pay scales were raised and special inducements for reenlistment were offered. In 1905 Congress authorized the commissioning as ensigns of twelve warrant officers a year, opening the way for an enlisted man to rise through the ranks.[5]

Promotion was still based on seniority, however, and the Navy List was encrusted with men who had reached the level of command long after their counterparts in other navies. Roosevelt tried to relieve the officer shortage by expanding the size of the entering classes at the Naval Academy. He also tried to make room for young men by retiring older officers and by basing promotion on merit rather than on seniority, but Congress refused to approve the latter change. The running battle between line and engineering officers concerning the status of the latter had been resolved by the Personnel Act of 1899, which Roosevelt drafted when he was assistant secretary of the navy. It provided for engineers to be incorporated into the line and for all officers to be qualified, in theory, to stand watch in the engine room as well as on the bridge.[6]

Following the Spanish-American War, far-seeing men called for the creation of a permanent body, a general staff, to provide centralized planning. This idea was strongly resisted by the entrenched bureau chiefs who feared that such a body would jeopardize their power and independence, and by their congressional supporters who feared the loss of opportunities for pork-barrel politics. Instead a General Board, with Admiral Dewey as its chief, was created in 1900 to prepare war plans and to make recommendations to the secretary of the navy regarding the operation of the fleet. But it was primarily an advisory body and the extent of its authority was not clear. Roosevelt continued to champion the idea of a general staff, and after 1903, when such a body was created for the U. S. Army, he made several unsuccessful attempts to persuade Congress that the navy should have a similar organization.[7]

Roosevelt's emphasis on a big navy coincided with a dramatic shift in the world balance of sea power. At the turn of the century, Imperial Germany began to threaten Great Britain's command of the sea, forcing the British to concentrate their ships in home waters. The vacuum thus created in the Caribbean was soon filled by the United States, while the Japanese, who had signed a treaty of alliance with Britain in 1902, extended their influence over Far Eastern waters, particularly after they defeated the Russians in the short and savage Russo-Japanese War of 1904–1905.

Technological obstacles, let alone distance, lay in the way of any German offensive against the Western Hemisphere, but Roosevelt was nevertheless obsessed with the idea of such a threat. German intervention in Venezuela in 1902 revived antagonisms that had been simmering since the Samoan dispute of 1889 and Dewey's brush with the German squadron in Manila Bay in 1898. As a result, American public opinion tilted toward Britain, and one of the first fruits of this understanding was the Panama Canal.[8]

Under the terms of the Clayton-Bulwer Treaty concluded between the United States and Britain in 1850, neither nation was to have exclusive control of such a canal. In 1901, that treaty was abrogated. Deciding that Panama, then part of Colombia, should be the site of the canal, the United States began negotiations for rights across the isthmus. In the summer of 1903 a price of $10 million plus a $250,000 annual payment was fixed for a six-mile-wide right-of-way, but the Colombians, hoping for more, delayed ratification of the treaty.

It was a fatal mistake. Impatient "to make dirt fly" before the 1904 election, Roosevelt denounced the Colombians as "inefficient bandits" and threatened to seize the canal strip by force. When revolution flared in Panama, he sent the gunboat *Nashville* to Colón to "protect American interests"—and to prevent Colombian troops from disembarking to put down the insurrection. Fifteen days after the revolution began, the government of newly independent Panama granted the United States control of a ten-mile-wide zone across the isthmus in perpetuity in return for the sum originally offered Colombia. Work on the canal was begun in May 1904—in plenty of time for the presidential election—and the waterway was opened to traffic in August 1914. "I took the Canal Zone," Roosevelt later declared in characteristic fashion.

To ensure the safety of the canal, the United States established a naval base at Guantánamo Bay, Cuba, and assumed a paternalistic role in Caribbean affairs. Roosevelt unilaterally proclaimed a "corollary" to the Monroe Doctrine, giving the United States "a moral mandate" to intervene in any dispute that might arise between a country of the Western Hemisphere and a European nation. Thus, the Monroe Doctrine, originally promulgated to prevent European interference in the Western Hemisphere, became a license for such interference by the United States. During the course of the following quarter-century, the navy was called upon to land marines in Santo Domingo, Cuba, Haiti, Mexico, and Nicaragua to restore economic and political order.[9]

Relations between Japan and the United States, friends since Commodore Perry's visit a half-century before, soured in the wake of the Russo-Japanese War. Most Americans cheered the victories of their Japanese protégés, and when the latter, despite their triumphs, were near exhaustion, Roosevelt stepped in to arrange a settlement. The Japanese failed to win all their demands at the peace table, however, and accused the United States of thwarting their ambitions.

With most of the U. S. Navy concentrated in the Atlantic, Roosevelt was anxious to avoid an open break with Japan. The United States was so ill prepared for war in the Far East that the Orange Plan, drafted by a joint army-navy board for use in the event of such a conflict with Japan, required that the Philippines be abandoned and the Asiatic Fleet be withdrawn to the West Coast until America had the strength to go on the offensive. Roosevelt hoped, therefore, through diplomatic negotiation, to freeze the status quo in the Far East before the balance of power tipped too far in Japan's favor.

Tensions between the two countries were fanned by a wave of anti-Japanese feeling that swept California. In 1906, the San Francisco Board of Education ordered the segregation of all Japanese schoolchildren. When this news reached Japan, it was regarded as an insult and there were violent anti-American demonstrations. Roosevelt considered the school board's action "foolish" and, with considerable difficulty, persuaded the Californians to rescind it in exchange for a "gentlemen's agreement" whereby the Japanese would slow the stream of emigrants to the United States.[10]

To impress Japan as well as other countries with American might, Roosevelt decided to send the entire battle fleet around the world. He wanted to find out what would happen if war broke out with Japan before the canal had been completed. With the disasters that a Russian fleet experienced when it steamed halfway round the world to its defeat at Tsushima in 1905 fresh in mind, he declared: "I want all failures, blunders and shortcomings to be made apparent in time of peace and not in time of war."

Enthusiastic crowds welcomed the Great White Fleet at ports along the Atlantic and Pacific coasts of South America, and by the time it reached San Francisco, arrangements had been made for it to visit Yokohama. The Japanese government seemed genuinely eager to dispel the bitterness created by past misunderstandings, and as the Americans paraded through the city, thousands of schoolchildren lined the streets singing in English "The Star-Spangled Banner." Sailing home by way of the Suez Canal and the Mediterranean, the fleet, having been at sea for fourteen months and steamed 46,000 miles, returned to Hampton Roads on February 22, 1909, just in time to usher out Teddy Roosevelt's administration in a blaze of glory. Later he declared that this demonstration of "big stick" diplomacy "was the most important service I rendered to peace."

The cruise of the Great White Fleet had tangible diplomatic and technical results. It satisfied American desires for recognition as a world power and proved that the fleet could steam long distances without experiencing serious difficulties. Shortly after its visit to Yokohama, both the United States and Japan agreed to maintain the status quo in the Pacific and to respect the independence and integrity of China. In 1909 Pearl Harbor, in the Hawaiian Islands, was selected for the establishment of a major base in the Pacific, a site in the Philippines having been rejected on the grounds that it would always be under the guns of the Japanese fleet.[11]

Within a few weeks of their return, the ships of the Great White Fleet were painted the dark gray that characterized most other battle fleets of the world—

but they were already obsolete. Late in 1906 Britain had commissioned a revolutionary new warship, the *Dreadnought*, which completely altered the design of all future capital ships. Displacing 17,900 tons, protected by eleven inches of armor, and propelled by newly designed steam turbines that gave her a speed of 21.6 knots, she was clearly superior to any existing battleship. But her most novel feature was her armament. Most battleships carried main batteries of four large guns, mounted in twin turrets fore and aft, secondary batteries of various sizes, and clusters of quick-firers for use against torpedo boats. For example, the U. S. Navy's *Virginia* class, commissioned in 1906 and 1907, carried five types of guns ranging from 3-pounders to 12-inch rifles. Realizing that future battles would be fought at ever greater distances, the *Dreadnought*'s designers gave her only ten 12-inch guns in twin turrets, three on the centerline and one on each beam, and a few 12-pounders for dealing with torpedo boats. With this arrangement, she had more than twice the firepower of other battleships and her fire control and munitions supply were greatly simplified.

Since the *Dreadnought* had reduced all existing battleships to second-class status at a single stroke, the Germans saw an opportunity to outbuild the Royal Navy, and new impetus was given to the Anglo-German naval race.

The United States missed laying down the first dreadnought by only a year. As early as 1901, Lieutenant Homer C. Poundstone had proposed an all-big-gun ship, but his conservative superiors ignored his suggestion. The 16,000-ton *Michigan* and *South Carolina*, which mounted eight 12-inch guns in twin turrets, two forward and two aft, were authorized before the *Dreadnought* was laid down but were not completed until 1909. Although they carried two fewer big guns than the *Dreadnought*, they fired a broadside equal to hers because all their guns were on the centerline and could be fired to either side, whereas four of the *Dreadnought*'s were in wing turrets that could be trained to one side only. The disposition of the U. S. guns was achieved by superimposing one turret above another. At first, European designers, fearing that the blast of the upper guns might affect the men in the lower turrets, looked upon this arrangement with misgivings, but when it proved itself in operation, this method of mounting guns was adopted universally.

The *Michigan* and *South Carolina* were followed by the *Delaware* and *North Dakota*. Laid down in 1907, displacing 20,000 tons and carrying ten 12-inch guns, they were at the time of their completion the biggest American warships. With all their guns mounted on the centerline, they fired a broadside 25 per cent greater than did any other ship. The *North Dakota* was the first American battleship to be driven by turbines. Although President William Howard Taft, who followed Roosevelt into the White House in 1909, was less naval-minded than his predecessor, the United States continued building its fleet of dreadnoughts. By 1912 the navy had six large battleships in commission, including the 26,000-ton *Arkansas* and *Wyoming*, which carried twelve newly designed 12-inchers in twin turrets.[12]

Improvements in gunnery and fire control accompanied all this construction, with two brilliant officers, William S. Sims and Bradley A. Fiske, playing a leading role in this country. American marksmanship was poor in the Spanish-American War, but the navy did little to correct the situation until shortly after the turn of the century when Sims, then a lieutenant, began to agitate for better gunnery. While serving in the Far East, he had observed the methods used by Sir Percy Scott to make the cruiser *Terrible* the crack gunnery ship of the Royal Navy. Scott perfected continuous-aim firing, a system that allowed a gunner to keep his sights fixed on a target despite the rolling of his ship. He also developed a training aid known as a "dotter," which enabled gun crews to practice continuous-aim firing without expending any ammunition.

Sims sent voluminous reports on his findings to the Navy Department, where they attracted little attention. In desperation, he wrote directly to President Roosevelt, a step that placed his career in jeopardy. Instead of ordering his dismissal for this effrontery, Roosevelt, always interested in matters concerning the navy, arranged for Sims to be appointed inspector of target practice. Applying the principles of continuous-aim firing and using the dotter, Sims made gunnery drills competitive and presented trophies and cash awards to outstanding gun crews. Within eighteen months, he reported that American standards of gunnery exceeded those of even the British, not only in accuracy but in rapidity of fire.

A handsome and active man with a fund of sailors' stories, Sims soon became a favorite of the president, who chose him as his naval aide. In this prominent position, he did not confine his criticisms to the navy's marksmanship. For some time, he had been pointing out to anyone who would listen that many of the battleships of the Great White Fleet had serious defects in design and construction: they had such low freeboards that it would be impossible to fight them in anything but a flat calm; in many cases the ammunition hoists connecting the powder rooms with the turrets were nothing more than open shafts into which flaming debris from the breeches of the guns could easily fall; some gunports were so large that the turrets provided little protection for the guns and their crews; and the armor belt on some of the ships was underwater. Sims recalled that a little girl he took on a tour of the *Kentucky* noticed one gaping gunport after another. "I thought you told me these guns were protected by armor," she said. "The armor is where the guns ain't."

In January 1908 all these criticisms—and more—appeared in an article in *McClure's Magazine* written by Henry Reuterdahl, a civilian commentator on naval affairs, but it required little detective work to trace most of his material to Sims. A congressional probe ensued. Angry over this washing of the navy's dirty linen in public, conservative bureau chiefs and officers responsible for the design of the ships hoped the investigation would club their critics into silence. Most of the charges were substantiated, however, and many of the same defects were found in ships that were still on the ways. From then on, resentment against

Sims was strong, and Roosevelt probably saved his career by seeing to it that he was given command of the battleship *Minnesota*.[13]

Bradley Fiske was another reformer whose steady flow of inventions and suggestions for change greatly irked his unimaginative superiors. As early as 1891, he had invented a telescopic gun sight. Among other inventions that flowed from his logical and inquiring mind were an optical range finder and a stadimeter for estimating ranges.[14] Through the efforts of Fiske and others, the effective range of naval guns was increased from about 6,000 yards in 1898 to nearly 20,000 yards by World War I. One of the great gunnery advances of the period was "director firing," which meant that an officer perched on a control platform high up on his ship's foremast laid her big guns by means of a director sight, which transmitted information on gun elevation and bearing to the turrets by an electrical circuit. When the sight—and the guns—were on target, he pressed a button and the guns fired simultaneously. With the shells falling about the target in a tight pattern, there was a strong possibility of hits being scored. Later, information obtained by the director was channeled to a gun-battery plot deep in the ship, where alterations in elevation, range, and course were worked out by electrical calculators and fed to the turrets.

In a vain attempt to keep up with Britain and Germany, both Roosevelt and Taft allocated most of the limited funds Congress appropriated for the navy to the building of battleships. For balance, the navy needed fast cruisers to serve as the "eyes of the fleet" and destroyers to screen capital ships, but it was reasoned that these smaller vessels could be built when the battleship race had subsided.

As a result, the U. S. Navy did not commission its first destroyer until 1902. Destroyers evolved from torpedo boats—in fact, they were developed primarily to counter the latter and were originally known as torpedo-boat destroyers. The invention in 1864 of a self-propelled torpedo by an Austrian naval officer, Commander Johann Luppis, and its improvement by Robert Whitehead, an English engineer, led to the development of the torpedo boat. This type of craft gained prominence in the world's navies when Japanese torpedo boats wreaked havoc upon a Chinese fleet during the Sino-Japanese War in 1895. The first torpedo-boat destroyer was simply a faster, larger, and better-armed torpedo boat and, before long, took over its function.

The *Bainbridge*, first of the line in the U. S. Navy, displaced 420 tons, had a maximum speed of almost twenty-nine knots, and was armed with a pair of 3-inch guns and two 18-inch torpedo tubes. Three dozen destroyers joined the fleet over the following ten years, and by the time World War I broke out, the type had more than doubled in size and its sea-keeping ability had vastly improved. The *Smith* (DD-17), which was commissioned in 1909, was the first American destroyer to have turbines instead of reciprocating engines, and the *Paulding* (DD-22), commissioned the following year, was the first to burn oil rather than coal. Slim, thin-skinned, and aquiver with energy, "tin cans" soon captured the imagination of the public.[15]

The U. S. Navy was also slow in accepting the submarine. From the time of David Bushnell onward, most of the advances in the development of undersea craft were the work of inventors who performed their experiments without government support. Among them was Irish-born John P. Holland, who produced several practical submarines and in 1888 won the Navy Department's competition for designing a submarine torpedo boat. He was not awarded a contract to build a submarine for the navy until seven years later. The long delay in getting the $200,000 contract drew from Holland the acid comment: "The Navy does not like submarines because there's no deck to strut on." Launched in 1897, the eighty-five-foot *Plunger* mounted two torpedo tubes and was designed to run, when submerged, on electricity drawn from storage batteries. To meet the navy's requirement for a surface speed of fifteen knots, however, she was fitted with a triple-screw steam plant, which turned the boat into a monstrosity; she was never commissioned.

Holland, convinced that the *Plunger* would be a failure even before she was completed, began work on a smaller and far less complex craft, the *Holland*, which was powered by a gasoline motor for surface operation. Built at the inventor's own expense, she was launched in 1897 and, after a series of tests, Theodore Roosevelt, then assistant secretary of the navy, recommended that she be purchased by the government. This suggestion was not followed until April 1900, when the boat was bought for $150,000—about half what it had cost to build her.

Considerably smaller than the *Plunger* and armed with a single torpedo tube and three 18-inch Whitehead torpedoes, the *Holland* displaced only seventy-five tons. She had a surface speed of about seven knots and a range of 1,500 miles. Submerged, she could travel fifty miles at a slightly lower speed. The maximum depth at which the boat could operate safely was seventy-five feet, but she had no periscope and was completely blind underwater. She had to surface every few minutes to allow her captain to take bearings through small ports in the conning tower. Even so, Admiral Dewey was sufficiently impressed with her performance to say that "if they [the Spaniards] had had two of these things in Manila, I could never have held it with the squadron I had."

Submarines grew in size, range, and offensive power, especially after the perfection of the gyrocompass in 1908 made sustained underwater cruising possible, and the substitution the following year of the diesel for the gasoline engine for running on the surface made the boats safer. Although questions were being raised as to whether the submarine had made the battleship obsolete, no navy correctly assessed the importance of the submarine's role, particularly as a commerce-destroyer. Large submarines were regarded primarily as weapons to be used in conjunction with the fleet against enemy fighting ships, while small ones were considered useful for harbor defense. In fact the Germans, who did not adopt the submarine until 1906, had fewer submarines in commission in 1914 than had the U. S. Navy.

Life on the early submarines was hazardous. Not only was there the ever-present danger that a boat might develop a leak and drown her crew, but there was also the possibility that the batteries used for underwater propulsion might generate hydrogen gas that could be exploded by a random spark, or, if contaminated by sea water, would give off deadly chlorine gas. Gasoline vapor posed an equal hazard. And the boats, with their low freeboard, were always in danger of being swamped or run down by a passing ship. Foul, crowded, a jungle of wiring, controls, and pipes, submarines were scorned by battleship sailors as "pigboats," but their crews had the faith and perseverance to prove the potential of their craft.[16]

Theodore Roosevelt also played a role in the application of manned flight to naval operations, and this as early as March 1898, when he was still assistant secretary of the navy. Taking note of the experiments that Professor Samuel P. Langley of the Smithsonian Institution was conducting with a steam-powered model "aerodrome," he wrote John D. Long, secretary of the navy: "The machine has worked. It seems to me worthwhile for this government to try whether it will not work on a large enough scale to be of use in event of war." A joint army-navy board investigated the project and returned a favorable report, but the Bureau of Construction and Repair refused to support Langley's efforts, saying that the "apparatus . . . pertains strictly to the land service and not to the Navy."

The army gave Langley some assistance but lost interest when his attempt to launch a full-sized airplane from a houseboat on the Potomac River did not succeed. A few months later, on December 17, 1903, two young bicycle mechanics from Dayton, Ohio, named Wilbur and Orville Wright succeeded where Langley had failed. Lying prone on the lower wing of a contraption that looked like a box kite, Orville Wright flew 120 feet over the sand dunes of Kitty Hawk, North Carolina, in twelve seconds—the first manned flight in a heavier-than-air craft. European nations immediately expressed interest in the military use of the airplane, but it was not until 1908, when President Roosevelt prodded the army into testing an advanced version of the Wrights' plane, that the American military seriously considered the possibility of flight. Navy Lieutenant George Sweet, who was observing the test, volunteered to fly with Orville Wright but was persuaded to give up his place to Lieutenant Thomas E. Selfridge, of the army. The plane crashed and Selfridge was killed. Despite his narrow escape, Sweet was enthusiastic about the possible uses of the airplane for the navy, particularly for scouting and spotting the fall of shells, and in his report suggested that more tests be held.

The army purchased one of the Wright machines, but Sweet's report was pigeonholed. However, on November 9, 1909, when he was taken up in the army's new airplane, Sweet became the first naval officer to fly in a heavier-than-air machine. Public interest in aviation was so great that the Navy Department could no longer ignore it, and the following year Captain Washington Irving Chambers, an experienced engineer, was assigned to deal with the flood of correspondence the navy was receiving on the subject. Chambers, who knew little about flying machines at the time of his appointment, soon became devoted to the cause of naval aviation. Late in 1910 he learned that as a publicity stunt aimed at winning more mail-carrying contracts, the German-owned Hamburg American Steamship Company was planning to launch a plane from a platform erected on one of its ships. Suspecting that the German navy was behind the project, Chambers resolved that the U. S. Navy should be the first to fly a plane from ship to shore.

Although the Navy Department claimed it had no funds for the experiment, Chambers was undaunted. He persuaded John Barry Ryan, a wealthy publisher and politician with an interest in aviation, to put up $1,000, and Eugene Ely, a civilian pilot employed by the aircraft designer Glenn H. Curtiss, volunteered to make the flight. An inclined platform was hastily erected on the bow of the cruiser *Birmingham*, and on November 14, 1910, as she lay in Hampton Roads, all was ready for the historic test. The plan called for Ely to take off as the ship was steaming into the wind, but with a squall blowing up, he decided not to wait for her to get under way. Revving up the engine of his frail biplane, he raced down the ramp and dropped out of sight. "Ely just gone," tapped out the cruiser's wireless operator. The plane staggered just above the water, then clawed its way into the fast-darkening sky. Snatching off his spray-splashed goggles, Ely discerned the shore not too far away. Five minutes later he landed near a row of beach cottages.

This first ship-to-shore flight was followed on January 18, 1911, by another demonstration, this one in San Francisco Bay. Taking off from the shore, with a bicycle inner tube wrapped about him as a life preserver, Ely landed his plane on a platform on the stern of the cruiser *Pennsylvania* as she lay at anchor. The aircraft was brought to a halt when hooks dangling below it snagged a primitive arresting gear that consisted of lines stretched across the deck and weighted with fifty-pound sandbags. An hour later Ely took off from the cruiser and landed ashore without mishap—having demonstrated the basic idea behind the aircraft carrier. That same month Glenn Curtiss demonstrated an airplane that could take off from and land on water. Soon after, Lieutenant Theodore G. Ellyson, who had been taught to fly by Curtiss, became the navy's first aviator.

With an eye on these advances, Congress was at last persuaded to bestow a modest $25,000 on naval aviation. Aircraft were purchased from Curtiss and from the Wrights, and two more lieutenants, John Rodgers, a member of the distinguished naval family, and John H. Towers qualified as pilots. More pilots were trained at an aviation camp established at the Naval Engineering Experimental Station, across the Severn River from the Naval Academy.

In 1913, when the aviation unit was ordered to Guantánamo Bay to be integrated into fleet exercises for the first time, the flyers proved that they could detect submerged submarines, sight "enemy" surface vessels without being seen, and take photographs from a height of 1,000 feet. The imaginative Bradley Fiske, now a rear admiral, concerned about the navy's ability to defend the Philippines in the face of a superior Japanese fleet, conjured up a vision out of Jules Verne with the suggestion that four air bases be established on Luzon, each equipped with at least 100 planes. Such a force, he said, would be able to drive off or destroy an attacking fleet.[17] To implement his proposal, he took out a patent in 1912 on a device that permitted an airplane to carry and release a torpedo.

The navy's handful of aviators got the chance to test their primitive flying machines under combat conditions in 1914. Nearly four years before, revolution had broken out in Mexico against the dictatorship of Porfirio Díaz, and in the kaleidoscopic violence that followed, a strongman named Victoriano Huerta shot his way to power. The new president, Woodrow Wilson, proclaiming his desire to see "an orderly and righteous government in Mexico," refused to recognize the "unspeakable" Huerta. To protect American lives and investments, he sent a squadron to show the flag off the Mexican coast. On April 9, 1914, some unarmed seamen went ashore at Tampico in search of gasoline and were arrested by the Mexicans. They were soon released, but Rear Admiral Henry T. Mayo, commander of the Fourth Division of the Atlantic Fleet, acting without authority, demanded an apology and a twenty-one gun salute to the American flag. Profuse apologies were forthcoming, but Huerta balked at giving the salute unless he had assurance that the Americans would similarly honor the Mexican flag—an assurance Admiral Mayo refused to provide.

The situation deteriorated quickly. Wilson, perhaps to counter charges that he was "soft," asked Congress for authorization to take "such action as may be necessary to enforce the respect due to the nation's flag," but before such authorization was granted, word was received that a German steamer had arrived off Veracruz carrying a large quantity of arms for Huerta. On April 21, the president ordered the seizure of the customs house to prevent the weapons from being unloaded, and the navy landed 800 sailors and marines at Veracruz. Three thousand more men were put ashore the next day and met heavy resistance. The cruiser *Chester* and the converted minelayer *San Francisco*, lying close inshore, were called upon to shell Mexican strong points, including the naval academy, whose cadets put up a bitter fight. "Opposed by an enemy they could not see, in the streets of a strange city where every house was an ambush and every church tower had a fighting top," the naval brigade fought its way into the city, Richard Harding Davis reported. By the time control of Veracruz had been won, seventeen Americans lay dead and sixty-three had been wounded. The action was futile because the navy had no legal right to hold the German ship and she steamed to another port to unload her cargo of arms. And Huerta, who was deposed a few months later, never ordered the salute demanded by Admiral Mayo.

Three days after the fighting had ended, the naval air unit arrived at Veracruz with five seaplanes and immediately began flying reconnaissance missions. These were the first patrols ever made by American naval aviators over hostile territory. Often flying at little more than tree-top height, the pilots took photographs and provided information on troop movements, terrain, and other matters of military interest. One of the machines returned with a bullet hole in its tail—proof that small-arms fire would not bring down an airplane unless it struck some vital part. Less than two months after its arrival, the unit was withdrawn as part of a general winding down of operations. In August of that year, the landing at Veracruz faded into insignificance as Europe was engulfed in war.[18]

For the U. S. Navy, the outbreak of the European War in 1914 created only a brief flurry of excitement. Experienced observers expected the conflict to be short, and President Wilson called upon the American people to be "impartial in thought as well as action." The navy was still growing in size and might and in 1914 the ships of the *New Mexico* class were authorized. They displaced 32,000 tons and mounted twelve 14-inch guns. Also launched was the *Nevada*, the first American battleship to be powered by oil rather than coal.[19]

Nevertheless, the opening years of the Wilson administration were stormy ones for the navy—and at the center of the uproar was its secretary, Josephus Daniels. A small-town Southern newspaper editor with radical agrarian and pacifist views, he was a hopeless landlubber. To compensate for his lack of knowledge about the navy, he chose for his assistant secretary, Franklin Delano Roosevelt, a thirty-one-year-old cousin of the former president and a disciple of Mahan. Daniels was a figure of fun in Washington—in the words of young Roosevelt, who had a great affection for his chief, "the funniest looking hillbilly I have ever seen"—but his appearance belied his political shrewdness.[20]

Daniels angered the navy by rejecting the General Board's request for 20,000 additional men, but Roosevelt won the confidence of naval officers with his love of the sea and his willingness to serve as a buffer between them and the secretary. On one occasion while sailing in a destroyer commanded by Lieutenant William F. Halsey, Jr., to inspect naval facilities in Frenchman's Bay, on the coast of Maine, Roosevelt suggested that, since he was intimately familiar with those waters, he should take the vessel through a strait between Campobello Island and the mainland. Reluctantly, Halsey yielded the conn, worried that this "white-flanneled yachtsman" might pile his vessel up on the rocks. He was surprised to find that the assistant secretary "knew his business" and took the ship safely through the treacherous channel.[21]

Seeming to regard the navy more as a vast school than as a fighting machine,

Daniels ordered every ship and shore station to establish classes in basic educational and technical subjects. Attendance at these classes, which were taught by officers, was compulsory. Advanced courses were offered on a voluntary basis. He also ordered that several appointments to the Naval Academy be set aside for enlisted men.

There was plenty of grumbling among officers about "mollycoddling," but that was nothing compared to the outrage that greeted the teetotalling secretary's order ending the wardroom wine mess as of July 1, 1914. The enlisted men's grog had been abolished in 1862, but officers were still permitted to buy wines and liquor on board ship—a situation that Daniels regarded as discriminatory. Wherever ships of the U. S. Navy lay, the eve of prohibition was marked by rollicking farewell parties for John Barleycorn. On the cruiser *Washington*, anchored off Veracruz, the "dead soldiers" were placed in a coffin and buried at sea, while a marine bugler sounded taps. During the bedlam on the *North Dakota*, the executive officer appeared in the wardroom wearing a baseball catcher's mask and chest protector and proposed a toast. "Here's to Josephus Daniels," he said—and was promptly bombarded with anything handy.[22]

Daniels, whose populist views made him suspicious of big business, tangled almost immediately with the three companies—U. S. Steel, Midvale Steel, and Bethlehem Steel—that produced armor plate for the navy. When contracts were advertised for armor plate for the battleship *Arizona*, Daniels was surprised to find that all three companies submitted identical bids of $454 per ton. Upon learning that Bethlehem Steel habitually sold the plate abroad at prices considerably below those charged the American government, he refused to accept the bids and ordered them resubmitted on a genuinely competitive basis. But once again the steel companies presented identical tenders. Daniels began negotiating with a British manufacturer, who made an offer so much lower than that of the American companies that the latter were forced to reduce their bids substantially before the contract was awarded. According to Daniels, enforced competitive bidding reduced the cost of armor plate for the *Arizona* by $1.1 million.[23]

Instead of ending quickly, the European war had bogged down into a bloody and almost motionless war of attrition. The Allies and Central Powers attempted to starve each other into surrender through naval blockade, just as the belligerents had done during the Napoleonic Wars. The Royal Navy rapidly swept German commerce from the high seas and seized neutral ships trading with Germany. Unable to contest Britain's command of the sea lanes, Germany struck back with the only weapon available to her—the submarine.

At the outset, American anger was directed primarily at Britain. The Royal Navy not only seized on the high seas neutral ships carrying contraband to Germany, but also diverted into British ports vessels merely suspected of carrying such trade—instead of conducting inspections at sea. Although officially neutral, the Wilson administration was sympathetic to the Allied cause, as the majority of the American people in time became. British and French purchases of war material in the United States lifted the country out of economic depression and American financial houses invested heavily in Allied victory. Past suspicions of German intentions in the hemisphere, reports of German machinations in volatile Mexico, and a flood tide of Allied propaganda all helped to crystalize public opinion against Germany.

Relations between the United States and the imperial government entered a new phase in February 1915, when the latter announced that the waters around Britain were to be considered a war zone and enemy ships found there would be sunk without warning. Unrestricted submarine warfare was one of the dubious blessings of twentieth-century technology. Under international law, warships were required to halt merchant vessels, verify their identity, and provide for the safety of passengers and crew before sinking them. But these rules, the Germans complained, pertained to the age of sail. After all, British merchantmen were armed, submarines were fragile, and it would be suicidal for a U-boat captain to surface and give warning. The United States warned the German government that it would be held to "strict accountability" should any American lives be lost. One after another, ships were sunk in the waters about Britain, but despite repeated German warnings, Americans continued to travel into the war zone on Allied vessels, including those carrying munitions.

Shortly after two o'clock on the afternoon of May 7, 1915, Kapitänleutnant Walter Schweiger of the U-20 was cruising off the coast of Ireland when he sighted a large steamer through his periscope. "Clean bow shot from 700 meters range," he later reported. "Shot hits starboard side right behind bridge. An unusually heavy detonation follows with a very strong explosion cloud. . . . She has the appearance of being about to capsize. Great confusion on board. . . . In the bow appears the name *Lusitania*."

Within little more than twenty minutes, the great Cunard liner plunged bow-first toward the bottom, taking with her 1,198 men, women, and children, 128 of them American citizens. The ship was carrying some munitions, but German attempts to justify the sinking were unavailing. Americans were incensed and President Wilson dispatched several strong notes of protest to Berlin. The Germans agreed to pay an indemnity for the American lives, and, realizing the danger of provoking the United States further, ordered U-boat captains to spare large ocean liners.[24]

The sinking of the *Lusitania* convinced many Americans, including Woodrow Wilson, that a preparedness movement which had been growing for some time, should be supported. In Congress, Richmond P. Hobson, who had sunk the collier *Merrimac* in the entrance to Santiago Harbor in 1898 and was now a Democratic representative from Alabama, led the fight for a new standard of naval power—a navy "second to none." Late in 1915 Wilson asked the General Board to prepare a five-year building program; it immediately produced a proposal for the construction of 156 ships at a total cost of nearly $500 million. This armada was to include 10 battleships, 6 battle cruisers, 10 scout cruisers, 50 destroyers, and 67 submarines. If the program were accepted, Wilson said, it would provide the nation with "incomparably the greatest navy in the world." Midway in the debate over the proposal, on May 31, 1916, the British and German battle fleets duelled off Jutland. In driving the Germans back into their harbors, the Royal Navy suffered such heavy losses that there was anxiety in the United States as to whether Britain would be able to maintain her traditional command of the sea. In this uncertain atmosphere, the Naval Act of 1916 was passed on August 29 with but one substantial change to the General Board's recommendation: the five-year program was speeded up to three years. Preparations began at once to build four battleships—the *Colorado, West Virginia, Maryland,* and *Washington*—which, with a displacement of 32,600 tons each and a main battery of eight 16-inch guns, were expected to be the world's most powerful ships. While the act represented a milestone in the development of the U. S. Navy, it did not mean that the United States was preparing to enter the war. In fact, Secretary Daniels refused to build ships for antisubmarine warfare or to make those on hand combat-ready, despite the pleas of ranking officers.[25]

One of the most important results of the preparedness movement was the creation of the office of Chief of Naval Operations, to provide central strategic planning in the mold of the long-sought general staff. Basically the work of Bradley Fiske, who was serving as an aide to Daniels, the proposal was introduced in Congress by Richmond Hobson. As drafted by Fiske, it called for the appointment of a chief of naval operations and fifteen assistants "who, under the Secretary of the Navy, shall be responsible for the readiness of the Navy for war and be charged with its general direction." Fearing that such an office would give the professionals too much control over naval policy at the expense of civilian leadership, Daniels persuaded Congress to water it down. As enacted on March 3, 1915, the law not only deprived the chief of naval operations of the fifteen assistants but also of the right to issue orders in his own name, either to the bureaus or to the commander in chief of the fleet. Consequently, he had no way of making certain that the plans he produced would be carried out.

Fiske might well have been appointed as the first chief of naval operations, but because of continued disagreements with Daniels over war-preparedness, he resigned a few weeks after passage of the bill, and the secretary appointed Rear Admiral William S. Benson, an officer regarded as less likely to press his authority. The Naval Act of 1916 improved the status of the chief of naval operations by giving him the fifteen assistants previously denied his office, by granting him permission to issue orders in the name of the secretary, and by providing that after the death of Admiral Dewey, he would be the navy's ranking officer.[26]

As the months went by, hope for peace was fading. The Battle of Jutland, although hailed as a great victory in Germany, had in reality demonstrated the inability of the Central Powers to break the Allied blockade by conventional means. In February 1917, in a desperate attempt to starve Britain into submission, Germany ordered the resumption of unrestricted submarine warfare against all neutral and belligerent merchant shipping found in the war zone. The German High Command fully realized that this would probably bring the United States into the conflict on the side of the Allies but gambled on defeating the enemy before the Americans could mobilize their vast resources. Within a few weeks several American merchantmen were torpedoed with loss of life, and Wilson, who had just been reelected with the campaign slogan, "He kept us out of war," asked Congress for a declaration of hostilities. On April 6, 1917, the United States took up arms to make the world "safe for democracy."

Less than a month later, on May 4, Destroyer Division 8 steamed in column through an opening in the anti-submarine nets guarding the British naval base at Queenstown (now Cobh), on the south coast of Ireland. Cheers and whistles echoed from the green hills surrounding the harbor as the six destroyers let go their anchors. After a stormy Atlantic crossing, the first American ships had arrived to join the battle against the U-boats. Caught in a gale that seemed to travel with them, the destroyers pitched and rolled so badly that the mess tables could not be rigged and the crews ate from their laps—if they ate at all. Soon after his ships were safely moored, Commander Joseph K. Taussig, the division's commander, reported to Vice Admiral Sir Lewis Bayly, commander in chief of the Western Approaches, under whom he was to serve.

The admiral's first question was to the point: "At what time will your vessels be ready for sea?"

"We are ready now, Sir," replied Taussig, "that is, as soon as we finish refueling."

Taussig's ships were in no condition to put to sea immediately, but he was not the sort of officer to tell that to his admiral. His words touched off a chord of appreciation on both sides of the Atlantic and helped cement bonds of friendship between the U. S. Navy and the Royal Navy—onetime adversaries, now allies. Four days later the American destroyers, fitted with British depth charges, began patrolling off the Irish coast, in fifty-mile squares, for German submarines. Taussig recalled:

> Things were looking black. In the three previous weeks the submarines had sunk 152 British merchant ships. The night before we entered the harbor, a German submarine had planted twelve mines right in the channel. Fortunately for us, they were swept up by the ever-vigilant British minesweepers before we arrived. The day following our arrival, one of the British gunboats from our station was torpedoed and her captain and forty of her crew were lost. Patrol vessels were continually bringing in survivors from the various ships as they were sunk.[27]

The war at sea was at the crisis stage. Allied merchantmen were being sunk faster than they could be replaced and Britain, with but a three-week supply of grain on hand, was in danger of being starved into submission. Few people knew this closely guarded secret, but one of them was William S. Sims, now a rear admiral. He had been summoned from the presidency of the Naval War College and sent to London, shortly before the United States entered the war, to open contacts with the British.

Travelling under an assumed name and with a single aide, Sims arrived in England under less than auspicious circumstances. His steamer struck a mine off Liverpool and her passengers were taken ashore in an excursion boat crowded with tipsy revellers who had been celebrating the Easter bank holiday on the Isle of Man. Sims hurried to the Admiralty and conferred on April 10 with his old friend Admiral Sir John Jellicoe, the First Sea Lord. With hardly a word, Jellicoe handed him a memorandum that revealed the ravages of the German submarine campaign. In the first three months of 1917, about 1.3 million tons, or 6 per cent of all available Allied and neutral shipping, had been sunk, and the toll for April was expected to be 900,000 tons. If the hemorrhage were not staunched, by October there would not be enough ships left to sustain the life-blood of Britain.

"It looks as though the Germans . . . [are] winning the war," said the astounded Sims.

"They will win," Jellicoe replied, "unless we can stop these losses—and stop them soon."

"Is there no solution for the problem?"

"Absolutely none that we can see now."

Before reporting this shocking news to Washington, Sims spent a few days finding out everything he could about the crisis. He was astonished to learn that the British were not escorting merchant vessels in the Western Approaches and the North Sea, although escorts had proved valuable in cross-channel operations and were used for troopships. Senior officers in the Admiralty argued that convoying was a defensive measure and the U-boats could be defeated only by offensive measures: by sending out destroyers to hunt them down, by arming merchantmen, by mining or otherwise blocking the approaches to submarine bases. Merchant ships, they claimed, were not disciplined enough to steam together at the fixed speed required by convoys; there would be collisions during the night, and the huddles of slow-moving vessels would provide tempting targets for the U-boats. Destroyers could not be spared from the vital task of screening the Grand Fleet.

With characteristic energy, Sims launched a two-pronged attack on the problem. He urged the Navy Department to send every destroyer it could lay its hands on to European waters. "We cannot send too soon or too many," he declared on April 28, 1917. At the same time, working with junior British officers who were convinced of the efficacy of convoys and with Prime Minister Lloyd

George, he helped persuade the Admiralty to give them a trial. In May experimental convoys that had assembled at Gibraltar and Hampton Roads and steamed
to British ports with the loss of only one straggler convinced the Admiralty that
the long-sought weapon for dealing with the U-boat menace lay at hand.

But Sims had better luck in London than with his superiors at home. They
were skeptical about the urgency of his requests, and they thought him too pro-
British. Admiral Benson apparently entertained latent if somewhat anachronistic
suspicions of Great Britain, and had, on the eve of Sims' departure, wagged a
cautionary finger at him and warned: "Don't let the British pull the wool over
your eyes. It's not our business pulling their chestnuts out of the fire."[28] More
importantly, despite the evidence on every hand of coming war, Secretary Daniels
had been reluctant to mobilize his men and ships. An investigation made after
the war showed that the United States went to war with "two-thirds of our fleet
not in proper condition for war service abroad."[29] Further, fearing that German
submarines would soon appear off the American coast, the Navy Department
resisted sending more than Taussig's token force of destroyers to Europe. Yet
in reality the Germans had few U-boats capable of crossing the Atlantic; even
when five of them did cross the following year, they sank only a handful of
small craft and laid some mines, one of which sank the old cruiser *San Diego*,
off Long Island.

Eventually the British and French managed to convince the Navy Department that Sims was not exaggerating. Ship after ship was sent to join Taussig's
division, and their work so pleased Admiral Bayly that he called the destroyermen
"my Americans." By July 1917, thirty-five U.S. destroyers and two tenders
were based at Queenstown, and before the war ended a total of eighty-five
American destroyers had crossed the Atlantic and were operating from Queenstown, Brest, Gibraltar, and other ports.[30]

World War I held little glamour for the U.S. Navy, whose primary mission
was to transport hundreds of thousands of troops and their equipment and supplies
safely across the U-boat-infested Atlantic to the battlefields of France. Vast
amounts of shipping were required for this operation—four times as much tonnage was needed to carry an army division's equipment and supplies as was
needed for the soldiers themselves. But the ships did not exist, thanks to years
of decline in the American merchant marine, and it was necessary to start
building. To mass-produce them, the Emergency Fleet Corporation was set up
in April 1917, only a few weeks after war was declared. In the interim, the
administration's eye fell upon some 600,000 tons of interned German shipping
that had been lying idle in American ports, some since 1914. Anticipating seizure
when war was declared, the German captains had sabotaged their vessels, but
such new techniques as electric welding made it possible quickly to repair the
damage. Twenty of them, including the 56,000-ton luxury liner *Vaterland*, renamed *Leviathan*, were converted to troopships and carried more than half a
million soldiers to France.

The task of ferrying the American Expeditionary Force was assigned to Rear Admiral Albert Gleaves, who was designated commander of the Cruiser and Transport Force. Flying his flag in the armored cruiser *Seattle*, he led the first convoy of American troops across the Atlantic in June 1917. U-boats tried to interfere but were driven off before they could do any damage. Gleaves' force soon grew to forty-five large transports, all manned by navy crews, and twenty-four cruisers that were assigned to escort them. Well-guarded and steaming at high speed, troop convoys proved to be such difficult targets that U-boat skippers wasted little time on them, preferring to devote their efforts to the sinking of freighters. Nevertheless, there was always the danger that German surface raiders or battle cruisers might slip through the blockade and play havoc with one of the convoys. By the summer of 1918, American troops were disembarking on the docks of Brest and other French ports at the rate of 10,000 men a day. In all, slightly more than two million men were transported to France without the loss of a single ship or a single man.[31]

In December 1917 five coal-burning battleships, the *New York, Florida, Delaware, Texas*, and *Wyoming* reinforced the British Grand Fleet, further tipping the balance against the Germans. These ships were selected rather than the more powerful oil-burning vessels because of a shortage of fuel oil in Britain. They were under the command of Rear Admiral Hugh Rodman and were designated Battle Squadron Six of the Grand Fleet. "Nothing could have been easier than a clash of ideas, of principles of fighting, of routine methods between two Services which had never been at sea together and had been trained in completely different environments," said a British officer. But the American squadron was integrated into the British fleet with a minimum of strain—thanks primarily to the efforts of Rodman himself. "I realized that the British fleet had had three years of actual warfare and knew the game from the ground up," he declared. "There could not be two independent commands in one force if our work was to be harmonious, and the only logical course was to amalgamate our ships and serve under the British commander-in-chief."

Most of the squadron's service was uneventful, but its arrival permitted the British to decommission five pre-dreadnought *King Edward*-class battleships and assign their crews to antisubmarine warfare. Later three other dreadnoughts, the *Nevada, Oklahoma*, and *Utah*, were stationed at Bantry Bay, on the west coast of Ireland, to keep watch against possible raids by German battle cruisers on the Atlantic supply and trade routes.[32]

The navy underwent an astonishing growth during World War I. By the end of 1917, it mustered 269,000 officers and men as compared to a strength of 67,000 when war was declared. At war's end, the figure had nearly doubled again to almost a half-million men—and women, because for the first time, the navy accepted women in its ranks. About 11,275 women served as "Yeomanettes" in the navy and another 300 enlisted as "Marinettes" in the Marine Corps.

Obtaining manpower was easy; it was a popular war. Turning the volunteers who flooded the recruiting stations into sailors was rather more difficult. To speed the flow of officers, classes at Annapolis were telescoped and training courses were hastily established at colleges in various parts of the country. "Boot camps" at Norfolk, Great Lakes, Newport News, and San Francisco were greatly expanded, but the cadres of experienced men were small and could barely keep up with the torrent of young men entering the camps. Often there were as many as 48,000 recruits undergoing training at one time.[33]

Because of the submarine menace, the building and manning of destroyers had the highest priority. Work was halted on the battleships authorized by the 1916 construction program and a fleet of 273 destroyers was laid down. Displacing about 1,200 tons, these four-stack vessels were larger than the destroyers that had crossed the Atlantic with Taussig. Their designed speed was thirty-five knots and they carried four 4-inch guns, one 3-inch antiaircraft gun, a dozen 21-inch torpedo tubes, and a pair of depth-charge racks. They were standardized for mass production—one was launched only seventeen days after her keel had been laid—but most were completed too late for combat service in World War I. During the postwar years these long, thin, so-called four-pipers, whose silhouettes became familiar around the globe, were the navy's workhorses, some of them serving through World War II.[34]

While waiting for destroyers to be built, the navy turned to 110-foot, wooden-hulled submarine-chasers. Displacing only seventy-seven tons, they made about fifteen knots on gasoline engines and were armed with a 3-inch gun forward, a "Y" gun for launching depth charges, and a depth-charge rack on the stern. Usually commanded by a newly minted ensign, they carried about twenty-five officers and men, almost all of whom were reservists and volunteers. For most of them, the Atlantic crossing was their first experience at sea. One sub-chaser had a quartermaster who enjoyed reading Greek tragedies in the original, a seaman who spoke fluent Arabic and four other languages, a chief engineer who had never been to sea before, and a cook who had hawked lemonade in a circus.

Sims related the story that someone told Captain Lyman A. Cotten, who commanded the first squadron of sub-chasers to arrive in Plymouth, "Those boys can't bring a ship across the ocean!" "Perhaps they can't," replied Cotten. "But they have." And then he pointed to thirty-six boats of the "splinter fleet" bobbing at anchor in Plymouth Harbor, near the monument commemorating the sailing of the *Mayflower* three centuries before. Nearly 400 submarine-chasers were built during the war and saw gallant and useful service from Murmansk to the Mediterranean, where they were part of the barrage established across the Strait of Otranto to prevent German and Austrian U-boats coming out of and entering the Adriatic.

To aid them in detecting enemy submarines, sub-chasers were fitted with hydrophones, a primitive underwater listening device. Hunting in three-boat units with code names like "corn-meal-mush" and "high-low-jack," which mystified not only the Germans but also the British, they tried to triangulate a submarine's position and then move in with depth charges for the kill. These tactics were often ineffective, however, because as soon as the U-boat captains learned that they could be tracked by the sound of their engines, they cut them and lay silent until the enemy wearied of the search.[35]

Escort duty and antisubmarine patrol in the North Atlantic were punishing work. Good weather was rare and the destroyers pitched and lurched constantly, throwing their crews careening against steel bulkheads. Most of the time the decks were awash and sometimes sea water sloshed down companionways and seeped into the living compartments. Hot meals were a rarity. So constant was the pounding that equipment broke down frequently. Collision with the ships they were escorting, particularly at night when running without lights, was sometimes a greater danger than the threat of submarine attack. The old *Chauncey* (DD-3), model for the destroyer in *Delilah*, Marcus Goodrich's novel of the prewar navy, was sunk in a collision with a British steamer off Gibraltar with a loss of twenty-one lives.

> But with all the uncertainty of the thing, together with the occasional excitement and interesting episodes, [recalled Commander Taussig] there was a great deal of monotony about the patrol. There were many days when our bright lookouts saw nothing that could give us a thrill. There were many days of discomfort when, owing to rough seas, the excessive rolling of the ship made eating off tables impossible, and sleeping in bunks difficult. The howling of the wind through the rigging had the tendency to get on one's nerves after several continuous days of it. Most of us slept in our clothes, not removing them during the tour of duty.[36]

Because there were not enough escort vessels to accompany every convoy across the Atlantic—except for outward-bound troopships—merchant convoys were protected only when they were actually in the danger zone, which extended about 200 miles out from the British coast. The assembling and movement of large numbers of ships required precise timetables. What Admiral Sims described as the "central nervous system" of the convoys was the Convoy Room of the Admiralty in London, where the positions of all convoys and of German submarines known to be at sea were plotted on a huge board. The convoy commodore, usually a retired admiral or captain, exercised general control from one of the merchant ships, frequently a passenger liner, but overall command was vested in the escort commander, who was in direct contact with the Admiralty. Formations of some thirty ships sailed from New York every sixteen days and from Hampton Roads every eight. Others departed from Halifax or Dakar or Gibraltar on their own schedules.

Zigzagging its way across the Atlantic to a rendezvous at the edge of the danger zone, a convoy would be met by a screen of destroyers that had just bid farewell to an outward-bound convoy. Timing had to be precise, because with their limited fuel capacities, destroyers could not wait long at sea for tardy arrivals. Formed up in several columns, with destroyers on each flank and one serving as a rear guard to keep track of stragglers, the convoy would steam at its best possible speed to its destination. U-boats often lurked off the major ports to attack single ships after the convoys had dispersed.

To detect U-boats, a destroyer depended on the keenness of her lookouts to catch the momentary feather plume of a periscope or the telltale track of a torpedo—by which time it might be too late. When a submarine was sighted, "general quarters" was sounded and the destroyer leaped at flank speed to the place where the periscope had been seen or where the destroyer captain, like a duck hunter "leading his target," estimated the U-boat would be when he could pass over it. Charges set for various depths were tumbled off her fantail or fired by her "Y" gun. After the water had calmed, she would cruise slowly in a circle, searching for an oil slick or a bit of debris that might indicate a hit. Only rarely, however, were crews rewarded with proof that they had made a kill.[37]

One such case occurred on November 17, 1917, when Coxswain David D. Loomis, caught a glimpse of a periscope from the pitching deck of the destroyer *Fanning* (DD-37) and called out, "Periscope on the port bow, 400 yards!" Breaking away from the convoy she was protecting, the *Fanning* raced to the spot and dropped a barrage of depth charges. A series of muffled detonations was followed by a geyser of discolored water. The *Nicholson* (DD-52) dashed in to assist, and as the two ships crisscrossed the area, the light gray conning tower of a submarine suddenly broke the surface, her bow seeming to rise from the sea. The U-boat's crew poured on deck through the hatches, hands in the air, shouting "Kamerad!" Only eighteen minutes had passed since Loomis sighted the periscope. The destroyers prepared to take the submarine in tow, but she was apparently scuttled by one of her crew. Kapitänleutnant Gustav Amberger, who was picked up with thirty-eight of his officers and men, identified his craft as the U-58. The *Fanning*'s crew was rewarded with the congratulations of Admiral Sims and the cheerful command, "Go out and do it again."[38]

Not all American destroyers were so lucky. The *Cassin* (DD-43) was on patrol off the coast of Ireland on October 15, 1917, when she sighted a submarine on the surface, but the U-boat submerged before contact could be made. A half-hour later, Gunner's Mate Osmond K. Ingram spotted a torpedo streaking for the ship's stern and ran aft to jettison the depth charges. The *Cassin*'s rudder was put hard over to port, and for a moment it looked as though the torpedo might miss. But just as Ingram was reaching the depth charges, the torpedo struck. The explosion killed Ingram and wounded nine other men, but the shattered *Cassin* made her way to port. Ingram was posthumously awarded the Medal of Honor, and a destroyer (DD-255) was named for him.[39]

The institution of the convoy system and the presence of more and more patrolling destroyers did not put an end to the U-boat menace but did make the task of submarine commanders more difficult. As Sir Arthur Hezlet, a veteran submariner, wrote:

> When all shipping sailed independently, U-boats were presented with a long succession of targets at which to fire, and they had time to take deliberate aim and then reload before the next victim appeared. With convoy there would be only one chance to fire as the enemy swept by *en masse*. Whilst the selected ship was being attacked, the rest of the convoy would slip by unscathed and a second shot was seldom possible even if the escorts permitted it. With only two, or sometimes four, torpedo tubes, only one ship, or at most two, would generally be hit. Moreover the attack was complicated by the presence of the escorts and the anticipation of the heavy counter-attack which was likely to descend on the U-boat after firing.[40]

Slowly the tide began to turn. From a peak of 881,000 tons of Allied shipping sunk during the bleak month of April 1917, losses dropped to 596,000 tons in May, increased slightly in June, and then began to fall steadily. By November, the month in which the Admiralty had feared a German victory, the toll of torpedoed ships dropped below 300,000 tons. During most of the remaining year of the war, it steadied at about that level, but these losses—tragic as they were for those sunk—were no longer a serious threat to Allied victory. America's vast industrial might had come into play and shipyards were turning out merchantmen faster than the Germans could send them to the bottom.[41]

"Why don't the British shut up the hornets in their nests?" complained Woodrow Wilson about the failure to prevent the U-boats from getting to sea. "We are hunting hornets all over the farm and letting the nest alone." Wilson had no specific plan in mind, but Assistant Navy Secretary Roosevelt envisioned a wall of mines extending 240 miles across the North Sea from Scotland to Norway, a wall so dense that no submarine could safely penetrate it or dive under it. Discussion of the project began within a few weeks of America's entry into the war, and the Navy Department sought the opinion of the British on its feasibility. Using mines, nets, and destroyer patrols, the British had made some progress in sealing the narrow Dover Strait against submarines, but attempts to mine the stormy North Sea extensively had failed because of the vastness of the area to be covered, the depth of the water, and the lack of effective mines. It was estimated that to close the northern passage, 400,000 mines would have to be sown—a task viewed by the Admiralty as beyond the range of possibility.

New life was breathed into Roosevelt's North Sea Barrage, however, when a Massachusetts inventor named Ralph C. Browne came forward with a device that made the antenna mine possible. Unlike the mines then in general use, it did not have to come into direct contact with a ship's hull in order to explode but would detonate if the vessel merely brushed a long wand, or antenna, that extended from it. Thus the antenna mine had a wider range of destruction than the old type, which meant that the North Sea could be closed with only 100,000 mines. Under Roosevelt's eager prodding, antenna mines, each containing 300 pounds of TNT, were soon pouring from the production lines. Actual mining began in June 1918 under the direction of Rear Admiral Joseph Strauss. By October some 70,000 mines had been sown, about 80 per cent by the U. S. Navy, the rest by the British, at a cost of some $80 million. The war ended before the effectiveness of the North Sea Barrage had been fully tested. U-boats passed through the North Sea throughout the mine-laying operation, but six of them are believed to have been sunk. Nevertheless, fear of the barrier contributed to the decline of morale in the German navy that led eventually to mutiny and defeat.[42]

Aircraft were also pressed into service in the antisubmarine campaign, and no branch of the navy grew faster during the war than its air arm. When the United States entered the war, naval aviation had 43 qualified pilots, 5 of them marines, 239 enlisted men, and 54 planes, most of which were not fit for wartime service. Nineteen months later, when the war ended, 6,716 officers wore the golden wings and forest green uniform associated with naval aviation. The number of enlisted men in aviation units totalled 30,693, and there were 2,107 planes, most of them of English and French manufacture. However, the navy was beginning to take delivery of huge flying boats that had been designed and built in the United States and were powered by the American-produced Liberty engine. There were also 282 officers and 1,180 enlisted men in the Marine Corps' aviation units.

Operating from twenty-seven bases in France, England, Ireland, and Italy, navy airplanes, blimps, and kite balloons patrolled submarine-infested waters, protected convoys, and performed scouting missions. They were credited with sinking at least one U-boat and with damaging several others. During the last ten months of the war, no convoy guarded by airplanes or blimps suffered loss, Secretary Daniels reported. Bombing missions were flown against submarine pens along the coast of Belgium, and canals, railroads, supply dumps, and airfields were raided. Navy flyers also flew from Italian bases on the Adriatic, paying particular attention to the Austrian submarine base at Pola.

On August 21, 1918, a flight of two bombers and three fighters—all floatplanes—led by Ensign George H. Ludlow was dropping propaganda leaflets on Pola when they were jumped by seven enemy aircraft. In the dogfight that followed, Ludlow shot down one of the Austrians, but his own plane was hit and burst into flames. Throwing it into a spin, he managed to put out the fire, but with his engine dead he was forced to land on the water, only about five miles from the Austrian base. Ensign George H. Hammann came to the rescue of his downed flight leader. He landed near Ludlow's sinking plane and shouted for him to swim over. With Ludlow clinging precariously to its struts, Hammann coaxed his plane into the air and made it back to base. For his gallantry, he was awarded the Medal of Honor—the first won by a navy flyer.

Two marine aviators, Lieutenant Ralph Talbot and his gunner, Corporal Robert G. Robinson, also received the Medal of Honor for single-handedly fighting off twelve German planes on October 8, 1918. They shot down two of the attackers and escaped from the rest by flying over the German trenches at an altitude of fifty feet. Nineteen-year-old Lieutenant David S. Ingalls was the navy's only official ace of World War I. Flying Sopwith Camels with a Royal Air Force squadron, he shot down the requisite five German planes in only a few weeks.[43]

The navy's long arm was felt on land as well as at sea and in the air. The first American force of any size to reach France included a regiment of marines; and the leathernecks served valiantly in the Allied cause. In late May 1918 two marine regiments, about 8,000 men in all, brigaded into the army's Second Infantry Division, helped blunt a German advance on Paris at Château-Thierry and then moved into Belleau Wood, where they were involved in some of the bitterest hand-to-hand fighting of the war. It was a battle of small units and quick, desperate rushes. Sometimes the ground gained was little more than the distance covered by a baseball player sliding into a base. Attacking under heavy fire, the marines cleaned out brushwood or thickets being used by the Germans as machine-gun nests, then turned the captured guns on the enemy. "Come on, you sons of bitches—do you want to live forever?" yelled Gunnery Sergeant Dan Daly.[44]

With German long-range guns shelling key positions and supply dumps behind their lines, the Allied commanders needed similar guns with which to retaliate, and the navy provided them. Five 14-inch naval rifles were mounted on special railway cars and sent to France along with gun crews, rolling machine shops, ammunition cars, barracks, and other equipment. Their natural target, the German "Paris gun" that rained death and destruction upon that city from seventy-five miles away, was taken out of action before the naval rifles arrived. Instead, the big guns, with the naval crews under army command and wearing the "Woozlefinch" insignia—the symbol of a species that was neither flesh, nor fish, nor fowl—were shunted up and down the Western Front as needed. Lobbing a 1,400-pound shell for as much as twenty-four miles, the guns went into action on September 6, 1918, and fired a total of 782 rounds during the next two months.

They were particularly effective against railroad marshalling yards, supply dumps, bridges, and highways well behind the enemy lines. The guns were laid as though they were being fired from ships. Once the position of the target had been established from the excellent French military maps, the gun was aimed and ballistic corrections made. One hit was enough to wreck a railroad line of three tracks for a distance of 100 yards. In some cases airplanes were used to spot the fall of the shells. The naval batteries fired their last shot at 10:57 on the morning of November 11, 1918. Three minutes later the war was over.[45]

8

THE LONG ARMISTICE

To the end that prohibition of the use of submarines as commerce destroyers shall be accepted universally as part of the law of nations, the signatory powers herewith accept that prohibition as binding between themselves, and invite all other nations to adhere thereto . . .
—Washington Naval Treaty, 6 February 1922

Battle flags flying, a great armada that included the U.S. Navy's Sixth Battle Squadron steamed out of the Firth of Forth on the morning of November 21, 1918. An armistice had been signed ten days before, but all hands were on the alert as the thirty-three dreadnoughts formed up in two parallel columns about six miles apart. Every eye was fixed on the eastern horizon. Out of the mists of the North Sea, there slowly emerged the outline of a ship . . . and then another and another . . . until nine German battleships and five battle cruisers came into view and passed between the two columns into captivity. Silently and without ceremony, the fleets returned to port, where the Allied commander in chief, Admiral Sir David Beatty, ran up a signal that marked the eclipse of German sea power: "The German flag will be hauled down at sunset today . . . and will not be hoisted again without permission."[1]

"Without the cooperation of the American Navy, the Allies could not have won the war," declared Admiral Sims.[2] Having met the test of battle, the navy emerged from World War I with enhanced power and prestige. The United States had become a first-class naval power with a balanced fleet at whose heart was a nucleus of highly skilled and thoroughly professional officers and men. Although still smaller than the Royal Navy, the U. S. Navy was expanding toward its announced goal of "second to none," whereas the former was entering a period of severe contraction.[3]

As soon as the war was over, President Wilson made a startling proposal to Congress. In 1916, it will be recalled, the United States had authorized a massive program of naval expansion that included ten 32,600-ton battleships,

193

each armed with eight 16-inch guns, and six battle cruisers. The battleships *Maryland, West Virginia, Colorado,* and *Washington* were laid down, but work on them was suspended to allow concentration on the building of destroyers and other craft needed to meet the U-boat menace. Wilson now urged not only that work on these ships be resumed but that the whole 1916 program be continued and even expanded. If his proposition were approved, by 1925 at the latest, the navy would have a matchless battle line of thirty-nine dreadnoughts and twelve battle cruisers.[4]

There were at least two reasons for advancing this proposal. First, the General Board of the navy pointed out that by virtue of the wartime revival of the American merchant marine the United States had become Britain's major commercial rival and, warned a staff paper: "Every great commercial rival of the British Empire has eventually found itself at war with Britain—and has been defeated."[5] Second, many strategists suspected Japanese intentions in the Pacific and were prophesying that war would eventually come. During World War I, Japan had begun a sizeable naval expansion, had seized German holdings in China and the Mariana, Marshall, and Caroline island groups, which lay astride the American line of communications between Hawaii and the Philippines, and had flouted the long-cherished Open Door policy by making aggressive demands on China.

Some historians say that Wilson's proposal was but a ploy to coerce a reluctant Britain into supporting the League of Nations, which he was promoting as a means of settling future international disputes.[6] The president, they suggest, fully realized that Congress was in no mood to approve funds for such a huge fleet and expected the proposal to be whittled down to more acceptable levels; in the meantime it would serve his purpose. Perhaps so, but it surprised, worried, and angered the British, planting between the former allies seeds of discord and suspicion that endured for a decade.[7]

In the end, the British did agree to support the League of Nations, and, as expected, Congress approved funds only for the resumption of the 1916 program. Wilson's hopes for an effective League of Nations foundered, however, when the Senate refused to approve American membership—a decision ratified in 1920 when Warren G. Harding was elected president by a landslide. Weary of Wilson's appeals to idealism and repelled by the prolonged maneuvering that had delayed the actual making of the peace, the American people retreated into isolationism. Harding's campaign slogan, "back to normalcy," suited the mood of the nation even though there was no such word as "normalcy."

Now that there was no longer any threat from Germany, American naval strategists turned full attention to the Pacific. The German fleet, interned at Scapa Flow, had been scuttled by its own officers and men on June 21, 1919, with Teutonic thoroughness. The opening of the Panama Canal in 1914 had made the two-ocean navy possible at last, and in the summer of 1919, the navy was divided into two fleets, the newest and most powerful units being sent to the Pacific.

This move, coupled with the large American construction program, galvanized Japan into action. Naval expenditures rose from $85 million in 1917 to $245 million in 1921, representing almost a third of the national budget. In 1920 the Japanese revived a dormant "eight-eight" building program that called for two squadrons, one of eight battleships and the other of eight battle cruisers—all to be completed by 1928. In 1917 and 1918 the formidable *Nagato* and *Mutsu*, both armed with 16-inch guns, had been laid down, and even larger super-battleships armed with 18.1-inch guns were said to be under consideration. Not to be outdone, Britain planned to build four 48,000-ton battle cruisers, the most powerful ships in her history, which were to be followed by four battleships mounting 18-inch guns.[8]

With the horror and waste of modern war fresh in the American mind, a revolt against mounting naval expenditures swept all before it. "Is it the logic of the situation that as dangers recede our preparations for war shall multiply?" asked Representative E. W. Saunders, a Virginia Democrat.[9] Feeling the same way and appalled by the cost of their own building program, the British put out feelers to Washington for a disarmament conference and indicated that they would accept naval parity with the United States—a step that was both truly historic and an admission of reality.

Although the Republicans had blocked Democratic attempts to lead America into the League of Nations, the Harding administration was anxious to show that it was, nevertheless, in favor of peace and adopted the British proposal as its own. Britain, Japan, France, and Italy were invited to Washington to attend a conference designed not only to seek a limitation on naval armaments but to resolve problems in the Pacific. This was a recognition of the fact that tensions in that area were to some extent responsible for the naval race and limitations on naval construction should be considered part of a wider settlement. Four nations that had no role in the naval discussions, China, Belgium, the Netherlands, and Portugal, were invited to participate in the talks concerning the Far East, where they all had a stake.

The Washington Conference for the Limitation of Naval Armaments got under way on November 12, 1921, with a proposal by Secretary of State Charles Evans Hughes that exploded among the delegates with the force of a 16-inch shell. He called for a moratorium on the building of capital ships and a scrapping of battleships afloat or on the ways that would leave the navies of Britain, the United States, Japan, Italy, and France with a tonnage ratio of 5:5:3:1.7:1.7. He made similar proposals for aircraft carriers, which were just entering the world's navies, as well as for cruisers, destroyers, and submarines.

The United States, Hughes continued, was ready to show its good faith by scrapping thirty capital ships, fifteen built and fifteen building, for an aggregate of 845,740 tons. He followed up this breathtaking gesture by calling on Britain to scrap nineteen capital ships, aggregating 583,375 tons, and Japan seventeen ships, aggregating 448,928 tons. In less than fifteen minutes, declared a British observer, Hughes sank sixty-six battleships and battle cruisers, "more than all the admirals of the world have sunk in a cycle of centuries."

Foreign diplomats and most American naval officers were stunned by the audacity of the move. Although it had been worked out in consultation with Admiral Robert E. Coontz, the chief of naval operations, and Theodore Roosevelt, Jr., assistant secretary of the navy, the actual details had been closely guarded. Hard bargaining followed but, no nation being willing to take responsibility for wrecking the conference, Hughes' proposal was accepted on February 6, 1922. The 5:5:3:1.7:1.7 ratio was fixed for battleships and carriers. No limitations were placed on the number of cruisers and smaller vessels, but cruisers were limited to 10,000 tons each and their guns to 8 inches.

Britain was allowed to retain twenty-two capital ships, totalling 580,000 tons, including the *Nelson* and *Rodney* still be be laid down; the United States eighteen, totalling 500,000 tons, among them the *Maryland, West Virginia*, and *Colorado*—the *Washington* was to be scrapped; and Japan ten, totalling 301,000 tons, including the *Mutsu* and *Nagato*. The United States and Britain were allocated 135,000 tons of aircraft carriers each, while Japan got 81,000 tons. A ten-year "holiday" in capital-ship construction was declared and vessels built after its expiration were not to exceed 35,000 tons or to mount guns greater than 16 inches.

Two other agreements came out of the conference: the Nine-Power Treaty, signed by all the participants and designed to preserve the territorial integrity of China, and the Four-Power Pact in which Japan, the United States, Britain, and France agreed to respect one another's rights in the Pacific. The latter agreement was a gesture to save face for Japan by making up for the abrogation of the Anglo-Japanese Alliance, which had become an embarrassment to the British in their efforts to improve relations with the United States.[10]

The conference was regarded by the general public as a triumph for American diplomacy and by many U. S. officers as an unmitigated disaster for the navy. In reality, the results were mixed. The halting of the battleship race, which had threatened to bankrupt the major powers, did defuse international tensions, give the United States its long-sought goal of parity in capital ships with Britain, and supposedly it locked Japan into a position of permanent inferiority. On the other hand, cruiser tonnage not having been restricted, the focus of the naval race shifted to this class of ship. It was also charged that whereas the United States had scrapped modern vessels and newly laid-down hulls, other nations had done no more than junk worn-out ships or tear up blueprints. Studies made since World War II have shown that the navy fared better at the conference table than was thought at the time, however. The battleships it retained were newer than those that remained in the British and Japanese fleets and they incorporated developments in firepower and protection that had resulted from wartime experience[11]

Nevertheless, in its eagerness to obtain Japanese consent to the limitations, the United States made concessions that, in effect, ratified the existing balance of power. Japanese dominance in the Far East was confirmed, while Great Britain retained primacy between the North Sea and Singapore and the United States controlled the Eastern Pacific. To strengthen the hand of a liberal government in dealing with its own restive military and to eliminate any threat to Japanese security, the United States agreed not to further fortify bases to the west of Pearl Harbor. Britain gave similar assurances with regard to Hong Kong. In return, Japan pledged to limit further fortification to her home islands and to maintain the status quo elsewhere, including the Pacific territories she had seized from Germany and now held under a League of Nations mandate. With the Japanese fleet normally operating close to home, this arrangement conferred a distinct advantage upon the Imperial Navy.[12]

In the years of the "long armistice" the major task of the navy was to maintain itself as a viable and balanced fighting force despite treaty limitations, cutbacks in spending, and public apathy. Although appropriations averaged about double those approved by Congress in 1916, the cost of keeping the fleet at sea was higher.[13] Most of the available funds were earmarked for the modernization and maintenance of the battleships, and there was little left over for other purposes. Naval construction techniques lagged because there were fewer opportunities for experimentation and for testing new designs. Manpower levelled off at about 100,000 officers and men, and prospects for promotion were limited. Members of the Naval Academy class of 1923 were warned upon graduation that they would be fortunate if they ever reached the rank of lieutenant commander.[14]

With economy the watchword of three consecutive Republican administrations, naval officers spent much of their time "bending the pencil," or working out ways to operate their vessels on as little fuel as possible. So pervasive was the passion for economy, relates a historian, that "in one ship a young officer suggested that the running lights be turned off at night, thus risking collision in order to save an amount of fuel so small that the engineers could not even measure it." Battle-efficiency competitions were often unrealistic and tactical originality suffered. As a senior officer told Samuel Eliot Morison: "The pencil became sharper than the sword, everyone tried to beat the target practice rules and too many forgot there was a war getting closer." Inadequate proving and testing procedures concealed torpedo defects that should have been corrected long before they were revealed to the navy's cost in the ruthless test of war.[15]

Unable to build up to treaty strength, the navy lagged behind the Japanese fleet, particularly in cruisers. The backbone of the cruiser force was the 7,500-ton *Omaha* class armed with 6-inch guns. In Japan, by contrast, national policies began to take on a military coloration, as festering interservice rivalry was fanned by the inferior status imposed by the Washington treaty ratios. The passage in 1924 of the Johnson Act, which all but excluded Japanese immigrants from the

United States, touched off a public display of anger that further strengthened the military. The laying down of a dozen cruisers mounting 8-inch guns and exceeding treaty limitations followed. Congress, paying heed at last to repeated warnings that the United States was being outclassed, appropriated funds for eight large cruisers, which were to be called the *Northampton* class after President Coolidge's hometown. The tight-fisted Yankee did not swallow this bait, however, and limited actual construction to two vessels.

Instead, he encouraged the attempt, in 1927, to impose limitations on cruisers, destroyers, and submarines. The Geneva Conference, which resulted from his efforts, foundered on the insoluble issue of large cruisers demanded by the United States, which lacked overseas bases, versus the desire for smaller cruisers by Britain, which was amply provided with refueling stations. Three years later, Coolidge's successor, Herbert Hoover, a Quaker who pursued disarmament for humanitarian as well as economic reasons, succeeded in securing such limitations under the pressure of the developing Great Depression. To prevent a new arms race, which none could afford, the United States, Britain, and Japan extended the battleship "holiday," which was scheduled to expire two years later, to 1936, and agreed to limit the number of warships in their fleets.[16]

The Washington treaty and its successors created a wide gap between U. S. commitments in the Far East and the ability to sustain them.[17] The American strategic position in the Western Pacific was never strong, anyway, because of the vast distance between Hawaii and the Philippines. Working over their game boards, the joint planners of the army and navy periodically overhauled the Orange Plan designed for use in case of war with Japan. On the eve of war in Europe, the Rainbow plans were developed to cover the eventuality of America's simultaneous involvement in the Atlantic and the Pacific. But as the planners watched the success of the German blitzkrieg in Poland and western Europe, they increasingly considered that the chances of holding the Philippines and the other islands would be slim, indeed, in the face of a massive Japanese onslaught. It was expected that a transpacific war would begin with a surprise attack on American naval forces in the Far East and that the U. S. island outposts would quickly fall. The navy would then have to fight its way back across 5,000 miles of open sea while under heavy Japanese attack—a task magnified by the lack of bases. Radical changes in tactical concepts and weapon systems were required if the navy was to compensate for its deficiencies and project its power into the Western Pacific. Naval aviation and the aircraft carrier filled the gap.[18]

Just as World War I was ending, the navy had taken delivery of four huge NC (Navy-Curtiss) flying boats, which were to be used in antisubmarine patrol work. Powered by four engines producing a total of 1,600 horsepower and with a wingspan only four feet less than that of a Boeing 707, these planes were designed to fly the Atlantic, even though that feat had not yet been accomplished. Six months after the armistice, on May 16, 1919, the NC-1, NC-3, and NC-4 lumbered into the air off Newfoundland and headed eastward toward the Azores. Only the NC-4, piloted by Lieutenant Commander Albert C. Read, made it, the others having been forced down in the Atlantic, happily without loss of life. The NC-4 completed its epoch-making flight by leapfrogging to Portugal and then to Plymouth, England.[19]

The flight of the NC-4 heightened the navy's interest in the airplane, and a month later the General Board announced that the development of fleet aviation was "of paramount importance and must be undertaken immediately if the United States is to take its proper place as a naval power." But how was this to be done? Sharp infighting developed between battleship admirals, who saw only that aircraft might be useful for reconnaissance and shell-spotting, and the advocates of the carrier, who foresaw a wider role for the airplane in naval operations.[20] Many strategists believed that if war with Japan came, it would be climaxed by a Jutland-style sea battle in which the big gun would be the decisive weapon. In fact, students at the Naval War College examined the engagement at Jutland in such minute detail that one officer humorously described it as "a major defeat of the United States Navy."[21]

Others, however, Admiral Sims among them, visualized the traditional role of the battleship being usurped by the aircraft carrier. Two decades before the debut of the fast carrier task force. Sims, as president of the War College, was including carriers in the school's war games. In future wars, he declared, the fleet with the strongest carrier force "will sweep the enemy fleet clean of its airplanes and proceed to bomb the battleships, and torpedo them with torpedo planes."[22]

When the navy finally got an aircraft carrier, she was right out of the bargain basement. The collier *Jupiter* was ordered converted into a carrier in 1919 and was renamed the *Langley* in honor of the air pioneer. Work on her proceeded at a slow pace, however, and she was not ready to join the fleet until 1922. Her flight deck was 534 feet long and 64 feet wide—about the same size as those on the escort carriers put in service during World War II. Bluff-bowed and broad-beamed, she was not a thing of beauty and was soon dubbed the "Old Covered Wagon."

Carrier advocates temporarily had an ally in Brigadier General William Mitchell, chief of the Army Air Service in Europe during the war. Billy Mitchell returned home with a vision of an independent air force similar to the newly created Royal Air Force, equal in stature to the army and navy—and with an equal claim on the national budget. Letting fly a scatter shot of claims, he announced that the airplane had made both of those services obsolete. "Air power has completely superseded sea power or land power as our first line of defense," he declared in a statement designed to raise the hackles of the admirals and generals. He zeroed in on the battleship, claiming it was "as obsolete as knights in armor after gunpowder was invented."

Much of what Mitchell had to say was not as revolutionary as it sounded —after all, Sims and others had been saying the same thing. As do most zealots, he resorted to exaggeration to attract public attention to his cause. "A superior air power will dominate all sea areas when they act from land bases," he said in summarizing his basic philosophy, "and no seacraft, whether carrying aircraft or not, is able to contest their aerial supremacy."

World War II, of course, proved Mitchell spectacularly wrong. Nevertheless, his charges could not have come at a worse moment for the navy, faced as it was with the threat of limitations and a Congress increasingly loath to make generous appropriations. This was not the time to have its reason for existence questioned.[23] Fearing popular acceptance of Mitchell's claim that, given the opportunity, bombers could sink any battleship afloat, the navy arranged a series of tests to determine the amount of punishment that could be absorbed by warships.

The most spectacular test took place in July 1921, when the old German dreadnought *Ostfriesland*, a 22,500-ton survivor of the Battle of Jutland, was towed out beyond the Virginia Capes to be a target. Much to the satisfaction of the navy, she survived two days of intensive bombing attacks. Finally, on July 21, Mitchell led over the ship a formation of seven twin-engined Martin bombers, each carrying a massive, specially designed, 2,000-pound bomb. The first bomb was a near miss. "Up came a spout of water, more than any geyser, more than any missile made by man had ever produced," declared Mitchell. "Three thousand feet above we felt the rush of air as it 'bumped' the wings of our planes." Five more bombs rained down on the *Ostfriesland* in quick succession, and amid a series of direct hits and near misses, her bow rose from the sea like a stricken thing. Assistant Secretary of War Benedict Crowell reported that some naval officers had tears in their eyes as they watched her capsize and sink.[24]

Officially, the navy was less impressed. It pointed out that the anchored ship was a sitting duck, the bombers knew her exact position, the weather and visibility were good, she could not return antiaircraft fire, and had no fighter cover or damage-control parties to work on her between raids. Three years later, the battleship *Washington*, which had been ordered scrapped under the Washington treaty, survived bombing and internal and underwater explosions designed to simulate the effect of bomb and torpedo hits, and had to be finished off by the 14-inch guns of the *Texas*.

The immediate response to the sinking of the *Ostfriesland* was not support for Mitchell's demand for an independent air force but advancement of the cause of naval aviation. "The lesson is that we must put planes on battleships and get aircraft carriers quickly," declared Rear Admiral William A. Moffett, an articulate spokesman for naval air power. The Bureau of Aeronautics was created on August 10, 1921, the first new bureau since the Civil War, and Moffett was named its chief.[25] The partially completed 33,000-ton battle cruisers *Lexington* and *Saratoga*, scheduled for scrapping under the terms of the Washington treaty, were converted into aircraft carriers and commissioned in 1927. The 14,500-ton *Ranger*, the navy's first ship designed and built as a carrier, was authorized that same year.

Even before the carriers became operational, the navy began experimenting with equipment, tactics, and procedures for the use of aircraft at sea. Dissatisfied with the arresting gear used by the British to brake airplanes landing on their carriers, Lieutenant A. M. Pride modified the wires and weights first used by Eugene Ely when he landed on the *Pennsylvania* in 1911 and developed a system that became standard on all carriers. American crews also learned how to crowd aircraft into their ships, and U. S. carriers have traditionally carried more planes than those of other nations. Some procedures were discovered by chance. Commander Kenneth Whiting, the executive officer of the *Langley*, once waved his cap over his head to signal a pilot that his landing approach was too steep. Recognizing that a man on the flight deck could better gauge the speed and angle of an aircraft than could its pilot, the navy created the billet of landing signal officer. Speed in launching and recovering planes was vital, and by constant drilling the *Langley*'s flight-deck crew had the takeoff interval between planes down to fifteen seconds and the landing interval to ninety seconds in 1926.[26] Brightly painted to make them visible when forced down at sea, the aircraft that flew from the "Lady Lex" and "Sister Sara"—Boeing F4Bs, Curtiss Helldivers, and Curtiss Hawks—were among the most graceful planes ever produced. Their highly skilled pilots were qualified to fly fighters, scout bombers, and dive bombers because the navy could not afford to train large numbers of specialists.

Although more convinced of the usefulness of aircraft than they had been, the battleship admirals—members in good standing of the "Gun Club" that dominated the navy—decreed that the primary task of the carrier should be to provide an aerial umbrella for their ships, and they insisted that the flattops be tied to the battle line. Others saw the carrier as an offensive rather than a defensive weapon. During the 1929 maneuvers off Panama, known as Fleet Problem IX, Rear Admiral Joseph M. Reeves was given permission by Admiral William V. Pratt, commander of the fleet, to experiment with offensive tactics. Breaking away from the main attacking force with the *Saratoga*, Reeves launched his sixty-six planes against the Panama Canal. Surprise was complete. Most of the defending aircraft were caught on the ground and two of the waterway's locks were theoretically destroyed. This experiment led eventually to the creation of the fast carrier task force. Three years later, planes from the *Lexington* and *Saratoga*, under the command of Rear Admiral Harry E. Yarnell, swept in from the sea one misty Sunday morning and launched a highly successful surprise "attack" on Pearl Harbor—an operation of intense interest to the Japanese.[27]

Under Admiral Moffett's enthusiastic direction, the navy also took an interest in the development of lighter-than-air craft. During World War I, blimps had been used with considerable success in antisubmarine warfare, and Moffett was interested in the possible uses of rigid lighter-than-air craft, or dirigibles, which were considerably larger than blimps. During the war, the German navy had used zeppelins for scouting and bombing missions with mixed results. One similar airship was acquired from Germany and three bigger ones were built in this country. The German-built *Los Angeles* remained in commission for eight years, often participating in fleet exercises. The three others, the *Shenandoah, Akron,* and *Macon,* were all lost on active service with heavy loss of life. Moffett himself was killed in the spectacular crash of the *Akron* in 1933.[28] His successor as chief of the Bureau of Aeronautics was Rear Admiral Ernest J. King, a combative, no-nonsense sailor who learned to fly at the age of forty-seven.

If the battleship admirals disliked the airplane, they positively detested the submarine—possibly because it was too vivid a reminder of the vulnerability of their beloved dreadnoughts. They disdained the strategy of commerce raiding, or *guerre de course,* despite the near-fatal success of the German U-boats during the previous war. Like British and Japanese admirals, they viewed the submarine as the weapon of the weak, not the strong. Besides, it was believed that aroused world opinion would never permit a return to the brutalities of unrestricted submarine warfare. If it did not, the conventional wisdom held that the introduction of convoys and later, Asdic or sonar, a system for detecting objects beneath the surface of the sea, had eliminated the submarine menace.

No effort was made to prepare for a war against commerce or to protect the nation's own maritime trade against underseas attack. Submarines were deployed as scouts and to protect the battle line in the annual war games. "Enemy" submarine captains who charged toward the battleships to make close-in attacks were branded as "reckless" violators of doctrine, and their fitness reports were damningly marked to reflect the stigma.

While the navy was evolving the theory and practice of carrier warfare, the Marine Corps was evolving the techniques of amphibious assault that were of vital importance in World War II. Following the disastrous failure of the British landing at the Dardanelles in 1915, military experts regarded any attack that included a landing on a hostile beach as doomed to defeat. But as early as 1921, Major Earl H. Ellis suggested that, in case of war, Marine Corps striking forces be used to seize advance bases in the Pacific from the Japanese. Landing exercises were held in the Caribbean and on the beaches of Hawaii. The "Good Neighbor" policy, which President Franklin D. Roosevelt announced upon his inauguration in 1933, meant that the marines would no longer be involved in "banana wars" in the Caribbean and Central America, and the Fleet Marine Force was organized that year. Thus, for the first time, sizeable numbers of marines were available for attachment to the fleet and could be used as amphibious forces.

Over the next eight years, navy and marine officers at the Marine Corps Schools at Quantico, Virginia, studied the failed landing at Gallipoli with the same avidity that the admirals gave to the duel between battleships at Jutland in

1916. Was the operation foredoomed or had there been a possibility of success? Gallipoli's failures and mistakes were minutely examined and the analysts found that despite appalling lapses in everything from security to leadership, the operation might have been a success had the planning been better.

Next, they examined every aspect of the problem of amphibious assault including organization, command and communications procedures, air and naval gunfire support, ship-to-shore movement, securing of the beachhead, and logistics. Fleet exercises in the Caribbean and off Panama as well as extensive staff work went into the creation of a comprehensive new amphibious doctrine that culminated in a landing manual produced in 1934. It was adopted almost without change by the army in 1941.

The key to an effective amphibious assault, however, was the development of suitable landing craft. The navy was still using standard ship's boats in amphibious exercises, boats that were built for seawater under the keel rather than the sand and surf of Pacific beaches. Some of those still in use in the 1930s had participated in the landings in Cuba in 1898. The marines had a difficult time convincing the Bureau of Ships to provide them with new landing craft. Lieutenant General Victor H. Krulak, later a Marine Corps commandant, related that while he was a young officer in China in 1939, he witnessed a Japanese beach landing. They had "a powerful, diesel-powered, 40–45 foot, ramp-bow boat," he related. "I took a lot of pictures of it and wrote a report and sent it back to Washington. . . . It got no consideration at all. When I got back to Washington, I went to the Bureau of Ships, and checked with them, and they finally found the report. And some fellow had written, had scribbled across it, 'this came from some nut out in China.' "

In 1936, the marines began testing a shallow draft "Eureka" boat developed by Andrew Jackson Higgins, a New Orleans boat builder, for use as a landing craft. Originally built for trappers and oil drillers in the Louisiana bayous, it had a "spoonbill" bow that enabled it to run up onto river banks and then back off and a tunnel stern that protected the propeller. Despite the craft's flat bottom, it was highly seaworthy. Although the marines wanted the Higgins boat, the Bureau of Ships turned it down several times, preferring an inferior craft from a long-favored East Coast builder. It was not until 1940 that the bureau finally recognized the superiority of the Higgins boat.

Krulak also showed Higgins the pictures of the ramped boat he had seen in China and suggested he try to produce his own version. Higgins cut away the bow of one of his original boats and replaced it with a ramp. It became the Landing Craft, Vehicle, Personal, or LCVP, which saw service in almost every theater of World War II. Amphibious tractors—or "amtracs"—capable of carrying troops and supplies over coral reefs and onto beaches were also developed just before the outbreak of the war. These experiments were not without their lighter moments: one of the first "amtracs" bogged down in the mud flats near Quantico with a full load of high-ranking officers.[29]

With the nation reeling under the impact of the Great Depression, President Hoover slashed government spending, and the navy was forced to trim manpower, lay up ships, reduce operations, place yards in caretaker status, and accept a 15 per cent cut in pay. Men were released on "furlough" without pay and only part of the Naval Academy class of 1933 was commissioned. Some officers doubted that the fleet, most of which dated from World War I, could be kept operative for very long under these conditions. Consequently, the election of Franklin Roosevelt, a former assistant secretary of the navy, to the presidency in 1932 was greeted by naval officers with relief and expectation. It was hoped that, as president, he would quickly take steps to brighten the gloomy picture.[30]

In the almost revolutionary first "hundred days" of his administration, Roosevelt earmarked for warship construction $238 million of the emergency relief funds provided by the National Industrial Recovery Act to put men back to work. Naval and private shipyards that had been all but abandoned again resounded to the clatter of rivet guns, as work began on thirty-two new ships, including the 20,000-ton aircraft carriers *Yorktown* and *Enterprise*, four cruisers, four submarines, two gunboats, and twenty destroyers, the first since the "four-pipers" of World War I vintage.[31]

To this was added a long-range building program sponsored the following year by Representative Carl Vinson, chairman of the House Naval Affairs Committee. The Vinson-Trammell Act authorized no less than 102 new ships by 1942.[32] Roosevelt was unhappy to learn, on taking office, that the U. S. Navy was considerably inferior to the Japanese navy in readiness, and the Vinson-Trammell Act was intended to build it up to the levels permitted by the naval-limitations treaties. Paradoxically, the buildup began just as the entire system of arms limitations was coming apart at the seams.

In 1931, Japan took the first step on the path that led to the Second World War. A reactionary military autocracy centered in the army and supported by fanatic nationalist associations had become convinced that the liberal ministries of the 1920s had betrayed the nation. Through a campaign of political terrorism and assassination, this faction gained predominant influence in the government and immediately set about establishing a new order in Eastern Asia under the political and economic domination of Japan. This campaign began with the seizure of Manchuria from China. Secretary of State Henry L. Stimson, restrained by President Hoover's reluctance to take overt action, tried to persuade Britain and France to join the United States in applying diplomatic pressure on Japan to withdraw from Manchuria, but nothing was done.

The unbridled Japanese gave the required two-year notice in 1934 of their intention to end their adherence to the agreements on naval limitations. The 5:5:3 ratio, said one Japanese official, sounded "to Japanese ears like Rolls-Royce: Rolls-Royce: Ford."[33] With both Japan and Fascist Italy, which had also adopted an expansionist foreign policy, refusing to participate, further attempts to limit naval armaments collapsed. In a shroud of secrecy, the Japanese began a massive program of warship construction, and in 1937, laid down the largest dreadnoughts ever built, the 68,200-ton *Yamato* and *Musashi,* which mounted nine 18.1-inch guns. That same year, the United States, not knowing that the Japanese were building these giants and itself abiding by the Washington treaty limitations, began work on two 35,000-tonners, the *North Carolina* and *Washington,* armed with nine 16-inch guns. These ships, although smaller than the Japanese giants, had an excellent combination of speed, protection, and fire-power.[34]

Ignoring international opinion, which had proven completely ineffective in halting either the Italian conquest of helpless Ethiopia or their own aggression in Manchuria, the Japanese launched an all-out invasion of China in 1937. Foreigners were not immune to attack. On December 12, 1937, Japanese planes bombed and strafed the American gunboat *Panay* in the Yangtze River and sank her with the loss of two crewmen and one civilian passenger. The Japanese Foreign Ministry apologized, attributing the sinking to a mistake by an over-zealous officer.

Tension was also mounting in Europe, where Adolf Hitler had come to power in Germany in 1933. With the intention of reversing his country's defeat in World War I and seizing control of Europe, he had rebuilt the German war machine. The Anglo-German Naval Agreement of June 1935 released Germany from the limitations imposed on her navy by the Treaty of Versailles—which had already been renounced by Hitler, anyway. It permitted Germany to rebuild her surface navy until it reached 35 per cent of the tonnage possessed by Britain and her Commonwealth. Despite Britain's narrow escape from defeat at the hands of the U-boats during World War I, Germany was to be allowed up to 45 per cent of British tonnage in submarines. An escape clause permitted the Germans to match Britain's submarine fleet after due notice had been given. Luckily, Hitler was a land-bound strategist and neglected submarine construction. When war broke out on September 3, 1939, Germany had only forty-three combat-ready U-boats and was producing no more than four a month. "A realistic policy would have given Germany a thousand U-boats at the beginning," said Admiral Karl Dönitz, chief of the German submarine force, after the war.[35]

In 1939 the American people were not neutral, as they had been in 1914. Together with President Roosevelt, they sympathized with the democracies in their struggle against dictatorship but were nevertheless wary of again being drawn into a European conflict. Shortly after the beginning of hostilities, the Neutrality Act of 1937 was modified to reflect these sentiments: the belligerents, which meant the Allies because Germany was again blockaded, were permitted to buy arms in the United States on a cash-and-carry basis. To prevent history from repeating itself, the U. S. government forbade American-flag ships to enter the war zone and Americans to sail in belligerent vessels. A neutrality patrol consisting of the old battleships *New York, Texas, Arkansas,* and *Wyoming,* the carrier *Ranger,* and a handful of cruisers and destroyers was organized to keep track of warships operating within 300 miles of the coast of the Americas.[36]

France, overwhelmed by the swift sword of the German blitzkrieg, collapsed in the summer of 1940, creating a crisis for the United States. Britain now stood alone against the full fury of the Nazi onslaught. Sooner than many other Americans, Roosevelt sensed the danger that the United States would face, should Britain fall. With the Royal Navy dominant in the Atlantic, the U. S. Navy had since 1922 been free to deploy its strongest units to the Pacific in readiness to deal with any threat from the Japanese. If Britain went under, the United States would be forced either to fight a two-ocean war without allies or to kowtow to the Nazis and Japanese. To keep Britain in the fight, the president decided to give her all assistance "short of war." The navy played a vital role in carrying out this policy—and for eighteen months provided the shield for the mobilization of America's resources and of her will to fight.

Three days after the German army entered Paris, Admiral Harold R. Stark, the chief of naval operations, went up to Capitol Hill with a request for $4 billion for a "two-ocean" navy. The appropriation, which was quickly approved, provided for a 70 per cent increase in the size of the fleet, or 257 additional ships, including several large, fast battleships and twenty-seven *Essex*-class carriers. But it would take time to build these ships—"dollars cannot buy yesterday" is the way Admiral Stark put it—and Britain was on the ropes.[37] German U-boats operating from the Atlantic coast of France were ripping the heart out of convoys and the British were short of escort craft. Prime Minister Winston Churchill urgently requested Roosevelt to let the Royal Navy have fifty of the old four-piper destroyers that were being overhauled for patrol duty. "Mr. President, with great respect," pleaded Churchill, "I must tell you that . . . this is a thing to do *now.*" In September 1940, by executive order, the ships were made available to the British in exchange for ninety-nine-year leases on a chain of air and sea bases extending from the coast of Canada to the Caribbean. The Royal Navy found the old ships, which rolled in any kind of sea, cantankerous and had some difficulty in getting accustomed to them. One sailor, used to sleeping in a hammock rather than a bunk, complained: "It's like lying on a bloody sack of jelly."[38]

Once he had been safely elected to a third term, Roosevelt sought new ways to help bombed, besieged, and nearly bankrupt Britain. In March 1941, the Lend-Lease Act was approved by Congress after a bitter fight by those who feared it was the president's intention to embroil the United States in the war by easy stages. Ending the "cash-and-carry" provisions of the Neutrality Act, this law permitted the lending of arms, munitions, and supplies to those nations "whose defense the President deems vital to the defense of the United States." The Lend-Lease Act marked the end of the fiction of neutrality and the beginning of an undeclared war on Germany. Hitler, who was preparing to unleash an attack on his ally, the Soviet Union, ignored these unneutral acts. The mistake made by the rulers of Imperial Germany in antagonizing the United States and the decisive effect that American intervention had on the outcome of World War I were in the forefront of his mind.[39]

The Germans, however, stepped up their attacks on convoys bound for Britain. Instead of operating independently, as in the previous war, the U-boats fanned out in wolf packs of from eight to twenty boats directed by radio from Admiral Dönitz's headquarters, which kept track of all convoys. They usually made their attacks at night while on the surface, where they could attain higher speeds, and then dived in the confusion. As soon as the escort had called off its search for them, they would renew their attack. Sometimes, harrowing convoy battles raged across the Atlantic for night after night and the sky was lit by flaming oil tankers. During the first half of 1941, 756 British merchantmen were sunk and another 1,450 were damaged. Had this toll continued unabated, the losses would have reached a phenomenal seven million tons for the year, double the combined capacity of American and British shipyards.[40]

"We cannot allow our goods to be sunk in the Atlantic," declared Frank Knox, the secretary of the navy. "We must make good our promise to Britain." An Atlantic Fleet, constructed around the nucleus of the old neutrality patrol and under the command of Admiral Ernest J. King, was given the task of escorting convoys as far as Iceland, which, along with Greenland, had been occupied by the Americans to prevent their seizure by the Germans. Despite increasing tension with Japan, Admiral Stark, convinced that the situation in the Atlantic was "critical," sent the battleships *Idaho, Mississippi,* and *New Mexico,* the carrier *Yorktown,* four light cruisers, and two destroyer squadrons from the Pacific to reinforce King's fleet. Seventeen naval aviators were assigned as "pilot-advisers" to fly American-built PBY Catalina patrol planes with British Coastal Command squadrons. One of them, Ensign Leonard B. Smith, found the German battleship *Bismarck,* which had dropped out of sight in the Atlantic after sinking the British battle cruiser *Hood* in the Denmark Strait, and summoned to the spot the Royal Navy ships and planes that ultimately sent her to the bottom.[41]

Most of the dangerous and unrewarding job of escorting convoys to Iceland was performed by four-pipers and modern 1,700-ton destroyers. In this twilight period between peace and war, the escorts were under orders to refrain from attacking German vessels but to signal the presence of any unfriendly craft they sighted. Thereafter, it was up to the British to get to the scene in time to make the kill. Although the Naval Academy class of 1941 was speeded up to graduate in January instead of June, reserves were called to active duty, and boot camps were absorbing 5,000 men a month, the fleet was shorthanded. The majority of crews were inexperienced and often younger than their ships, some of them getting their training in antisubmarine warfare while on escort duty. As always, the sea was an enemy. Wirt Williams, a novelist, later wrote:

The days ground you with dull and unvarying cruelty. The watches on the bridge struck as inexorably as the bells of a clock. Half your life you spent on the bridge; no night passed but that the hard hand on your shoulder and the malevolent light in your face jerked you from sleep made troubled and uneasy by the tossing of that steel shell that encased you and with whose destiny yours was so irrevocably welded. And the clanging call of the general alarm rasped you to battle stations, night and day, from sleep and from meals, always with the same emptyhandedness of failure in the end. . . .[42]

The shooting war began for the Atlantic Fleet on September 4, 1941. After being tracked for three hours by the old destroyer *Greer,* a U-boat skipper, obviously weary of the game of hide-and-seek, aimed a torpedo at his tormentor. It missed, and the *Greer* dropped a pattern of depth charges. Spotting another torpedo coming her way, she evaded this one, too, but she lost contact with her quarry. Little more than a month later, a convoy being escorted by the modern destroyer *Kearny* came under heavy night attack by a wolf pack. Silhouetted against a burning merchantman, the *Kearny* was struck amidships by a torpedo and badly damaged, but she managed to limp into port with eleven dead within her shattered hull. The *Reuben James* was next. Just after dawn on October 31, 1941, the four-piper was hit by a torpedo forward of her No. I stack. Perhaps because the explosion touched off a magazine, the old ship broke in half, her bow section sinking immediately and her after part going down within five minutes. Only 45 of her crew of about 160 men were pulled from the icy water. With no time to mourn its dead, the navy girded for war in the Atlantic—but it erupted instead in the Pacific.[43]

Bogged down and being drained of resources by the continued resistance of the Chinese, Japan looked southward to the oil and mineral wealth of Southeast Asia and the Dutch East Indies. The summer of 1941 seemed favorable for such a move. Britain was fighting desperately to defend the Suez Canal, German armies were rolling across the plains of Russia, and the attention of the United States was fixed on the grim events unfolding in the Atlantic. In fact, under the ABC- 1 Plan worked out by the ranking military and naval officers of the United States, Britain, and Canada in March 1941, it was agreed that the defeat of Germany would have the highest priority in case the United States became involved in a two-ocean war. All other theaters would be secondary. This plan established the "Europe first" strategy that governed Allied operations throughout the war.[44]

The Japanese began their drive to the south by occupying Indo-China in July 1941, with the acquiescence of the hapless Vichy regime then in control of defeated France. When its demand that the Japanese withdraw immediately was refused, the American government froze Japanese assets in this country and tightened an existing embargo on the shipment to Japan of oil and scrap metal—

materials vital to the Japanese military machine. The United States and Japan had moved to the brink of war.[45]

The basic Japanese strategy, which was devised by the chief of the navy's general staff, Admiral Osami Nagano, was to head for the Dutch East Indies, striking at American bases in the Philippines en route, and then fend off a counterattack by the U. S. Pacific Fleet. Submarines and aircraft would harass this fleet as it moved through the Marshalls and Carolines, and the survivors would be destroyed in a battle in Japanese-controlled waters. That strategy might have worked, but in 1941 Admiral Isoroku Yamamoto, the commander in chief of the Combined Fleet, came up with a much more daring plan. He proposed a surprise carrier strike on the Pacific Fleet as it lay at Pearl Harbor, similar to the one launched by Harry Yarnell during the fleet exercises of 1932. There was ample precedent for such an attack. Japan had struck both China and Russia before hostilities had been declared and had done well in both cases.

Yamamoto recommended launching an attack while Japan had a larger navy in the Pacific than did the United States—ten battleships and ten carriers to nine battleships and three carriers. "If we are to have war with America," he said, "we will have no hope of winning unless the U. S. fleet in Hawaiian waters can be destroyed." With the Pacific Fleet knocked out, Japan would be able to seize the Philippines, Malaya, and the Dutch Indies without interference. Once she had secured these territories, she would establish a defense line extending southward from the Kurile Islands, through the Marshalls, and along the fringes of Malaysia to the Burmese-Indian border. Using interior lines of communication and supply, the Imperial Navy would be able to beat back attacks on this barrier until the Western nations, weary of fighting a two-ocean war and suffering heavy losses, would be forced to accept Japan's conquests and the establishment of a "Greater East Asia Co-Prosperity Sphere."[46]

Guarded by a pair of fast battleships, six carriers, crammed with 425 planes and the most experienced air crews in the Japanese navy, slipped into the thick fog of the North Pacific on November 26, 1941. As they moved ghostlike toward Oahu the final scenes in a diplomatic shadow play were being acted out in Washington where a special Japanese envoy, Saburo Kurusu, was trying to negotiate a last-minute settlement of differences with the United States. Ominous reports of Japanese troop movements along the coast of Southeast Asia filtered into Washington, however, and on November 27, a "war warning" was sent to Admiral Husband E. Kimmel, commander of the Pacific Fleet. "An aggressive move by Japan is expected within the next few days" against the Philippines, or Thailand, or Borneo, the message read. Believing no attack was planned on Pearl Harbor, Kimmel did not put his fleet on full alert.[47]

Eight battleships were at Pearl Harbor, seven of them moored in Battleship Row, along the east side of Ford Island. The flagship *Pennsylvania* was in dry dock. None of the three carriers was in port. The *Lexington* and *Enterprise* were ferrying planes to Wake and Midway islands and the *Saratoga* was undergoing repair on the West Coast. Early on the morning of December 7—a Sunday—American cryptologists who had broken the Japanese diplomatic code learned that the Japanese ambassador to Washington Admiral Kichisaburo Nomura, and Kurusu had been instructed to seek a meeting with Secretary of State Cordell Hull at one o'clock that afternoon—7:30 A.M. Pearl Harbor time.

At about the time this message was being decoded, the Japanese carrier force, having penetrated to within 230 miles of Oahu without being discovered, turned into the wind to launch its planes. With the *Akagi,* flagship of Vice Admiral Chuichi Nagumo, flying the flag flown by Admiral Heihachiro Togo at Tsushima in 1905, the first wave of 183 bombers, torpedo planes, and fighters roared off the pitching decks of the carriers and headed south.[48]

Shortly after 7:00 A.M., Private Joseph Lockard, a radar operator on Oahu detected a swarm of aircraft coming in from the northeast. His superiors took it to be an expected flight of B-17 Flying Fortresses from the West Coast. A report from the destroyer *Ward* that at 4:00 A.M. she had made contact with an unidentified submarine and had depth-charged it was delayed in transit to Admiral Kimmel's headquarters. "Pearl Harbor was still asleep in the morning mist," reported one of the Japanese flight leaders. "It was calm and serene inside the harbor, not even a trace of smoke arising from the ships at Oahu. The orderly groups of barracks, the wiggling white line of automobiles climbing up to the mountaintop; fine objectives of attack lay in all directions. . . ."[49]

The ninety-four ships in the harbor were just coming to life. Many officers and men were ashore on weekend liberty and a good number of those on board had slept late and were having breakfast. Some had found a quiet place for the Sunday ritual of reading the comics or for writing Christmas cards to the folks back home, and awnings were being rigged for church services. Only a few of the fleet's antiaircraft guns were manned and ammunition was locked up.

In the *Nevada,* at the tail end of Battleship Row, Ensign Joseph K. Taussig, Jr., was worried as the hour crept towards eight o'clock. As officer of the deck, he was responsible for raising the colors, but he had never handled this duty before and was not sure which size flag should be used. He sent a man over to the next ship in line, the *Arizona,* to find out what size she was using. As the *Nevada's* band and marine guard lined up on the fantail at 7:55, they idly noted a line of aircraft coming in from over the mountains behind the base. Suddenly, the planes swooped down on the air station on Ford Island and the sound of explosions was heard. At eight o'clock the band automatically crashed into the national anthem. Midway in the ceremony, one of the attacking planes, having let go a torpedo, pulled away over the *Nevada,* spraying her afterdeck with machine-gun fire. The flag that had just been raised was cut to ribbons, but the color party remained rooted to the spot until the band had sounded the last note. "Air raid! This is no drill!" Taussig repeatedly shouted into the public-address system. "Air raid! This is no drill!"[50]

Men raced to their battle stations. Keys to some of the ammunition boxes had been taken ashore by officers on liberty, others could not be found. Enemy planes were ripping the ships with gunfire, trying to wipe out the crews before they could get into action. An eternity seemed to pass before the locks were broken and the guns began an irregular fire. In the destroyer *Monaghan,* Boatswain's Mate Thomas Donahue threw several monkey wrenches at low-flying planes, as he waited for ammunition for his 5-inch gun. Asked what he needed, he replied: "Powder! I can't keep throwing things at them!"[51]

Airfields scattered around Oahu were the first targets of the Japanese. Lined up wing-to-wing as if for inspection—it was easier to guard them from sabotage this way—dozens of army, navy, and marine aircraft were caught on the ground and blasted into twisted piles of scrap metal. Some men fought back with machine guns salvaged from their wrecked planes, but to little avail. As soon as the airfields had been knocked out, Kate torpedo planes and Val dive bombers swept in from several directions and concentrated on the battleships. So complete were Japanese preparations for the attack that their highly effective "long lance" torpedoes had been fitted with special wooden fins to make them run true in the shallow waters of Pearl Harbor, and their pilots had charts showing exactly where each U. S. battleship was.

Zooming in at little more than forty feet above the water, the Kates dropped their torpedoes with devastating precision. Every one of the outboard ships was hit several times. The *Arizona* was moored inboard of the repair ship *Vestal* but projected so far beyond her that she took a torpedo hit just under her forward turret. An armor-piercing bomb—in reality a 16-inch shell with fins—smashed through her steel deck and touched off a magazine before it could be flooded. Huge chunks of the *Arizona* were hurled hundreds of feet into the air. Broken in half and swept by towering flames, she became a tomb for nearly 1,100 of her officers and men. The *West Virginia,* a gash 120 feet long and 15 feet wide torn in her port side by six or seven torpedoes, was taking on great amounts of water. Counterflooding saved her from capsizing and she settled into the mud. The *Oklahoma* was struck by a spread of three torpedoes and immediately began to roll over. The capsizing ship was hit by two more torpedoes and turned turtle, stopping only when her masts struck bottom. Crawling to safety on her barnacle-encrusted keel, her men were strafed by the Zero fighters that followed up the torpedo planes and bombers. Two torpedoes hit the *California* but she was saved from capsizing by the superhuman efforts of her damage-control crews.

The battleships *Maryland, Tennessee,* and *Pennsylvania* escaped serious damage but were unable to get to sea, the first two being wedged in by sinking ships and the flagship being in dry dock. The *Nevada* was the only battleship to get under way. Her topside a shambles and taking on water from a torpedo hit in her bow, she backed out of the flaming oil that was spewing from the shattered *Arizona* and through columns of oily, black smoke made her way toward the harbor mouth. Hoping to sink her in the channel, wave after wave of Japanese dive bombers attacked her, but she survived by throwing up a heavy barrage of antiaircraft fire. She was too badly damaged to maintain way, however, and was run aground.

For nearly two hours, until 9:45, successive waves of Japanese planes had the skies over Pearl Harbor to themselves. In all, 343 planes participated in the attack. By the time they returned to their waiting carriers, the harbor was dotted with the wreckage of nineteen ships, including almost the entire battle line of the Pacific Fleet. An estimated 265 aircraft had also been lost, most of them on the ground. American casualties totalled 2,403 dead and 1,178 wounded; the Japanese lost 29 planes and 55 airmen.[52]

Pearl Harbor is the worst disaster in the history of the U. S. Navy, and as President Roosevelt said, December 7, 1941 is "a date which will live in infamy." Nevertheless, the Japanese success was only temporary. Except for the *Arizona,* all the battleships were raised from the mud of Pearl Harbor, and all but the *Oklahoma* returned to action. The Japanese made a mistake in not destroying the oil tanks and shops at Pearl Harbor, which were vital to continued American naval operations. Even more important, the U. S. aircraft carriers escaped the attack and became the spearhead of the navy's offensive against Japan.[53] But the biggest mistake made by the Japanese was that they unified the nation in a war against Japan. The shock and anger of Pearl Harbor created the mightiest navy the world has ever seen.

9
"THE WAY TO VICTORY"

Victory at all costs, victory in spite of all terror, victory however long and hard the road may be; for without victory there is no survival.

—Winston Churchill
(To the House of Commons, 13 May 1940)

Swooping in under low rain clouds, a navy flying boat landed on the oil-covered waters of Pearl Harbor early on Christmas morning 1941 and taxied to a halt. A whaleboat came alongside and took off a ruddy man in civilian clothes who had an unmistakable air of authority about him. Admiral Chester W. Nimitz had arrived to take up his duties as commander in chief of the U. S. Pacific Fleet. Even though he had studied reports of the devastation inflicted by the Japanese eighteen days before, the admiral was shaken by the scene that met his eyes. The anchorage was dominated by one of the sunken *Arizona*'s tilted tripod masts and by the capsized hull of the *Oklahoma*, looking like a giant whale that had tried to beach itself. Small boats moved slowly about, retrieving the bloated bodies of sailors and marines. "This is a terrible sight," the admiral remarked to no one in particular.[1]

On December 7, Nimitz, a rear admiral and chief of the Bureau of Navigation, and his wife were enjoying a radio broadcast of the New York Philharmonic Orchestra when news of the Japanese attack was flashed to the world. He rushed to the Navy Department only to find that the war plans he wanted to consult were stowed in a safe with a time lock that would not be released until Monday morning. It made no difference, however, because with most of the battle fleet resting in the mud of Pearl Harbor, none of the plans the navy had so carefully prepared for the eventuality of war with Japan had any relevance.[2]

Like a dark stain spreading over the sea, the Japanese widened their control over East Asia and the Pacific with a rapidity that astounded even themselves. Within a few weeks of the attack on Pearl Harbor, they invaded the Philippines, captured Guam and Wake Island, the latter despite spirited resistance from a

213

small marine detachment, seized control of Thailand, took Hong Kong, and were threatening Singapore and the Dutch East Indies.

To revitalize the navy and restore confidence, President Roosevelt shook up the top command. Admiral Ernest J. King, commander in chief of the Atlantic Fleet, was named to the newly created post of commander in chief, U. S. Fleet, which was separated from an actual fleet command, and the job of chief of naval operations was added to it, making him the navy's ranking officer. Few men had King's breadth of experience, for he had been an aviator, a submariner, a staff officer, a bureau chief, and a member of the General Board.

Nimitz was raised over the heads of twenty-eight seniors to be appointed commander in chief of the Pacific Fleet in place of Admiral Husband E. Kimmel, who was saddled with a large part of the blame for the debacle at Pearl Harbor. When a spent bullet struck him on the chest during the attack, Kimmel commented, "Too bad it didn't kill me."

Two more dissimilar men than King and Nimitz could not have been chosen. Samuel Eliot Morison describes the sixty-three-year-old King as "a hard man with little sense of humor . . . more respected than liked in the Navy," and Nimitz, seven years his junior, as "the most accessible, considerate and beloved of fleet commanders." A story current in the navy was that when Admiral King went to his heavenly reward, a naval officer who followed him was told by St. Peter that the place had been reorganized and placed on "combat readiness" since the admiral's arrival. "I'm not surprised," replied the officer. "Ernie King always thought he was God Almighty." St. Peter shook his head. "That's not our trouble. It's far worse. God Almighty thinks he's Ernie King."[3]

Despite the great contrast in their personalities and the distance between them—King was in Washington and Nimitz at Pearl Harbor—they complemented each other and together devised the strategy that brought Imperial Japan to her knees. Admiral King's first statement as commander in chief of the U. S. fleet was forceful:

> The way to victory is long. The going will be hard. We will do the best we can with what we've got. We must have more planes and ships—at once. Then it will be our turn to strike. We will win through—in time.

"In time." These were the key words in King's statement. As a new year began, an American offensive in the Pacific seemed a long time in the future. It would take time to repair the vessels crippled at Pearl Harbor, to build enough ships, manufacture enough planes, and train enough seagoing officers, pilots, and men to overcome Japan's superiority. And with the navy committed to fighting a two-ocean war—the campaign against the U-boats in the Atlantic having been formalized by a German declaration of war after Pearl Harbor—it appeared that the Japanese had won sufficient time to strengthen their defense perimeter and, by use of interior lines of communication, make it impregnable to the American onslaught that would one day come. The "Europe first" strategy agreed upon by the Allies in the ABC-1 Plan of 1941 called for full concentration on the early defeat of Germany before mounting an attack on the Japanese. In the meantime, the navy's task was to hold a line running from Midway to Samoa to Fiji to Australia by what Admiral King called "defensive-offensive" operations—"hold what you've got and hit them where you can."[4]

Nimitz ordered carrier strikes against advanced Japanese bases in the Gilbert and Marshall islands. On February 1, 1942, aircraft from a carrier task force led by the pugnacious Vice Admiral William F. Halsey, Jr., who flew his flag in the *Enterprise*, raided Kwajalein in the Marshalls, sinking a transport and two other vessels and damaging eight smaller craft. Attacks were launched on Wake and Marcus islands, and a carrier task force built around the *Lexington* attacked the newly seized Japanese base at Rabaul, on New Britain, in the Bismarck Archipelago, to the northeast of Australia. Japanese planes tried to interfere and in the ensuing battle on February 21, Lieutenant Edward H. O'Hare shot down five of the enemy, becoming the navy's first ace of World War II.

The most spectacular of these raids occurred on April 18, when sixteen twin-engined B-25 bombers were coaxed from the flight deck of the *Hornet* and headed for Tokyo, 668 miles away. Army bombers were chosen for this mission because no navy plane had sufficient range. The army pilots, under the command of Lieutenant Colonel James H. Doolittle, a pioneer speed and test pilot, had been specially trained in short takeoffs but not in deck landings. When their mission had been accomplished, they were to fly to airfields in China, another 1,100 miles away. Halsey, whose task force had met the *Hornet* at sea, looked down on the launching operation from the bridge of the *Enterprise* and later described the tense minutes of the takeoff:

> The wind and sea were so strong that morning that green water was breaking over the carriers' ramps. Jimmy led his squadron off. When his plane buzzed down the *Hornet*'s deck at 0725, there wasn't a man topside who didn't help sweat him into the air. One pilot hung on the brink of a stall until we nearly catalogued his effects. . . .[5]

Doolittle's raiders achieved complete surprise, but the damage they did— like that in most of the early raids—was small compared to that inflicted by the Japanese at Pearl Harbor. Nevertheless, these operations provided a much-needed shot in the arm for American morale, kept the enemy off balance, and served as valuable tests of fast carrier tactics.

Following the Japanese invasion of the Philippines in December 1941, Admiral Thomas C. Hart's Asiatic Fleet, deprived of its bases, withdrew south-ward to bolster the defense of the Dutch East Indies, in accordance with previous plans. The admiral, a veteran of forty years' service, had been kept on beyond his retirement date because of his experience and competence. He was appointed commander of the ABDA (American-British-Dutch-Australian) fleet, which was based on Batavia and Soerabaja and consisted of nine cruisers, including the *Houston, Boise*, and *Marblehead*, twenty-six destroyers, and thirty-nine submarines. The British battleship *Prince of Wales* and battle cruiser *Repulse*, which would have made this a powerful force, had been sunk by torpedo planes off Malaya on December 10, 1941, and a British carrier, the *Indomitable*, which had been assigned to join it, had run aground in the West Indies. Before this motley Allied group had time to do much about coordinating differences of communications, language, gunnery, and tactics, it was forced to fight two powerful Japanese squadrons working their way down into the East Indies from the east and west like the tentacles of an octopus, to use Morison's analogy. Having no hope of reinforcement, the ABDA fleet was doomed. The only question was how many of the enemy could it take with it.[6]

First blood was drawn by the four-pipers *John D. Ford, Pope, Parrott*, and *Paul Jones* when they attacked a large Japanese convoy at anchor off Balikpapan, Borneo, in the Makassar Strait, on the night of January 24, 1942. Oil tanks set afire by the retreating Dutch illuminated the Japanese ships, and the American destroyers dashed in firing torpedoes and guns like a bunch of cowboys shooting up a town and sped away, leaving behind them four sinking ships, three transports, and a patrol boat. Although this success—first surface action fought by the U. S. Navy since 1898—buoyed Allied morale, it did not slow the Japanese invasion of the Dutch Indies. A few days later, enemy bombers roared over the Allied airfields on Java and destroyed most of the planes on the ground. Left with little air cover, the *Houston* and *Marblehead*, two Dutch cruisers, and seven destroyers tried to smash another convoy in the Makassar Strait on February 4 and came under attack by bombers. Twisting and turning in an effort to confuse the enemy bombardiers, they threw up clouds of antiaircraft fire, but the *Marblehead* was hit so badly that she was lucky to be able to limp home to the United States, and the *Houston*'s after 8-inch gun turret was knocked out, causing heavy casualties. Damaged or not, she was the last American cruiser left in the Java Sea, the *Boise* having struck a reef a few days before and been put out of action.

Rear Admiral Karel W.F.M. Doorman, of the Royal Netherlands Navy, led the remnants of the ABDA force from its much-bombed base at Soerabaja on February 27 to attack a large Japanese convoy that was approaching Java. Besides his flagship, the *De Ruyter*, he had with him four other cruisers: the battered *Houston*, which the enemy claimed so many times to have sunk that her crew called her "The Galloping Ghost of the Java Coast"; the British *Exeter*; the Australian *Perth*; and the Dutch *Java*. They were screened by nine destroyers, four of which were four-pipers that had to strain to keep up with the much faster cruisers.

Doorman hoped to raise havoc among the convoy's forty-one transports, but he could not get past its escort. The two sides seemed roughly equal, with the Japanese having two heavy cruisers, the *Nachi* and *Haguro*, two light cruisers, and fourteen destroyers. The Japanese, however, had control of the air, their ships were in good repair and their crews fresh, whereas Doorman's vessels were badly in need of overhaul and his men's nerves were frazzled. The Battle of the Java Sea began with a salvo of 8-inch shells fired from one of the Japanese cruisers at the extreme range of 30,000 yards. This was answered by the guns of the *Houston* and *Exeter*. Commander Walter G. Winslow, in the *Houston*, provides a graphic account of what happened next:

> The sound of our guns bellowing defiance is terrific, the gun blast tears my steel helmet from my head and sends it rolling on the deck. The range closes rapidly and soon all the cruisers are in on the fight. Salvos of shells splash in the water ever closer to us. Now one falls close to the starboard followed by another close to port. . . . Shells from our guns are observed bursting close to the last Jap heavy cruiser. We have her range and suddenly one of our 8-inch bricks strikes home. There is an explosion aboard her. Black smoke and debris flies into the air and a fire breaks out forward of her bridge. We draw blood first as she turns out of the battle line making dense smoke.[7]

But the ABDA squadron's luck did not hold. About an hour after the action began, the thin-skinned *Exeter* was hit by an 8-inch shell that penetrated to one of her firerooms and severed a main steam line but did not explode. With her speed suddenly cut to seven knots, the cruiser turned away from the enemy, creating considerable confusion in the Allied battle line. The Japanese loosed a shoal of torpedoes, one of which sundered a Dutch destroyer. An Allied torpedo attack on the Japanese line resulted in the loss of another destroyer and damage to two enemy destroyers. At nightfall the Japanese commander withdrew to check on the safety of his convoy, while Doorman ordered the crippled *Exeter* to return to Soerabaja. Still resolved to attack the convoy, he set about finding his quarry with his four remaining cruisers. Before he succeeded in doing this, enemy reconnaissance aircraft spotted him and dropped flares that bathed his ships in an eerie white light. Shortly after midnight the *Java*, about 900 yards astern of the *Houston*, was racked by an explosion. Flames enveloped her and she dropped out of line. More torpedoes fired by Japanese cruisers that had been summoned by the planes slashed through the dark sea. The *De Ruyter* was making a change in course when she was hit and quickly sank. Ordered by Doorman not to risk themselves by stopping to pick up the *De Ruyter*'s survivors, the *Houston* and *Perth* escaped into the darkness, leaving Doorman and 344 officers and men of the Dutch navy to perish.

The following night, as the two cruisers, short of ammunition and badly in need of repairs, steamed into Sunda Strait, they came upon the main Japanese invasion force. Sweeping into Banten Bay, they caught the enemy flat-footed.

In the wild melee that followed, the Japanese fired torpedoes indiscriminately, some of them striking their own ships. One transport was sunk and three others so badly damaged that they had to be beached. But the hour of the *Perth* and *Houston* had come. A torpedo hit the Australian cruiser in her forward engine room and, lying dead in the water, she was given the coup de grâce by Japanese gunners. Now it was the *Houston*'s turn. Caught in the white glare of searchlights that stabbed through the darkness, she shuddered under the impact of hit after hit. Let Commander Winslow finish the story:

> A torpedo penetrated our after engine room, where it exploded, killing every man there and reducing our speed to fifteen knots. . . . Power went out for the shell hoists. . . . Number Two turret, smashed by a direct hit, blew up, sending wild flames flashing up over the bridge. . . . Slowly we listed to starboard as the grand old ship gradually lost steerageway and stopped. The few guns still in commission continued to fire, although it was obvious that the end was near. . . .

Of the *Houston*'s 1,064 officers and men, only 368 survived. Captain Albert H. Rooks, who went down with his ship, was posthumously awarded the Congressional Medal of Honor for "extraordinary heroism," and the unit citation given his ship tells its own story: "Often damaged, but self maintaining, the *Houston* kept the sea and went down, gallantly fighting to the last against overwhelming odds." Proud of her record, the citizens of Houston raised funds to build a namesake. The day after the *Houston* made her last stand, the *Exeter* was sunk in a battle with four Japanese heavy cruisers. The *Pope* and another accompanying destroyer were lost with her. The old *Langley*, the navy's first carrier and now a seaplane tender ferrying fighters from Australia, was sunk by enemy bombers. In a few weeks, the Japanese had wiped out the ABDA fleet and captured the riches of the East Indies.

The time had come for them to consolidate their conquests and strengthen their defense perimeter. But so infected were the Japanese strategists with "Victory Disease" that they gambled on a new campaign of conquest.[8] To complete their domination of the Coral Sea and to threaten Australia, they decided to capture Port Moresby, in New Guinea, and Tulagi, in the Solomons.

Fortunately, the Americans, having by now broken the enemy naval code, were aware of the Japanese threat to Port Moresby and Australia. Early in May 1942 Admiral Nimitz ordered Rear Admiral Frank Jack Fletcher, commander of the *Yorktown* task force, into the Coral Sea. He sent the *Lexington* task force under Rear Admiral Aubrey W. Fitch to join Fletcher, and as soon as Halsey, with the *Hornet* and *Enterprise*, returned from the Tokyo raid, he, too, was ordered to the area. The Battle of the Coral Sea, the first naval action in history in which surface ships did not exchange a single shot, or, indeed, ever see one another, began on May 4, when the *Yorktown*'s planes struck the Japanese landing force at Tulagi. Little damage was inflicted and the next two days were spent in searching the placid waters in the hope of finding the main Japanese force en route to Port Moresby.[9]

On May 7, the day after the Americans surrendered the island of Corregidor in Manila Bay, marking the end of the Philippines campaign, the two fleets made contact. Planes from the *Yorktown* and *Lexington* sank the small carrier *Shoho* with the loss of but a single dive bomber. "Scratch one flattop!" exuberantly radioed one of the pilots. Upon receiving word of the loss of the *Shoho*, the Japanese commander ordered the Port Moresby invasion force to turn back and wait until the Americans had been cleared from the area. That same morning, aircraft from the large carriers *Shokaku* and *Zuikaku*, mistaking the American fleet oiler *Neosho* and the destroyer *Sims* for a carrier and cruiser, sank them at a cost of six planes, which diverted their attention from the presence of the nearby American carriers. Both sides were learning their deadly trade, and that was not the only mistake made. Land-based B-17s twice attacked Allied surface ships, and at nightfall that same day, six of the Japanese planes sent to attack the American carriers got confused and tried to land on the *Yorktown*.

Early on May 8 the opposing carrier groups—almost equally matched in strength—located each other and launched their aircraft. The *Zuikaku* was hidden in a rain squall and the Americans did not see her, but they damaged the *Shokaku*'s flight deck so badly that she could not handle her planes. The *Yorktown* and the *Lexington* were both damaged. Hit by two torpedoes, the *Lexington* was afire but did not appear to be too badly hurt to carry on. Suddenly, she was shattered by a terrific explosion. Fumes from her aviation-fuel supply lines, ruptured by the bombing, had been ignited by a chance spark. Captain Frederick C. Sherman was finally forced to order her abandoned. This was done in good order and most of her crew of some 3,000 were saved before she was sunk by escorting American destroyers to make sure that she did not fall into the hands of the enemy.

When the score was totalled up, the Japanese had taken the greater toll of tonnage. The Americans had lost three ships, including the *Lexington*, and seventy-seven planes; the Japanese had lost the much less valuable *Shoho* and several smaller vessels as well as ninety-seven planes. Strategically, the Battle of the Coral Sea was an American victory, however, because for the first time a Japanese thrust had been thwarted. The *Yorktown* was soon back in action, but the *Zuikaku*'s planes were not immediately replaced nor was the *Shokaku* immediately repaired. Thus, neither carrier took part in the next moves in the Pacific war.

Having studied in the United States and served in Washington as a naval attaché, Admiral Yamamoto realized that it was essential for Japan to bring the war to a victorious conclusion before America's industrial might could come into play. "If I am told to fight regardless of the consequences," he had declared in 1941, "I shall run wild for the first six months or a year, but I have utterly no confidence for the second and third years of the fighting."[10] He was obsessed with the need to prevent there being "second and third years of fighting." One of his desires was to lure the U.S. Pacific Fleet into a decisive battle while Japan still had a chance of demolishing it.

Through coded Japanese messages, Nimitz knew that the enemy was planning a sizeable operation somewhere in the central Pacific. The enemy's radio traffic bore numerous references to "AF," which some officers thought was Midway. In order to find out whether it was or not, Lieutenant Commander Joseph J. Rochefort, who was in charge of the decoding operation at Pearl Harbor, went to Lieutenant Commander Edwin T. Layton, one of Nimitz's aides, with a plan to sound out Japanese intentions. The admiral approved, and Midway was ordered to transmit to Pearl Harbor in plain English a message stating that its water-distilling machinery was out of order. Two days later a Japanese message reported that "AF" was short of water.[11] Thereupon, Nimitz redoubled efforts to strengthen the defenses of Midway and prepared to concentrate his forces in the central Pacific.

The *Yorktown* was patched up in record time and Admiral Halsey was ordered to bring the *Enterprise* and *Hornet* back from the Coral Sea. By June 1 Nimitz had a fleet of three carriers, eight cruisers, fourteen destroyers, and about twenty submarines deployed to the west of Midway. They were divided into two task forces, one under the command of Rear Admiral Raymond A. Spruance, one of the navy's leading strategists, who had replaced Halsey when the latter was hospitalized with a skin rash, and the other under Admiral Fletcher. The approaching Japanese force, commanded by Admiral Yamamoto, was divided into three major parts: a striking force of four carriers, the *Akagi, Kaga, Hiryu,* and *Soryu*, under Admiral Nagumo who had led these same vessels in the attack on Pearl Harbor; a dozen transports carrying 5,000 troops and escorted by two battleships and a light carrier, the *Zuiho*, as well as cruisers and destroyers; and a main body consisting of seven battleships, including the *Yamato*, Yamamoto's flagship. Preceding this armada to sea was a diversionary force of two carriers, the *Ryujo* and *Junyo*, a pair of cruisers, and some transports assigned to bombard Dutch Harbor in the Aleutians and seize Adak, Attu, and Kiska.[12]

The Battle of Midway began on the morning of June 3, 1942, when Japanese planes suddenly dropped out of the foggy sky over Dutch Harbor and raked the base with bombs and machine-gun fire. A small cruiser force that had been sent north by Nimitz to deal with the expected Japanese attack was outmaneuvered, and four days later the Japanese landed troops on bleak Attu and Kiska. While the attack on Dutch Harbor was under way, Ensign Jewell H. Reid was on patrol in his PBY about 700 miles to the west of Midway when he spotted a large formation of ships on the horizon. "Do you see what I see?" he asked his co-pilot. "You're damn right I do" was the reply.[13] Because of heavy cloud cover, the exact composition of the enemy fleet could not be ascertained, but army B-17s based on Midway immediately attacked it. They did not, however, achieve anything. Nimitz greeted the news of the sighting of what turned out to be the occupation force with "a brilliant white smile," according to Commander Layton.

Early the next morning, June 4, another PBY got a fleeting glimpse of the Japanese carrier strike force as it emerged from the overcast about 200 miles to the northwest of Midway. Shortly before being sighted, it had launched 108 bombers and fighters against the atoll. Fletcher ordered Spruance to take the *Enterprise* and *Hornet* and hit the enemy flattops as soon as their position had been fixed; he would follow when he had recovered his search planes. Except for twenty-seven obsolescent F2A Buffalo fighters flown by marines that were being held in reserve to meet the incoming enemy bombers, every plane on Midway that could get into the air was sent to attack the enemy carriers. Although completely outclassed by the Zeros attempting to reduce the island, the marines and ground fire shot down or damaged about a third of the enemy planes at a cost of fifteen of their own. By contrast, planes from Midway that simultaneously attacked the Japanese carriers suffered heavy losses and failed to damage the strongly defended ships.

So far, the honors had gone to the Japanese, but the decisive moment of the battle—and of the entire war in the Pacific—occurred at this point. A cruiser reconnaissance plane signalled Admiral Nagumo that an American carrier was approaching from the northeast. Surprised because he had not suspected that there were any enemy carriers in his area, he hastily considered his options. Ninety-three planes of his second wave were arming with bombs for use against ground targets. At the urgent request of his air operations officer, Commander Minoru Genda, he ordered them to reload with torpedoes and armor-piercing bombs suitable for use against ships. Before the reloaded planes could be brought up from the hangar decks and launched, those that had struck Midway returned and had to be recovered, refueled, and rearmed. Soon the flight decks of the Japanese carriers were crisscrossed with gas hoses, and bombs, ammunition, and torpedoes were strewn about as the deck crews worked frantically to get their charges into the air again.

On the *Hornet* and *Enterprise*, pilots in the ready rooms joked nervously as they awaited word that the enemy carriers had been sighted. They tried to brush aside the thought that there would be empty seats in the wardroom that night. "Pilots, man your planes!" ordered the metallic voice through the squawk box, "Pilots, man your planes!" Realizing that there would be confusion on the Japanese ships as they refueled and rearmed, Spruance had waited for this moment to launch his air groups.[14] The Japanese had changed course, however, and when the Americans arrived at the position where they expected the enemy to be, they saw only empty sea. But a squadron of fifteen old TBD Devastator torpedo planes from the *Hornet*—Torpedo 8—found the carriers and, without fighter cover, courageously pressed home an attack. Waiting Zeros and a barrage of antiaircraft fire met them and sent them splashing into the sea, trailing flames as if they had hit a stone wall. Ensign George Gay, the sole survivor of the squadron, whose craft was also shot down, recalled that the falling planes looked like bits of orange peel being thrown into the water from a speedboat.[15]

Torpedo 8's sacrifice was not wasted. They had diverted the attention of the Japanese fighter pilots and antiaircraft gunners from fifty-four SBD Dauntless dive bombers that swooped down undetected on the *Kaga*, *Soryu*, and *Akagi*, whose decks were crowded with planes. Lieutenant Clarence E. Dickinson, one of the dive-bomber pilots, reported:

> As I put my nose down I picked up our carrier target below in front of me. I was making the best dive I had ever made. The people who came back said it was the best dive they had ever made. We were coming down from all directions on the port side of the carrier, beautifully spaced. . . . I recognized her as the *Kaga*; and she was enormous. . . . The target was utterly satisfying. . . . I saw a bomb hit just behind where I was aiming. . . . I saw the deck rippling, and curling back in all directions exploding a great section of the hangar below. . . . I dropped a few seconds after the previous bomb explosion . . . I saw the 500-pound bomb hit right abreast of the island. The two 100-pound bombs struck in the forward area of the parked planes. . . . Then I began thinking it was time to get myself away from there and try to get back alive.[16]

The *Kaga* was hit by four bombs which fed on gasoline and touched off secondary explosions among her parked planes. Engulfed in soaring flames, she sank that evening after being abandoned by what was left of her crew. One bomb ruptured the *Akagi*'s flight deck, another fell among her planes, and she was turned into a flaming pyre. As soon as Admiral Nagumo had shifted his flag from her to a cruiser, she was sunk by escorting destroyers. Three bombs landed on the flight deck of the *Soryu* and she later sank. The fourth Japanese carrier, the *Hiryu*, which had not been sighted at the outset, launched eighteen dive bombers against the *Yorktown*. Most of them were shot down, but three of their bombs struck the carrier and she was rocked by internal explosions. Enemy torpedo planes evaded the carrier's fighter screen and put a pair of torpedoes into her. Listing badly, she was abandoned but, refusing to sink, she was taken in tow. She had already been avenged, however. An attack group from the *Enterprise* found the defenseless *Hiryu*—she had lost most of her fighters during the battle—and so badly damaged her that she had to be scuttled the next day. Having lost his four carriers with their crack air groups and about 250 planes, the shaken Admiral Yamamoto withdrew.

Admiral Spruance, who had handled his carriers brilliantly, turned away rather than risk a night action against the big guns of the Japanese battleships, which had not been damaged.[17] Two days later, on June 6, American planes, nipping at the heels of the retiring Japanese, attacked the cruisers *Mikuma* and

Mogami, sinking the former and crippling her consort. That same day a submarine picked off the *Yorktown*, along with one of her escorting destroyers. And so the curtain came down on the Battle of Midway—the first decisive defeat suffered by the Imperial Japanese Navy since 1592. The tide of Japanese conquest had been stopped in both the Coral Sea and the central Pacific, and Japan was faced with the kind of war that Yamamoto had warned against. Now, the time had come for the United States to shift from the "defensive-offensive" to the "offensive-defensive."

To implement the "Europe first" strategy, the Allies were marshalling all available men and material for an impending invasion of North Africa, and only limited resources could be devoted to a Pacific offensive. Nevertheless, to keep the Japanese from consolidating their gains without hindrance and to provide a staging area for attacks on Japan's defense perimeter when more resources became available, an advance through the Solomons was planned. Simultaneous with the capture of the Solomons, American and Australian troops commanded by General Douglas MacArthur were to launch an offensive against Rabaul, the center of Japanese strength in the Southwest Pacific.[18]

Under the guns of five American and three Australian cruisers and planes from the *Enterprise, Wasp,* and *Saratoga*, some 19,000 men of the First Marine Division (Reinforced) were landed on Guadalcanal and Tulagi on August 7, 1942. Japanese resistance was unexpectedly light, and the marines had little difficulty in seizing Tulagi and the uncompleted airfield on Guadalcanal, which was the key to control of the whole Solomons chain and the adjacent seas. Using steamrollers and other equipment left behind by the Japanese who had vanished into the jungle, the navy's newly organized construction battalions went to work preparing the landing strip, later called Henderson Field, for marine fighter planes.

The construction battalions, or CBs, consisted of civilians employed by the navy to build advance bases in the Pacific. The Seabees, as the battalions soon came to be called, were put into uniform to provide them with some ability to defend themselves. "Can Do" was their motto, and they lost no time in demonstrating their abilities to outbuild the Japanese in any climate and under any conditions. The top strength of the Seabees was about 240,000 men, all with considerable experience in a wide variety of building trades. They took part in every amphibious operation in the Pacific, usually landing soon after the first wave of marines, and set up temporary bases in short order. At Guadalcanal, the Seabees, many of whom were older men, made Henderson Field fit for operations in five days and kept it going even in the face of desperate Japanese attacks. Young marines who had seen Seabees deal with Japanese machine-gun nests with bulldozers had a saying: "Never hit a Seabee. He may be your grandfather."[19]

Although surprised by the landing on Guadalcanal, the Japanese on Rabaul managed to launch sizeable air attacks on the invasion fleet as it lay off the island unloading reinforcements and supplies. At high cost to themselves, the attackers sank a transport and a destroyer. Vice Admiral Gunichi Mikawa assembled a striking force of five heavy cruisers, including his flagship, the *Chokai*, two light cruisers, and a destroyer and raced south from Rabaul. He took the daring step of sailing down the passage through the central Solomons —"the Slot"—in broad daylight in order to attack the ships in Savo Sound in the darkness of the early morning hours of August 9. His intention was both to surprise the Allies and to capitalize on his crews' thorough training in night operations.[20]

Blunders on the part of the Allies assisted him. Admiral Fletcher had chosen this moment to withdraw his three carriers for refueling, leaving the fleet without air cover. Australian reconnaissance aircraft sighted the Japanese while they were in the Slot, but their reports were delayed or incomplete, and the crews of the radar picket destroyers, fatigued by thirty-six hours on duty, were not on the alert. Rear Admiral Richmond Kelly Turner, commander of the South Pacific Amphibious Force, confident that his fleet was safe from attack, called away his ranking officers for a conference. By the time the alarm was sounded, the Japanese were already plunging into Savo Sound.

"Warning! Warning!" broadcast the destroyer *Patterson*. "Strange ships entering the harbor!" It was too late. A spread of torpedoes was speeding toward its targets, and float planes were dropping parachute flares to illuminate their victims. The Australian cruiser *Canberra* was so badly damaged by two torpedoes and a rain of shells that struck her while general quarters was still being sounded that she was scuttled the next morning. With her port bow blown away by a torpedo, the *Chicago* steamed about erratically. The cruisers *Vincennes, Astoria*, and *Quincy*, which were completing one leg of a patrol, had not yet got all their men to battle stations when the Japanese gunners turned their attention on them. Struck by salvo after salvo, the *Astoria* soon became a flaming wreck, and the *Vincennes*, victim of several torpedoes, was hammered into wreckage. The *Quincy*, ablaze from several hits and her hull ripped open by torpedoes, managed to fire a few rounds that damaged the *Chokai* before rolling over and plunging to the bottom.

Not knowing that Fletcher had taken his carriers to sea and wary lest they launch an attack, Mikawa abruptly ordered a withdrawal, leaving the helpless American transports untouched. In just one frenzied half-hour, he had sunk or left sinking four Allied cruisers and severely damaged a fifth. Two thousand men either went down with their ships or were wounded. Except for the damage inflicted on his flagship by the *Quincy*, Mikawa escaped unscathed, although his triumphant return to Rabaul was marred by an American submarine, the S-44, which sank one of his ships. The Battle of Savo Island, says Morison, was "probably the worst defeat ever inflicted on the United States Navy in a fair fight."[21]

Without air cover and with his force dangerously weakened, Admiral Turner abandoned the beachhead on August 9, eliciting bitter comment from the marines and Seabees left to fend for themselves ashore. Until both sides began slipping in reinforcements more than a week later, Guadalcanal was suspended in a vacuum. The island, itself of no importance, became a symbol. To the Americans it represented their determination to remain on the offensive; to the Japanese its loss would represent failure. Six more naval battles were fought for possession of this dreary speck of malaria-infested jungle, and Savo Sound was so littered with sunken ships that it became known as Ironbottom Sound.

The first of these battles occurred on August 24 when Japanese and American carrier groups struck at one another 150 miles to the east of the island.[22] During the Battle of the Eastern Solomons, bombers from the *Saratoga* sank the small Japanese carrier *Ryujo*, and enemy planes persisted through heavy fire to maul the *Enterprise* severely. One of the Japanese planes that was shot down was a German-built Messerschmitt-109, an oddity in the Pacific.

Both sides continued building up their forces on the island. Under cover of aircraft from the carriers or from Henderson Field, the Americans sent in a constant stream of freighters. On September 15 the carrier *Wasp*, protecting a convoy of six transports, was torpedoed and sunk by a submarine, and the *North Carolina* was damaged. The "Tokyo Express," consisting of light cruisers and destroyers, made nightly runs to unload men and supplies on Japanese-held beaches, shelled marine positions, and then scooted to safety. By the end of the month, the Japanese had put some 20,000 men on the island.

On the night of October 11, a task force of cruisers and destroyers under Rear Admiral Norman Scott attempted to derail the Tokyo Express off Cape Esperance, at the northern tip of Guadalcanal. Scott capped the enemy's T—a classic maneuver equivalent to "raking" in the age of fighting sail—and, at the cost of one of his own destroyers and extensive damage to the *Boise*, sank a heavy cruiser and a destroyer. Despite these losses, the Express continued to deliver troops and heavy artillery. Three nights after the marines had been reinforced by an army regiment from General MacArthur's command, two Japanese battleships pounded Henderson Field, sending its supply of aviation fuel up in flames, smashing the landing strip, and destroying forty-eight planes. "It now appears that we are unable to control the sea in the Guadalcanal area," was Admiral Nimitz's grim estimate of the situation. "Thus our supply of the positions will only be done at great expense to us. The situation is not hopeless, but it is certainly critical."[23]

Nimitz dealt with the problem by naming Admiral Halsey, his health restored and eager for action, as overall commander of naval forces in the South Pacific. "I'll never forget it," one officer said when the news of the aggressive Halsey's appointment spread. "One minute we were too limp with malaria to crawl out of our foxholes; the next, we were running around whooping like kids."[24] In

Washington, Admiral King persuaded President Roosevelt to earmark more ships, planes, and men for the Guadalcanal campaign.

Admiral Yamamoto, believing that his enemy was on the ropes, moved in for a knockout punch. While the Japanese launched a massive sea-land offensive aimed at capturing Henderson Field, a striking force of four carriers cruised to the northeast of Guadalcanal. On October 26 this force made contact with the *Hornet* and *Enterprise* forces, which were sweeping the waters to the north of the Santa Cruz Islands. Planes from the American carriers damaged the *Zuiho* and *Shokaku* but the Japanese gave as much as they got, sinking the *Hornet* and damaging the new battleship *South Dakota*. They lost about 100 planes, however, along with their experienced air crews. Nor did things go well on land, their troops being driven back from the airfield in hand-to-hand fighting.

In the dark hours of the morning of November 13—a Friday—the Tokyo Express, led by the battleships *Hiei* and *Kirishima*, came down the Slot to shell American positions on Guadalcanal. Since the *Enterprise, Washington,* and *South Dakota* were a day's steaming away, a cruiser-destroyer force led by Rear Admiral Daniel J. Callaghan, flying his flag in the heavy cruiser *San Francisco*, courageously offered battle. "We want the big ones," Callaghan told his captains. At a range of less than 3,000 yards there followed a melee, in which both sides fired at anything that came under their guns. Early in the action, Norman Scott was killed on the bridge of the *Atlanta*, which was hit and engulfed in flames. The *San Francisco* traded salvos with the *Hiei* and was scoring until she was hit by 14-inch shells that killed Callaghan and forced her to limp out of action. The cruiser *Portland* concentrated her 8-inch fire on the *Hiei*, taking hits in exchange. Two destroyers, the *Laffey* and *Cushing*, joined the attack on the *Hiei* and, when they were wrecked, the *O'Bannon, Sterett,* and *Monssen* continued the fight.

This action, which Admiral King described as "one of the most furious sea battles ever fought," lasted exactly twenty-four minutes. At daylight the *Hiei* was discovered to the northeast of Savo Island, turning in circles, and was finished off by aircraft from the *Enterprise* and from Guadalcanal. She was the first Japanese battleship to be sunk in the war. American losses were heavy; except for one destroyer, every ship in Callaghan's force was sunk or damaged. Following the battle, the already battered cruiser *Juneau* was torpedoed by a Japanese submarine and exploded with the loss of 700 men, including five brothers from the Sullivan family.

The Japanese returned with the *Kirishima*, a large number of cruisers and destroyers, and eleven transports loaded with reinforcements.[25] Planes from the *Enterprise* and Henderson Field sank seven transports and damaged the other four so badly that they had to be beached. The *Washington, South Dakota,* and four destroyers under Rear Admiral Willis A. Lee had taken up station in Iron-bottom Sound to deal with the heavy ships, and the climactic battle for Guadalcanal began on the night of November 14, with the roar of the *Washington's* 16-inch guns. Ripped apart by one of her salvos, a Japanese destroyer burst into flames and sank, as did three of the four American destroyers that tried to press the advantage. The *South Dakota* had an electrical failure, leaving the brunt of the fighting to the *Washington*. With her radar-directed guns locked on the *Kirishima*, she hurled salvo after salvo at the enemy battleship, which within seven minutes was a blazing wreck and was scuttled by her crew.

Even though the U. S. Navy had suffered heavy losses, the American position in the Solomons was not seriously threatened again. The Tokyo Express continued its runs, however, and on the night of November 30, eight Japanese destroyers bloodied an American force of five cruisers and six destroyers that intercepted them off Tassafaronga. The *Northampton* was sunk by torpedoes, and three other cruisers were damaged at the cost of a single Japanese destroyer.[26] Nevertheless, as the Americans absorbed the bitter lessons of war, their strength was increasing, while that of the Japanese was waning. Fifty thousand army troops—the marines on Guadalcanal were relieved in December—stepped up the pressure on the enemy, and unknown to the Americans, about 12,000 of the nearly starving survivors were evacuated from the island before they could be hunted down. On February 9, 1943, six months after the marines had landed, General Alexander M. Patch radioed Admiral Halsey: "Tokyo Express no longer has terminus on Guadalcanal."

The British steamer *Cyclops*, splotches of red lead showing on her weather-beaten sides, wallowed along at her best speed about 300 miles northeast of Cape Cod on January 12, 1942. Germany had declared war on the United States a month before and, although no U-boats had yet been detected off American shores, her captain was undoubtedly anxious about being at sea alone. Suddenly the wake of a torpedo appeared, and the hapless *Cyclops* went down. Operation *Paukenschlag*—roll of drums—had begun. This was the name Admiral Karl Dönitz, Commander, U-Boats, had given to his offensive against American coastal shipping. The Germans having been just as surprised as the Americans by the Japanese attack on Pearl Harbor, only six long-range submarines were immediately available to open this new front in the Battle of the Atlantic.[27]

With the attention of the U. S. Navy in the Atlantic fixed on the transocean route plied by convoys bound for Britain and on the even more difficult route to the Soviet Union, the U-boat skippers reaped a rich harvest of undefended coastal shipping. They lurked off the heavily travelled shipping lanes where before the blackout went into force in April, their targets were sometimes silhouetted against the glow of bright city lights. Victims were being torpedoed only thirty miles out of New York or off the Virginia Capes. Sometimes three or more ships were sunk in a day, some within sight of spectators on shore. Thick oil from blasted tankers and debris from wrecked ships covered the Atlantic beaches. In little more than two weeks, a good portion of the nation's coastal tanker tonnage was sent to the bottom. Supported by 1,700-ton "milch cow" submarines, which supplied fuel oil and torpedoes, the U-boats could remain on station for weeks. Their skippers gleefully called this the "American Shooting Season." Reporting his success to Dönitz by radio, one captain, Jochen Mohr of U-129, resorted to doggerel:

> The new-moon night is as black as ink.
> Off Hatteras the tankers sink.
> While sadly Roosevelt counts the score.
> Some fifty thousand tons—by Mohr.[28]

The navy was ill prepared to meet this challenge. In prewar years, it had earmarked most of its limited funds for large ships with the expectation of building escorts in a hurry if they were ever needed. Consequently, there was a crippling shortage of escorts, and most of those available were already in service on the Atlantic convoy routes. President Roosevelt had prodded the Bureau of Ships, successor to the Bureaus of Engineering and of Construction and Repair, to build small craft before the emergency, but little had been done. "The Navy couldn't see any vessel under a thousand tons," commented the president.[29]

Top priority was hastily given to the construction of destroyer escorts and escort carriers, the latter built on freighter and tanker hulls, but none of them would be ready for months. As a stopgap, a ragtag of Eagle boats and submarine chasers left over from World War I, Coast Guard cutters, and various other types of small craft, including private yachts, were pressed into service to establish inshore convoy escorts. "I have begged, borrowed or stolen every vessel of every description over eighty feet," Roosevelt told Churchill. Although the Coast Guard was not placed under the navy's control until November 1941, its ocean-going vessels had been on Neutrality Patrol since July of that year. In all, it supplied some seventy-five large vessels for ocean escort work and a much greater number of small vessels, as well as aircraft, for inshore escort duty. "Their performance was glorious; their casualties heavy," says Morison.[30]

By degrees, blimps and airplanes, some of them bombers borrowed from the army to make up for the shortage of naval patrol planes, were added to the forces that protected the inshore convoys. When the Atlantic coast became too "hot," Dönitz, whose policy was to operate in areas of least resistance, ordered his boats into the Gulf of Mexico and the Caribbean. Concentrating off the mouth of the Mississippi and in the area of Aruba and Trinidad, his boats met with considerable success. In May, forty-one ships, totalling 219,867 tons, went down in the Gulf alone, more than in any area during the entire war. Many of the victims were freighters laden with vital bauxite, but more than half of them were tankers whose cargoes turned the sea black. One survivor pulled from the water by the Coast Guard was "so coated with thick congealed oil that we had to cut his clothes and his life jacket off with knives. They were so weighted with oil we couldn't get him aboard. Even his mouth was filled with a blob of oil."[31]

When stepped-up antisubmarine warfare, particularly air cover for convoys, brought the days of easy pickings in the Caribbean to an end, Dönitz shifted his efforts back to the North Atlantic. As in World War I, the well-defended, high-speed troop convoys had little to fear from the U-boats—in fact, the Cunard liners *Queen Mary* and *Queen Elizabeth,* with speeds in excess of twenty-six knots, raced across the Atlantic in five days without escort. The full brunt of the German onslaught was borne by the convoys of stormbeaten merchantmen and their escorting destroyers, corvettes, and cutters. Day after day, week after week, cold food, little sleep, and the monotonous "ping . . . ping . . . ping" of the sonar gear probing the depths for U-boats was their lot. Although land-based aircraft provided cover for convoys at both ends of the voyage, there was a 600-mile-wide gap in mid-Atlantic that in 1942 was beyond the range of such craft. It was called the Black Pit—and with good reason.

From August to December 1942, the U-boats sank an average of over 500,000 tons of shipping a month around the world, and the toll reached nearly 700,000 tons in November. Bad weather in January and February 1943 reduced the Allied losses, but in March the toll was up to 567,000 tons against a loss of only six U-boats. Convoys would escape from one wolf pack only to be attacked by another. The Germans were now achieving results comparable to April 1917, and this against convoys, not against ships sailing independently. "The Germans never came so near disrupting communications between the Old World and the New as in the first twenty days of March 1943," according to an Admiralty report.[32]

These successes marked the high tide of the German submarine campaign, for the war at sea was not only a battle between U-boats and escorts but also a race between rival technologies. At first, the Germans held the edge. B-Dienst, the German navy's codebreaking operation, had broken the British naval codes before the war, giving Admiral Donitz access not only to the position, course, and speed of every convoy but also to the admiralty's estimated position of all U-boats. The British did not realize what was happening until July 1943 and changed their codes.

On the other hand, the British cryptanalysts at Bletchely Park had difficulty breaking into the German naval ciphers. The naval version of the Enigma ciphering machine, used by the German military, was complex and the rotor settings were changed every twenty-four hours, which forced the British to break a new cipher every day. In mid-1941, the Royal Navy captured the submarine U-110 before her crew could scuttle the boat or destroy her Enigma machine, which gave the British insight into its operation. Now that the British had an Enigma machine plus its rotor settings, they were able to plot the positions of individual U-boats and wolfpacks.

Armed with advance warnings of impending German submarine operations, convoys were diverted from lurking wolf packs. Long-range B-24 Liberator bombers, equipped with sophisticated new radar systems and depth charges, and escort carriers provided continuous air cover across the Atlantic. More and more ships were fitted with high-frequency direction finders (HF/DF), known as "huff duff," which allowed them to home in on the considerable radio traffic between the wolf packs and Dönitz's headquarters and thus determine the submarines' bearings. Destroyer escorts carrying the forward-firing "hedge-hogs," which were more effective than ordinary depth charges, began to join the convoys in increasing numbers, with 260 in commission by the end of 1943.

The passage of ONS-5, a slow convoy of forty-two ships westward-bound across the North Atlantic, whose escort commander was Peter W. Gretton, one of the Royal Navy's ace escort leaders, is generally accepted as the turning point in the Battle of the Atlantic. Despite bad weather, no less than four groups totalling fifty-six U-boats attacked the convoy, and the ensuing struggle raged over a wide stretch of ocean from April 28 to May 6, 1943. Twelve merchantmen fell victim to the U-boats, but eight of the latter were sunk, three of them by patrol planes, and two more sank after colliding with each other, for a total loss of ten boats. This was merely the shadow of things to come. Forty-one submarines—one third of those at sea—failed to return from combat patrol during the U-boat's "Black May." Dönitz later stated that at this point he became convinced that Germany had lost the Battle of the Atlantic.[33]

Driven from the North Atlantic, he once again shifted his sights to the south, where the waters were teeming with troop-laden transports and supply ships preparing for the invasion of Sicily and Italy. The U. S. Navy, which had major responsibility for the defense of these ships, was ready for him. "Hunter-killer" groups built around escort carriers and operating in support of the convoys took their toll of the raiders. The *Bogue, Card, Core,* and *Santee* groups sank thirteen U-boats in two months, and the destroyer escorts *Bronstein* and *Thomas* sent three to the bottom in a three-week period.

Some of these battles recalled the ship-to-ship duels of an earlier age. Captain Daniel Gallery's escort carrier group forced the U-505 to the surface and sent a boarding party swarming aboard to capture her before she could be scuttled. One of the most bizarre encounters was a fight to the death between a blimp and a U-boat. Lighter-than-air enthusiasts could boast of the excellent record of the blimp as a deterrent—none of the ships on the 89,000 voyages they escorted fell victim to a direct submarine attack—but no blimp had ever made an unassisted kill of a submarine. Lieutenant N. G. Grills, commander of the airship K-34, tried to better this record on July 18, 1943, when he sighted a U-boat on the surface off the coast of Florida. Before the blimp could get into position to drop her depth charges, however, the Germans unlimbered their guns and began pouring hot lead into her. Grills tried to launch his attack even though his craft was lurching crazily from the impact of enemy shells. They passed through the airship's envelope without exploding but sliced it open, and, as the helium drained out, she lost altitude. Suddenly a fluky wind blew the K-34 directly over the submarine, and Grills ordered his depth charges dropped. Nothing happened; the releasing gear had jammed. The blimp slowly settled into the sea and the U-boat sailed away, only to be sunk by British aircraft as she tried to reach home.[34]

On November 1 the four-piper *Borie* blew the U-405, which had attacked a Gibraltar-bound convoy, to the surface with depth charges. Lieutenant Charles H. Hutchins, her captain, trying to ram the submarine, ran the *Borie*'s bow right up on her foredeck. The vessels were locked together like the *Bonhomme Richard* and the *Serapis*. Unable to depress their 4-inch guns enough to take the U-boat in range, the *Borie*'s men opened up with anything they could get their hands on: machine guns, rifles, shotguns, and Very pistols. Someone threw a sheath knife and it caught a German sailor in the stomach; someone else dropped empty shell casings on the enemy. The pounding and grinding of the two steel hulls opened up the old destroyer's weakened plates and she began taking on water. After ten minutes of fury, the U-boat managed to wrench free. Too battered to submerge, she tried to make her getaway on the surface. Hutchins signalled for flank speed and the men in the engine room, working in water up to their chests, responded. "Like tomcats in the dark," the two vessels circled each other and both tried to ram. By skillful maneuvering, Hutchins got into position to straddle the submarine with a brace of depth charges, which damaged the U-boat so badly that her crew abandoned her. The *Borie* was in bad shape, too, and went down in heavy seas with twenty-seven of her men before the rest were taken off by other destroyers.[35]

With the teeth of the wolf packs drawn, Dönitz scattered his U-boats about the seas to attack targets of opportunity, while he awaited the development and production of a new and more deadly type of submarine. Fitted with diesels for greater speed and with "snorkels," standpipe-like devices that permitted them to draw air from the surface, the boats could remain submerged for longer periods and thus avoid detection by radar and air patrols. Some of the older boats were equipped with snorkels, but the almost undetectable new boats that would have played havoc with Allied convoys did not come into service before the Germans surrendered on May 7, 1945: In all, they lost seven hundred and eighty-one U-boats, 191 being accounted for by American ships and planes.[36]

The U. S. Navy played a leading role in the breaching of Fortress Europe. Landings under hostile fire in North Africa in November 1942, in Sicily in July 1943, and on the mainland of Italy two months later, provided opportunities to test and perfect tactics and techniques before the assault on the beaches of France was made. In these operations, the navy's role was to organize the safe passage of the transports, landing craft, and supply ships, land the troops on the beaches and provide supporting gunfire.

The invasion of North Africa was designed to provide bases for operations in the Mediterranean and to open that sea to Allied shipping. The operation revealed serious shortcomings in training and equipment, particularly landing craft, which were remedied for later invasions. The new LST was used for the first time in the landing in Sicily, where it permitted large numbers of tanks, troops, and artillery to be put ashore so quickly that within a few hours the invaders were in control of substantial beachheads. Gunfire from destroyers and cruisers, including the *Boise,* which had been badly damaged off Guadalcanal, was so accurate during the invasion of Sicily that it repeatedly destroyed enemy tank columns ashore.

Yet, when the time came for a landing at Salerno on the Italian boot, the army, hoping to achieve surprise, insisted that there be no preliminary naval bombardment. Vice Admiral H. Kent Hewitt, the amphibious force commander, protested that such a plan was hopeless, but he was ignored. As a result, the Allied troops were met with withering German fire and suffered heavy casualties. For the first time, the Germans used radio-directed glide bombs controlled by accompanying aircraft, and one heavily damaged the cruiser *Savannah.* [37]

Operation Neptune, the naval side of the Normandy invasion, began before dawn on D-Day, June 6, 1944. From Milford Haven in Wales, from Plymouth, Portsmouth, and Southampton on England's south coast sailed the greatest invasion fleet that the world has ever seen.[38] As far as the eye could see, the English Channel was covered with ships and small craft bound for the beaches of France under the watchful protection of the navies of Britain and the United States. Almost 200,000 men were crowded into these tossing vessels. With the impatience of sheepdogs chivvying a dim-witted flock, sleek destroyers darted about, keeping order among the wallowing landing craft. Several battleships rode on the horizon, ready to lend support with their big guns, among them the venerable *Texas* and *Arkansas,* and the *Nevada,* risen from the mud of Pearl Harbor. Thousands of bombers and fighters rumbled overhead.

The guns of almost 800 warships bombarded key sectors of the forty miles of beach from Le Ravre to Cherbourg for upward of fifty minutes. The battleships fired methodically at targets spotted by fighter planes, an innovation introduced during the Sicilian campaign; the cruisers, closer inshore, fired at such a rapid rate that their muzzle flashes looked like summer lightning; the destroyers shouldered their way in among the landing craft, searching out targets. Bank after bank of rockets from specially designed landing craft shrieked toward the beaches, trailing streams of orange-red flame. This curtain of fire was lifted as the landing craft moved in.

On Utah Beach, the western flank of the American disembarkation area, where the Germans were taken by surprise and momentarily stunned by the intensity of the bombardment, the landing was made in good order. But at Omaha Beach the enemy was prepared, and the landing craft were snagged by underwater obstacles, blown up by mines, or blasted out of the water by gunfire. Rough seas made it impossible for amphibious tanks to get ashore.

Men who managed to struggle to the beach were cut down before they could get clear of the area.

The destroyer *Corry,* standing off Utah Beach, was firing so fast that water hoses had to be played on the barrels of her guns.[39] As the German gunners in well-placed bunkers that dominated the landing areas began to concentrate their full fury on her and the sea around her boiled with near misses, Lieutenant Commander George D. Hoffman decided to increase the range, but before he could make his getaway, the destroyer struck a mine. Within seconds the *Corry* was transformed from a smoothly functioning fighting ship into a shattered wreck. Some of her gun crews continued to fire until water lapped over her decks and she was abandoned—one of the major losses suffered by the navy on D-Day.

The destroyers *Frankford, Doyle, Harding, Thompson, Baldwin, McCook,* and *Emmons* ventured in so close to Omaha Beach, where it appeared the invaders might be driven into the sea at any moment, that their gunners were able to select targets with the naked eye. Rear Admiral Alan G. Kirk, the American naval commander, said "they had their bows against the bottom."[40] At the same time, the battleships created a ring of fire around the beachhead cutting it off from the interior and prevented the Germans from moving up reinforcements. Slowly, the enemy guns were suppressed, and the Allied forces, by this time supplied with tanks and artillery, enlarged their footholds and broke out of the beachheads. "The fire curtain provided by the guns of the Navy . . proved to be one of the best trump cards of the Anglo-United States invasion armies," according to an assessment of the breaching of Fortress Europe made by the German army.[41]

> I was up on the bridge. I was just standing there looking out to sea. . . . All of a sudden I noticed something. Little black spots on the horizon. I looked through the glasses and it was a formation of our ships that stretched for miles! Carriers and battleships and cans—a whole task force. . . . They came on and passed within a half a mile. . . . Carriers so big they blacked out half the sky! And battlewagons sliding along—dead quiet. . . riding west across the Pacific.

This is the way "Mr. Roberts," the hero of Thomas Heggen's and Joshua Logan's now-classic play about the wartime navy, described the passage of a fast carrier task force—a sight that was becoming familiar in the Pacific in 1943. With *Essex*-class carriers, which carried 100 planes, and larger battleships, including the 45,000-ton *Iowa* class, joining the fleet along with new cruisers and destroyers, all bristling with antiaircraft guns, it became possible to create large task forces. Rather than the one or two carriers of the hard-pressed days of 1942, these formidable new forces might consist of a dozen carriers, a half-dozen battleships, and corresponding numbers of cruisers and destroyers.[42] By mid-1943 the navy had approximately 18,000 aircraft of all types, and this number had reached 30,000 by the end of 1944, with an accompanying improvement tn quality. The Grumman F6F Hellcat and Vought F4U Corsair were superior to the latest Japanese fighters, and the lumbering Devastator torpedo plane had been replaced by the Grumman TBF Avenger. Dive-bomber pilots' still swore by the reliable old Douglas Dauntless, however, and preferred it to the new Curtiss SB2C Helldiver.[43]

The navy went to war with 325,000 officers and men, and by war's end its ranks had increased almost tenfold to some 3.4 million people, about 100,000 of whom were Women Accepted for Volunteer Emergency Service, a name carefully worked out to produce the acronym WAVES.[44] Lieutenant John F. Kennedy, Lieutenant Commanders Lyndon B. Johnson, Richard M. Nixon, and Gerald R. Ford, Midshipman James Earl Carter, Jr., and Lieutenant George Bush were among those who served. Training such enormous numbers of people was a monumental task and, by June 1944, the navy was operating no less than 947 schools of various kinds with a daily attendance of 303,000. Seven boot camps absorbed raw youths, many of whom had never seen anything remotely resembling a warship until they clambered over the mockups of destroyer escorts erected on dusty drill grounds, and within a few weeks turned them into the semblance of sailors.

The war in the Pacific was a war of logistics. Fought across thousands of miles of blue water, it required a smooth-working system to keep the fleet supplied with food, fuel, and ammunition, and to repair damaged ships without time-consuming journeys back to the United States.[45] Although little attention had been given to logistics planning in the interwar years, the navy had begun experimenting with underway refueling during World War I, when the oiler *Maumee* replenished destroyers alongside while crossing the Atlantic to Queenstown. Refueling carriers at sea began in 1939. When World War II came and the navy was short of tenders, oilers, ammunition ships, and transports, it took civilian vessels into the fleet train and manned them with navy crews, while it awaited the completion of new construction. Along with the organization of the fast carrier task force itself, this floating logistics service was a unique American contribution to the art of war. As the carriers sailed westward, they were accompanied by squadrons of oilers, tenders, and freighters, ready to turn any remote atoll into a major base, complete with a floating dry dock and repair shops. Like Mr. Roberts' old *Reluctant,* the slow-moving freighters plowed the backwaters of the Pacific with "food and trucks and dungarees and toothpaste and toilet paper . . . from Tedium to Apathy [with] . . . an occasional trip to Monotony."

By the beginning of 1944, naval and amphibious forces under Admiral Halsey had fought their way up the northern Solomons and, combined with MacArthur's army and air forces which had worked around the southern tip of New Guinea, they seized New Britain and the Admiralty Islands, which lay just beyond. Rabaul, the key Japanese base in the area, was isolated and bypassed.

The Americans were poised for a return to the Philippines.[46] The main thrust against Japan, however, was launched across the central Pacific, through the strategically located and heavily defended Gilbert, Marshall, and Mariana islands, which the Japanese regarded as "unsinkable aircraft carriers" for their land-based planes.

The offensive began on November 20, 1943, when the newly created Fifth Fleet under the command of Vice Admiral Spruance, with Rear Admiral Marc A. Mitscher, a pioneer naval aviator, in charge of carriers and Rear Admiral Kelly Turner leading its amphibious forces, attacked Tarawa, in the Gilberts. Strongly entrenched and fighting to the last man, the Japanese had to be rooted out in three days of desperate hand-to-hand fighting in which about 1,000 marines were killed and another 2,000 were wounded. The entire Japanese garrison of some 4,800 men was wiped out. Kwajalein and Eniwetok, in the Marshalls, were captured in January and February 1944. Mitscher then, with Task Force 58 composed of carriers and fast battleships, raided the major Japanese base at Truk and destroyed most of the defending planes. Admiral Nimitz decided not to try to capture Truk and, instead, to capture Guam, Saipan, and Tinian, in the Marianas, a 1,000-mile leap across the Pacific—and only about 1,500 miles from Japan itself.[47]

The capture of these islands, which were to be used as springboards for long-range bomber and submarine attacks on Japan, was to be a joint army-navy venture and, as in most such operations, bickering and interservice rivalry arose. Nimitz quieted one such dispute with a story. "This all reminds me," he said, "of the first amphibious operation—conducted by Noah. When they were unloading from the Ark, he saw a pair of cats come out, followed by six kittens. 'What's this?' he asked. 'Ha, ha,' said the tabby cat, 'and all the time you thought we were fighting.' "[48]

Japanese carriers were sent to help resist the invasion of the Marianas, which began with a bitterly contested landing on Saipan on June 15, 1944. They had been provided with new planes but most of their air crews were inexperienced. "The Navy was frantic for pilots," said a Japanese flying instructor. "Men who could never have dreamed even of getting near a fighter plane before the war were now thrown into the battle."[49] As soon as Spruance received word from his submarines of the approach of a Japanese fleet of nine carriers and five battleships, he postponed a landing on Guam, scheduled for June 18, and deployed Mitscher's task force of fifteen carriers and seven battleships to the west of Saipan to meet the oncoming enemy. The Japanese commander, Admiral Jisaburo Ozawa, had certain factors in his favor: his options were not restricted, as were Spruance's by the need to defend the Saipan beachhead; his planes were longer-legged than those of the Americans; and although outnumbered two-to-one (956-473) in carrier aircraft, he intended to fight within reach of the squadrons based on the adjoining islands. The aggressive Mitscher wanted to attack the Japanese before they drew close enough to the Marianas to use those islands as bases for their carrier planes, but Spruance refused him permission to do this on the grounds that it would draw the ships away from the primary task of defending the beachhead and Turner's transports.[50]

The Battle of the Philippine Sea—or "The Great Marianas Turkey Shoot," as American fighter pilots later called it—began on the morning of June 19, when Admiral Ozawa launched sixty-nine planes against the American carriers. Hellcats shot down about twenty-five of them even before they came within sight of the American vessels, and most of the rest fell victim to the combat air patrols and antiaircraft guns firing shells fitted with the deadly new VT, or proximity fuse, which automatically detonated them within seventy feet of a target. With supreme courage, wave after wave of inexperienced Japanese pilots tried to break through the American defenses, only to be splashed in coveys into the sea. In all, a phenomenal 373 Japanese planes went down during the day. The submarine *Albacore* sank the 33,000-ton carrier *Taiho,* Ozawa's flagship, while the *Cavalla* dispatched the *Shokaku.*

The Japanese withdrew and were not found again until late the following afternoon, when they were just within range of Mitscher's air groups. Were he to launch his planes, they would probably have to return in the dark with nearly empty tanks, and few of his pilots had training in night landings. On the other hand, this might be the last opportunity to hit the enemy fleet. "Launch 'em," ordered Mitscher.[51] In six-inch-high letters, orders were chalked on all the ready-room blackboards: "Get the carriers!"

Just before sunset, 216 of Task Force 58's planes caught up with a part of Ozawa's retreating fleet. In the face of heavy antiaircraft fire, they sank the carrier *Hiyo,* along with a pair of fleet oilers, and damaged the *Zuikaku.* As Mitscher had foreseen, by the time they returned to their carriers, night had closed in and only a few of the more skilled—or luckier—pilots managed to land on the darkened decks. Men in the ships could hear the planes circling, the engines coughing and failing to catch again, and the heavy splashes as they ditched in the dark sea.

In the *Lexington*'s flag plot, every eye was on "Pete" Mitscher, his long-billed cap framing his gnarled face, slumped in his chair, quietly smoking a cigarette. He was torn between his identification with his pilots, most of whom would probably be lost if the fleet did not turn on its lights, and the possibility that the ships might be sunk by submarines if they were lit up. Suddenly he looked up at his chief of staff, Captain Arleigh Burke, and in a soft voice gave an order. "Turn on the lights."

Red masthead lights came on, glow lights outlined the flight decks of the carriers, and searchlights lit up the sky. One pilot said it was like "a Hollywood premiere, Chinese New Year's, and the Fourth of July rolled into one." Planes landed on any flight deck they could find, and some crashed into aircraft that had already landed. By 2200, when every plane had either landed or "ditched" in the sea, the carriers steamed away. Float planes and destroyers remained behind to search for downed airmen, and although about a hundred aircraft were lost, almost 90 per cent of the flyers were saved.[52]

From the start the patrol had gone badly for the submarine *Sealion.* First, she had failed to make contact with a Shanghai-bound convoy that should have been easy pickings. Then she had suffered a series of mechanical breakdowns that had put one of her stern torpedo tubes out of action. So, when three large pips appeared on her radar screen on the night of November 21, 1944, as she cruised the Formosa Strait, her skipper, Commander Eli T. Reich, hoped that his boat's luck was about to change. Making twenty knots on the surface, she closed on the targets, which turned out to be the old battleships *Haruna* and *Kongo* escorted by only a few destroyers. Reich fired six torpedoes at the lead battleship and three at the second. He scored three hits on the *Kongo* and the last spread hit one of the destroyers which exploded and sank. The battleships were only slightly slowed, however, and the *Sealion* gave chase. After a while the *Kongo* began to drop behind her consort, and Reich got into position to fire again. Before he could get off another shot, he reported, there was a

> tremendous explosion dead ahead—sky brilliantly illuminated, it looked like a sunset at midnight. Radar reports battleship pip getting smaller—that it has disappeared. . . . Destroyers seem to be milling around vicinity of target. Battleship sunk—the sun set.[53]

The *Sealion* was the first American submarine to sink a battleship—and she did it with only three torpedoes fired at extreme range. Six days later, off Honshu, the *Archerfish,* under Commander Joseph F. Enright, put four torpedoes into the largest aircraft carrier in the world, the 59,000-ton *Shinano.* Laid down as a sister ship of the *Yamato* and the *Musashi,* the *Shinano* had been converted to a carrier and had just been commissioned. As the sea poured into her ripped hull, it turned out that some of her watertight doors did not work and her inexperienced crew was too panic-stricken to make any serious effort to control the damage. She went down, taking 500 of her men with her.[54] These were the two most spectacular victories scored by American submarines in the war in the Pacific.

As an island nation, Japan depended on her maritime commerce for the oil and raw materials that fuelled her war machine, and much of the internal trade between the home islands was carried on by sea. Thus, she was particularly vulnerable to the ravages of a submarine war. In World War I, the United States had denounced unrestricted submarine warfare against shipping, but, immediately after Pearl Harbor, launched just such a campaign to cut Japan's strategic jugular. The primary weapon of this campaign was the 1,500-ton fleet submarine, which carried twenty-four torpedoes and had a cruising range of 10,000 miles.

In the early stages of the war, the navy could keep only about thirteen of its sixty-seven submarines on patrol at any given period and, because of the huge distances to be covered in the Pacific, half of the time they could remain at sea was spent on passage to the theater of war. Furthermore, the shortage of other vessels made it necessary for submarines often to be diverted to rescue missions and to supplying guerrillas in the Philippines. Another problem American submariners had to face was defective torpedoes, which had a tendency to run deeper than set, thus missing the target, and often failed to explode. It was not unknown for submarine skippers to have the unnerving experience of seeing their own tin fish double back on them because their gyroscope had failed.[55]

Vice Admiral Charles A. Lockwood, who in 1943 was appointed to command the Pacific Fleet's submarines, made aggressive use of his force. New boats, fitted with radar that enabled them to attack at night, came on the line and the defective torpedoes were replaced. The toll of Japanese merchant shipping began to mount, rising to 231,000 tons in November 1943 alone. Japanese antisubmarine efforts were surprisingly weak and ineffective. Apparently unwilling to face the reality that it would have to fight a defensive war, the Imperial Navy placed little emphasis on the building of escorts, and convoys were poorly defended. American intelligence having broken the Japanese codes, submarine commanders were often supplied with the positions of ships.

Beginning in 1944, Lockwood launched an all-out attack on the tankers that were carrying oil from Borneo and the East Indies to the home islands for distribution to various bases about the Pacific. Soon the tankers were being sunk at a faster rate that they could be replaced, the *Jack*, known as "Jack the Tanker Killer," disposing of four out of five of them in one convoy. Packs of three or four submarines, such as "Hydeman's Hellcats," "Blair's Blasters," and "Wilkins' Wildcats," roamed the seas around Japan. In October 1944, when sixty-eight U. S. submarines were on patrol, 320,900 tons of Japanese shipping, a third of it tankers, were sunk—the highest monthly score of the war.

In all, 288 American submarines accounted for 4,861,000 tons of Japanese merchant shipping, or 1,150 vessels, excluding small craft. By the end of the war the Japanese merchant marine had virtually ceased to exist. The submarines' toll of warships was 276, including a battleship and eight carriers. The U. S. Navy lost fifty submarines in action. In addition, mines planted by submarines, surface minelayers, and aircraft sank or damaged 1,075 ships, or a total of 2,250,000 tons of shipping—a significant portion of it in Japan's home waters. "The American submarine campaign against commerce was probably the most important single factor in the defeat of Japan," says Admiral Sir Arthur Hezlet. The "unrestricted campaign against sea communications . . . weakened Japan to an extent which enabled an amphibious drive supported by carrier-borne air power to succeed."[56]

With the Marianas safely in the bag and Rabaul isolated, the Philippines became the next American target. Originally, the navy planned to bypass the archipelago except for Mindanao on the southern rim, and to attack Formosa preparatory to the final assault on Japan. But General MacArthur argued that Luzon should be the springboard to the Japanese home islands and made the emotional appeal that the United States was honor-bound to liberate the Philippines. MacArthur's argument prevailed, and a landing was scheduled for Mindanao in mid-November 1944 and Leyte, in the center of the islands, a month later. The question of whether Luzon or Formosa would follow was left open.

The Leyte landing was speeded up to October 20 and the Mindanao operation abandoned when Admiral Halsey, succeeding Spruance in command of the Fifth Fleet, which had been redesignated the Third Fleet, raided the islands and reported that Japanese resistance was surprisingly weak. In preparation for the assault, Mitscher gave Japanese airfields and other installations on Formosa a severe pasting, in which more than 500 aircraft were destroyed at a cost of 79 American planes. To bolster morale at home, the Japanese claimed to have sunk the entire American fleet, prompting Halsey to report that he was "retiring toward the enemy following the salvage of the Third Fleet ships recently reported sunk by Radio Tokyo."[57]

When an army under the command of General MacArthur landed on Leyte with little difficulty, the Japanese put into effect the Sho, or Victory, Plan. Like most Japanese naval planning it was a complex blend of stealth, ruse, and division of forces intended to keep the enemy off balance. Two fleets were to converge on Leyte Gulf, sink the amphibious vessels of Vice Admiral Thomas C. Kinkaid's Seventh Fleet, and cut off the American beachhead. The stronger of these fleets, under the command of Vice Admiral Takeo Kurita and consisting of five battleships, including the *Yamato* and *Musashi,* was to pass through San Bernardino Strait, to the north of Leyte. The other, to include two old battleships under the command of Vice Admiral Shoji Nishimura, was to transit Surigao Strait, to the south, with the support of Vice Admiral Kiyohide Shima's three cruisers and two destroyers. Ozawa's four remaining carriers, which had been all but stripped of their aircraft at the Battle of the Philippine Sea, were to form a third group and to come in from the home islands to lure Halsey and his ships away from Leyte. The four actions that resulted are known collectively as the Battle for Leyte Gulf, which, in terms of numbers of men, planes, ships, and distances covered, still stands as the greatest naval battle in history.[58]

The heavy toll of tankers taken by American submarines had created such a shortage of fuel that it took the Japanese units involved in the Sho Plan nearly a week to arrive off Leyte. This delay caused them to miss the chance to attack the American invasion fleet while it was unloading. Admiral Kurita's force lost the advantage of surprise when two submarines, the *Darter* and *Dace,* detected it in the South China Sea and sank two cruisers, one of them the flagship *Atago,* and heavily damaged another. Japanese land-based planes attacked Halsey's carriers off Luzon the next day and so badly damaged the light carrier *Princeton* that she was abandoned and sunk. Kurita's main body, which had no air cover, was attacked by American planes in the Sibuyan Sea, to the west, and the *Musashi* was sunk. She absorbed nineteen torpedo and seventeen bomb hits before slipping beneath the waves.

Forewarned of the approach of Nishimura's southern force and surmising correctly that it was heading for the Surigao Strait, Admiral Kinkaid ordered Rear Admiral Jesse B. Oldendorf to deploy his half-dozen old battleships—the *West Virginia, Tennessee, California, Maryland, Pennsylvania,* and *Mississippi*—across the northern end of the strait and await its arrival. Entering the passage shortly after midnight on October 24, Nishimura was promptly harassed by destroyers and PT-boats. Destroyer Squadrons 54 and 23 launched a series of daring torpedo attacks that sank the battleship *Fuso* and two destroyers and damaged the *Fuso*'s consort, the *Yamashiro*—all without sustaining any damage themselves. At the end of the passage, neatly crossing the Japanese T, lay Oldendorf's battleships, which poured down a storm of radar-directed 14- and 16-inch shells upon the remains of Nishimura's hapless squadron. A pair of torpedoes fired by the destroyer *Newcomb* just before daylight finished off the flaming *Yamashiro*. Admiral Shima's cruiser and destroyer squadron arrived at the strait several hours after Nishimura, and upon meeting the battered survivors of the retreating force turned tail without firing a shot. During the entire action the Japanese managed to hit only one American destroyer. The last naval battle ever to be fought in a formal line had ended in a sweeping victory for the U. S. Navy—a victory particularly sweet because it was won by ships that had been put out of action at Pearl Harbor.[59]

Earlier on the evening of October 24, Halsey had received reports that Ozawa's carriers were approaching, and, not knowing they were almost devoid of planes, swallowed the bait dangled before him. As the Japanese intended him to do, he regarded the flattops, rather than Kurita's force, as his primary target. Accepting the overly optimistic reports of his pilots concerning the damage they had inflicted on the enemy, Halsey easily convinced himself that Kinkaid had enough strength to deal with Kurita. In his memoirs, he recalled: "I went into the flag plot, put my finger on. . . [Ozawa's] charted position, 300 miles away, and said, 'Here's where we're going . . . start them north.' "[60]

Kinkaid was informed of Halsey's decision to go north, but having picked up a confusing directive that Halsey had transmitted earlier, he thought Task Force 34 was being left to guard San Bernardino Strait—which was not the case. Halsey, in turn, was under the impression that Kinkaid was maintaining surveillance of the area. In fact, the strait was left wide open, and Kurita steamed through in the dark undetected. The Sho Plan appeared to be working, in spite of heavy losses.

Escort Group "Taffy-3"—six small escort, or "jeep," carriers and seven destroyers and destroyer escorts—commanded by Rear Admiral Clifton A. F. Sprague had begun operations off Samar at sunrise on October 25. Avenger bombers and old Wildcat fighters were taking off to attack Japanese positions on Leyte when a scout plane radioed that four enemy battleships, seven cruisers, and eleven destroyers were approaching at high speed. "Air plot, tell him to check his identification," replied Sprague, irritated that the pilot had obviously misidentified some of Admiral Halsey's ships. Back came the answer: "Identification of enemy forces confirmed. Ships have pagoda masts!"[61]

Kurita's powerful force suddenly loomed up and the sea about the jeep carriers began to spout geysers made by falling shells. But if Sprague was startled by the unexpected appearance of the Japanese, Kurita was equally surprised to see him and mistook Taffy-3 for Halsey's fast carriers and battleships. Instead of leaving a few cruisers behind to finish them off and pressing on to attack Kinkaid's transports and cargo vessels thought to be lying 100 miles to the south, he diverted his entire force to an attack on Sprague.

"I didn't think we'd last fifteen minutes," said Sprague, but "I thought we might as well give them all we've got before we go down." He launched his remaining planes against the oncoming enemy with anything that could be crammed into them—heavy bombs, fragmentation bombs, torpedoes, depth charges. When his planes had been launched, his ships dodged in and out of series of squalls and took refuge behind a smoke screen. Help was sought from Kinkaid and from nearby escort groups under Rear Admirals Felix B. Stump and Thomas L. Sprague. When the pilots of Taffy-3's motley collection of planes had dropped their bombs, they strafed the Japanese ships, and when they ran out of ammunition, they made passes over them to distract the gunners. Sprague also ordered his destroyer escorts to make torpedo attacks. "Small boys . . . intercept!" he radioed. The *Hoel, Heerman,* and *Johnston* dashed in close to the enemy cruisers before loosing their tin fish. "We need a bugler to sound the charge," said Commander Amos T. Hathaway in the *Heerman.*[62] When the destroyers had expended their torpedoes and hit a cruiser, they peppered the well-armored Japanese ships with 5-inch shells.

The big guns of Kurita's battleships soon found the range and hit the *Johnston* with a salvo of 14-inch shells. "It was like a puppy being smacked by a truck," said one of her officers. In the hope of diverting fire from the fragile carriers, the *Heerman* engaged all four of the big ships, including the *Yamato.* To confuse the enemy gunners, Hathaway zigzagged and ran from splash to splash, believing the Japanese would not fire twice at the same place. A shell struck a locker full of dried navy beans, reducing them to pulp, which was sucked up through an intake and dumped on an officer on the bridge. "He lost his taste for beans right there," said Hathaway. Now, the carriers were taking hits, reported Sprague, and one, the *Kalinin Bay,* was struck sixteen times:

> The shells created a shambles below decks . . . only the heroic efforts of her
> crew kept the little ship going. Bos'n's crews wrestled under five feet of
> water to plug up big holes in the hull; engineers worked knee-deep in oil,

choking in the stench of burned rubber; quartermasters steered the ship for hours from the emergency wheel below, as fire scorched the deck on which they stood; and all hands risked their lives to save mates in flooded or burning compartments.

Where was Halsey? That morning, his carriers had located Ozawa's decoy force off Cape Engaño, at the northeastern tip of Luzon, and he had launched repeated attacks that led to the sinking of four carriers, including the *Zuikaku*, last survivor of the Pearl Harbor attack force. Ozawa continued his race to the north with the survivors. While Halsey, hoping to bring his battleships in range of the Japanese, pounded along astern, Kinkaid was filling the airwaves with frantic pleas for assistance. At Pearl Harbor, Nimitz, anxiously monitoring the situation, sent a message, with copies to Admiral King, in Washington, and to Kinkaid, seeking information from Halsey. The communications officer who encoded the message added the usual padding to distract enemy cryptographers. Perhaps thinking of "The Charge of the Light Brigade," as E. B. Potter suggests in his biography of Nimitz, he used the words "the world wonders." However, when the message was received on board Halsey's flagship, the *New Jersey*, the final phrase was thought to be part of the message and it was handed to the admiral in the following form: "Where is Rpt Where Is Task Force Thirty Four RR The World Wonders."[63]

"I was as stunned as if I had been struck in the face," Halsey wrote later. "The paper rattled in my hands. I snatched off my cap, threw it on the deck."[64] Furious at what he thought was public criticism from Nimitz, the admiral delayed for an hour—he says he was refueling his ships—before leading the task force south. Ozawa's ships were only forty-two miles away when he put about, Halsey claimed. In any case, it was too late to catch Kurita who, having disposed of only one of Taffy-3's gallant escort carriers, escaped through the San Bernardino Strait.

The Battle for Leyte Gulf—fought almost entirely outside that body of water—cost the Japanese four aircraft carriers, three battleships, nine cruisers, and ten destroyers, or more tonnage than was lost by both sides at Jutland. For all practical purposes, it marked the end of the Imperial Japanese Navy as an organized fighting force.

The Rising Sun was setting, but many more brave men were to die and many more gallant ships were to be lost before it went down in a blood-red sea. While the advance through the Philippines was in progress, the United States began planning for the capture of island bases to be used as staging areas for the invasion of the Japanese home islands. Iwo Jima, a small island of volcanic origin lying midway between the American base on Saipan and Tokyo, was pinpointed as an airfield for fighters accompanying the B-29 Superforts that were levelling Japan's cities in fire raids and as a halfway house for damaged bombers. It was pocked with caves that proved impervious to aerial bombing and naval gunfire, and the 20,000 defenders had to be dug out, almost man by man, in a month-long battle that cost the lives of some 6,000 marines, the Corps' costliest campaign yet in the Pacific war.

On Easter Sunday, April 1, 1945, the highly experienced amphibious team of Spruance and Turner landed an army-marine force that eventually reached more than 200,000 men on Okinawa, largest island of the Ryukyu chain, only 350 miles from Kyushu.[65] Early resistance was light, but as the Americans fanned out from their beachheads, they found that the defending garrison of some 100,000 men intended to contest every foot of the island. The Japanese were going to bleed and exhaust the Americans and prevent their invading the home islands of Japan.

For the U. S. Navy, the Okinawa operation proved to be the deadliest of the war. Unlike Guadalcanal, where the marines complained that Admiral Turner had abandoned them on the beaches, the fleet came to stay—and it did, without flinching, through the most harrowing assault any navy has ever suffered. This offensive did not come from the Japanese fleet, for it had all but ceased to exist since the Philippines campaign. And it did not consist of massive aerial bombing, for Japan had lost most of her experienced air crews. It was launched by the Kamikaze—"Divine Wind"—Corps, which tried to crash its planes into the American ships. This tactic was completely foreign to the Western mind, and no matter how alert the combat air patrols or how effective the curtain of anti-aircraft fire thrown up by the ships, some suicide planes got through. The kamikazes first appeared during the Philippines campaign, where they wrecked and sank several ships, causing heavy casualties.

During the softening-up of Japan prior to the Okinawa landing, the carrier *Franklin* was severely damaged by bombs and set afire. Racked by explosions and transformed into a fiery hell, she would have been lost had it not been for the skill and courage of her officers and men. As it was, she lost 724 men killed and 265 wounded. The *Wasp* and *Yorktown*, new carriers named for old fighters, were also mauled, but none of these setbacks upset the invasion timetable.

The Japanese also used the remnants of their surface fleet as kamikazes. The *Yamato*, carrying only enough fuel for a one-way trip, was steaming toward Okinawa on April 7 to annihilate the invasion fleet with her huge guns when she was caught in the East China Sea by Mitscher's planes. Wave after wave of dive bombers, torpedo planes, and fighters swooped to the attack, and in little more than two hours, the *Yamato* rolled over and sank, taking 2,488 of her crew with her. A light cruiser and four of eight accompanying destroyers were also sent to the bottom. Only ten of the attacking planes were lost.

The day before, the kamikazes had unleashed their full fury against the fleet riding off Okinawa, the brunt being borne by the destroyers, escorts, gunboats, and minesweepers that formed a radar picket circle around the island.

From every quarter of the compass, kamikazes and conventional bombers bored in to attack. More than 400 were splashed by fighters before they even reached the target area, or by heavy flak when they came within range of the ships, but nineteen vessels were hit, some of them several times, and six were sunk. Commander Albert O. Momm, of the destroyer *Mullany,* reported that even a direct hit failed to halt one plunging kamikaze:

> The plane crashed into the ship at the after deckhouse between the two high 5-inch gun mounts, and exploding with a spray of gasoline started huge fires, leaving the deckhouse, gun mounts, and gun directors a mass of torn wreckage. We lost steering control and communications abaft the after deckhouse. Attempts to sprinkle the after magazines and ammunition handling rooms were useless; the fire mains had been pierced and sprinkler valves destroyed by the crash and explosions that followed it.[66]

The *Mullany* was dead in the water, but her consorts helped put out the fires and with emergency pumps rigged, she limped away under her own power. The destroyer *Laffey* was attacked on April 16 by twenty-two suicide planes. In less than eighty minutes, six of them crashed into her and she was hit by four bombs. Eight of the attackers were shot down by her guns. "Probably no [other] ship has ever survived an attack of the intensity that she experienced." Morison observed.

Over the next three months, the attacks continued—despite heavy losses and the pounding given the airfields from which the kamikazes flew. The suicide planes were devastating against cruisers, destroyers, and lightly armored vessels but were relatively ineffective against the heavy armor of battleships. In all, the Okinawa campaign cost the navy 34 ships sunk and 368 damaged. More than 4,900 sailors were killed or reported missing, and another 4,800 were wounded. Through it all, the crews of the picket vessels managed to keep their sense of humor. One gunboat crew, weary of being attacked while larger ships were ignored, erected on her deck a large sign with a pointing arrow and the words: "To Jap Pilot—This Way to Task Force 58."[67]

After the conquest of Okinawa, American carriers ranged almost at will in Japanese waters, raking airfields beyond the reach of the B-29s, bombing rail yards, and attacking vital facilities. The home islands had been all but isolated by the submarine and mine, in preparation for the invasion, when the awesome flash of an atomic bomb burst over Hiroshima on August 6 and over Nagasaki three days later. In the interim the Soviet Union entered the war and invaded Manchuria. Convinced at last of the futility of further resistance, the Japanese surrendered on August 14, 1945. The formal ceremony of capitulation took place on September 2 on the deck of the *Missouri,* as she rode in Tokyo Bay, not far from where Commodore Matthew Calbraith Perry had anchored nearly a century before. She flew the flag that had flown over the Capitol on December 7, 1941.[68]

10

"CHALLENGING YEARS"

*When the animals had gathered, the lion looked at the eagle
and said gravely, "We must abolish talons." The tiger
looked at the elephant and said, "We must abolish tusks."
The elephant looked back at the tiger and said, "We must
abolish claws and jaws." Thus each animal in turn proposed
the abolition of the weapons he did not have, until at last
the bear rose up and said in tones of sweet reasonableness:
"Comrades, let us abolish everything—everything but the
great universal embrace."*

—Attributed to Winston Churchill

Wreathed in the acrid white smoke of her salutes, the *Missouri* swung to her anchors off Istanbul on April 5, 1946, as the morning sun brightened the domes and minarets of the old city's countless mosques. Thousands of Turks crowded the shore to welcome the famous battleship, and small craft swarmed about her with lighthearted curiosity. Officially, the *Missouri* had steamed into the Bosporus to bring home the body of a Turkish ambassador who had died in Washington. In reality, she was there to demonstrate American support for Turkey's steadfast refusal to allow the Soviet Union a share in the control of the Dardanelles. Less than a year had passed since the defeat of Nazi Germany and Imperial Japan, but suspicion and fear among the wartime allies had already planted the seeds of cold war.[1]

The duel between the United States and the Soviet Union and their respective allies was precipitated by the collapse of Europe and the disintegration of the old colonial order in Asia. Mixing their sense of insecurity with their goal of world revolution, the Russians moved to fill this strategic vacuum, while the United States slowly committed itself to defense of the West from Soviet ambitions. Over the next quarter-century the navy, returning to the days when it maintained distant stations, showed the flag from the Mediterranean to the South China Sea—wherever the Communists were found to be fishing in troubled

245

waters. As Walter Lippmann, the most widely respected foreign-policy analyst of the day, noted, a call by a warship at some crisis point—such as the visit of the *Missouri* to the eastern Mediterranean—was an effective instrument of diplomacy even in the nuclear age. The atom bomb is "a weapon for the extermination of civilians," he said, and "it cannot replace a regiment of Marines or a visit of a warship to a troubled spot."[2]

With the Russians pressing hard to force the barrier that contained them to the north of the Mediterranean, President Harry S Truman sent vessels into the area to bolster the Greek and Turkish governments, both of which were faced with internal and external Communist threats. The presence of these warships assured them that the United States supported their struggles to remain free of Soviet domination. Under the newly enunciated Truman Doctrine, which broke with America's traditional foreign policy of noninvolvement in the affairs of Europe, substantial amounts of military and economic assistance were made available to both countries. "Our policy [was] to support the cause of freedom wherever it was threatened," said Truman.[3]

After many ebbs and flows of strength, the American naval force in the Mediterranean was slowly built up and was eventually designated the Sixth Fleet, successor to the Mediterranean Squadron of the previous century. Effective use was made of naval power during the Italian elections of 1948, when it was thought that the Communists might stage a coup. American ships paid courtesy calls at ports on the east and west coasts of Italy, and the air group of the 45,000-ton carrier *Franklin D. Roosevelt* swept over the peninsula to indicate that the United States would not sit silently by and allow the Italian government to be overthrown. A few months later, naval aircraft joined the air force in maintaining a life line to West Berlin, land access to which had been cut off by the Russians. This airlift of food and supplies lasted a year, and about 25 per cent of the cargo flown into beleaguered Berlin was brought in by navy planes.[4]

While it was serving as the strong arm of American foreign policy, the navy was engaged in a struggle for its very existence. For it, the years immediately following the war were a period of conflict, confusion, and contraction. When the Japanese surrender was signed within the shadow of the *Missouri's* big guns, the navy was the most powerful maritime force ever seen, but within a year, it had been reduced to a shade of its wartime self. Oblivious of its global responsibilities as the guarantor of the United Nations, an organization formed to ensure permanent world peace, the American people had no desire to maintain sizeable military or naval forces and allowed them to be dismantled.

War's end was greeted by a clamor to "bring the boys home" and was followed by the institution of Operation Magic Carpet, during which even battleships and aircraft carriers were pressed into service as troopships. In spite of the fact that the navy was itself in the process of demobilization, between October 1, 1945, and May 1, 1946, it carried more than two million men home to the

United States. Of the more than three million men and women on active naval service at the time of the Japanese surrender, only about half a million remained a year later. This drastic reduction made it difficult at times to man even the relatively few ships still on active service. Construction was halted on 9,800 ships and small craft, another 2,000 were decommissioned and "mothballed," and even larger numbers were declared surplus.[5]

Sea power had played a vital role in the defeat of Germany and Japan, yet the navy suffered more than the other services from the strategic fallout of the atom bomb. The American public, fed the false claim that strategic bombing had won the war, regarded the air force, with its long-range bomber, as the nation's first line of defense. Assured that bombing would provide a quick and cheap victory in any future war, many people did not see any need to maintain a strong fleet. In the age of atomic warfare, the fast carrier task force was regarded as an anachronism, and such a massive concentration of ships was seen as being more vulnerable to the bomb than any other weapon system. Because carrier aircraft were not big enough to carry the primitive "Fat Man" bombs of the period, the air force had a monopoly on the delivery of the bomb, and some strategists doubted that the navy would have an important role to play in the future.[6]

"Why should we have a Navy at all?" asked General Carl A. Spaatz, who had directed the bombing of Germany. "The Russians have little or no navy. . . . The only reason for us to have a Navy is because someone else has a navy and we certainly do not need to waste money on that."[7] Taking a more realistic view, Admiral Nimitz, then chief of naval operations, pointed out that the same thing had been said about the navy when the submarine, the torpedo, and the airplane were introduced. "While the prophets of naval doom are shouting themselves hoarse, the Navy will be at work to make the changes needed to accommodate American sea power to the new weapons," he declared. "The American genius for the exercise of sea power will not be allowed to languish."[8]

Faced with this threat to its existence, the navy launched an all-out effort to obtain a share of nuclear capability. Because the *Essex*-class carriers and the three ships of the 45,000-ton *Midway* class that were coming into service at war's end were too small to embark large jet planes, supercarriers that could handle multiengine aircraft capable of carrying the atom bomb were planned. While these ships and planes were under development, the Lockheed P2V anti-submarine patrol plane was converted to carrier use to provide the navy with a nuclear-air-strike capability.[9]

Some officers, including Admiral Forrest P. Sherman, Nimitz's deputy chief of naval operations, saw an opportunity for the navy in the challenge of the atomic age. Describing the warship of the future, Sherman envisioned "a large armored vessel firing guided missiles with atomic warheads." Before World War II, the Naval Research Laboratory had made preliminary studies of nuclear propulsion, and almost immediately after the end of hostilities discussions were begun about the possibility of producing a nuclear-powered submarine. However, there were significant technological barriers to such a project: a shortage of nuclear fuel; inability to design a reactor small enough to fit inside a submarine hull; and, even more important, a complete lack of naval personnel with nuclear training. The first step toward acquiring such expertise was the assignment of a small group of officers to the nuclear laboratory at Oak Ridge, Tennessee— among whom was a fiercely energetic and prickly engineering captain named Hyman G. Rickover.[10]

Plans for the unification of the armed forces also caused problems for the navy. Various proposals for the creation of a single department of defense had been discussed since the early 1920s when Billy Mitchell had tried to drum up support for an independent air force, but the army and navy had successfully resisted all such moves. With the end of World War II, however, unification was an idea whose time had come. Public opinion supported it in the belief that it would lead to economies in military procurement and would prevent a repetition of the lack of coordination between the army and navy that had contributed to the disaster at Pearl Harbor. The army, convinced of the efficacy of unified command, now supported a merger, and so did the air force, which believed that this would bring about its independence from the army. Only the admirals held back.[11]

There were several reasons for the navy's position. With the air force in possession of a monopoly of the atom bomb and the means of delivering it, the navy feared that in a merged defense establishment it would be subordinate to the air force. It also feared that the army and air force, neither of which understood the realities of sea power and maritime strategy, would gang up on it when the defense budget was being allocated. The army had been antagonistic to the marines, particularly since the battle for Saipan, where its operations were criticized by the marines, and there were indications that the corps might be abolished or absorbed into the army. The air force, contending that "the air is indivisible," was eyeing the naval air arm and the navy was concerned that it would be stripped of control of its shore-based aircraft, as the British, German, and Italian navies had been before World War II—with dire results for their operations. The navy's fears seemed to be summed up in a speech that Air Force General Frank A. Armstrong, Jr., made at a goodwill dinner arranged by Norfolk businessmen:

> You gentlemen had better understand that the Army Air Force is tired of being a subordinate outfit. It was a predominant force during the war, and it is going to be a predominant force during the peace . . . and we do not care whether you like it or not. The Army Air Force is going to run the show. You, the Navy, are not going to have anything but a couple of carriers which are

ineffective anyway, and they will probably be sunk in the first battle. Now as for the Marines, you know what the Marines are, a small bitched-up army talking Navy lingo. We are going to put those Marines in the Regular Army and make efficient soldiers out of them.[12]

Such remarks raised the hackles of the admirals, and only after considerable maneuvering was the National Security Act, which provided for unification, finally approved by Congress and signed into law by President Truman on July 26, 1947. The air force achieved its long-sought goal of independence from the army, but the navy obtained important concessions. Legal assurances were given that land-based naval antisubmarine aircraft would not be merged into the new air force and the marines were provided with statutory protection against any future raids by the army. James V. Forrestal, a Wall Street financier who had come to Washington to serve as the navy's first undersecretary and had been named secretary of the navy in 1944, following the death of Frank Knox, was appointed the first secretary of defense. In that position, Forrestal became a cabinet member, while the secretaries of war, navy, and air force were downgraded to sub-cabinet level.[13]

Under Forrestal's strong leadership, this compromise arrangement proceeded on a more-or-less-even keel, in spite of backstage bickering over the allocation of the diminishing defense budget. In March 1949, however, a nervous breakdown resulting from overwork forced Forrestal to resign. The new secretary of defense, Louis A. Johnson, was a lawyer-politician active in veterans' affairs who was rewarded with the post for his activities as a fund-raiser in behalf of Truman during the presidential campaign of 1948. He proved to be tactless and overbearing, and within a few weeks of his assumption of office, the defense establishment was shaken by what came to be known as the "admirals' revolt."[14]

Throughout the unification struggle, with the approval of the White House and Congress, planning for the proposed 60,000-ton supercarrier *United States* had continued. Funds for construction were appropriated and the keel of the vessel was laid at Newport News, Virginia, on April 18, 1949. Five days later, when Secretary of the Navy John L. Sullivan was out of town, Johnson ordered all work on the carrier halted, ostensibly for budgetary reasons. Admiral Louis E. Denfeld, the chief of naval operations, learned of the action through a press release. The navy was flabbergasted. Sullivan resigned immediately in protest. When the admirals recovered from the shock, they interpreted Johnson's action as part of a campaign by the air force to sabotage the navy's only hope for a future. Whether correct or not, this conspiratorial view of events was given credibility when funds allegedly saved by cancellation of the *United States* were earmarked for the purchase of greater numbers of the air force's huge new intercontinental bomber, the B-36.

Repeatedly outvoted in the meetings of the Joint Chiefs of Staff and with its appropriations being whittled away, the navy feared that it would be reduced to a convoy-escort service. The crisis boiled over when Captain John G. Crommelin, a distinguished naval combat pilot, supplied the press with documents showing that key naval officers, including Admiral Denfeld, were sharply critical of Johnson's management of defense policy and were concerned about what they considered to be the perilous state of the nation's security. The resulting uproar led to a congressional investigation in which naval officers, led by Admiral Arthur W. Radford, commander in chief of the Pacific Fleet, attacked Johnson's budgetary policies and the air force's claims for the effectiveness of strategic bombing.[15]

Much of the navy's fire was concentrated on the B-36, which was characterized as "a billion dollar blunder." With a range of 5,000 miles, the plane was designed to carry an atom bomb from American bases to any target on the globe without refueling. Critics pointed out, however, that the B-36, which had been designed as early as 1940 and had piston engines, was capable of a top speed of only about 375 miles an hour, and its service ceiling of 40,000 feet made it vulnerable to the new Russian MIG-15 jet fighters. Just as the congressional hearings got under way in October 1949, it was learned that the Russians had exploded a nuclear device, ending U. S. control of the atom bomb. The new dimension that this added to the discussions was quickly exploited by the navy. With both superpowers now in possession of the ultimate weapon of destruction, it was foolhardy to talk of atomic warfare, Admiral Radford declared. "In planning to wage a war . . . we must look to the peace to follow . . . a war of annihilation might possibly bring a Pyrrhic military victory, but it would be politically and economically senseless."[16]

Testimony from ranking naval officers on active duty, as well as from those on the retired list such as Admirals King, Nimitz, Halsey, and Spruance, attacked the B-36, questioned the validity of air force claims about strategic bombing, and warned of the effects Louis Johnson's budget cuts would have on the navy's combat readiness. In the end, the budget cuts remained in effect and even the B-36 program was trimmed. Although Admiral Denfeld had given only lukewarm public support to Johnson's critics, he was relieved as chief of naval operations. But the admirals' revolt was successful in that it focused public opinion on the navy's plight and put the claims of the air force into proper perspective.

Perhaps the outstanding feature of the episode was the clarity with which it revealed America's basic strategy in the Cold War.[17] The navy's efforts to emphasize the nation's need to be prepared to fight limited, as well as atomic, wars in an age of nuclear stalemate fell on deaf ears; all scenarios were based on the assumption that the next war would be an all-out atomic struggle and that the "one possible enemy" was the Soviet Union. When the Cold War did erupt into actual fighting, however, the opponent proved to be a Soviet satellite, and the war was fought below the atomic threshold—a situation for which the United States was not prepared. In spite of Louis Johnson's claims that his reductions in defense spending amounted to cutting away "fat not muscle," when the armed forces were put to the test, it was found that only five years after World War II, the American military machine had painfully little muscle.

The Cold War flamed into a hot war in East Asia where the end of World War II had not brought peace.[18] After the Japanese surrender, the Chinese Communists and Nationalists, the latter supported by the United States, fought a civil war for control of China, a struggle that ended in 1949 with the victory of the Communists and the retreat of the Nationalists to Formosa, or Taiwan. A Communist victory resulted in the closing of the Open Door, which had been the keystone of American policy in the Far East and one of the major reasons for the war with Japan. Containment of Communist expansion took its place, and the first implementation of this policy was costly—the Korean War.

This conflict was an outgrowth of the settlement that followed the capitulation of Japan. The Russians accepted the surrender of Japanese forces in Korea north of the 38th parallel, and the United States accepted the surrender of those south of it. Plans for free elections to determine Korea's future government fell through when the Russians refused to allow a United Nations observation team to enter their zone. The peninsula was divided along the parallel into two rival nations—a Russian-backed Communist regime in the north and an American-supported regime in the south, both claiming to be the legitimate rulers of all Korea.

In the early morning hours of June 25, 1950, the North Koreans crossed the 38th parallel, justifying their action on the grounds that they were repelling an invasion. Outclassed militarily, the South Koreans were driven from Seoul, and it appeared that the entire country would soon be overrun. Acting swiftly, the United States went before the United Nations Security Council with a resolution branding the invasion a breach of international peace and demanding that the North Koreans withdraw. In the absence of the Russians, who were boycotting the organization, the resolution was approved. Two days later, on June 27, the Security Council, acting on another American resolution, directed the member states of the United Nations to "furnish such assistance to the Republic of Korea as may be necessary to repel the armed attack."

President Truman immediately instructed General Douglas MacArthur, the commander in chief in the Far East, to deploy naval and air units to help the South Koreans to stem the invasion, and on June 30 issued an order permitting the use of American ground forces. Troops from Britain, Greece, Turkey, and other nations also sent troops to fight under the blue and white banner of the United Nations. Worried that the attack by the North Koreans might be the start of a general Communist offensive, the president ordered the Seventh Fleet, which had been maintained in Asian waters since World War II, into the Formosa Strait to prevent both the Chinese Communists from invading Taiwan and the Nationalists from using the emergency to harass the mainland.

With most of America's naval strength deployed in the Atlantic, the Seventh Fleet, commanded by Vice Admiral Arthur D. Struble, consisted of only one *Essex*-class carrier, the *Valley Forge*, the heavy cruiser *Rochester*, and eight destroyers. Task Force 96, based on Japan and under the command of Vice Admiral C. Turner Joy, included the antiaircraft cruiser *Juneau* and four destroyers. A handful of mine sweepers and auxiliary craft was also in Far Eastern waters. Although by World War II standards these units were insignificant, they were far superior to those of the North Korean navy, which consisted of about forty-five small craft, including a few Russian-built torpedo boats.

While American troops and supplies poured into the small defense perimeter around Pusan, on Korea's southeastern coast, the *Valley Forge* and the British light carrier *Triumph* ranged up and down the coasts of Korea, launching their planes against the North Korean army and its supply lines. Since there were few targets in Korea for strategic bombers, much of the brunt of the action was borne by fighter-bombers. Air force jets based in Japan lacked the range required to attack objectives in North Korea and there were not enough airfields in the south to accommodate them. Consequently, it was left to the jets and piston planes from the carriers to take the war to the enemy. With bombs and rockets, they blasted the main air base near Pyongyang, the capital of North Korea, shooting down or wrecking on the ground most of the enemy's air force. British and American cruisers and destroyers also shelled shore batteries and enemy forces moving along coastal roads, destroyed bridges, and broke up formations of small craft carrying supplies and ammunition. On July 2, three of four torpedo boats that attacked the *Juneau* and the British cruiser *Jamaica* were sunk or put out of action. That was the first—and last—time the North Korean navy made any attempt to contest Allied command of the sea.

By the end of the summer of 1950, the situation having stabilized, General MacArthur saw the time as ripe for a decisive blow—an amphibious landing in the enemy's rear.[19] Ironically, only a few months earlier, Louis Johnson had unburdened himself of the opinion that "amphibious operations are a thing of the past. We'll never have any more amphibious operations."[20]

Inchon, a port city near Seoul and Kimpo, South Korea's largest airfield, was the site selected, and the strategy was that when marines had been landed, the Eighth Army would break out of the Pusan perimeter, and the North Koreans would be crushed between the hammer and anvil of the two forces. The amphibious phase of the operation was a daring gamble because the phenomenal tides at Inchon not only created unusually strong currents but limited the period in which a landing could be made to only a few days each month—and to only a few hours on each of those days. Furthermore, the approach to the city, which was guarded by substantial fortifications, was via a twisting and treacherous channel with wide mud flats that could cause landing craft to ground well offshore. Unlike the amphibious landings of World War II, which had been made on beaches, the one at Inchon required the assault troops to clamber over sea walls and piers while under enemy fire.

D-Day for the assault by the First Marine Division was set for September 15, and on September 10 the softening-up process began. Planes from Task Force 7 launched a series of strikes on Wolmi-do, an island fortress connected with Inchon by a causeway, and concentrated bombardment by destroyers lured the enemy gunners into showing themselves. Three destroyers, the *Lyman K. Swenson*, *Collett*, and *Gurke*, sustained hits before the heavier guns of the American and British cruisers began pounding the fortifications with considerable effect.

As the pre-dawn gloom of September 15 began to fade, the bulky outlines of 230 ships appeared out of the Yellow Sea, like the ghosts of some great invasion fleet of World War II. A lookout was kept for Russian submarines but none appeared. By the standards of 1945, the Inchon invasion force was not overwhelming, but considering the state of the navy and the short time in which the ships had been gathered, its existence was nothing less than phenomenal. Every combat ship available in the Pacific was pressed into service, and American and even some Japanese merchant ships were chartered. The attack force under Rear Admiral James H. Doyle gingerly threaded its way up the channel toward Inchon with the command ship *Mount McKinley* in the rear. On board her were General MacArthur and what Marine Corps Colonel Robert D. Heinl, Jr., called "a star-studded galaxy of admirals and generals" who were "soon dubbed 'VIKs' (Very Important Kibitzers) by the working staffs."[21]

Wolmi-do, with its garrison of 400 men and elaborate fortifications, was to be taken on the morning tide and the assault against Inchon itself launched on the evening tide. Planes and naval guns pounded the island and the first marines were ashore by 6:30 A.M. Within a half-hour the Stars and Stripes was broken atop the highest point of the island. "That's it," said MacArthur to his retinue. "Let's get a cup of coffee." During the long, tense wait for the evening tide, planes and naval gunfire continued to hammer at the North Korean positions, rockets whooshing in with devastating effect. Just as twilight was falling, landing craft loaded with marines headed for the shore. Marguerite Higgins, of the *New York Herald-Tribune*, reported:

> As we strained to see . . . more clearly, a rocket hit a round oil tower and big, ugly smoke rings billowed up. The dockside buildings were brilliant with flames. Through the haze it looked as if the whole city was burning.[22]

The sea wall seemed "as high as the RCA Building" wrote another correspondent, but the marines, equipped with crude scaling ladders, were ready. Looking like soldiers going "over the top" in World War I, they climbed over the wall and drove off the enemy. By midnight, all of Inchon was in American hands. It was a thrifty victory gained at the cost of 22 men killed and 174 wounded. Before the enemy could regroup, Kimpo airfield had been taken and the marines were closing in on Seoul, despite stiffened resistance inland. "The Navy and the Marines have never shone more brightly," commented General MacArthur.

With the trap closing, as intended, between the marines and the Eighth Army, the North Koreans fled back across the 38th parallel. Sweeping along in hot pursuit, despite warnings that an invasion of the north would result in Chinese Communist intervention, MacArthur decided to make another amphibious landing, at Wonsan, about 115 miles northeast of Seoul. This operation was complicated by the fact that the entrances to Wonsan had been seeded with some 3,000 mines. With only a handful of sweepers available to clear a channel, more than 200 transports and supply ships were forced to wait offshore for more than a week until it was safe to enter the port, which had been taken from the rear by the South Korean army. "Those damn mines cost us eight days' delay in getting the troops ashore and more than two hundred casualties," said Admiral Sherman, chief of naval operations. "When you can't go *where* you want to, *when* you want to, you haven't got command of the sea."[23]

The navy was soon forced to support an amphibious operation in reverse. Disregarding the repeated warnings of the Chinese, MacArthur, having defeated the North Korean army, ordered a two-pronged advance toward the Yalu River. On the night of November 25, 1950, both prongs of the American advance, which were widely separated by twisting mountain defiles, were attacked by the Chinese. Suffering heavy losses, the column advancing in the west beat a hurried retreat and did not regroup until it was below the 38th parallel. The marines advancing on the eastern side of the peninsula near the Chosin Reservoir, faced with isolation and destruction by six Chinese divisions, fought their way to the coast at Hungnam, about thirty-five miles away, under cover of close support from carrier aircraft. Every available vessel was dispatched to Hungnam, and as planes and ships, among them the *Missouri*, established a curtain of fire about the town, Admiral Doyle carried out the evacuation in good order. By Christmas Eve, some 105,000 American and Korean troops along with their equipment and supplies and 91,000 Korean civilians had been sea-lifted to Pusan.

Warships and naval aircraft were employed in the seesaw war of attrition that followed, and by the early summer of 1951, the battle line lay just inside North Korea. In the face of the stalemate that ensued, truce talks began on July 10, 1951, and with the exception of a few months when negotiations broke down and fighting was briefly resumed to win local advantages, the war ebbed away. A formal truce was not signed until July 27, 1953—three years, one month, and two days after the conflict had erupted.

For the navy, the war in Korea had positive results. The wide scope of the fleet's activities off the coast of Korea provided an irrefutable answer to those who contended that navies were obsolete: shore bombardment; carrier strikes against bridges, supply depots, and transport; close air support for ground troops; amphibious landings—and evacuations—and logistical support for the army. (Much to the chagrin of the pilots, however, the rules of engagement forbade attacks north of the Yalu in Chinese territory.) These operations underscored the remarks made by Admiral Nimitz during the unification crisis. "Our country is dependent on our sea power for its external influence," he had declared. "With control of the sea lanes we have influence; without that control we are limited to the boundaries of our continent."[24] The navy had met its challenges so well that within two years of the cancellation of the supercarrier *United States*, six even larger carriers, the 78,000-ton *Forrestal* class, were laid down.

These vessels were the tangible result of a secret National Security Council report, known as NSC-68, that predicted continued tension and Communist aggression and called for a "rapid and sustained build-up" of American military and naval strength. Fitted with canted flight decks and steam catapults that had originally been developed by the British, they could launch aircraft capable of carrying nuclear bombs. Surface-to-air missiles were developed, and in 1952 the *Boston* and *Canberra* were designated as guided missile cruisers, their after batteries being replaced by Terrier missile installations. That same year, the navy also activated its first air squadron fitted with radar-guided Sparrow missiles, and later added heat-seeking Sidewinder missiles.

Blunt-bowed and black-hulled, the submarine *Nautilus* moved silently out into the Thames River, off Groton, Connecticut, on the morning of January 17, 1955. No deck guns marred the sleekness of her lines, and her periscopes and radar antennae were enclosed in her streamlined sail, replacing the old conning tower, which was crowded with visitors. As soon as she had passed out into Long Island Sound, her captain, Commander Eugene P. Wilkinson, flashed a message to an escorting tug, "Under way on nuclear power."[25]

The trials of the world's first nuclear-powered submarine were a triumph for Hyman G. Rickover, who observed them from her bridge. In the eight years since he had studied nuclear propulsion at Oak Ridge, he had become the navy's leading expert on the subject and was chief of both the Nuclear Propulsion Division of the Bureau of Ships and the Naval Reactors Branch of the Atomic Energy Commission. In his dual role of naval officer and civilian official, Rickover helped create a technological revolution at sea that ranks in importance with the introduction of steam, armored ships, and the airplane. Unlike earlier submarines, which were nothing more than surface craft that could submerge for brief periods, the *Nautilus* could remain submerged as long as her crew could endure it. The nuclear reactor that generated steam for her turbines required no oxygen and produced no exhaust: purification equipment cleansed the air breathed by her crew.

Like many innovators, Rickover was impatient with bureaucratic routine and traditional chains of command.[26] Caustic and quick-tempered, he left in his wake a trail of bruised feelings and damaged egos, but he drove no one harder than he drove himself in translating the nuclear submarine into reality. His background was as unconventional as his methods. The son of a Polish immigrant tailor, he graduated from the Naval Academy in 1922 and was an anomaly in a period in which few Jews sought military careers. As assistant engineering officer in the *New Mexico* in the mid-thirties, he showed signs of the individuality that marked his later career. "Bending the pencil" to lower fuel consumption, he reduced the amount of oil allowed for heating the battleship's living quarters to such low levels that when an admiral's staff came on board they pointedly wore their bridge coats in the wardroom. Rickover was not to be deterred, however, and his ship won the fleet award for fuel economy. Despite the work he had done on the nuclear submarine, when he came up for promotion to rear admiral, he was passed over twice by selection boards, and at the age of fifty-three faced mandatory retirement. The antagonisms his methods aroused among his seniors are thought to have been at the root of the problem, but an outcry from the public and from Congress forced Rickover's promotion in 1953.

In 1958, the *Nautilus*, skippered by Commander William R. Anderson, sailed from the Pacific to the Atlantic under the polar ice cap, and later that year, the *Skate*, under Commander James F. Calvert, broke through the ice to surface at the North Pole. Two years later, Captain Edward L. Beach sailed the *Triton* on the first submerged circumnavigation of the globe, covering 36,000 miles in eighty-three days. Beach periodically rose to periscope depth to take "fixes" on the sun or stars so that the *Triton*'s position could be plotted, but this was merely a check on her new inertial navigation system. Now used on all nuclear submarines, the system automatically calculates longitude and latitude without the need for taking celestial sights.[27]

With nuclear propulsion in submarines making giant strides, it was not long before similarly powered surface ships went to sea. The keel of the 17,000-ton cruiser *Long Beach* was laid on December 2, 1957, and she joined the fleet four years later. Besides being the first navy surface ship with a nuclear engineering plant, she was the first new cruiser since World War II and the first to be built to carry guided missiles rather than guns as her main battery. She was followed into service by the carrier *Enterprise*, at 89,600 tons the largest warship in the world, her flight deck being the size of three football fields. Powered by eight reactors, the giant vessel can make thirty-five knots and steam for years without refueling. Using her four steam catapults, she can launch one of her 100 planes every thirty seconds and in all but the heaviest seas. Embodiment of modern technology that she was at the time of her launching, the *Enterprise* contains a link with the past: her only three portholes, mounted in the captain's cabin, are from her namesake, the "Big E" of World War II. Third of the nuclear flotilla, the guided-missile frigate *Bainbridge* bears the same name as the navy's first destroyer, but at 7,600 tons, she is a far cry from her 420-ton predecessor. In

1964 these three ships, formed into the first all-nuclear-powered task force, sailed round the world without refueling or reprovisioning.[28]

Early nuclear-powered submarines were armed with conventional torpedoes, but almost from the beginning there were plans to outfit them with guided missiles. The first such missile was the Regulus, whose range was 500 miles. In order to fire it, however, the submarine had to surface and thus lose momentarily her inherent advantage of concealment. Under the direction of Admiral Arleigh Burke, an aggressive destroyer officer during World War II who became chief of naval operations in 1955, the highest priority was given to producing a ballistic missile that could be fired from under the sea and a platform from which to launch it. The missile, named Polaris, was developed by a special projects group under the leadership of Rear Admiral William F. Raborn.[29] The submarine *George Washington* fired the first Polaris missile from a submerged position off the coast of Florida on July 20, 1960, raising the curtain on a new age in warfare. Over the next several years, a total of forty-one Polaris submarines, each armed with sixteen nuclear-warhead missiles capable of hitting targets in the Soviet Union, put to sea. The Polaris submarine fleet became one of three basic components of the nation's deterrent to nuclear attack. The other two elements of the "triad" are the long-range bombers of the Strategic Air Command and a covey of land-based intercontinental missiles kept in silos in the Middle West. By the late 1970s, the Polaris missile had been replaced on most submarines by the more powerful Poseidon, with a range of 2,900 miles and up to fourteen MIRVs, or multiple independently targeted re-entry vehicles.

Each submarine has two complete crews—the Blue and the Gold—so that the ships can spend most of their time on station. When one crew returns from a two-month patrol, the other crew can take the ship out again. Hidden by the sea and constantly moving to keep their whereabouts unknown, they are always ready to launch their missiles in retaliation for a nuclear attack. Almost undetectable at the current level of technology and with its missiles capable of reaching any target ashore, the Polaris-Poseidon weapon system, and the Trident with its range of 4,000 miles which followed, vastly broaden the navy's role in the national defense.

In the decade following the end of the Korean War, the navy was repeatedly called upon to meet the challenge of Communist expansionism in the Mediterranean, the Caribbean, and the China Sea. Standing in from over the horizon, the silent gray sentinels of the Sixth and Seventh fleets and the ships assigned to the North Atlantic Treaty Organization kept the peace without firing a shot, launching a missile, or dropping a bomb. As Admiral Richard L. Conolly, one-time commander of American naval forces in European waters and the Mediterranean, pointed out: "In a critical period, if you send a naval force into an area, it is really a warlike gesture; whereas if you already have forces there and you merely reinforce them, that's not significant at all."[30]

American sea power was frequently used as a stabilizing force in the volatile Middle East, where the ambitions of the United States and the Soviet Union were in direct conflict. The Americans were trying to balance support of Israel with the need to ensure access to Arab oil, while the Russians were trying to dominate the land bridge between Europe, Asia, and Africa, and to deny oil to the West. The most significant of the operations in which the navy figured during this period occurred in Lebanon.[31]

The affair began on July 14, 1958, when an army revolt toppled the pro-Western government of Iraq with considerable bloodshed. In neighboring Lebanon, President Camille Chamoun, believing that the coup had been staged with the support of Russia's ally, President Gamal Abdel Nasser of Egypt, and fearing a similar blood bath in his own country, immediately asked for American military assistance. This request was made in line with President Dwight D. Eisenhower's promise, known as the Eisenhower Doctrine, to furnish such aid to any legitimate Middle Eastern government that considered itself threatened.

Within a few hours, the Sixth Fleet, which included the large carrier *Saratoga*, the smaller carriers *Essex* and *Wasp*, and escorting cruisers, destroyers, and amphibious ships laden with marines, was moving into action under the overall command of Admiral James L. Holloway, Jr. In the afternoon of July 15, the marines began landing on the white-sand beaches near the Beirut airport, while navy fighters screamed in from the sea. Instead of being confronted by an armed enemy, the marines were met by girls in bikinis and an army of ice-cream vendors selling Eskimo pies at triple the prices they had charged that morning. Undaunted, the sweating invaders moved on in the ninety-degree heat to capture the airport and to take over Beirut. "How do you tell a rebel from a good guy?" asked a marine corporal. Shortly afterward, the British sent an army of 2,600 men to Jordan to help prop up King Hussein, who was convinced that the aftershock of developments in Iraq was also being felt in his own uneasy country. The situation in Lebanon was stabilized, elections were held, and the Americans withdrew.

Because no insurrection took place—it may have been thwarted by the American landing—and because of the comic-opera overtones surrounding the arrival of the marines, many Americans overlooked the significance of the operation. But Nasser and his Russian allies understood its implications. Although the Soviet Union had pledged unlimited assistance to the Egyptians, her promises turned out to be empty, resulting in a loss of prestige for the Russians in the Arab world. As Richard K. Smith points out in his study of the Cold War navy, the American operation in Lebanon demonstrated dramatically that the Sixth Fleet was not a "showboat organization" but a force "capable of incredibly swift and decisive action."[32] The Soviet Union did not have the unrestricted maneuverability that such a force bestowed, but the success of the intervention in Lebanon was a prod to her to remedy this deficiency.

While the Sixth Fleet was effectively supporting American policy in the

Middle East, the Chinese Communists, quiescent since the Korean War, tested America's resolve in the Far East.[33] Intelligence reports disclosed a military build-up on the Chinese coast near Amoy, across from the Nationalist-held islands of Quemoy and Matsu, only four miles off the mainland. These tiny islands were a centerpiece in the propaganda war between the Communists and the Nationalists. The latter, claiming that they were steppingstones for their eventual return to the mainland, had garrisoned them with 100,000 men. Conversely, the Communists regarded the islands as the key to their conquest of the Nationalist stronghold on Taiwan. Expecting trouble, Admiral Burke reinforced the Seventh Fleet just as the storm broke.

On August 23, 1958, the Communists began an intensive bombardment of Quemoy, firing some 40,000 shells at the island in two hours. As the shelling continued day after day, the position of the defenders appeared vulnerable. The United States had formally agreed to defend Taiwan itself, but it was not clear whether this pledge extended to the offshore islands. The Eisenhower administration tried to keep the Communists guessing as to its intentions. Without actually committing the Seventh Fleet to turning back an invasion, it supported the Nationalist attempts to hold the islands. Admiral Burke described the American position in pungent language:

> As soon as the Quemoy incident started, I moved the 7th Fleet to the vicinity of Taiwan so that they would be ready. Again we began reinforcing the 7th Fleet and we made preparations so that if battle ensued the pipelines would be formed and would be filled and that we would commit enough military force to prevent not only the Communists from achieving their purposes but also to convince the Communists that if they started anything we would kick hell out of them.[34]

With all the beaches of Quemoy constantly under fire from the Communist guns, the major problem was to keep the Nationalist defenders supplied. Repeated attempts by large Nationalist landing craft to reach the island having failed, the navy provided Taiwan with amphibious tractors and similar craft that were able to land safely. These vehicles, loaded aboard larger landing craft, were convoyed by elements of the Seventh Fleet to within three miles of Quemoy. The vessels ventured as close to shore as the enemy batteries permitted and then launched the tractors. Communist gunners were careful not to fire on the American ships, although they were within range. At the same time, air groups from five carriers flew defensive missions over Taiwan, freeing the Nationalist air force to take on Communist air power. Fitted with Sidewinder heat-seeking missiles, the Nationalist planes had little trouble in dealing with Communist MIGs that tried to attack the offshore islands. The combination of the Seventh Fleet's presence and the use of American convoys and equipment to supply Quemoy thwarted any designs that the Chinese Communists had on the islands.

* * *

The navy also played a key role in the Cuban missile crisis of 1962, when a single miscalculation could have brought about a thermonuclear holocaust.[35] Throughout that summer, reports filtering into Washington told of unusual activity in Cuba, which had been a thorn in the side of the United States since Fidel Castro seized power in 1959 and moved the island into the Communist orbit. Soviet-flag freighters laden with electronic gear and construction equipment were calling at Cuban ports; large numbers of Russians were on hand; photographs taken by high-flying U-2 reconnaissance planes indicated that surface-to-air missile batteries were being erected, and refugees arriving in the United States told about the mysterious activities they had seen. Since the Soviets were not known to have deployed long-range missiles outside their own borders, President John F. Kennedy and his advisers discounted the evidence that they were doing so in Cuba.

Proof that this assumption was false came from photographs provided by a U-2 that flashed through the high, thin air over western Cuba in the dawn of October 14, its cameras taking picture after picture of Soviet missile bases under construction. American officials were appalled. With ranges up to 2,200 miles, the missiles and IL-28 bombers, which were also arriving on the island, could reach many targets in the United States. Soviet Premier Nikita S. Khrushchev appeared to be trying with a single stroke to overcome the superiority of America's arsenal of ballistic missiles, including the 144 at sea in Polaris submarines. President Kennedy had to make an agonizing choice—do nothing and face the charge that the United States was, indeed, a "paper tiger," or get the missiles removed, even if it meant risking nuclear war. In the week that followed, he and his advisers considered their options: a naval blockade of Cuba, an air strike against the missile bases, an invasion of the island, or diplomatic negotiation through the United Nations. The president opted for the blockade, to be euphemistically known as a "quarantine."

"You are certain that this can be done?" he asked Admiral George W. Anderson, Jr., chief of naval operations.

"Yes, sir," answered Admiral Anderson.

"Well, it looks as if everything is in the hands of the Navy."

"Mr. President," responded the admiral, as he left the White House to give the necessary orders, "the Navy will not let you down."[36]

The following evening, October 21, Kennedy went on television to inform the nation and the world that the Soviet Union had placed in Cuba rockets that endangered the security of the United States. He announced that "a strict quarantine on all offensive equipment under shipment to Cuba is being initiated" and any ship carrying such cargo would be turned back. The speech ended with an appeal to Khrushchev to withdraw the weapons from Cuba. By the time the president spoke, the ships of Task Force 136, under the command of Admiral Robert L. Dennison, had already taken up station in an arc about 500 miles to the northeast of Cuba. Some 483 ships participated in the operation. To give the Russians time to weigh the consequences, the actual blockade was not to begin until the morning of October 24. "Send the order in the clear," said the president, probably recalling the problems he had with coded messages when he was a junior officer.

Khrushchev branded the American charges as lies and warned that if the Americans carried out any act of "piracy" the Soviet Union would react accordingly. Tension mounted as the work on the missile sites continued unabated and the first of some two dozen ships en route to Cuba neared the quarantine line. "There wasn't one of us [in the White House] who wasn't pretty sure that in a few hours we'd have to sink one of those Russian ships," a presidential aide recalled. Suddenly, word was received that perhaps half the ships had either stopped or had put about. "We're eyeball to eyeball and I think the other fellow just blinked," said Secretary of State Dean Rusk.[37]

Shortly after dawn on October 26, the destroyers *John R. Pierce* and *Joseph P. Kennedy, Jr.*, the latter named after the president's older brother who had lost his life in World War II, halted the Lebanese-flag freighter *Marucla*, chartered by the Russians, as she arrived at the quarantine line. Boarding parties searched her and, finding no contraband, let her proceed. Nevertheless, the incident served to underscore the navy's right to stop and search vessels suspected of violating the quarantine. In the meantime, preparations were being made for an invasion of Cuba by some 30,000 marines poised offshore. Fortunately, this proved to be unnecessary. Unable to challenge the flexibility and mobility provided by American sea power, Khrushchev was faced with the alternative of submitting to Kennedy's demands or precipitating a nuclear war. He submitted. In exchange for an American pledge not to invade the island, the Russians dismantled the missiles and removed them from Cuba. The humiliating failure of Khrushchev's bold gamble to overcome America's nuclear superiority was undoubtedly one of the major reasons for his ouster from power two years later. As Admiral Anderson had promised, the navy had not let the nation down.

President Kennedy, emboldened by his success in the Cuban missile crisis, embarked on a vigorous effort to blunt Russian- and Chinese-sponsored probes wherever they might be met, with special emphasis on Indochina. Bloody conflict had raged in this remote sector of the globe ever since World War II—first a war against the French colonial authorities who had tried to regain control after the ouster of the Japanese, and then a struggle between Communist-controlled North Vietnam and anti-Communist South Vietnam. Throughout the remainder of that struggle, the U.S. Navy was to play a key role in helping to prevent what successive American presidents regarded as an attempt by the Communists to take over not only the Indochinese peninsula but all of Southeast Asia.

The first American naval mission—eight officers and men—arrived in Saigon in August 1950 and over the next four years helped supply the French with $2.6 billion in military and naval assistance, including two light aircraft carriers.[38] In 1954, responding to the desperate pleas of the French who were trying to hold on to an isolated bastion at Dien Bien Phu, American carrier-based planes were readied for an attack against the besieging Viet Minh forces. Reconnaissance flights were actually launched over the area before President Eisenhower, convinced that the political risks outweighed the possible benefits, decided against intervention. The fall of Dien Bien Phu and public clamor at home forced France to abandon its colonial claims to Indochina to the triumphant Viet Minh. The area was partitioned at a conference in Geneva into North and South Vietnam, with a Demilitarized Zone (DMZ) along the 17th parallel. Hundreds of thousands of Vietnamese fleeing from the North to the non-Communist South were evacuated by a massive U.S. Navy sealift known as "Passage to Freedom."

But the end of that war did not bring peace. The Communists, now called the Viet Cong, opened a guerrilla war in the South and infiltrated neighboring Laos and Cambodia. Regarding Vietnam as a testing ground for counterinsurgency tactics designed to suppress brush-fire wars being waged by the Communists, the United States poured economic and military assistance into South Vietnam and dispatched increasing numbers of advisers to the region. When Kennedy was inaugurated in 1961, there were about 800 Americans in South Vietnam; by the time of his assassination on November 22, 1963, the American presence had grown to 23,000 men, two-thirds of them in the armed forces. The North Vietnamese–sponsored guerrilla campaign was not checked, but the American commitment to the Saigon regime was steadily escalating.[39]

On August 2, 1964, the destroyer *Maddox* was carrying out an electronic-surveillance mission in the Gulf of Tonkin, off the coast of North Vietnam, when she was attacked by three North Vietnamese motor torpedo boats. With the assistance of planes from the carrier *Ticonderoga*, she beat off and damaged the attacking craft. President Lyndon B. Johnson, already committed to stepped-up support for the faltering South Vietnamese government, declared that American ships would continue to sail where they wished and warned that the United States would "take whatever measures are appropriate for their defense." The destroyer *Turner Joy* joined the *Maddox* on her next patrol of the Tonkin Gulf on August 4. That night, the destroyers reported they were under attack by unidentified small craft. Unlike the previous incident, this one occurred in the dark amid considerable confusion, giving rise to a lingering uneasiness that the tense and inexperienced destroyer crews might have imagined the attack.[40]

Nevertheless, Johnson immediately ordered retaliatory air strikes against North Vietnamese torpedo-boat and oil-storage facilities. Two of the sixty-four attacking planes from the *Ticonderoga* and *Constellation* were shot down by heavy enemy fire. One of the pilots was lost, while the other, Lieutenant (j.g.) Everett Alvarez, Jr., was pulled out of the water by the North Vietnamese, becoming their first American prisoner of war. He remained in captivity for eight years. Congress put its stamp of approval on Johnson's actions by a joint resolution passed on August 10, 1964, with only two dissenting votes. The Tonkin

Gulf resolution gave the president blanket authority "to take all necessary measures to repel any armed attack against the forces of the United States and to prevent further aggression."

Although Johnson assured the nation that "we seek no wider war," the number of Americans in Vietnam continued to rise steadily until there were more than a half-million men there, 85,000 of whom were marines and 38,000 sailors. Over the quarter century that began in 1950, about 2 million U.S. Navy personnel, of whom 2,511 gave their lives, served in Vietnam. American strategy was double-pronged: the South Vietnamese armed forces were to be strengthened to withstand the Communist attack behind a U.S. military shield, while the American armed forces would destroy enemy forces within the country and interdict the infiltration of reinforcements and supplies until the North Vietnamese abandoned their designs on the South.

But along with many Americans, some naval officers doubted the wisdom of massive intervention in the ground war in Vietnam. For example, Admiral Elmo R. Zumwalt, Jr., on duty at the Pentagon in 1964 and later Commander, Naval Forces, Vietnam, and chief of naval operations, states that some of his superiors argued within the government that "a Communist takeover of the whole of Vietnam . . . did not pose an immediate or direct threat to the safety of the United States." Major assistance to the South Vietnamese should be restricted to naval and air forces, and only a small number of advisory ground troops, they said. Serious doubts were expressed about the chances of winning a guerrilla war unless the Saigon regime could capture the wholehearted support of its own people. There was also considerable concern that funds needed to modernize and replace the navy's aging ships—most of them dating back to World War II—would be earmarked instead for operations in Vietnam.[41]

The navy played a many-faceted role in the "unplanned, unwanted, undeclared and unpopular" war that followed.[42] Marines supported by 26,000 Seabees carried the brunt of the fighting in the I Corps Tactical Zone abutting the DMZ. Planes from the carriers of Task Force 77, which lay about a hundred miles offshore, ranged over both Vietnams, flying missions in close support of the army and marines and striking at Hanoi's industrial base and supply lines as part of Operation Rolling Thunder. The battleship *New Jersey* joined the cruisers and destroyers of the Seventh Fleet in providing naval gunfire support against targets ashore. Minesweepers, LSTs, patrol boats, and Coast Guard cutters, formed into Task Force 115, were deployed along the thousand-mile coastline of South Vietnam in the unceasing task of hunting down junks and other craft carrying supplies to Viet Cong guerrillas. And in a startling throwback to the Civil War, flotillas of shallow-draft boats patrolled the rivers of South Vietnam.

Task Force 77 conducted operations from "Yankee Station," in the Gulf of Tonkin, where three carriers were usually in position with the object of projecting power ashore.[43] Although their attacks on enemy positions were closely coordinated, the flattops did not steam together, as in World War II, but operated independently, accompanied only by their escorts. Each ship launched and recovered planes for twelve hours, then paused for twelve hours to rest and rearm before resuming operations. Thus, except in the poorest weather, navy planes were always in action over North Vietnam. During the first year of the war, when there were not enough fields to accommodate land-based aircraft, a fourth carrier operated from "Dixie Station," off South Vietnam.

These continuous operations were made possible by a system of underway replenishment carried out by the Service Forces of the Pacific Fleet.[44] With their main base, Subic Bay, in the Philippines, about 700 miles away, it was impractical for the carriers and other ships to return there every time they ran low on fuel, ammunition, and supplies. Two fast combat support ships, the *Sacramento* and *Camden*, which performed the functions of several different types of older supply vessels, made their first appearance off Vietnam. They carried fuel oil, gasoline, jet fuel, shells, rockets, bombs, and foodstuffs, and usually remained in position for two or three weeks at a stretch before returning to reload. A pair of navy hospital ships, the *Repose* and *Sanctuary*, each with 560 beds, also lay off the war zone, and casualties were sometimes carried out to them by helicopters within a half-hour of being injured. Eighty-seven per cent of the wounded who required hospitalization during the Vietnam War were returned to duty and less than 1 per cent died—the lowest mortality rate of any war.[45]

The first navy strike of Rolling Thunder occurred on March 18, 1965, when aircraft from the *Coral Sea* and *Hancock* bombed supply depots in the North. All aircraft returned safely, but successive attacks brought mounting casualties. Moving up and down North Vietnam, the planes took out such targets as railroads, highways, canals, bridges, power stations, industrial plants, petroleum storage facilities, and supply convoys. In defense, the Communists stopped supplying their units during daylight and moved only at night along what became known as the Ho Chi Minh Trail, which eventually stretched from North Vietnam through Laos into South Vietnam.

The bombing campaign against the North was hindered by what Vice Admiral Malcolm W. Cagle described as "self-imposed bombing pauses, self-inflicted restrictions and self-designated sanctuaries."[46] Military and naval operations were shackled by political factors and controlled by civilians in Washington who even selected daily targets while having only a rudimentary understanding of what was actually happening on the scene. Learning that the American rules of engagement forbade the bombing of villages, the Viet Cong sometimes pulled their trucks into these areas and parked them in the open in broad daylight where they could be seen and still be safe from attack.[47] Restricted areas included most cities, a thirty-mile buffer zone along the Chinese border, and the harbor of Haiphong, the country's most important port, where Russian supplies were unloaded. Fearing that Soviet advisers might be hit, which would create an incident with the Russians, the White House prohibited strikes against any target where Soviets were likely to be present. Haiphong Harbor itself was not mined until May 8, 1972, despite repeated pleas from the naval high command.

"You don't think the Vietnamese are going to use them!" scoffed one Pentagon official when asked to approve the bombing of surface-to-air missile (SAM) sites that were under construction. "Putting them in is just a political ploy by the Russians to appease Hanoi."[48] Forbidden to attack, one frustrated pilot from the *Midway* actually watched the building of the SAM site that eventually shot him down.[49]

U.S. flyers had control of the air, and the threat from the North Vietnamese MiGs was minimal. In all, navy and marine pilots shot down sixty-one MiGs of various types while losing sixteen planes in aerial combat. The navy's first and only aces—in fact, the first team aces in aerial warfare—were Lieutenant Randall H. Cunningham and his radar intercept officer, Lieutenant (j.g.) William Driscoll, who shot down five enemy MiGs, including three kills during a single mission. Low on fuel, they were nursing their F-4J Phantom back to the *Constellation* when it was heavily damaged by a SAM that exploded nearby. Cunningham and Driscoll ejected safely and were pulled from the sea by a marine helicopter. A key factor in American aerial success was the radar controlmen on the ships of Task Force 77, who picked up the presence of MiGs and vectored fighters to meet their threat. One man, Chief Radarman Larry H. Nowell of the *Chicago*, was cited for having participated in intercepts that resulted in the downing of twelve enemy planes.[50]

Enemy MiGs represented only a small part of the peril to attacking planes, however. Antiaircraft fire over North Vietnam was the most intense in the history of aerial warfare, and pilots on low-level missions found themselves flying into murderous curtains of hot steel. "There was no way to defeat barrage fire," observed Commander John B. Nichols. "Pilots could dodge and jink to evade aimed fire, but in a dive through a sector filled with smoking, crackling flak there was no point."[51] Naval aircraft losses to gunfire amounted to 59 per cent of total combat losses. The radar-guided SAMs added immeasurably to the hazards. The first navy planes to fall victim to the missiles were lost on the night of August 11, 1965, when the pilots of a pair of A-4Es from the *Midway* spotted what appeared to be two flares glowing in the sky. Not realizing their danger, they watched with interest as the lights approached them. By the time they tried to take evasive action, it was too late: the missiles had locked on them, and their planes were rocked by successive explosions. One plane was destroyed and the other, badly damaged, limped back to the carrier—raising the curtain on a new era in air warfare.

A SAM did not have to strike its target to be lethal. If it exploded within 300 feet of an aircraft, the damage was likely to be serious; detonation inside 200 feet of the target was almost certain to be fatal. The missiles were usually fired in pairs, with a few seconds' separation. A pilot might have little difficulty in evading the first missile if he spotted it in time, but in dodging it, he would be caught by the second. Timing was crucial in evading a SAM, according to Commander Nichols.[52] If a pilot began evasive tactics too soon, the missile had time to correct and continue tracking him. If he waited too long, he might not be able to avoid it. "Surviving a SAM launch became an exercise in sweaty-palm patience and pulse-pounding judgment," he recalled.

Pilots learned to deal with the SAMs by confusing the radar guidance systems, and the missiles were responsible for far fewer kills than conventional flak. But the missiles dictated the conduct of strike operations. To avoid them, attacking planes were forced to fly lower, where they became targets for fierce gunfire from the ground. In all, Task Force 77 lost 83 pilots and crewmen over North Vietnam and approximately 200 were captured or reported missing in action before President Johnson, on March 31, 1968, called a halt to air strikes north of the 20th parallel, in the hope of getting the North Vietnamese to the peace table. About 300 planes were lost and 1,000 more damaged. With much of his industrial base and transportation network destroyed, the enemy had been unable to conquer South Vietnam, but his morale was high and his will to win undiminished.

Few of the navy's blue-water sailors foresaw that much of their work in Vietnam would be done in the maze of rivers and canals and around the network of offshore islands by a rough-and-ready "brown-water navy" in which Andrew H. Foote and David D. Porter would have been at home.[53] The steamy Mekong Delta, south of Saigon, contained the largest part of South Vietnam's people and was the source of much of its food production; inland waters connected the vital population centers. Strategists on both sides realized that control of these waterways meant control of the heart of South Vietnam, and a long and bitter struggle ensued.

A century after the Yankee tinclads had broken the back of the Confederacy, the shallow-draft boats of Task Force 117 performed similar missions in the Mekong and in the Rung Sat Special Zone, a delta area adjacent to the South Vietnamese capital. Converted landing craft fitted with armored gun turrets that made them look like Civil War monitors worked with the U.S. Army's Ninth Division and navy and army helicopters in carrying out raids against enemy forces. Such operations as Market Time, Stable Door, and Game Warden disrupted the flow of reinforcements and supplies to the Viet Cong.[54] The activities of the "brown-water navy" were not limited to the South, however. Ninety per cent of the supplies delivered to the marines in the I Corps sector were brought up from the main base at Da Nang by LSTs and smaller amphibious vessels that navigated the meandering, narrow Cua Viet and Perfume rivers despite floating mines and carefully laid ambushes.

River patrol boats (PBRs) assigned to Task Force 116 patrolled the winding rivers and mangrove swamps of the Mekong Delta to interrupt the enemy's line of communications. The PBRs were manned by crews of four and were usually under the command of petty officers, of whom most were deck ratings but some were former cooks or yeomen. Long hours were spent in checking junks and sampans for contraband, and the boredom and fatigue of blockade duty soon settled in. In the words of Commander Sayre A. Swarztrauber, who led River Squadron 5: "The routine of a standard 12-hour patrol is waiting . . . drifting . . . searching . . . verifying cargo manifests . . . checking ID cards against black lists . . . putting on the rain gear . . . taking off the rain gear. . . ."

Routine patrol duty might turn into high adventure in a twinkling. One crewman, searching a junk, ran into the latest twist in booby traps when he opened a bilge compartment and was confronted by a deadly tropical snake. Another sailor, suspicious of a floating C-ration box, tossed a hand grenade at it and was showered with a cascade of water from a hidden mine. Patrol boats ran into Viet Cong ambushes and fought their way out again. In one such action, Boatswain's Mate First Class James E. Williams won the Medal of Honor while leading a two-boat patrol. Williams destroyed sixty-five enemy craft and inflicted numerous casualties despite taking fire from a battalion-sized guerrilla unit surprised as it attempted to cross the Mekong. Overall, one out of every three patrol-boat sailors was wounded, and in one year they were awarded a Medal of Honor, six Navy Crosses, twenty-four Silver Stars, and more than five hundred Purple Hearts.

Beginning in September 1967, the war took a new turn. Supplied with modern Soviet weapons, the North Vietnamese launched attacks on American positions in the highlands of central Vietnam near the DMZ. In the face of some of the heaviest bombing of the war, the enemy concentrated about thirty-five thousand men against Khe San, a major American forward firebase manned by the marines. General William Westmoreland, the U.S. military commander in Vietnam, sent in six thousand marines with strong artillery support and backed up the marines with an uninterrupted torrent of bombing.

The attack against Khe San was a feint. While the Americans concentrated on the highlands leaving the defense of Saigon to the South Vietnamese, in effect no protection at all, the North Vietnamese and their Viet Cong allies planned an uprising in the South. On January 31, 1968, during the Tet lunar new year celebrations, the cities of South Vietnam exploded. Vietcong commandos shot their way into the American Embassy in Saigon before being rooted out by the marine guards. Others attacked South Vietnamese Navy headquarters where the dead were stacked up like cordwood. The old imperial capital of Hue was captured and towns and villages in the central highlands and Mekong Delta were attacked.

In the Delta, TF 116, the most readily available force, stiffened the defenses of numerous towns and villages that were under siege. River patrol boats were the key element in many such stands. Two army battalions landed by the riverine force recaptured My Tho from the Viet Cong after fierce street fighting. They also took part in the fighting in Van Long Province where a joint American task force overran three Viet Cong battalions during a campaign for control of Can Tho, the major city of the Delta. Offshore, where the North Vietnamese mounted a major shipping effort to support the Viet Cong, patrol boats shot up and intercepted this traffic. Fighting around Saigon lasted until February 20 and Hue was recaptured four days later by the marines after bitter, door-to-door street combat in which both sides suffered heavy casualties.

The Tet Offensive was a costly military failure for the Communists. Some forty thousand Viet Cong were killed and their tactical leadership was wiped out. But the battle appeared different on the color television sets in America's living rooms where the chaotic images did not convey a sense of triumph. The major casualty of Tet was public faith in President Johnson's repeated assurance of "light at the end of the tunnel." Growing antiwar fervor and demands by Westmoreland for an additional 200,000 troops caused Johnson to order an end to the bombing of the North with the hope of bringing Hanoi to the peace table and to announce that he would not seek reelection.

The navy's last areas of involvement in the Vietnam War were the Linebacker bombing offensives and the mining of North Vietnam's harbors. Both operations were designed to throttle the enemy's military buildup in the South while forcing Hanoi to accept a cease-fire at the bargaining table in Paris. Navy planes sowed some 8,500 mines and destructive devices in North Vietnamese waters in May 1972. They also joined Air Force B-52 bombers in bombing overland supply routes from China and a widening number of military and economic targets in both North and South as part of Linebacker I. The attacks were halted in October 1972, when it appeared Hanoi would compromise, but Linebacker II marked the resumption of heavy bombing at year's end after the talks bogged down. On January 27, 1973, the North Vietnamese agreed to a cease-fire, and the U.S. Navy's active role in the Vietnam War was over.

Peace brought the release of some 600 American prisoners held by the Communists, many of them navy and marine airmen. Their captivity in the "Hanoi Hilton" and other jails had been bitter and brutal. The ranking naval officer downed, Commander James B. Stockdale, who had suffered a broken back when he ejected from his A-4E, was repeatedly beaten and tortured for inspiring fellow captives to resist enemy attempts to force them to broadcast antiwar statements—statements often excerpted from the American press. Stockdale survived more than seven years of imprisonment and was awarded the Medal of Honor.[55]

But the American-backed regimes in South Vietnam and Cambodia enjoyed only a brief respite. Two years after the American military withdrawal, they collapsed under a fresh onslaught from the North Vietnamese. The navy's final mission was to evacuate American nationals and the Vietnamese who were able to escape. In the confusion, the Cambodian Communists seized the

American-flag container ship *Mayaguez* on May 12, 1975, along with thirty-nine crewmen, on charges of having violated Cambodian territorial waters. Keeping in mind the *Pueblo* incident, in which the North Koreans had seized a naval vessel that had been collecting intelligence electronically off their shores, the United States responded quickly. Branding the seizure of the *Mayaguez* as "an act of piracy" and reaffirming America's traditional policy of freedom of the seas, President Gerald R. Ford ordered an attack on the vessel's captors. Planes from the carrier *Coral Sea* sank three Cambodian patrol boats that tried to interfere with the operation, and a marine boarding party recaptured the ship. All her men were safely returned to American custody.[56]

Even as the Vietnam War was being fought, the U.S. Navy was undergoing a period of turmoil as great as any in its history. Sweeping changes were made in personnel policy, administration, technology, the balance and number of its ships, and its weaponry. The old bureau system was abolished as of May 1, 1966, the enormous technological advances since the end of World War II having revealed its inadequacies.[57] For example, such new weapons systems as the Polaris-Poseidon submarine missile had cut across the lines of separation between the bureaus. The four material bureaus—Naval Weapons, created in 1959 by the merger of Aeronautics and Ordnance; Ships; Yards and Docks; and Supplies and Accounts—were replaced by six material commands. These commands—Air Systems, Ships Systems, Ordnance Systems, Electronics Systems, Supply Systems, and Facilities Engineering—were all placed under the chief of naval material, who reported to the chief of naval operations. The last two remaining bureaus, Personnel, and Medicine and Surgery, reported directly to the CNO.

The advent of Admiral Zumwalt as chief of naval operations in 1970, at forty-nine the youngest man ever to fill the billet, raised the curtain on a period of controversy. Zumwalt immediately launched a two-front campaign to modernize the navy's personnel policies and the fleet itself. From his office in the E ring of the Pentagon came a blizzard of "Z-grams" that delighted younger officers and enlisted men but alarmed traditionalists who contended they encouraged permissiveness. Zumwalt, who sported bushy eyebrows and long sideburns himself, was convinced the navy could not remain aloof from the social revolution sweeping the nation in the wake of the Vietnam War. Niggling "Mickey Mouse" regulations were eliminated; sailors were permitted to wear beards, have "mod" hairstyles, wear civilian clothes on liberty, and keep motorcycles on naval bases. More important, steps were taken to ensure that officers and men would have longer tours of duty ashore, and there was more "homeporting" of ships overseas so the families of the crews could join them. Efforts were also made to make the navy, heretofore a predominately white, male service, more attractive to women, blacks, and other minorities.[58]

The worst fears of the traditionalists were soon realized. Late in 1972 at least four ships were beset by racial violence, and there were reports of rioting, disobedience, and threats of sabotage. Drug use was almost endemic, reenlistments of first-timers amounted to only 10 per cent, and the rate of desertion was alarming. Some officers blamed the incidents on Zumwalt's reforms, which they thought had gone too far too fast and should be slowed to preserve discipline. Zumwalt insisted, however, that the navy's problems reflected the turmoil abroad in the nation as a whole and continued the fight for equality of opportunity for all those on the navy's rolls.[59]

By the mid-1970s, many of the U.S. Navy's ships were obsolescent; only the unstinting efforts of their overworked officers and crews kept them steaming. Several hundred vessels were retired in the winding-down after Vietnam, reducing the number of ships in commission to 460, the lowest level since before Pearl Harbor. Funds for new construction were slashed, and in an age of supposed detente with the Soviet Union, force levels continued to decline. Many of the remaining ships were of World War II vintage, and a significant number were smaller "low-option" vessels such as frigates that were suited to only a single mission. Naval aviation was beset by similar problems as more planes were lost through attrition and retirement than were procured. Some ships were manned at only 80 per cent of full complement, and mid-career officers and petty officers were in short supply. Undermanning forced a higher tempo of operations and extended overseas deployments, further depressing reenlistment rates.

Even as it was contracting, the U.S. Navy faced complex problems created by rapid changes in technology and policy. Ever since World War II, when the fast carrier task forces had played a crowning role in the victory at sea, the navy had been dominated by the flattop and carrier admirals seeking ever-larger ships. Advocates of greater emphasis on the submarine, antisubmarine warfare, heavy-hitting surface ships, and speedy hydrofoils argued, however, that this concentration on large carriers made the navy as unbalanced as it had been when the big gun and the battleship dominated strategic thought. In statements remarkably similar to those voiced by aviators who once pointed out the vulnerability of the battleship, they questioned the wisdom of diverting limited resources to the construction of such giant nuclear-powered carriers as the 91,000-ton *Nimitz* class in an age of highly accurate cruise missiles and torpedoes of increasingly long range and deadliness.

The imaginative Admiral Zumwalt suggested a "high-low mix" fleet to meet the problems of cost and survivability. Large carriers and nuclear-powered cruisers would constitute the high end of the mix, while sea-control ships of 7,000 to 10,000 tons equipped with a few vertical short takeoff and landing (VSTOL) aircraft would make up the low end. The large-deck carriers would be positioned in less threatened areas until sea-control task groups had won control of a specific sector. Then the heavy carriers could steam in and launch air strikes against enemy targets in relative safety.

As these arguments raged, the U.S. Navy was faced with a new challenge.

The Soviet Union, which had previously been satisfied with a navy designed primarily for coastal defense, was building a blue-water fleet. Graceful new Soviet ships began showing the red flag in waters where it had rarely been seen before, and the Soviet Navy eventually outnumbered the U.S. Navy in every class of warship except for aircraft carriers and amphibious warfare vessels. The Russians were particularly strong in submarines and antiship missiles, which had been neglected by the U.S. Navy. Thus, for the first time since World War II, the United States was confronted by a rival whose objective was to limit American freedom to use the seas. "The flag of the Soviet Navy flies over the oceans of the world," proclaimed Admiral Sergei G. Gorshkov, commander in chief of the Russian navy. "Sooner or later, the United States will have to understand it no longer has mastery of the seas."[60]

11

"THE VIOLENT PEACE"

When bad men combine, then good men must associate;
else they will fall one by one, an unpitied sacrifice in a
contemptible struggle.

—Edmund Burke

With the election of Jimmy Carter to the presidency in 1976, U.S. naval officers hoped that the advent of the first Naval Academy graduate to the White House would boost the service's depleted fortunes. A member of the war-accelerated Class of 1947, which was graduated the previous year, Carter had served in submarines and been accepted into the nuclear submarine program where he had been strongly influenced by Admiral Hyman Rickover. But in 1953, following the death of his father, Lieutenant Carter resigned to manage his family's peanut farm and warehouse and later was elected governor of Georgia.

The U.S. Navy, battling creeping obsolescence since the end of the Vietnam War, needed all the help it could get. Rather than "second to none," the fleet maintained only a thin edge of superiority over the Soviet Union, based mostly on its twelve carrier battle groups—the successor to the old task forces. Instead of dealing with such problems as Soviet military capability, force levels, and the manpower drain, Pentagon analysts focused on budget-driven assessments based on how much defense we could afford not on how much defense the nation needed and should have. Indecision, inflation, cost overruns, and financial constraints nibbled at the fleet's capability.[1]

Even the survivability of the ballistic-missile submarine, the nation's primary deterrent against attack by an aggressor, was in question as the Russians increased the efficiency and number of the nuclear-attack submarines targeting the "boomers." They were assisted by the secret data supplied by the Walker family spy ring and the sale of forbidden equipment by foreign concerns. The forty-one original strategic-missile submarines were aging, and the first of the replacement *Ohio*-class boats was not launched until 1979. These vessels, which have a displacement of 18,700 tons, carry twenty-four C-4 Trident missiles, each with a 4,000-mile range and eight independently targeted warheads.

It was hoped that Carter would reverse the trends running against the navy but the new president turned out to be a disappointment to his old service. Unlike his predecessors, he did not regard communism as the nation's chief adversary. The United States was giving too little attention to the dangers of the arms race, he said, and too much support to repressive, right-wing dictatorships. In winning election, Carter played upon the widespread public resentment of big government in Washington and the desire of many Americans for a less-activist, less-involved foreign policy. He promised no more Watergates, no more Vietnams, and a government "as idealistic, as decent, as competent, as compassionate, as good" as the American people. "I'll never tell a lie," he pledged.

Rather than upgrade the navy, Carter took the position that, in effect, if the United States provided a good example by limiting defense spending, the Russians would do the same. The outgoing Ford administration had submitted a budget for fiscal years 1978–1982 that would have produced 153 new and modernized ships, including a fourth *Nimitz*-class supercarrier. Carter slashed this program in half; the carrier would have been dropped had Congress not insisted upon building it. Although the navy asserted 600 ships were needed to fulfill the missions imposed upon it by geography, political commitments, and the Soviet threat, by 1977 it was reduced to 459 ships. If the United States continued to build ships at the then-current rate, analysts said, the number of combat vessels would drop to 285 by the turn of the century.[2]

Under the Carter strategy, the bulk of America's military resources were to be used to strengthen the North American Treaty Organization. If the navy was to have any role in a conventional war, it was to serve merely as a ferry system for the army and to prevent Russian submarines from cutting the nation's sea lines of communication in such areas as the sea passages between Greenland, Iceland, and the United Kingdom. Marine divisions would be "heavied-up" to create clones of the existing army divisions for service in Europe. Naval strategists warned to little avail that such a plan meant the surrender of the Pacific and other seas to the Soviets without a fight. "The naval equivalent of the Maginot Line has been constructed," declared the Navy secretary, Graham Claytor, Jr.[3]

Most of the top leadership of the navy and Marine Corps had served in Southeast Asia, and were seared by the war and the hard peace that followed. In the post-Vietnam years, they vowed not only to restore the honor and competence of America's military but also to repair the shattered bond between the people and their defenders. Forced to rethink their position in a period of reduced expectations, the sea services gave urgent priority to retooling strategies. Under the leadership of Vice Admiral Stansfield Turner, the course of study at the Naval War College was broadened. Because of the influence of Admiral Rickover and the nuclearization of the navy, promotion policies had been skewed in favor of narrowly focused nuclear-power officers. Turner, however, recognized that more than technical expertise was required to ensure that an officer would be a fine tactician, an expert strategist, and a leader. Fresh emphasis was placed upon the works of Mahan and Sir Julian S. Corbett, the British naval strategist, particularly the relationship of sea power to armies and land operations.

The marines also returned to fundamentals. "We are pulling our heads out of the jungle and getting back into the amphibious business," said General Robert E. Cushman.[4] A fresh look was taken at amphibious tactics, and new equipment—ranging from 50-knot air-cushion landing craft and heavy helicopters to AV-8B Harrier short-take-off and landing jets—was introduced. These provided the marines with the ability to make wider and deeper assaults that leapfrog or outflank an enemy's defenses. There was also a reemphasis on war fighting—a doctrine that seeks to shatter an enemy's ability to fight through a series of rapid and violent shocks that create a turbulent and swiftly deteriorating situation with which the enemy cannot cope.[5]

In 1979, with the intention of reversing the trends running against the navy, Admiral Thomas B. Hayward, the chief of naval operations, outlined in a widely discussed essay, "The Future of U.S. Sea Power," what later became known as the Maritime Strategy. Hayward offered an alternative to the NATO-centric policy of the Carter administration, which updated Mahan and postulated that the navy's mobility could prevent the Soviets from restricting the locale of the conflict. In the event of a conventional war with the Soviet Union, Hayward wrote, the navy's first objective would be to carry the war to the enemy by destroying the enemy's submarine forces before they could interfere with efforts to supply allied forces on the Central Front in Europe.

No region would be ceded to the Soviets, and Russian ground and tactical forces, at the far ends of the Eurasian land mass, in the Norwegian fjords and Barents Sea, would be pinned down to divert them from the main front. "Horizontal escalation," as it was called, was aimed at convincing the Soviets there would be no protected havens for their forces and was intended both as a deterrent and as a means of building a spirit in the navy of "carry the fight to the enemy."[6]

Unexpected events in the Persian Gulf and the Indian Ocean lent force to the navy's proposals and global view. The region had long been dominated by Britain, but following the withdrawal of the Royal Navy from east of Suez by 1968, the United States moved to fill the vacuum. The gulf was the source of much of the petroleum consumed by the industrialized West. Every fifteen minutes, a loaded tanker steamed through the Straits of Hormuz toward Europe, Japan, or the United States. To ensure against interference with this vital trade, the navy established a continuing logistical presence in the Indian Ocean based on Diego Garcia, a British-owned atoll south of India.

Rather than being drawn directly into the gulf, however, successive U.S. presidents relied upon Iran as the pillar of western interests in the region. Shah Mohammed Reza Pahlavi was lauded for his efforts to modernize his country and was freely supplied with arms and advisers. Visiting Teheran at the end of 1977, President Carter described Iran as "an island of stability in one of the most troubled areas of the world."

But little more than a year later, as a confused and helpless United States looked on, the shah was swept from the Peacock Throne by a revolution of fanatically anti-American Islamic fundamentalists led by the aged Ayatollah Ruholla Khomeini. Youthful militants seized the U.S. Embassy in Teheran on November 4, 1979, and took fifty-two Americans hostage. They demanded that the terminally ill shah, who had been given asylum in the United States, be returned for trial along with his "stolen" wealth—conditions that Washington found unacceptable. The Carter administration was jolted again on Christmas Eve 1979, when Soviet forces invaded Afghanistan to prop up a Marxist dictatorship that was about to be overthrown by Moslem tribesmen.

The upheaval in Iran and the Afghan invasion raised the specter of a Soviet stranglehold on the Persian Gulf and much of the world's proven oil reserves. Reversing his previous position, Carter took a hard line toward the Soviets. Grain and high-technology sales were curtailed, a strategic arms limitation agreement was withdrawn from Senate consideration, and the president declared that the Persian Gulf was within the zone of America's vital interests. Under what became known as the Carter Doctrine, he said the United States would repel a Russian assault on the region "by any means available—including military force."

This crisis marked a turning point for the navy. Forced to rethink his Eurocentric strategic views, Carter created a rapid deployment force of three marine brigades, plus transportation and support, for emergency use anywhere in the world, which ultimately evolved into Central Command, headquartered at MacGill Air Force Base in Florida. Two carrier battle groups moved into the Arabian Sea to put teeth into the Carter Doctrine and a steady stream of ships followed. For all practical purposes, these developments put an end to the preoccupation with strategic forces in Europe.

To make up for the shortage of ships, vessels had to be withdrawn from the Western Pacific and the Mediterranean, confirming the navy's arguments in support of a fleet capable of meeting the nation's commitments. The gulf region was also an extremely difficult place in which to sustain continuous fleet operations. Transit times from American bases were measured in weeks, and once on station, the ships were almost completely dependent on at-sea replenishment.

Only 550 miles long and 217 miles at its widest point, the gulf was ideal for mining. It could be closed easily by land-based missiles.

"Weather conditions are poor," declared Vice Admiral Sylvester R. Foley, Jr. "It's hot. You have a lot of sand and humidity in the wintertime and you get high waves. It's a miserable operating area. . . . There is no potential for change. You aren't popping into a Spanish port or the Riviera the following day." Ships were required to remain so long on what the sailors dubbed "Camel Station" that the Navy Department broke a long-standing taboo against alcohol on board ship and approved the issuance of two cans of beer to each man after a vessel had been at sea for sixty straight days. "That's a hell of a tough way to get a cold beer," observed Admiral Foley.[7]

Obsessed with the hostages' plight, Carter made their safe return his first priority, paradoxically enhancing their value to the Iranians. Unable to negotiate freedom for the captives, he eventually approved a rescue attempt that was aborted amid questions about the capability of the military and the readiness of its equipment. Three of the eight helicopters assigned to the mission experienced mechanical failures that caused the cancellation of the operation. In the withdrawal from Desert One, the staging area within Iran, a helicopter collided with a transport, and eight soldiers died in the blazing wreckage. The last shreds of Jimmy Carter's credibility were also consumed by the flames. Ronald Reagan, a one-time movie star and governor of California, defeated him for reelection; the hostages were not released until the exact moment when Carter left office.

The inauguration of President Reagan resulted in another of those periodic swings that have marked American foreign and defense policy. Vowing never again to be humiliated by the Iranians and regarding the Soviets as "the focus of evil in the modern world," he dedicated his administration to renewed military containment, a lesser reliance on detente, and muscular intervention in the Middle East, Latin America, and the Western Pacific. Reagan intended not only to fulfill the traditional Cold War commitment in Europe, but also to develop the capacity to execute several other missions, and launched the largest and most costly peacetime military buildup in the nation's history.

The navy was a principal beneficiary of this program; nearly $500 billion was earmarked for the construction of a three-ocean navy of six-hundred plus ships by 1989. To preside over this massive buildup, Reagan selected the boyish-looking, thirty-nine-year-old John Lehman, a Wall Street operator and one-time navy pilot. Aggressive, abrasive, and a consummate bureaucratic infighter, Lehman saw himself as a warrior-statesman cast in the mold of Theodore Roosevelt.

While not universally admired, he was the most influential secretary of the navy since World War II. "I am naval aviation," Lehman was quoted as saying. "I run surface warfare and ASW. I run naval personnel. I run shipbuilding, procurement, and research and development. I let Watkins [Admiral James D.

Watkins, then chief of naval operations] run submarines."[8] Among Lehman's most notable moves was to loosen the dictatorial grip of the aging Admiral Rickover upon the navy by pushing him into retirement, and to try to reform the Pentagon's uncompetitive and often corrupt procurement process.

Lehman's new fleet was to include fifteen carrier groups; four surface action groups centered on refurbished *Iowa*-class battleships fitted with Tomahawk cruise and Harpoon antiship missiles; nearly two hundred antiaircraft and antisubmarine cruisers, destroyers, and frigates; ten underway replenishment groups; enough amphibious shipping to lift one-and-a-half marine divisions; and at least one hundred nuclear attack submarines. Naval aviators received updated versions of their planes. Work began on an improved Trident D-5 missile intended to increase the range and survivability of the nation's nuclear submarines. Beginning in 1984, cruise missiles were installed on a wide variety of ships turning what had been single-purpose ASW or antimissile ships into powerful shipkillers as well. One of the most significant additions to the fleet was the *Ticonderoga*-class guided missile cruisers fitted with the sophisticated Aegis long-range air-defense missile and phased-array radar system capable of tracking one hundred targets and engaging up to twenty at the same time.

But many of these programs were troubled. The *Arleigh Burke* class of superdestroyers, which were intended to be the workhorses of the new battle groups, were seriously flawed and far exceeded expected costs. Cost overruns and mismanagement meant that less than half the planned sixty-three vessels would be built. The *Oliver Hazard Perry* antisubmarine warfare frigates were found to be less effective than hoped. Moreover, it was charged that Lehman had paid scant attention to mine warfare. Minesweeping lacked the panache of nuclear submarines and naval air and was neglected even though the Russians were known to be proficient in minelaying—a failure that struck home when the navy became involved in the Persian Gulf.

The Soviet submarine threat was also "advancing at a rate greater than our current ability to counter the threat," according to Admiral Carlisle A. H. Trost, the chief of naval operations. This problem was particularly acute because the complex, new *Seawolf* attack boats, designed to replace the old *Los Angeles* class and to destroy Soviet ballistic-missile submarines under the polar ice, were plagued by huge cost overruns and described by critics as inferior to the best Soviet craft.

Some analysts also derided the Maritime Strategy, which had been adopted by Lehman as a master plan for fighting a conventional war with the Soviet Union. They saw it as more of a rationalization for a six-hundred-ship fleet than a serious plan for deploying these vessels.[9] "Forward operations"—the proposal for the immediate launch of strikes against Soviet submarine bases on the Kola peninsula northeast of Norway and in the Sea of Okhotsk near Vladivostok—in the face of wretched weather, enemy submarines, land-based bombers, and missiles—was likened to the Charge of the Light Brigade. And the intention to target and destroy Soviet missile submarines at the outset of a war was labeled a folly that would virtually guarantee escalation of a conventional conflict into a nuclear holocaust.

By concentrating on supercarriers, the critics also charged, the navy was preparing to fight the wrong war. The carrier, they argued, had taken the place of the nineteenth-century gunboat, and large vessels were too sophisticated for the contingencies they were likely to face. Moreover, the critics alleged that the large-deck carriers not only were vulnerable to attack, but also did not produce a big enough bang for the buck. Each *Nimitz*-class carrier cost about $2.5 billion; an entire battle group costs about $17 billion to operate. Instead of calling for large-deck carriers, the critics called for building smaller vessels outfitted with VSTOL fighters. Two of these vessels could be sent to sea, it was said, for about the cost of one of the large vessels, which not only would multiply the threat against the Soviets but also would make it more difficult to counter.

Large-carrier advocates countered that the small carriers were a false economy because most of the navy's top-of-the-line aircraft, including the F-14 Tomcat, could not operate from their flight decks. They also pointed out that many Third World countries possess advanced air forces and precision-guided missiles that could put small carriers out of commission. Supercarriers, on the other hand, with their armored flight decks, side armor, full compartmentalization, and efficient damage control, would have little difficulty in surviving missile hits similar to those that had caused the loss of several small British ships during the Falklands war with Argentina.

In an age described by Admiral Watkins as "a permanent state of violent peace," large-carrier advocates contended these vessels coupled the vital element of air superiority with the advantage of rapid concentration of forces without reliance upon bases under foreign control.[10] In recent years, they said, the United States had lost access to bases in the Philippines and in the future might be denied use of bases in Panama, Greece, Spain, and Portugal. This made the navy's floating airfields even more indispensable in backing America's words with force.

The sheer size of the carrier battle group was also a defense, it was argued. If a fully deployed group were superimposed upon a map of the United States with its center in Washington, D.C., the forward ships would range as far north as Trenton, New Jersey; its western ships as far as Harrisburg, Pennsylvania; its eastern ships would be well out into the Atlantic; and the southernmost ships would be on the Virginia–North Carolina border. Combat air patrols could be vectored out to Detroit and air strikes made north of Chicago.[11]

Marine Lance Corporal Henry P. Linkkila heard the speeding truck before he saw it. As the bright yellow vehicle crashed through a wire barricade early on the morning of October 23, 1983, he slammed a clip into his M-16 rifle and chambered a round. But it was already too late to fire at the onrushing truck. It had smashed into the headquarters of the 24th Marine Amphibious Unit near Beirut Airport and exploded with the force of more than twelve thousand pounds of TNT. Within seconds, the building was transformed into a heap of dusty rubble in which 241 Americans died, the victims of a suicide bomber.[12]

Tumbled out of his cot in a nearby billet by the force of the explosion, Lieutenant Commander George W. Pucciarelli, the unit's Catholic chaplain, raced to the scene. "I kept looking for the building," he recalled. "As I came around the edge of the shrubbery, I found out that the building wasn't there anymore. It was leveled. . . . And then suddenly, I began to see things move within the rubble, and then I realized that these things . . . moving were our fallen comrades, were those who were wounded." For the U.S. Marine Corps, it was the highest loss of life sustained in a single day since the bloody landing on Iwo Jima in 1945.

Tragically, the marines had come to Lebanon as peacekeepers. They were part of a multinational force sent to restore order to the strife-torn country—a role that the navy found itself playing increasingly in the 1980s. But Lebanon dissolved into a vicious civil war between various political and religious factions while Israel and Syria occupied part of the country. Infuriated at foreign interference, fanatics focused their attention upon the peacekeepers—particularly the 1,500 marines—and the situation deteriorated rapidly. Blundering as badly as Carter in Iran, the Reagan administration had no coherent policy in Lebanon except to maintain a "presence," and the marines were all but held hostage at the Beirut airport.

In the meantime, Reagan took the side of the Christian-dominated Lebanese government, and the situation grew even more confused. Marine forward observers were directing naval gunfire on Moslem militiamen while only a few miles away, fellow marines were expected to behave as if they were neutral. With the country having all but ceased to exist as a viable political entity, few Americans saw any point in remaining in Lebanon. Congress talked of invoking the War Powers Act, which would have forced the president to withdraw the marines within ninety days. Reagan tried to deal with the crisis by beefing up the task force off Lebanon. Naval gunfire reduced the frequency of the attacks on the marines, but each salvo also raised the level of violence.

Although he expressed shock and anger at the bombing of the marine barracks, the president vowed that the marines would remain in Lebanon because their presence was "central to our credibility on a global scale." The battleship *New Jersey* opened up with its big guns, and air strikes against Moslem positions were stepped up; but without adequate policy support, these were empty gestures. Following the complete breakdown of order in Lebanon, Reagan announced early in February 1984 that the severely mauled marines were being "deployed" to the ships off Beirut. One by one, the vessels of the task force were recalled, bringing down the curtain on this unhappy adventure in peacekeeping. If there was a lesson to be learned from the debacle, it was, as in

Vietnam, the inadvisability of sending naval and or military forces into danger without adequate strength or a clearly defined mission. Such forces are only a means of executing a coherent policy, not a substitute.

Two days after the Beirut bombing, on October 25, 1983, Americans were startled by President Reagan's announcement of the completion of another exercise in gunboat diplomacy.[13] The night before, elements of the 22nd Marine Amphibious Unit and the army's 82nd Airborne Division had landed on the tiny, impoverished Caribbean island of Grenada to "restore order and democracy" and ensure the safety of some one thousand Americans, mostly medical students at St. George's University Medical School. The marines were on the way to Lebanon but were diverted to the former British colony amid reports that a radical leftist group had seized control of the government.

Washington was already concerned by reports that the Cubans were helping to build a 10,000-foot runway on Grenada—reportedly to bring in tourists—and viewed it as a threat to sea lanes in the Caribbean basin. The Cuban workers and troops, about eight hundred in all, tried to resist but were quickly overwhelmed. The operation was clouded by a lack of intelligence—some units had to rely upon tourist maps—and poor communications and coordination, which resulted in unnecessary casualties. Within a few days, however, the marines were on their way again to Lebanon. Even if imperfect in practice, the Grenada operation clearly showed the rapidity with which forces from the sea could be brought to bear upon a crisis point—and then disappear back into the sea.

Recurrent crises also erupted in the Mediterranean where President Reagan added an explosive exclamation point to his expressed determination to confront the Soviet Union and its acolytes from the Gulf of Sidra to the South China Sea. Following numerous incidents, the full brunt of American power fell upon the erratic dictator of Libya, Colonel Mu'ammar Gadhafi, the fountainhead of world terrorism.

In the early morning darkness of April 15, 1986, planes from the Sixth Fleet carriers *Coral Sea* and *America* rendezvoused with twenty-four U.S. Air Force F-111 attack bombers from Britain, to attack targets in Tripoli and Benghazi. "Try to make the world smaller for the terrorists," Reagan ordered. The action was precipitated by the recent murders of several Americans in the bombing of a Berlin disco and the hijacking of a TWA airliner. But the navy, returning to the waters where it had won early victories against the Barbary pirates, had been preparing for a showdown with Gadhafi for some time. As early as 1981, Sixth Fleet F-14s had splashed two Libyan fighters that had fired on them over the Gulf of Sidra, which Gadhafi claimed as Libyan territory. In the intervening years, he had obtained new and more sophisticated hardware from the Soviets and the French, including modern fighters and SAM batteries. Late in March 1986, navy planes had thwarted attacks by several Libyan missile boats, sinking at least two of them.

Surprise was complete. The bombing runs of the planes that attacked the airport outside Benghazi were illuminated by the shining runway lights. After dumping sixty tons of bombs on barracks and airfields, the American planes streaked out to sea and safety. One F-111 and its two-man crew were lost. Quick, effective, and leaving no prisoners to be held as hostages by terrorists, Operation El Dorado Canyon was a model of its kind. The attack on Libya proved that the best countermeasure against terrorism is a certain and creditable response. Now painfully aware of the long reach of American power, Gadhafi at least temporarily tamped down his open support of terrorism.[14]

The U.S. Navy's role as a peacekeeper was further tested in the Persian Gulf, at the opposite end from Lebanon in the Middle Eastern crescent of violence. War had been raging between Iraq and Iran since 1980 when the Iraqi dictator, Saddam Hussein, had taken advantage of the confusion in Iran to attack his neighbor. A seaborne guerrilla campaign aimed at interdicting each other's oil exports threatened stoppage of the free flow of oil from the gulf and President Reagan expanded the Carter Doctrine to include a pledge to deal not only with external threats from the Soviets, but also with internal threats—particularly from Iran.

As the Iranians deployed Chinese-made Silkworm surface-to-surface missiles on the narrow Strait of Hormuz, able to reach any ship on the main tanker route, the United States assumed the role of policeman and moved warships into the war zone to protect friendly vessels. Once again the peacekeepers became the target. On the evening of May 17, 1987, the guided-missile frigate *Stark*, part of the navy's Middle East Force, was steaming north of the Strait of Hormuz on radar picket duty when she was hit by two Exocet missiles fired by an Iraqi jet.[15] Thirty-seven crewmen lost their lives in the explosion and fire that followed, and only heroic damage control efforts saved the ship. An inquiry indicated that the attack was probably accidental; an inexperienced Iraqi pilot had been confused as to his location and had fired at a radar blip without checking the identity of his target. Questions were raised about the readiness of the *Stark*, her design, and the rules of engagement issued to her captain. Following the attack, these rules were changed to permit U.S. warships to fire on nearby aircraft that were acting "suspiciously."

In the confusion that followed, Kuwait, which had been financing the Iraqi war effort and was concerned about Iranian attacks on its tankers, indicated that it might seek Soviet escorts for the vessels. To prevent the Russians from obtaining a long-sought foothold in the Persian Gulf, the United States offered the protection of the American flag to eleven Kuwaiti vessels. Iranian mines were known to be a threat, but no effort was made to reinforce the Middle East Force with minesweepers because there was a shortage of such craft and equipment. As a result, an Iranian mine of World War I vintage damaged the supertanker *Bridgeton* during the maiden convoy of reflagged tankers up the gulf. No lives were lost, but the navy was embarrassed.

Quickly adapting to the Iranian challenge, the United States increased the number of ships in the gulf and adjacent waters, with the total reaching forty-eight vessels, the largest deployment since Vietnam. An innovative array of surveillance patrols, offensive power, and intelligence capabilities forced the Iranians to abandon attacks in the northern gulf. Several European nations that initially had been reluctant to become involved—Britain, France, Italy, Belgium, and the Netherlands—united against the common threat and contributed combat ships, minesweepers, and support vessels to the operation. Most analysts credited the presence of American and western ships with preventing total Iranian isolation of the waterway.

U.S. reaction to Iranian attacks was governed by a policy of "measured response" to avoid direct confrontation and preserve the possibility of improved relations with Teheran after the death of the Ayatollah Khomeini. As a result, many ship commanders expressed frustration at the limited role allowed them. The navy made it clear, however, that no interference with the American-escorted convoys would be tolerated. Several Iranian frigates and gunboats were sunk after the craft fired on American helicopters. A minelayer was seized in a daring night raid, and when the frigate *Samuel B. Roberts* was severely damaged by a mine on April 14, 1988, two oil platforms were destroyed in retaliation.

No war can be fought without miscalculation, however, and the possibility of a mistake in the gulf was increased by the heavy traffic in the waterway and the skies overhead. The Iranian practice of refusing to acknowledge the challenges of U.S. patrols compounded the danger. On July 3, 1988, several Iranian gunboats opened fire on the helicopter belonging to the Aegis cruiser *Vincennes*, and she replied with her two 5-inch guns. In the heat of battle, her radar picked up an approaching aircraft and the crew classified it as hostile because the plane appeared to be descending toward their ship, as if for an attack, and giving off an identifying signal typical of a military aircraft. Missiles locked on the target. Captain Will Rogers delayed giving the order to fire until the aircraft was ten miles out; but with the near-fatal example of the *Stark* before him and worried about a suicide attack timed for the Fourth of July, he launched a pair of missiles. The target was destroyed.

Elation quickly gave way to horror. The downed aircraft was a regularly scheduled airliner, Iranian Air Flight 655, and all 290 passengers and crew on board were killed. The United States readily agreed to pay compensation to the families of the dead. Following a lengthy investigation, the navy concluded that the downed plane had not been descending as reported, and the identifying signal may have been emitted by an Iranian military aircraft parked on an airfield. The inquiry held that the crew of the *Vincennes* had misread its equipment in the excitement of battle, but others questioned the efficiency of the Aegis radar system itself.

Within a few months of this tragedy, Iran and Iraq, both worn out by the long and agonizing struggle, agreed to sit down at the negotiating table under

United Nations auspices, and the war ended with the belligerents not far from the positions that they had occupied when the struggle began. The U.S. Navy had played a critical role in ending the struggle. It kept oil flowing from the Persian Gulf, blocked Iran's attempt to intimidate Iraq's allies, and reinforced the stalemate on the ground that led to an end to the fighting.

The navy's successful operations in the gulf also helped restore some of the prestige lost by President Reagan as a result of the botched efforts to trade arms to the Iranians for American hostages and the failed policy in Lebanon. America's Arab allies were also provided with proof of the staying power of the United States when the chips were down—and soon they received even more convincing evidence.

Even as George Bush, who as a naval aviator had been shot down during a World War II bombing raid and picked up by a submarine, was being inaugurated as president in 1989, the world was being turned upside down by the end of the Cold War. Bankrupt, plagued by declining productivity and a demoralized populace, the Soviet Union collapsed and the tide of democracy spilled over Eastern Europe with a swiftness that was breathtaking. The drain on Soviet resources caused by the effort to match the Reagan arms buildup—including the six-hundred-ship navy—was a major factor in the disintegration of the Soviet empire and its replacement by a pride of independent nations. "The world has changed at a fantastic pace, with each day writing a fresh page of history before yesterday's ink has even dried," Bush declared.[16]

Nowhere was the crumbling of the Soviet state more evident than in the rapid decline of the Red Navy. Having abandoned global adventurism, the Russians slashed funds for shipbuilding and operations, and also abandoned overseas bases. Much of the fleet, including the attack boats that had tracked the U.S. Navy's ballistic-missile submarines, disappeared from the sea lanes. The Black Sea Fleet, rusting and immobilized in port, was divided between the Russian Federation and the newly independent Ukrainian Republic. Officers and men faced hard times as pay and even basic equipment and supplies were late in arriving or were not to be had at all.

Paradoxically, the Bush administration met the end of the Cold War with a significant reduction in the size of the navy and an increase in the nation's foreign policy obligations. Plans were announced to slash the navy to the level preceding the Reagan-era buildup. The 545 warships and major auxiliaries that constituted the fleet in 1990 were to be slashed to 451 in 1995, including a reduction in the number of attack carriers from fourteen to eleven and the decommissioning of all four battleships. Naval aviation also faced a bleak future with a reduction in carrier air wings and cancellation of new aircraft types including replacements for the aging A-6 and F-14. In all, by 1995, defense spending was slated to shrink to 3.6 per cent of the gross national product, the lowest level since the 1930s.

Yet despite these reduced capabilities, American policymakers continued to project U.S. power abroad. "We'll need to control the seas regardless of what happens in Moscow," said Defense secretary Richard Cheney. President Bush proclaimed a New World Order in which "brutality will go unrewarded and aggression will meet collective resistance."[17] Under this doctrine, the United States soon found itself intervening directly in various quarters of the world in a new version of gunboat diplomacy—in the Philippines, in Panama, in Liberia, and once again in the Persian Gulf where the world was shocked by an Iraqi invasion of Kuwait.

Iraq had emerged in a badly battered state from the savage war with Iran and most observers thought it would take some time until the nation was on its feet again. But almost immediately, Saddam Hussein, the Iraqi dictator, began pressuring the Kuwaitis and accused them of having stolen $2.4 billion of oil from an underground deposit straddling the border between the two countries. Nevertheless, even though Saddam Hussein had massed troops and tanks on the Kuwaiti border, U.S. intelligence regarded these moves as mere blackmail and played down the possibility of an attack. Rather than issuing a warning, the State Department took a hands-off attitude toward the situation—which Saddam may have seen as a green light for an invasion. U.S. officials also came to Baghdad to fawn on Saddam in search of trade deals.[18]

On August 2, 1990, the Iraqi army attacked Kuwait, sending the emir and his entourage fleeing into Saudi Arabia. Overrunning the country with little difficulty, Saddam declared that Kuwait had been annexed to Iraq as its nineteenth province. An angry Bush considered his options. Twenty-five per cent of the oil imported by the United States came from Kuwait, and Saddam's annexation of Iraq not only gave him control of some of the world's richest petroleum reserves but also put him 250 miles from Saudi Arabia's largest oil fields. Urged on by Margaret Thatcher, Britain's iron-willed prime minister, Bush not only denounced Saddam's action but called for the organization of an international coalition to defend Saudi Arabia and to free Kuwait from the Iraqi grip. But the prospects for intervention were not encouraging.

Most of the muscle would have to come from the United States but the American people were hardly in a warlike mood. The day before the invasion, on August 1, the Pentagon and Congress had announced massive cuts in the defense budget. The Democratic leadership in Congress, still paralyzed by the Vietnam syndrome, flatly opposed military intervention. And analysts were not all that certain that the Iraqi army was a paper tiger. Although it had performed poorly in the war with Iran, Saddam had lavished sophisticated new weaponry upon the elite Republican Guard, and he was known to be trying to develop nuclear, chemical, and biological weapons. By the time the Americans and their allies would be ready to dislodge the Iraqis from Kuwait, Saddam's troops would probably be well dug in. Iraq's naval strength was negligible, but it possessed two weapons that might redress the balance: a large stock of Exocet and Silkworm missiles and sea mines ranging from crude contact versions to modern pressure and magnetic mines.

With a masterful display of diplomacy, Bush convinced the United Nations Security Council to approve resolutions condemning Iraqi aggression and compelling Saddam to disgorge Kuwait under the threat of economic sanctions and military force. The Soviet Union and China supported the American initiative for their own reasons. A coalition of twenty-eight nations agreed to provide ground forces, ships, planes, supplies, or financial support in proportion to their dependence on Persian Gulf oil.

On August 6, the president ordered General H. Norman Schwarzkopf, commander in chief of the Central Command (CINC), to begin Operation Desert Shield, so named to emphasize that it was intended to protect Saudi Arabia from invasion. Schwarzkopf immediately shifted headquarters of CENTCOM from Florida to a bunker in Riyadh, the Saudi Arabian capital, and began to orchestrate the deployment of 200,000 soldiers and marines and more than 1,000 aircraft to the Arabian peninsula. CENTCOM exemplified the "joint" character of U.S. command and control called for by the Goldwater-Nichols Military Reform Act of 1986. Schwarzkopf as CINC had the power to direct all the forces in the theater in an effort to end interservice rivalries and jealousies, which had often plagued American military operations.

In spite of the UN vote, Saddam Hussein was convinced that the United States was powerless to do anything about the invasion of Kuwait. Ironically, many top American military officers shared his conviction. The nearest substantial U.S. forces were in Germany and the Philippines. At best, some marines and aircraft, possibly some airborne troops, might be deployed to the gulf. To move enough troops to drive the Iraqis out of Kuwait would require resources and efforts equal to the commitment in Vietnam. Saddam was also known to have a stockpile of chemical and biological weapons. Yet there were some positive factors. Preparations had been made over the years for the defense of Saudi Arabia. The largest airbase in the world had been built at Dhahran, and bunkers there were crammed with engine assemblies, munitions, and avionics equipment. Modern ports had been constructed at Al Jubail and Dhahran, both with giant cranes and roll-on/roll-off capacity.

The closest U.S. ships to the crisis area were those of the small Joint Task Force Middle East, which included a cruiser, several frigates, and a destroyer, and the even smaller British Armilla patrol. They provided an immediate show of force by shutting down Iraqi trade with the outside world through the Persian Gulf with the exception of ships carrying food. The *Independence* carrier battle group, which had been exercising in the Indian Ocean near Diego Garcia, steamed north to the Gulf of Oman while the *Eisenhower* group, already in the Mediterranean, transited the Suez Canal and took up station in the Red Sea.[19]

For the first two weeks of the crisis, aircraft flying from these two carriers provided the shield that prevented Iraqi action against Saudi Arabia—had any been intended. Until late fall, naval aircraft provided the bulk of ready U.S. tactical air in the region. "Without the instant availability of the maritime forces there would have been no five-month buildup, no military option," states one authority. "The Iraqi force in Kuwait would surely have been sufficient to pressure Saudi Arabia to preclude any use of its territory to launch a counterattack."[20]

Other vessels, including additional carriers and the battleships *Wisconsin* and *Missouri*, began arriving to add muscle to the naval force. The naval component of CENTCOM (NAVCENT) under the command of Vice Admiral Stanley Arthur, commander of the Seventh Fleet who flew his flag in the command ship *Blue Ridge*, grew into a multinational naval force of about 120 U.S. and 50 allied warships, including British, French, Canadian, Dutch, Spanish, Argentine, and Italian vessels.[21]

The first mobile ground units capable of immediate sustained operations, the 1st and 7th Marine Expeditionary Brigades were on their way to Saudi Arabia by air within days of the decision to defend that country. Tanks, artillery, ammunition, and supplies to sustain thirty days of fighting arrived on preloaded Marine Prepositioning Ships from Diego Garcia and Guam. The 15,248 desert-trained troops of the 7th MEB were in place on the Saudi-Kuwait border and ready for combat by August 20. They were augmented by 123 tanks, 425 artillery pieces, and 124 aircraft, including helicopters and Harrier jets, which could operate equally well from the decks of small carriers and the desert. The 1st MEB was deployed at the front shortly after.

While these units were "marrying up" with their equipment, an amphibious task force brought the 4th MEB totaling 16,000 troops to the gulf where it was joined by the 13th Marine Expeditionary Unit. The Iraqi and Kuwaiti coasts seemed well suited for amphibious landings, so General Schwarzkopf decided to keep them afloat where they were a constant threat to the uneasy Iraqis, who positioned 50,000 troops just to the east of Kuwait City to oppose a landing. Other units arrived to fill out the MEBs to two full divisions—the 1st and 2nd Marine divisions—with their own air wings. Lieutenant General Walter E. Boomer was named commander of the 1st Marine Expeditionary Force, which eventually included 92,000 troops—the largest deployment of U.S. Marines since the Pacific campaign of World War II.[22]

In the meantime, the herculean task of mounting a military operation from scratch seven thousand miles from home was underway. A 2,300-strong ready brigade of the 82nd Airborne was flown to Saudi Arabia where it took a place in the line along the frontier with the marines. Yet, even with increasingly powerful air support, the marines and lightly equipped airborne troops were no guarantee against a preemptive Iraqi drive south. They needed reinforcements—the tanks, armored personnel carriers, and big guns of the army's 24th Mechanized Infantry Division and other heavy units.

The responsibility for getting this force to the gulf rested upon Vice Admiral Francis R. Donovan, the director of the Military Sealift Command.[23] The key elements of his operation were eight 55,000-ton roll-on/roll-off transports held in reserve at ports along the southeastern coast of the United States for just such a contingency. Computerized simulations had demonstrated that each ship could be loaded in 24 hours, and at a steady cruising speed of 30 knots, they could move a mechanized division to the gulf in 14 days. But no realistic exercises had ever been held to test these assumptions. One naval officer graphically summed up the problem: "Imagine taking a 1978 car, draining the gasoline and all the fluids and putting it up on blocks for twelve years. Then you get a call saying the car has been taken off the blocks and has to be ready for a long trip in one week."

Against all odds, the first of the transports docked in Savannah only four days after the activation order was issued and she sailed on August 14, more or less combat loaded. The second vessel sailed the following day, but after maintaining a grueling 27 knots for 48 hours her engines burst into flames and she had to be ignominiously towed into Rota, Spain. Realizing that these ships were inadequate for the task, Donovan activated the ninety large freighters of the Ready Reserve Fleet (RRF). These vessels were purportedly to be ready for sea in two or three weeks after activation, but it took more than two months for some ships to be made ready. Several suffered spectacular boiler explosions; critics sardonically noted that the Iraqis had no need for submarines because the U.S. merchant fleet seemed ready to self-destruct on its own.

This logistical nightmare came as no surprise to those who had followed the steep decline of America's merchant fleet in the post-Vietnam era. The last commercial ship built in an American yard had been completed in 1986 and only one had been placed on order since then. Not only was there a shortage of ships but also of crews, particularly crews familiar with the technology of the 1960s and 1970s when the reserve ships were built. Although Congress had voted $7 billion to maintain the military sealift, a considerable share of these funds had been diverted to nuclear submarines and to pay for military dependents' health insurance. Nevertheless, the navy's Sealift Command delivered from a standing start over three million tons of materiel to Saudi Arabia when the land battle began in February 1992, and another 600,000 tons was on the way. Nothing like it had been seen since the buildup for the Normandy invasion in World War II.

Even as this buildup continued, the marines conducted frequent practice landings on the coast that kept the Iraqis on edge and the navy enforced the blockade of Iraq. While carrier aircraft provided cover, destroyers and frigates monitored the traffic in the gulf in search of contraband. The first Iraqi ship was intercepted on August 17 and by the time of the ceasefire, almost seven thousand had been inspected—between thirty and forty a day. Most of these inspections were made by U.S. Coast Guard teams who had become accustomed to boarding and searching ships during antidrug patrols in the Caribbean. Although the Iraqis tried to evade the sanctions by bringing in supplies over land through Jordan and by air, the blockade effectively deprived them of military and civilian spare parts. Food supplies were so tight that the Iraqi government ordered strict rationing on September 1. History records no example of economic sanctions forcing an aggressor to relinquish his prize, however, and it was inevitable that military pressure would eventually have to be brought to bear. In the interval, the naval blockade maintained a stranglehold on the Iraqi economy.

In November, President Bush announced that an additional 200,000 troops would be sent to the Persian Gulf to join the 230,000 already there. Three more carrier battle groups built around the *America*, *Ranger*, and newly commissioned *Theodore Roosevelt* were also deployed making a total of six. The reinforcements signified a shift in overall strategy from the defense of Saudi Arabia to the eventual expulsion of the Iraqis from Kuwait. Following extensive debate, the UN passed a resolution giving the Iraqis six weeks—until January 15—to withdraw from the occupied territory or be driven out. As the deadline approached, debate in the United States sharpened. Security was stepped up throughout the country in anticipation of terrorist attacks. Saddam blustered that if the coalition forces attacked they "would swim in their own blood." Out in the desert, the troops practiced offensive maneuvers, while in the air the pilots sharpened their skills and at sea, the ships steamed on.

Shortly after 0200 on January 16, 1991, the Aegis guided-missile cruiser *San Jacinto* in the Red Sea, was brilliantly illuminated by the fiery plume of a blunt-nosed Tomahawk missile as it leaped with a low roar from its launcher. A mile from the ship the missile's rocket motor dropped away, stubby wings and tail control fins popped out of its sides, and a jet engine ignited in a coil of smoke. Having settled in at an altitude of a thousand feet, the Tomahawk streaked northward toward the command and control centers of Saddam Hussein's military establishment. Operation Desert Storm, the liberation of Kuwait, had begun.

Soon afterward, missile after missile blazed skyward from the *Wisconsin* and other vessels of the U.S. Navy battle groups operating in the gulf as well as the Red Sea. Commander R. J. Turner, the battleship's dentist who was manning his battle station in a triage center, remembered a quotation from general William Tecumseh Sherman: "War is the remedy our enemies have chosen, and I say let us give them what they want."[24]

The Tomahawks led off a volley of more than a hundred missiles that whiplashed Baghdad and the surrounding area with devastating accuracy. Eighty per cent scored direct hits on their designated targets. A British television correspondent standing on a sixth-floor balcony of his hotel reported seeing a Tomahawk whizzing past at eye level and slamming into the nearby Iraqi Defense Ministry.[25] Much of Iraq's first-line communications capability was shattered by the initial barrage, along with the nation's vital electrical grid and main defensive systems.

Navy F-14 and F/A-18 fighters, A-6 and A-7 strike craft, and EA-6B electronic jammers followed the missiles into Iraqi air space. They joined U.S. Air Force planes and the aircraft of six nations—Britain, France, Italy, Canada, Saudi Arabia, and the Kuwaiti government in exile. High-speed antiradiation missiles (HARMS) smothered the Soviet-built radars guiding the Iraqi defenses. Although antiaircraft fire was in some cases intense, it was largely inaccurate because the gunners feared "getting a HARM down the throat" if they turned on their radars. Few fighters rose to challenge the attackers and allied losses were light.

This attack was followed by the most powerful and sustained air assault in history. Unlike the Vietnam conflict where civilians in Washington had insisted upon choosing targets, air operations were planned and orchestrated by the theater commanders based upon local conditions. Moreover, the launching of an immediate overwhelming strike allowed the Iraqis no time to become acclimatized to attack or to repair their air-defense system. It was far more effective than the gradual buildup of the air war against Vietnam. The primary aim of the bombing campaign, Schwarzkopf later explained, was to offset purported Iraqi superiority in numbers of men and tanks.

Over the next thirty-eight days, coalition aircraft, including navy and marine planes, joined in isolating the Kuwaiti theater of operations by taking out all the bridges, roads, and supply lines between northern Kuwait and southern Iraq.[26] Key ground targets were destroyed and the Iraqi air force was driven from the sky. Many of the Iraqi planes took refuge in Iran and by January 23, the coalition had won complete air superiority over Kuwait and the lower third of Iraq. While sophisticated missiles were used with great effect, including the new laser-guided SLAM, a land-attack version of the Harpoon, about 95 per cent of the ordnance delivered to the target consisted of conventional bombs.

Naval and marine aircraft performed about 30 per cent of the 2,000 sorties a day of Desert Storm. When attacking land targets, a carrier launched "strike packages" of twenty to thirty aircraft, and each ship averaged 150 sorties a day. Despite efforts at "jointness," the air war was complicated by incompatible computer systems, which delayed communication between the air force air-war controller at CENTCOM and the carriers at sea. Each morning, the Air Tasking Order for the day, a nine hundred page document detailing air operations for the day, had to be carried manually from Riyadh to the battle force commanders at sea and then by helicopter to each of the carriers.

Flying in from the Red Sea, the air groups of the carriers *Kennedy* and *Saratoga* outflanked the Iraqi air defenses, which were expecting attacks from the four carriers in the gulf. Some carrier planes flew to Saudi bases where they refueled and were fully armed with twenty-eight 500-pound bombs. Others refueled in midair from Air Force tankers. This intensive, around-the-clock pace created what one writer described as a certain "lunatic charm" on the carriers. Some pilots suited up in the ready rooms to the strains of the Rolling Stones or "The William Tell Overture," and watched "motivational tapes" of bare-breasted blondes.[27]

Each fleet as well as each carrier developed a unique personality. The Red Sea armada, which was composed largely of Atlantic Fleet ships used to working closely with allies in the Atlantic and Mediterranean, was considered cooperative on the *Blue Ridge* and by CENTCOM in Riyadh. On the other hand, the gulf armada, drawn from the Pacific and used to steaming independently, was regarded by both headquarters as tending to act autonomously.

Admiral Stanley Arthur, the overall naval commander, also had his problems with higher command. Before the fighting began, he had asked permission to sink Iraqi craft suspected of laying mines in the international waters of the northern gulf, itself an act of war. If an army general looked outside his tent and saw someone planting a mine, the admiral argued, he would be justified in shooting the intruder. Schwarzkopf denied the request, saying it might trigger an all-out war while Washington was still seeking a diplomatic solution to the crisis. After the bombing started, Schwarzkopf threatened to court martial the pilots of a flight of A-6 bombers from the *Midway* who strafed and set aflame an Iraqi tanker that was warning the enemy of the approach of navy planes because he had issued orders placing tankers off limits to attack to avoid polluting the gulf.[28]

The Iraqi Navy consisted of about fifty *Osa* patrol boats armed with Exocet and Styx missiles and a handful of minelaying and other miscellaneous craft. Avoiding direct combat with the coalition ships in the northern gulf, the Iraqis devoted most of their naval effort to laying mines. Carrier planes attacked the Iraqi naval base at Umm Qasr early in the campaign, and most of the missile boats were sunk or damaged. Vigorous steps were also taken to clear the offshore islands and oil platforms used by the Iraqis as observation posts. The guided-missile frigate *Nicholas* deployed army special forces who cleared eleven platforms of troops that had been firing missiles at approaching aircraft. On January 29, a convoy of seventeen small boats carrying Iraqi commandos tried to make a landing on the Saudi coast, apparently in support of a sizable foray against the town of Khafji. Carrier planes and helicopters operating with the British frigate *Cardiff* destroyed the entire convoy. U.S. Marines and Saudi and Qatari forces turned back the ground attack with heavy Iraqi losses.

By early February, all of Iraq's missile boats had been accounted for, but an estimated 1,200 mines of various types sown by the Iraqis were a significant threat to the freedom of passage in the northern gulf. Some American ships were fitted with a high-definition mine-avoidance sonar that had been developed as a result of experience gained while escorting the reflagged Kuwait tankers during the Iran-Iraq War. Minesweeping ships and helicopters provided by the coalition partners made up some of the deficiencies in the U.S. Navy's capabilities, but the mines slowed the pace of naval operations. Both the helicopter/ carrier *Tripoli* and the Aegis cruiser *Princeton* were extensively damaged by mines. Nevertheless, on February 3, the *Missouri* was led through a minefield by the *Nicholas* to bombard Iraqi bunkers and artillery batteries on the coast of southeastern Kuwait with its 16-inch guns. Three days later, the *Wisconsin* supported a marine probe into southern Kuwait. With the battleships in firing position, it was clear that the final battle was about to begin.

"Our strategy is . . . very simple," General Colin L. Powell, chairman of the Joint Chiefs of Staff, proclaimed as the land war burst into full fury at 0400 February 24. "First, we are going to cut it [the Iraqi army] off, and then we are going to kill it." Schwarzkopf's plan of attack called for a three-pronged ground offensive while the threat of a giant amphibious assault was maintained to keep the six Iraqi divisions pinned down to the coast. The 1st and 2nd Marine divisions plus the Tiger Brigade of the army's 2nd Armored Division and five Arab mechanized infantry brigades were to punch northward to Kuwait City. In the center, the British 7th Armored Division and the heavy units of the U.S. Army's VII Corps, the main strike force, were to surge north and then east to take the Republican Guard on the flank. To the west, the French 6th Light Armored Division and the U.S. XVIII Airborne Corps were to make a sweeping end run around the Iraqi defense line. Advancing rapidly through the desert, these units were to swing north and east toward the Euphrates River to cut off the Iraqi retreat.

The marines had the unenviable task of breaching the strongest part of the much vaunted Saddam Line. They had to cross two belts of minefields, sand berms, and barbed-wire defenses, all the while under Iraqi artillery fire. But these "impenetrable defenses" were less impregnable than reported. The Iraqi gunners had no forward observers or airborne spotters, and their fire was sporadic and ineffectual. M-60 tanks fitted with mine plows and steel rakes rumbled ahead cutting six lanes through the mine belts. The tanks of Task Forces Ripper, Grizzly, and Papa Bear poured through these breaches and thousands of marines followed. Numbed, starved, and isolated by the air campaign, the Iraqis were stunned and whole battalions surrendered.[29]

"It was a classic, absolutely classic military breaching," Schwarzkopf later observed. "They went through the first barrier like it was water. Then they brought both divisions streaming through that breach. Absolutely superb operation—a textbook, [operation] and I think it will be studied for many, many years to come as the way to do it."[30]

Once clear of the defense line, Task Force Ripper wheeled westward toward Al Jabar Air Base while Papa Bear angled northeast on a trajectory toward Kuwait City International Airport. Marine Lieutenant William Delaney of Ripper spotted the first Iraqi tanks. "They knew we were coming," he later reported. "We didn't wait to get closer. We destroyed them—in all, our company got fifteen tanks. It was unbelievable. Tanks blew up with tremendous explosions. Turrets flipped off. . . . Everybody in my platoon got a tank kill. There were dead bodies all over the place. . . . If it didn't have a white flag, we shot it—trucks, vehicles, bunkers."[31]

Overhead, Cobra helicopters fitted with TOW antitank missiles, rockets and cannon, Harriers, and A-6 Intruders provided close air support for the marines as they pushed forward. Iraqi armor launched a counterattack against the 1st Marine Division but it was beaten back as marine and navy planes attacked in waves. The 2nd division enjoyed equal success. Brushing aside mortar and small-arms fire, it drove into Kuwait, taking more than five thousand prisoners. Only five Americans and four allied soldiers were reported killed in the breaching action, an extraordinarily small number in view of the magnitude of the operation.

On the second day of the ground war, both marine divisions pushed farther into Kuwait. The 1st Marine Division destroyed fifty to sixty Iraqi tanks with a hail of artillery fire during a fight near the Burgan oilfield. As the remnant of the Iraqis sought to disengage, they were blasted by marine armor and Cobras. Similarly, Iraqi tanks standing in the way of the 2nd Marine Division and the Tiger Brigade as they pushed farther north to the Kuwait airport fell victim to American firepower. Afloat, the two battleships and other vessels shelled targets designated by navy and marine spotters on the ground and in the air. In all, the battleships fired over 1,100 16-inch shells in what would be their farewell to combat. The amphibious force made a feint toward the Faylaka Islands to keep the Iraqis off balance, but no landing was made. By day's end, the marines were only ten miles from Kuwait City.

At daybreak on the third day, the Iraqis began a panicked retreat from the capital. North of the city, A-6s from the *Ranger* caught a bumper-to-bumper stream of military vehicles and stolen civilian cars and trucks, most crammed with loot, on the Al Jahra highway and strafed and bombed the convoy. Harriers, FA-18s, and Air Force fighter-bombers swarmed in, turning the road into the "Highway of Death." Navy pilots also blasted another convoy on the coastal road.

Elsewhere, the Iraqi army continued to disintegrate as U.S. and British forces turned eastward to the Euphrates to pin the retreating enemy between the advancing allied forces. One Iraqi battalion of five hundred men even encircled themselves with concertina wire and waited patiently for American scouts to take them prisoner. Elements of the 2nd Marine Division cut the highway from Kuwait City to Basra, in southern Iraq. The 1st Marine Division secured the airport after a fierce tank battle on the outskirts of the city in which more than three hundred Iraqi tanks were destroyed. But the marines were forbidden by Schwarzkopf to enter Kuwait City. With a sense of diplomatic etiquette and a prudent reluctance to risk American troops in what could be costly street fighting, he reserved this honor for the Arabs. With all Iraqi troops having been driven from Kuwait, the ground war came to an end the following day, February 27, 1991, after one hundred hours of fighting. The two marine divisions and the Tiger Brigade, supported by navy, marine, and coalition aircraft, had destroyed or damaged 1,060 tanks, 608 artillery pieces, and 7 missile launchers and captured over 20,000 Iraqi soldiers.

If there should be a next war, however, the enemy will probably not be as cooperative as Saddam Hussein. Future enemies are unlikely to watch passively as an American-led coalition uses Saudi Arabian ports and airfields unimpeded for five months to mobilize 620,000 troops to ready an attack, or to build four enormous "iron mountains" of supplies in the open desert to fuel a rapid-fire offensive. Nor are the United States and its partners likely to have such an overwhelming superiority in training and equipment and an enemy so unskilled in modern warfighting techniques as Saddam. While the allies were planning, thinking, and fighting in three dimensions, the Iraqis were digging in as if for World War I. Moreover, he did not use his stockpile of biological and chemical weapons.

Sea power played a vital—if unpublicized—role in the final victory in the Gulf War.[32] The U.S. Navy's carriers and their planes, plus the thin line of marines, blocked the Iraqis from immediately pressing on into Saudi Arabia after the conquest of Kuwait, and served as its shield for several months afterward. The navy enforced an effective trade embargo on Iraq, prepared the way for the air and ground campaign, conducted a massive sealift that brought in 95 per cent of all the supplies used to fight the war, provided 30 per cent of the air assets, and furnished a significant strategic threat to the seaward flank of the Iraqi positions. In the final analysis, both the air and land campaigns rested upon a foundation constructed by the naval forces.

For the U.S. Navy , however, Desert Storm was a paradox. While the service performed well in crisis, its doctrine, weapons, and systems proved ill-suited to the Gulf War. Desert Storm hardly supported the assumptions of the Maritime Strategy. No opposing naval force worthy of the name challenged the coalition fleet nor did waves of enemy aircraft attack its carriers. No submarines threatened the flow of troops and materiel to the gulf. No battles were fought on the open sea of the kind for which the navy had been preparing for twenty years. Instead, mines were the primary threat in a war fought in a confined area. The navy was successful because the high-quality force painstakingly created after Vietnam made it possible to modify its operating doctrine under emergency conditions. For the U.S. Navy, more than any other service, Desert Storm was the midwife of change.

EPILOGUE

*Tradition, valor, and victory are the navy's heritage from
the past. To these may be added dedication, discipline, and
vigilance as the watchwords of the present and the future.*
                                            —*All Hands* magazine

With engines droning, the crew of a patrol bomber searches the ocean below for a warship they know is out there somewhere. But they are unable to locate it. Even the sophisticated radar comes up blank. One crewman makes out what he thinks is a "blip" on the radar screen but it is gone before he can be certain. As the sky brightens, another man catches a momentary glimpse of a vessel down below but it quickly disappears. It is proceeding at high speed and has a strangely shaped superstructure like no other ship he has ever seen.

Warships embodying such stealth technology have yet to take to the sea but they point the way to the future as the U.S. Navy sets its course for a new century. Such vessels are in line with the changes in naval weaponry and warfighting doctrine adopted to meet changed conditions resulting from the collapse of the Soviet Union. The entire direction of war at sea has been transformed. Yet, even though the Soviet threat has disappeared, the world is an increasingly disorderly and unpredictable place, a world in which the navy has a vital role in protecting the national interest.

Rogue nations threaten the peace and in all too many regions of the world, chaos in the form of ethnic, civil, and religious strife has become a way of life. Libya, Iran, and Iraq are a threat to American interests in the gulf region and the Mediterranean. North Korea, strained by famine and heavily armed, may seek relief from the pressures upon it by renewing hostilities on the Korean peninsula. China clearly intends to become a major military power in coming decades. Terrorism is a constant danger. Growing populations and widening gaps between rich and poor nations are likely to incite new conflicts—and the need to send American troops and naval forces abroad on peacekeeping missions will arise with increasing frequency. Somalia, Haiti, Bosnia, and Sierra Leone are merely the beginning.

To deal with these problems, naval strategists have placed fresh emphasis on the creation of forwardly deployed ready forces able to intervene in regional conflicts where less than maximum force is required. In such scenarios, containing conflict is likely to be more important than defeating an enemy. This has resulted in a turning away from the Cold War strategic doctrine of sea control. Promulgated during the height of the struggle with the Soviets, this doctrine is ill suited for an environment in which there is no countervailing military superpower with a bluewater fleet.

Under ". . . From the Sea," the U.S. Navy's new warfighting doctrine, naval forces are shifting from confrontation with another superpower on the open sea to the projection of power from the sea. The navy, along with the army, air force, and marines will strive to control events in littoral regions—on or near the shore—rather than on the blue water. Influencing events ashore is hardly a fresh concern for naval forces. But the new operational concept goes far beyond the traditional notion of power projection to a broader concept known as battlefield dominance.

Although the navy will still be concerned with an enemy's maritime capabilities, ". . . From the Sea" postulates that the primary purpose of U.S. naval power will be "expeditionary warfare"—to assist in winning a victory on land. Reversing traditional roles, the marines—and the army—are now seen as the spearhead of naval operations. Large carrier battle groups and missile submarines have a reduced role in such a strategy.

The navy's role in world affairs is increasingly that of an instrument of preventive diplomacy, for tamping down crises before they get out of hand and for conventional deterrence in situations of low- and midlevel intensity rather than battling for control of the high seas. By controlling the seas adjacent to the littoral battlefields, the navy can project—with the assistance of embarked marines or army troops—missiles, shells and bombs, bullets and bayonets to match the situation in hand. By being forward deployed and ready to fight, the navy can prevent some fights from occurring by arriving on the scene before tensions get out of hand. Ships do not need the permission of any country to remain on station, and can bring to bear a complete package of military force to resolve a crisis. Moreover, they can be withdrawn with less trouble than an onshore buildup.

Yet as the leadership of the navy tries to maintain its focus as a fighting force, it faces problems on several fronts at century's end. Force levels, manpower, and spending are all subject to drastic revision although missions are multiplying. The number of ships in commission is being reduced to little more than half the levels of the Reagan years. Debate rages over whether the navy's weapons mesh with the service's post–Cold War strategy. With the emphasis shifting to littoral warfare, critics point out that the navy should increase its ability to clear mines in shallow waters and to lay down a curtain of gunfire from sea to shore to cover amphibious landings. Yet, they claim, the mine warfare budget is declining and the latest ships lack sufficient gun power for effective shore bombardment. Instead, the navy is promoting a new missile-ladden arsenal ship, even though some analysts charge that million-dollar missiles are an expensive substitute for gunfire and inadequate against such targets as tank columns. The arsenal ship itself is described by critics as vulnerable to submarine and air attack.

Like the other armed forces, the navy is also struggling to provide women with a more equitable role in what has been largely a male-dominated service. Incidents of sexual harassment such as those that occurred at the Tailhook Association convention in September 1991, prompted official announcement of zero tolerance for such conduct, yet further incidents have occurred. The decision to assign half of all female sailors to sea duty on combat ships by the end of the century has been particularly controversial. Critics charge that the plan's supporters outside the navy are less interested in the navy's reason for existence—a readiness to fight—than to use it as an instrument for social engineering. Nevertheless, Admiral Jay L. Johnson, the chief of naval operations, has insisted that except for submarines and SEALS teams all career billets will be opened to women.

One thing is certain, however. The navy of the new century will bear little resemblance to what has gone before. The navy looks ahead to warships built like catamarans, which will skim the surface at sixty knots, are powered by turbine-generated electricity, are armed with directed-energy weapons such as lasers, and use stealth technology to evade radar detection. Submarines will run so quietly they will be nearly impossible to detect; their weapons will include supersonic antiaircraft missiles fired from beneath the sea.

But there is a unity between these craft and the past. No ship sails alone. The vessels of the future—and the men and women serving in them—will continue to fulfill the navy's historical mission of preserving the peace and keeping open the sea lanes of the world. For the foreseeable future, the navy will remain a major factor in supporting American political, economic, and military objectives in a world dependent upon the free flow of commerce on the seas. In the words of Admiral Nimitz, the U.S. Navy will continue to be, as it has been for more than two centuries, "the nation's instrument of policy in peace and its first line of defense in war."

NOTES

CHAPTER 1—A NAVY IS BORN

1. Commodore Esek Hopkins' signals for the first Continental Fleet, *Naval Documents of the American Revolution* (Washington, D.C.: Government Printing Office, 1964–) Vol. 3, pp. 1287–1291, cited hereafter as *Naval Documents.* Journal of *Andrew Doria*, February 18, 1776, *Ibid.*, p. 1349.

2. Naval Committee to Commodore Esek Hopkins, January 5, 1776, *Ibid.*, Vol. 3, pp. 637–638.

3. Hopkins to John Hancock, April 9, 1776. *Ibid.*, Vol. 4, pp. 735–736.

4. Nicholas Biddle to James Biddle, May 10, 1776, *Ibid.*, Vol. 5, p. 27.

5. Washington to Comte de Grasse, October 28, 1781, *The Writings of George Washington*, John C. Fitzpatrick, ed. (Washington, D.C.: Government Printing Office, 1937), Vol. 23, p. 285.

6. John Adams, *Diary and Autobiography*, L. H. Butterfield, ed. (Cambridge, Mass.: Belknap Press, 1961), Vol. II, p. 198.

7. Edmund Burke, "Speech on Conciliation with America," *Burke's Speeches* (Westport, Conn.: Greenwood Press, 1974), p. 77.

8. Lawrence H. Gipson, *The Coming of the American Revolution: 1763–1775* (New York: Harper & Row, 1954), p. 15; and Howard I. Chapelle, *The History of the American Sailing Navy* (New York: W. W. Norton and Co., 1949), p. 5.

9. Debates in the House of Lords, *Naval Documents*, Vol. 1, pp. 444–445.

10. For detailed accounts of the founding of the Continental Navy, *see* Charles O. Paullin, *The Navy of the American Revolution* (Cleveland: Burroughs,

1906), Chapters I and III; J. Adams, *op. cit.*, Vol. II, pp. 192–198, 201–202, 205, 220, 229–230; and Nathan Miller, *Sea of Glory: The Continental Navy Fights for Independence, 1775–1783* (New York: David McKay Company, Inc., 1974), Chapter III.

11. The organization of this force can be traced in *Naval Documents*, Vols. 2 and 3; and in William Bell Clark, *George Washington's Navy* (Baton Rouge, La.: Louisiana State University Press, 1960).

12. "Rules for the Regulation of the Navy of the United Colonies," *Naval Documents*, Vol. 2, pp. 1174–1178.

13. For the administrative history of the Continental Navy, *see* Charles O. Paullin, *Paullin's History of Naval Administration: 1775–1911* (Annapolis, Md.: U. S. Naval Institute, 1968), Chapter One.

14. John Trevitt, "Journal of John Trevitt," printed in Charles R. Smith, *Marines in the Revolution* (Washington, D.C.: U.S. Marine Corps, 1975), p. 321; and *Naval Documents*, Vol. 4, p. 1360.

15. For impressment in the Continental Navy, *see* William M. Fowler, Jr., "The Non-Volunteer Navy," U.S. Naval Institute *Proceedings*, August 1974; and *Archives of Maryland*, William H. Browne, ed. (Baltimore: Maryland Historical Society, 1879), Vol. XVI.

16. Alfred T. Mahan, *Major Operations of the Navies in the War of American Independence* (Boston: Little, Brown & Co., 1913), pp. 60–61; and Edgar S. Maclay, *A History of American Privateers* (New York: D. Appleton and Company, 1899), p. ix.

17. For operations on Lake Champlain, *see* Mahan, *op. cit.*, Chapter I; and Willard M. Wallace, *Traitorous Hero: The Life and Fortunes of Benedict Arnold* (New York: Harper and Brothers, 1954), Chapter X.

18. Committee of Secret Correspondence to Lambert Wickes, October 24, 1776, *Naval Documents*, Vol. 6, pp. 1400–1403.

19. William Bell Clark, *Lambert Wickes: Sea Raider and Diplomat* (New Haven: Yale University Press, 1932).

20. *Letters and Papers Relating to the Cruises of Gustavus Conyngham*, Robert W. Neeser, ed. (New York: Naval History Society, 1915).

21. For details of Jones' early life, *see* Samuel Eliot Morison, *John Paul Jones: A Sailor's Biography* (Boston: Little, Brown & Co., 1959); and Lincoln Lorenz, *John Paul Jones: Fighter for Freedom and Glory* (Annapolis, Md.: U.S. Naval Institute, 1943).

22. John Kilby, "John Kilby's Narrative as Seaman on the *Bonhomme Richard*," Dunard T. Stokes, ed., *Maryland Historical Magazine*, Spring 1972.

23. There are four accounts of the cruise of the *Bonhomme Richard*: Jones' report to Franklin, October 3, 1779, in John H. Sherburne, *The Life and Character of John Paul Jones* (New York: Adriance, Sherman & Co., 1851), pp. 108–160; an account by Richard Dale, *Ibid.*, pp. 120–123; Nathaniel Fan-

ning, *Fanning's Narrative* (New York: Naval History Society, 1912); and Kilby, *op. cit.*

24. Dale's account, Sherburne, *op. cit.*, p. 121.

25. For Biddle's career, *see* William Bell Clark, *Captain Dauntless: The Story of Nicholas Biddle of the Continental Navy* (Baton Rouge, La.: Louisiana State University Press, 1949).

26. Mary Barney, *A Biographical Memoir of the Late Commodore Joshua Barney* (Boston: Gray and Bowen, 1836), pp. 65–67. Nicholson's account is in the *Pennsylvania Packet*, April 15, 1778.

27. The events leading up to the Battle of the Chesapeake Capes are described in Francis E. Chadwick, ed., *The Graves Papers and Other Documents Relating to the Naval Operations of the Yorktown Campaign* (New York: Naval History Society, 1916); and Harold A. Larrabee, *Decision at the Chesapeake* (New York: Clarkson N. Potter, 1964).

CHAPTER 2—IN PURSUIT OF PRIVATEERS AND PIRATES

1. George Claghorne to James McHenry, September 24, 1779, *American State Papers*, Naval Affairs (Washington, D.C.: Gales and Seaton, 1834), Vol. I, p. 56.

2. For background of the Barbary pirates, *see* Gardner W. Allen, *Our Navy and the Barbary Corsairs* (Boston: Houghton Mifflin Co., 1905), Chapters I and II, cited hereafter as *Corsairs*.

3. *Ibid.*, pp. 36–37.

4. Charles O. Paullin, *Paullin's History of Naval Administration, 1775–1911* (Annapolis, Md.: U.S. Naval Institute, 1968), pp. 90–91; Harold and Margaret Sprout, *The Rise of American Naval Power, 1776–1918* (Princeton, N.J.: Princeton University Press, 1966), pp. 26–27.

5. *Naval Documents Related to the United States Wars with the Barbary Powers*, Dudley W. Knox, ed. (Washington, D.C.: Government Printing Office, 1939), Vol. I, p. 56, cited hereafter as *B.W.*

6. Marshall Smelser, *The Congress Founds the Navy* (South Bend, Ind.: University of Notre Dame Press, 1959), Chapter IV.

7. Joseph G. Henrich, *The Triumph of Ideology: The Jeffersonians and the Navy 1779–1807.* (Unpublished doctoral dissertation, Duke University, 1971). Microfilm in U.S. Naval Academy Library. *See also* J. H. Macleod, "Jefferson and the Navy: A Defense," *Huntington Library Quarterly*, February 1944, pp. 153–184.

8. Howard I. Chapelle, *The History of the American Sailing Navy* (New York: W. W. Norton and Co., 1949), pp. 118–134; Allen, *Corsairs*, pp. 50–51.

9. Paullin, *op. cit.*, pp. 94–96.

10. Smelser, *op. cit.*, p. 79.

11. Gardner W. Allen, *Our Naval War with France* (Boston: Houghton Mifflin Co., 1909), Chapter I, cited hereafter as *France*; Thomas A. Bailey, *A Diplomatic History of the American People* (New York: Appleton-Century-Crofts, Inc., 1946), Chapter V.

12. *Naval Documents Related to the Quasi-War Between the United States and France*, Dudley W. Knox, ed. (Washington, D.C.: Government Printing Office, 1935), Vol. I, p. 6, cited hereafter as *Q.W.*

13. Smelser, *op. cit.*, Chapter VIII; and Knox, *Q.W.*, Vol. I, pp. 7–9.

14. Charles W. Goldsborough, *United States Naval Chronicle* (Washington, D.C.: J. Wilson, 1824), pp. 109–111.

15. Allen, *France*, Chapter IV.

16. Robert G. Albion, "The First Days of the Navy Department," *Military Affairs*, Spring 1948; and Smelser, *op. cit.*, Chapter XI.

17. Robert F. Jones, "The Naval Thought and Policy of Benjamin Stoddert, First Secretary of the Navy, 1796–1801," *The American Neptune*, January 1964; Albion, *op. cit.*

18. Goldsborough, *op. cit.*, p. 86.

19. Paullin, *op. cit.*, pp. 110–111; Albion, *op. cit.*; Knox, *Q.W.*, Vol. II, p. 116.

20. Knox, *Q.W.*, Vol. II, pp. 129–134; Jones, *op. cit.*, p. 64.

21. Allen, *France*, is the most complete history of operations during the Quasi-War.

22. Eugene S. Ferguson, *Truxtun of the Constellation* (Baltimore: The Johns Hopkins Press, 1956); David F. Long, *Nothing Too Daring: A Biography of Commodore David Porter, 1780–1843* (Annapolis, Md.: U.S. Naval Institute, 1970), p. 7.

23. Knox, *Q.W.*, Vol. II, pp. 326–330; Allen, *France*, pp. 96–97.

24. Knox, *Q.W.*, Vol. V, pp. 159–172.

25. Allen, *France*, pp. 200–208, 210–214.

26. Bailey, *op. cit.*, pp. 87–89.

27. Peace Establishment Act, Knox, *Q.W.*, Vol. VII, pp. 134–135; Goldsborough, *op. cit.*, p. 181.

28. Sprout, *op. cit.*, pp. 45–47, 53–54; Henrich, *op. cit.*

29. Henry Adams, *History of the United States of America During the First Administration of Thomas Jefferson* (New York: Charles Scribner's Sons, 1921), Vol. I, p. 222.

30. Paullin, *op. cit.*, pp. 128–132; Chapelle, *op. cit.*, pp. 175–180; Henry Adams, *op. cit.*, p. 223.

31. Bainbridge's account is in Allen, *Corsairs*, pp. 76–77.

32. Knox, *B.W.*, Vol. I, pp. 463–469; Allen, *Corsairs*, pp. 88–104.

33. Truxtun to Smith, in Knox, *B.W.*, Vol. II, p. 76.

34. Goldsborough, *op. cit.*, pp. 211–212; Knox, *B.W.*, Vol. II, pp. 526–531; J. Fenimore Cooper, *The History of the Navy of the United States of America* (Paris: A. and W. Galignani and Co., 1839), Vol. I, pp. 235–240; Allen, *Corsairs*, pp. 120–121.

35. Preble's orders are in Knox, *B.W.*, Vol. II, pp. 474–477. His personality is fully discussed in Christopher McKee, *Edward Preble* (Annapolis, Md.: U.S. Naval Institute, 1972); Cooper, *op. cit.*, Vol. II, p. 53.

36. McKee, *op. cit.*, pp. 134–136, 173.

37. *Ibid.*, pp. 140–141; Allen, *Corsairs*, pp. 139–140; Fletcher Pratt, *Preble's Boys* (New York: William Sloane Associates, 1950), pp. 28–29.

38. Knox, *B.W.*, Vol. III, pp. 171–176, 189–194; Allen, *Corsairs*, pp. 146–157.

39. McKee, *op. cit.*, pp. 180–181.

40. Knox, *B.W.*, Vol. III, pp. 414–425; Allen, *Corsairs*, pp. 164–177; Goldsborough, *op. cit.*, p. 259.

41. Knox, *B.W.*, Vol. IV, pp. 192, 293–298; Allen, *Corsairs*, pp. 185–195.

42. Knox, *B.W.*, Vol. IV, pp. 347–348.

43. Allen, *Corsairs*, pp. 198–201; McKee, *op. cit.*, pp. 276–281.

44. Knox, *B.W.*, Vol. IV, pp. 305–307; Allen, *Corsairs*, pp. 206–210.

45. Allen, *Corsairs*, pp. 227–243.

46. *Ibid.*, pp. 246–257.

CHAPTER 3—"A HANDFUL OF FIR-BUILT FRIGATES"

1. William O. Stevens, *An Affair of Honor, The Biography of Commander James Barron, U.S.N.* (Norfolk, Va.: Norfolk County Historical Society, 1960), p. 55.

2. Edwin M. Gains, "Outrageous Encounter: The Chesapeake-Leopard Affair of 1807." (Unpublished doctoral dissertation, University of Virginia, 1960). Microfilm in U. S. Naval Academy Library.

3. *Correspondence between Thomas Jefferson and Pierre Samuel duPont de Nemours, 1798–1817*. Dumas Malone, ed. (Boston: Houghton Mifflin Co., 1920), p. 94.

4. Francis F. Beirne, *The War of 1812* (New York: E. P. Dutton & Co., 1949), p. 17.

5. Theodore Roosevelt, *The Naval Operations of the War Between Great Britain and the United States, 1812–1815* (Boston: Little, Brown & Co., 1901), p. 23.

6. For a full discussion of impressment, *see* Alfred T. Mahan, *The Influence of Sea Power in its Relation to the War of 1812* (Boston: Little, Brown & Co., 1905), Vol. I, pp. 114–127. Numbers of Americans impressed are in James F.

Zimmerman, *Impressment of American Seaman* (New York: Columbia University, 1925), Appendix I. *Also see* J. R. Hutchinson, *The Press Gang Afloat and Ashore* (London: E. Nash, 1913), p. 326, for Nelson's estimate of the number of deserters.

7. *American State Papers*, Naval Affairs (Washington, D.C.: Gales and Seaton, 1834), Vol. I, p. 169, cited hereafter as *ASP. See also* Howard I. Chapelle, *The History of the American Sailing Navy* (New York: W. W. Norton and Co., 1949), pp. 189–209, 218–233.

8. *ASP*, p. 163; Harold and Margaret Sprout, *The Rise of American Naval Power, 1776–1918* (Princeton, N.J.: Princeton University Press, 1966), pp. 58–61; Charles W. Goldsborough, *United States Naval Chronicle* (Washington, D.C.: J. Wilson, 1825), pp. 322–329.

9. Mahan, *op. cit.*, Vol. I, p. 298; Goldsborough, *op. cit.*, p. 329.

10. Thomas A. Bailey, *A Diplomatic History of the American People* (New York: Appleton-Century-Crofts, Inc., 1946), pp. 118–119.

11. Mahan, *op. cit.*, Vol. I, pp. 256–259.

12. Bailey, *op. cit.*, Chapter IX; Reginald Horsman, *The War of 1812* (New York: Alfred A. Knopf, Inc., 1969), Chapter I.

13. Irving Brant, *The Fourth President: The Life of James Madison* (Indianapolis: Bobbs-Merrill Co., 1970), p. 505; Adams is quoted in Leonard F. Guttridge and Jay D. Smith, *The Commodores* (Harper & Row, 1969), p. 172.

14. For the strength of the opposing forces, *see* Roosevelt, *op. cit.*, pp. 40–48. Brant, *op. cit.*, p. 506.

15. Brant, *op. cit.*, p. 505.

16. Edward K. Eckert, *The Navy Department in the War of 1812* (Gainesville, Fla.: University of Florida, 1973), pp. 18–19; Mahan, *op. cit.*, Vol. I, pp. 314–321.

17. Roosevelt, *op. cit.*, pp. 49–51; Mahan, *op. cit.*, Vol. I, pp. 322–326.

18. Roosevelt, *op. cit.*, p. 52; Eckert, *op. cit.*, pp. 45, 49.

19. Christopher McKee, *Edward Preble* (Annapolis, Md.: U.S. Naval Institute, 1972), pp. 214–219, 221–224; George Jones, *Sketches of Naval Life* (New Haven: H. Howe, 1829), Vol. I, pp. 96–105; John Masefield, *Sea Life in Nelson's Time* (New York: Macmillan, Inc., 1925), Chapter VIII.

20. *The Naval Monument*, A. Bowen, ed. (Boston: George Clark, 1840), pp. 3–9; Roosevelt, *op. cit.*, pp. 53–55; Mahan, *op. cit.*, Vol. I, pp. 328–329.

21. Bowen, *op. cit.*, pp. 9–16; Roosevelt, *op. cit.*, pp. 55–59; Mahan, *op. cit.*, Vol. I, pp. 330–335; Eckert, *op. cit.*, p. 49.

22. Sprout, *op. cit.*, p. 87; Eckert, *op. cit.*, pp. 75–76.

23. Bowen, *op. cit.*, pp. 16–23; Roosevelt, *op. cit.*, pp. 60–64; Mahan, *op. cit.*, Vol. I, pp. 411–415.

24. Samuel Leech, *Thirty Years from Home* (Boston: Charles Tappan, 1844), pp. 87, 127–140; Bowen, *op. cit.*, pp. 23–28; Roosevelt, *op. cit.*, pp. 65–74; Mahan, *op. cit.*, Vol. I, pp. 415–423.

25. Bowen, *op. cit.*, pp. 28–37; Roosevelt, *op. cit.*, pp. 75–83; Mahan, *op. cit.*, Vol. II, pp. 1–9; Quote from William James is in Mahan, *op. cit.*, p. 8.

26. Roosevelt, *op. cit.*, pp. 91–102; Mahan, *op. cit.*, Vol. II, pp. 9–26.

27. For the *Chesapeake-Shannon* engagement, *see* Bowen, *op. cit.*, pp. 44–68; Mahan, *op. cit.*, Vol. II, pp. 131–148; Roosevelt, *op. cit.*, pp. 122–139.

28. Bowen, *op. cit.*, pp. 69–77; Roosevelt, *op. cit.*, pp. 139–143; Mahan, *op. cit.*, Vol. II, pp. 217–219.

29. The saga of the *Essex* can be followed in David F. Long, *Nothing Too Daring: A Biography of Commodore David Porter*, 1780–1843 (Annapolis, Md., U.S. Naval Institute, 1970), pp. 73–162; Roosevelt, *op. cit.*, pp. 160–174; Mahan, *op. cit.*, Vol. II, pp. 244–252.

30. Edgar S. Maclay, *A History of American Privateers* (New York: D. Appleton and Company, 1899), pp. 506–507.

31. *Ibid*, p. xvi; Henry Adams, *History of the United States During the Second Administration of James Madison* (New York: Charles Scribner's Sons, 1921), Vol. I, pp. 318–320; John Philips Cranwell and William Bowers Crane, *Men of Marque* (New York: W. W. Norton and Co., 1940).

32. Sprout, *op. cit.*, pp. 79–86; Mahan, *op. cit.*, Vol. II, pp. 221–222, 241–244.

33. Mahan, *op. cit.*, Vol. II, Chapter XVI; Walter Lord, *The Dawn's Early Light* (New York: W. W. Norton and Co., 1972).

34. Roosevelt, *op. cit.*, pp. 176–189.

35. *Ibid*, pp. 189–207; Chapelle, *op. cit.*, pp. 268–269; Bowen, *op. cit.*, pp. 85–97; Mahan, *op. cit.*, Vol. II, Chapter XI; Eckert, *op. cit.*, p. 50; Charles O. Paullin, *Paullin's History of Naval Administration: 1775–1911* (Annapolis, Md.: U.S. Naval Institute, 1968), p. 153.

36. Bowen, *op. cit.*, pp. 145–157; Roosevelt, *op. cit.*, pp. 210–229; Mahan, *op. cit.*, Vol. II, pp. 355–381; Chapelle, *op. cit.*, p. 298; E. B. Potter, and Chester W. Nimitz, *Sea Power* (Englewood Cliffs, N.J.: Prentice Hall, Inc., 1960), pp. 219–221.

37. Mahan, *op. cit.*, Vol. II, pp. 382–396; Naval History Division, *Riverine Warfare* (Washington, D.C.: Government Printing Office, 1969), pp. 10–12; Fletcher Pratt, *Preble's Boys* (New York: William Sloane Associates, 1950), pp. 385–389.

38. Bowen, *op. cit.*, pp. 158–174; Roosevelt, *op. cit.*, pp. 268–273.

39. Bowen, *op. cit.*, pp. 174–186; Roosevelt, *op. cit.*, pp. 273–276.

40. Roosevelt, *op. cit.*, pp. 279–283; Pratt. *op. cit.*, pp. 290–292; Bowen, *op. cit.*, pp. 186–192.

CHAPTER 4—DISTANT STATIONS

1. *American State Papers*, Naval Affairs (Washington, D.C.: Gales and Seaton, 1834), Vol. I, p. 365, cited hereafter as *ASP*.

2. Gardner W. Allen, *Our Navy and the Barbary Corsairs* (Boston: Houghton Mifflin Co., 1905), Chapter XVII; *The Naval Monument*. A. Bowen, ed. (Boston: George Clark, 1840), pp. 297–307.

3. Harold and Margaret Sprout, *The Rise of American Naval Power, 1776–1918* (Princeton, N.J.: Princeton University Press, 1966), pp. 88–89; Charles O. Paullin, *Paullin's History of Naval Administration: 1775–1911* (Annapolis, Md.: U. S. Naval Institute, 1968), pp. 176–177; Howard I. Chapelle, *The History of the American Sailing Navy* (New York: W. W. Norton and Co., 1949), p. 314.

4. *ASP*, pp. 354–359; Paullin, *op. cit.*, pp. 164–174; Sprout, *op. cit.*, pp. 91–93; David F. Long, *Nothing Too Daring: A Biography of Commodore David Porter 1780–1843* (Annapolis, Md.: U. S. Naval Institute, 1970), pp. 175–180.

5. Robert G. Albion, "The Naval Affairs Committees," U. S. Naval Institute *Proceedings*, November 1952.

6. *Report of the Secretary of the Navy*, 1841, p. 5; Thomas A. Bailey, *A Diplomatic History of the American People* (New York: Appleton-Century-Crofts, Inc., 1946), p. 451.

7. Robert G. Albion, "Distant Stations," U. S. Naval Institute *Proceedings*, March 1954, cited hereafter as "Distant Stations."

8. Frank M. Bennett, *The Steam Navy of the United States* (Pittsburgh, Pa.: W. T. Nicholson, 1896), pp. 8–16.

9. James P. Baxter, *The Introduction of the Ironclad Warship* (Cambridge, Mass.: Harvard University Press, 1933), pp. 23–32.

10. Russell F. Weigley, *The American Way of War* (New York: Macmillan Publishing Co., 1973), pp. 59–61; Sprout, *op. cit.*, pp. 99–101.

11. Gardner W. Allen, *Our Navy and the West Indian Pirates* (Salem, Mass.: Essex Institute, 1929), cited hereafter as *Pirates*.

12. Long, *op. cit.*, pp. 203–227; Allen, *Pirates*, p. 55.

13. Long, *op. cit.*, pp. 227–258.

14. Allen, *Pirates*, pp. 86–89.

15. Robert E. Johnson, *Thence Round Cape Horn: The Story of United States Naval Forces on Pacific Station, 1818–1923* (Annapolis, Md.: U. S. Naval Institute, 1963), Chapter I; Albion, "Distant Stations."

16. Dudley W. Knox, *A History of the United States Navy* (New York: G. P. Putnam's Sons, 1948), pp. 151–152; Bailey, *op. cit.*, pp. 320–322.

17. Samuel Flagg Bemis, *A Diplomatic History of the United States* (New York: Henry Holt, 1955), pp. 344–345.

18. Earl E. McNeilly, "The U. S. Navy and the Suppression of the West African Slave Trade." (Unpublished doctoral dissertation, Case Western Reserve

University, 1973). Microfilm in the Library of Congress, pp. 1–34; Albion, "Distant Stations."

19. Edgar S. Maclay, *Reminiscences of the Old Navy* (New York: G. P. Putnam's Sons, 1898), pp. 9–10.

20. Christopher Lloyd, *The Navy and the Slave Trade* (London: Frank Cass & Co., 1968), p. 176.

21. William F. Lynch, *Naval Life; or, Observations Afloat and On Shore* (New York: Charles Scribner's, 1851), p. 149.

22. Andrew H. Foote, *Africa and the American Flag* (New York: D. Appleton Co., 1854), p. 260.

23. McNeilly, *op. cit.*, p. 146.

24. *Ibid.*, p. 231.

25. Francis P. Prucha, *The Sword of the Republic* (New York: Macmillan, Inc., 1969), p. 269.

26. George E. Buker, *Swamp Sailors* (Gainesville, Fla.: University of Florida, 1976), pp. 105–106; Naval History Division, *Riverine Warfare* (Washington, D.C.: Government Printing Office, 1969), pp. 15–18; Prucha, *op. cit.*, p. 301.

27. Albion, "Distant Stations"; Paullin, *op. cit.*, pp. 191–192.

28. George Jones, *Sketches of Naval Life* (New Haven: H. Howe, 1829), Vol. I, pp. 2–3.

29. Paullin, *op. cit.*, pp. 190–191; Harold D. Langley, *Social Reform in the United States Navy, 1798–1862* (Urbana, Ill.: University of Illinois Press, 1967), p. 23.

30. William O. Stevens, *Pistols at Ten Paces* (Boston: Houghton Mifflin Co., 1940), pp. 186–211, 50–72.

31. Reuben E. Stivers, *Privateers & Volunteers* (Annapolis, Md.: U. S. Naval Institute, 1975), pp. 170–171; Peter Karsten, *The Naval Aristocracy* (New York: The Free Press, 1972), p. 80.

32. Charles Nordhoff, *In Yankee Windjammers* (New York: Dodd, Mead & Co., 1940), p. 105.

33. Samuel Eliot Morison, *"Old Bruin," Commodore Matthew Calbraith Perry* (Boston: Little, Brown & Co., 1967), p. 91.

34. James C. Tily, *The Uniforms of the United States Navy* (New York: Thomas Yoseloff, 1964), pp. 94–97; Morison, *op. cit.*, pp. 93–94.

35. Herman Melville, *White-Jacket* (London: Oxford University Press, 1966), pp. 9, 13.

36. Langley, *op. cit.*, pp. ix, 131–269; Paullin, *op. cit.*, pp. 231–235.

37. Morison, *op. cit.*, pp. 126–132; Bennett, *op. cit.*, pp. 16–31.

38. Bennett, *op. cit.*, Chapter III; Bernard Brodie, *Sea Power in the Machine Age* (New York: Greenwood Press, 1969), pp. 23–24, 32–38.

39. Bennett, *op. cit.*, Chapter V; Henry C. Watts, "Ericsson, Stockton, and the *USS Princeton*," U. S. Naval Institute *Proceedings*, September 1956.

40. A. H. Miles, "The 'Princeton' Explosion," U. S. Naval Institute *Proceedings*, November 1966; Robert Seager II, *And Tyler Too* (New York: McGraw-Hill Book Co., Inc., 1963), pp. 204–207.

41. Vincent Ponko, Jr., *Ships, Seas, and Scientists* (Annapolis, Md.: U. S. Naval Institute, 1974), p. xi.

42. Quoted *Ibid.*, p. 21.

43. *Ibid.*, p. 23.

44. *Ibid.*, p. 24.

45. *Ibid.*, p. 31.

46. "Matthew Fontaine Maury," *Dictionary of American Biography*; Matthew F. Maury, *The Physical Geography of the Sea and its Meteorology* (Cambridge, Mass.: Belknap Press, 1963), p. 23.

47. Robert G. Albion, "Makers of Naval Policy, 1798–1947." Unpublished manuscript, Harvard University Library. pp. 42, 23–24.

48. *Ibid.*, pp. 143–144; Paullin, *op. cit.*, pp. 208–214.

49. Morison, *op. cit.*, pp. 139–140; Langley, *op. cit.*, pp. 103–115; Stivers, *op. cit.*, pp. 177–178.

50. Frederic F. Van de Water, *The Captain Called It Mutiny* (New York: Ives Washburn, Inc., 1954). Hanson W. Baldwin, "Mutiny on the Brig Somers," in *Sea Fights and Shipwrecks* (Garden City, N. Y.: Hanover House, 1955), pp. 182–206.

51. F. M. Brown, "A Half Century of Frustration," U. S. Naval Institute *Proceedings*, June 1954, pp. 631–635.

52. James R. Soley, *Historical Sketch of the United States Naval Academy* (Washington, D.C.: Government Printing Office, 1876), pp. 38–97.

53. K. Jack Bauer, *Surfboats and Horse Marines: U. S. Naval Operations in the Mexican War* (Annapolis, Md.: U. S. Naval Institute, 1969), pp. 135–136.

54. Knox, *op. cit.*, p. 170; Morison, *op. cit.*, pp. 179–180, 186. Bauer, *op. cit.*, pp. 23–24.

55. Raphael Semmes, *Service Afloat and Ashore During the Mexican War* (Cincinnati: W. H. Moore & Co., 1851), p. 76.

56. Stivers, *op. cit.*, pp. 174–175; Langley, *op. cit.*, pp. 79–80; Morison, *op. cit.*, pp. 189–190.

57. Bauer, *op. cit.*, pp. 138–204; Knox, *op. cit.*, p. 172.

58. Bauer, *op. cit.*, pp. 75–98.

59. Morison, *op. cit.*, pp. 261–269.

60. *Ibid.*, p. 270.

61. Francis L. Hawks, ed., *Narrative of the Expedition of an American Squadron to the China Seas and Japan*, Exec. Doc. No. 79, U. S. Senate, 33rd Congress, 2nd Session (Washington, D.C.: Beverly Tucker, Senate Printer, 1856), p. 231.

62. *Ibid.*, pp. 253–255.

63. Quoted in Arthur C. Walworth, *Black Ships Off Japan* (New York: Alfred A. Knopf, Inc., 1946), p. 103.

64. Morison, *op. cit.*, p. 429.

65. Hawks, *op. cit.*, pp. 357–358; Morison, *op. cit.*, pp. 357–402.

66. Quoted in Edgar S. Maclay, *A History of the United States Navy* (New York: D. Appleton and Company, 1898), Vol, II, p. 132.

CHAPTER 5—DIVIDED WATERS

1. Reuben E. Stivers, *Privateers and Volunteers* (Annapolis, Md.: U. S. Naval Institute, 1975), p. 199.

2. Russell F. Weigley, *The American Way of War* (New York: Macmillan Publishing Co., 1973), pp. 92–93; Bern Anderson, *By Sea and By River: The Naval History of the Civil War* (New York: Alfred A. Knopf, Inc., 1962), pp. 33–34; Theodore Ropp, "Anaconda Anyone?" *Military Affairs*, Summer 1963, pp. 71–76.

3. *Official Records of the Union and Confederate Navies in the War of the Rebellion* (Washington, D.C.: Government Printing Office, 1890), Series I, Vol. 4, pp. 272–305, cited hereafter as *ORN*, all Series I; Richard S. West, Jr., *Mr. Lincoln's Navy* (New York: Longmans, Green and Company, 1957), Chapter 3.

4. *New York Times*, April 26, 1861.

5. James Russell Soley, *The Blockade and the Cruisers* (New York: Charles Scribner's Sons, 1885), pp. 8, 11–14.

6. Charles O. Paullin, *Paullin's History of Naval Administration: 1775–1911* (Annapolis, Md.: U. S. Naval Institute, 1968), pp. 251–258; John Niven, *Gideon Welles: Lincoln's Secretary of the Navy* (New York: Oxford University Press, 1976), Appendix I.

7. Nathan Miller, *The Founding Finaglers* (New York: David McKay Company, Inc., 1976), pp. 184–185; Paullin, *op. cit.*, pp. 280–288.

8. C. B. Boynton, *History of the Navy During the Rebellion* (New York: D. Appleton and Company, 1867), Vol. I, p. 139. J. Thomas Scharf, *History of the Confederate States Navy* (New York: Rogers and Sherwood, 1887), pp. v–vi.

9. Stivers, *op. cit.*, pp. 199–213, 217–220; *ORN*, Vol. 6, p. 252.

10. Paullin, *op. cit.*, pp. 259–263, 299–303.

11. *Report of the Secretary of the Navy*, December 1, 1862, p. 2.

12. Carl Sandburg, *Abraham Lincoln, The War Years* (New York: Harcourt Brace & Co., 1939), Vol. I, pp. 332–333.

13. *ORN*, Vol. 6, pp. 119–127; West, *op. cit.*, pp. 75–80.

14. *Samuel Francis DuPont, A Selection From His Civil War Letters*, John D. Hayes, ed., (Ithaca, N.Y.: Cornell University Press, 1969), Vol. II, p. 33.

15. *ORN*, Vol. 12, pp. 262–265.

16. *Ibid.*, pp. 300–307; West, *op. cit.*, pp. 82–88; E. B. Potter and Chester W. Nimitz, *Sea Power* (Englewood, N.J.: Prentice-Hall, Inc., 1960), pp. 252–253.

17. Anderson, *op. cit.*, pp. 58–60; John D. Hayes, "Sea Power in the Civil War," U. S. Naval Institute *Proceedings*, November 1961.

18. Quoted in Frank L. Owsley, *King Cotton Diplomacy* (Chicago: University of Chicago Press, 1959), p. 234.

19. Anderson, *op. cit.*, p. 222; Soley, *op. cit.*, p. 167. Howard P. Nash, Jr., *A Naval History of the Civil War* (New York: A. S. Barnes and Company, 1972), pp. 34–36; Alfred T. Mahan, *From Sail to Steam* (New York: Harper Brothers, 1907), p. 192.

20. Charles A. Post, "A Diary of the Blockade in 1863." U. S. Naval Institute *Proceedings*, October 1918.

21. James M. Merrill, "Men, Monotony, and Mouldy Beans—Life on Board a Civil War Blockade," *American Neptune*, January 1956, p. 57; Harold D. Langley, *Social Reform in the United States Navy, 1798–1862* (Urbana, Ill.: University of Illinois Press, 1967), p. 266.

22. West, *op. cit.*, Chapter 7.

23. William C. Davis, *Duel Between the First Ironclads* (New York: Doubleday & Co., Inc., 1975), p. 85.

24. J. P. Baxter, *The Introduction of the Ironclad Warship* (Cambridge, Mass.: Harvard University Press, 1933), pp. 224–225.

25. Davis, *op. cit.*, pp. 9–12, 33–34, 36–37.

26. *ORN*, Vol. 7, p. 44.

27. *Ibid.*, pp. 23–24, 45; West, *op. cit.*, p. 114.

28. Sandburg, *op. cit.*, pp. 479–480.

29. Davis, *op. cit.*, pp. 117, 20. Baxter, *op. cit.*, pp. 247–284; Frank M. Bennett, *The Steam Navy of the United States* (Pittsburgh, Pa.: W. T. Nicholson, 1896), pp. 264–282.

30. *Aboard the USS Monitor: 1862*, Robert W. Daly, ed. (Annapolis, Md.: U. S. Naval Institute, 1964), pp. 28–29.

31. *Ibid.*, p. 31.

32. *Ibid.*, p. 34.

33. *Ibid.*, p. 37.

34. Nash, *op. cit.*, p. 96; Robert W. Daly, *How the Merrimac Won* (New York: Thomas Y. Crowell Company, 1957).

35. John D. Milligan, *Gunboats Down the Mississippi* (Annapolis, Md.: U. S. Naval Institute, 1965), pp. xvii–xxv.

36. Phyllis F. Dorset, "James B. Eads: Navy Shipbuilder, 1861," U. S. Naval Institute *Proceedings*, August 1975; Naval History Division, *Riverine Warfare* (Washington, D.C.: Government Printing Office, 1969), pp. 21–34.

37. Milligan, *op. cit.*, pp. 31–44; Bruce Catton, *Grant Moves South* (Boston: Little, Brown & Co., 1960), pp. 142–145.

38. Milligan, *op. cit.*, pp. 44–49.

39. *Ibid.*, pp. 53–60; Alfred T. Mahan, *The Gulf and Inland Waters* (New York: Charles Scribner's Sons, 1883), p. 34.

40. Naval History Division, *Civil War Naval Chronology, 1861–1865* (Washington, D.C.: Government Printing Office, 1971), Vol. II, p. 45, cited hereafter as *NC*: Milligan, *op. cit.*, pp. 73–77.

41. West, *op. cit.*, pp. 130–136; "David Glasgow Farragut," *Dictionary of American Biography*.

42. *ORN*, Vol. 18, p. 160; West, *op. cit.*, pp. 148–149.

43. Quoted in *Quarter-Deck and Fo'c's'le* James M. Merrill, ed. (Chicago: Rand, McNally & Company, 1963), pp. 191, 199.

44. *ORN*, Vol. 18, pp. 154–159; West, *op. cit.*, pp. 151–154.

45. *ORN, op. cit.*, pp. 519–521.

46. *Ibid.*, p. 641; Allan Westcott, ed., *American Seapower Since 1775* (Philadelphia: J. B. Lippincott Company, 1947), pp. 162–163; West, *op. cit.*, pp. 200–204.

47. *NC*, Vol. II, pp. 81–82; West, *op. cit.*, pp. 179–193; Westcott, *op. cit.*, p. 163.

48. "David Dixon Porter," *Dictionary of American Biography*.

49. *NC*, Vol. II, p. 113; Mahan, *op. cit.*, p. 118.

50. *NC*, Vol. III, pp. 44–45; West, *op. cit.*, pp. 217–218.

51. *Ibid.*, pp. 67, 72, 75–76; West, *op. cit.*, 220–223; *ORN, op. cit.*, Vol. 19, p. 669.

52. *NC*, Vol. II, pp. 18–20.

53. *Ibid.*, pp. 59–61; George E. Belknap, "Reminiscences of the Siege of Charleston" in *Papers of the Military Historical Society of Massachusetts*, XII, 1902.

54. Alvah F. Hunter, "A Year on a Monitor." (Unpublished typescript in The Library of Congress, Chapter 6, p. 5.)

55. Anderson, *op. cit.*, pp. 163–177; *NC*, Vol. V, p. 32; Nash, *op. cit.*, p. 186.

56. *NC*, Vol. III, pp. 143–144.

57. *Ibid.*, pp. 147, Vol. IV, p. 21.

58. Robert G. Albion and Jeanie B. Pope, *Sea Lanes in Wartime* (New York: W. W. Norton and Co., 1942), p. 171; George W. Dalzell, *The Flight From the Flag* (Chapel Hill, N.C.: University of North Carolina Press, 1940), Chapter XII.

59. Raphael Semmes, *The Confederate Raider Alabama*, Philip Van Doren Stern, ed. (Bloomington, Ind.: Indiana University Press, 1962), pp. 34–35.

60. Dalzell, *op. cit.*, p. 128.

61. Semmes, *op. cit.*, pp. 152–157.

62. *Ibid.*, pp. 163–173.

63. *Ibid.*, pp. 366–376; *ORN*, Vol. 3, pp. 59–81; *NC*, Vol. IV, pp. 74–78; Westcott, *op. cit.*, pp. 201, 204.

64. *ORN*, Vol. 21, pp. 404–428; *NC*, Vol. IV, pp. 95–97.

65. West, *op. cit.*, pp. 288–289.

66. *NC*, Vol. IV, pp. 124–126, 149–150; West, *op. cit.*, pp. 289–299.

67. *ORN*, Vol. 11, pp. 430–442; *NC*, Vol. V, pp. 11–16; West, *op. cit.*, pp. 299–302.

68. *The Collected Works of Abraham Lincoln*, Roy Basler, ed., (New Brunswick, N.J.: Rutgers University Press, 1953), Vol. VI, pp. 409–410.

CHAPTER 6—A NAVAL RENAISSANCE

1. Foxhall A. Parker, "Our Fleet Maneuvers in the Bay of Florida and the Navy of the Future," *The Record of the U. S. Naval Institute*, 1874.

2. Thomas A. Bailey, *A Diplomatic History of the American People* (New York: Appleton-Century-Crofts, Inc., 1946), pp. 423–424; Charles O. Paullin, *Paullin's History of Naval Administration 1775–1911* (Annapolis, Md.: U. S. Naval Institute, 1968), p. 336.

3. Alfred T. Mahan, *From Sail to Steam* (New York: Harper Brothers, 1907), p. 197; Peter Karsten, *The Naval Aristocracy* (New York: The Free Press, 1972), pp. 278–279.

4. Stanley Sandler, "A Navy in Decay," *Military Affairs*, December 1971; Kenneth J. Hagan, "Admiral David Dixon Porter, Strategist for a Navy in Transition," U. S. Naval Institute *Proceedings*, July 1969.

5. Caspar F. Goodrich, *Rope Yarns from the Old Navy* (New York: Naval Historical Society, 1931), pp. 65–67; Frank M. Bennett, *The Steam Navy of the United States* (Pittsburgh, Pa.: W. T. Nicholson, 1896), p. 614; Harold and Margaret Sprout, *The Rise of American Naval Power 1776–1918* (Princeton, N.J.: Princeton University Press, 1966), pp. 166–168; Robeson is quoted in Sandler, *op. cit.*

6. Edward W. Sloan III, "Isherwood's Masterpiece," U. S. Naval Institute *Proceedings*, December 1965; Bennett, *op. cit.*, Chapter XXII.

7. Lance C. Buhl, "The Smooth Water Navy; American Naval Policy and Politics 1865–1876," (Unpublished doctoral dissertation, Harvard University, 1968.) Microfilm in the U. S. Naval Academy Library; Sprout, *op. cit.*, p. 181; Paullin, *op. cit.*, pp. 342–345.

8. Paullin, *op. cit.*, pp. 359–360; Karsten, *op. cit.*, pp. 280–286.

9. Paullin, *op. cit.*, pp. 361–363; Albert Gleaves, *Life and Letters of Rear Admiral Stephen Luce* (New York: G. P. Putnam's Sons, 1925), pp. 134–148.

10. K. Jack Bauer, "The Korean Expedition of 1871," U. S. Naval Institute *Proceedings*, February 1948.

11. Bennett, *op. cit.*, Chapter XXXIV; Dudley W. Knox, *A History of the United States Navy* (New York: G. P. Putnam's Sons, 1948), pp. 323–324.

12. Roy C. Smith III, "The First Hundred Years Are . . .", U. S. Naval Institute *Proceedings*, October 1973.

13. Robert Seager II, "Ten Years Before Mahan: The Unofficial Case for the New Navy, 1880–1890," *The Mississippi Valley Historical Review*, December 1955; Kenneth J. Hagan, *American Gunboat Diplomacy and the Old Navy* (Westport, Conn.: Greenwood Press, 1973), pp. 188–291.

14. Sprout, *op. cit.*, pp. 183–188; Paullin, *op. cit.*, pp. 387–392; Donald W. Mitchell, *History of the Modern American Navy* (New York: Alfred A. Knopf, Inc., 1946), pp. 9–14.

15. Mitchell, *op. cit.*, p. 15.

16. William Hovgaard, *Modern History of Warships* (Annapolis, Md.: U. S. Naval Institute, 1971), pp. 174–175; George T. Davis, *A Navy Second to None* (Westport, Conn.: Greenwood Publishers, 1971), pp. 23–24.

17. John D. Alden, *The American Steel Navy* (Annapolis, Md.: U. S. Naval Institute, 1972), pp. 13–22.

18. Leonard A. Swann, Jr., *John Roach, Maritime Entrepreneur* (Annapolis, Md.: U. S. Naval Institute, 1965), Chapters VII and VIII.

19. Alden, *op. cit.*, pp. 25–29.

20. *Ibid.*, pp. 31–37; Davis, *op. cit.*, pp. 44–48; Paullin, *op. cit.*, pp. 378–379.

21. J. Richard Thomas, "The Birth of the Naval War College," U. S. Naval Institute *Proceedings*, March 1953; *The Writings of Stephen B. Luce*, John D. Hayes and John B. Hattendorf, eds. (Newport, R.I.: Naval War College, 1975), pp. 11–13.

22. Richard S. West, Jr., *Admirals of American Empire* (Indianapolis: The Bobbs-Merrill Company, 1948), pp. 18–22, 81–97.

23. Mahan, *op. cit.*, pp. 276–278; Sprout, *op. cit.*, pp. 202–205; *Letters and Papers of Alfred Thayer Mahan*, Robert Seager II and Doris D. Maguire, eds. (Annapolis, Md.: U. S. Naval Institute, 1975), Vol. II, p. 9.

24. West, *op. cit.*, pp. 146–161.

25. Walter LaFeber, *The New Empire* (Ithaca, N.Y.: Cornell University Press, 1963).

26. Walter R. Herrick, Jr., *The American Naval Revolution* (Baton Rouge, La.: Louisiana State University Press, 1966), pp. 54–58; Mitchell, *op. cit.*, pp. 18–20; Sprout, *op. cit.*, pp. 205–209.

27. Sprout, *op. cit.*, pp. 207–213; Alden, *op. cit.*, pp. 77–89.

28. Bailey, *op. cit.*, pp. 452–455.

29. Sprout, *op. cit.*, pp. 213–222; Alden, *op. cit.*, pp. 89–91, 135–141.

30. Paullin, *op. cit.*, pp. 422–426.

31. Quoted in *Quarter-Deck and Fo'c's'le*, James M. Merrill, ed. (Chicago: Rand, McNally & Company, 1963), p. 251.

32. Hyman G. Rickover, *How the Battleship Maine was Destroyed* (Washington, D.C.: Naval History Division, 1976).

33. H. W. Wilson, *Battleships in Action* (Boston: Little, Brown & Co., 1926) Vol. I, pp. 120–124.

34. David H. Burton, *Theodore Roosevelt, Confident Imperialist* (Philadelphia: University of Pennsylvania Press, 1968), pp. 42–52.

35. Frank Freidel, *The Splendid Little War* (New York: Bramwell House, 1958), pp. 13–31; Wilson, *op. cit.*, pp. 153–159; West, *op. cit.*, pp. 197–210.

36. West, *op. cit.*, pp. 271–273.

37. *Ibid.*, pp. 222–250; Wilson, *op. cit.*, pp. 128–134; Freidel, *op. cit.*, pp. 43–52.

38. Freidel, *op. cit.*, pp. 52–54.

39. *Ibid.*, pp. 96–97.

40. Walter Millis, *The Martial Spirit* (Cambridge, Mass.: The Riverside Press, 1931), pp. 293–300.

41. West, *op. cit.*, pp. 258–266; Wilson, *op. cit.*, pp. 138–157; Freidel, *op. cit.*, pp. 193–231.

42. Sprout, *op. cit.*, pp. 241–245.

CHAPTER 7—A NAVY SECOND TO NONE

1. Robert A. Hart, *The Great White Fleet* (Boston: Little, Brown, & Co., 1965), pp. 58–60.

2. Gordon C. O'Gara, *Theodore Roosevelt and the Rise of the Modern Navy* (Princeton, N.J.: Princeton University Press, 1943), pp. 3–12.

3. Harold and Margaret Sprout, *The Rise of American Naval Power, 1776–1918* (Princeton, N.J.: Princeton University Press, 1966), pp. 257–259; *American Sea Power Since 1775*, Allan Westcott, ed. (Philadelphia: J. B. Lippincott Company, 1947), p. 293.

4. Robert G. Albion, "Distant Stations," U. S. Naval Institute *Proceedings*, March 1954.

5. Frederick S. Harrod, "Enlisted Men in the United States Navy, 1899–1933." (Unpublished doctoral dissertation, Northwestern University, 1973.) Microfilm in the Library of Congress.

6. Charles O. Paullin, *Paullin's History of Naval Administration, 1775–1911* (Annapolis, Md.: U. S. Naval Institute, 1968), pp. 461–462.

7. Henry P. Beers, "The Development of the Office of the Chief of Naval Operations," Part I, *Military Affairs*, Spring 1946.

8. Richard D. Challener, *Admirals, Generals and American Foreign Policy* (Princeton, N.J.: Princton University Press, 1973), pp. 26–29; Sprout, *op. cit.*, pp. 252–257.

9. Thomas A. Bailey, *A Diplomatic History of the American People* (New York: Appleton-Century-Crofts, Inc., 1946), pp. 533–546.

10. *Ibid.*, pp. 569–575.

11. Sprout, *op. cit.*, p. 301.

12. William Hovgaard, *Modern History of Warships* (Annapolis, Md.: U. S. Naval Institute, 1971), pp. 136–140, 146–147; Richard Hough, *Dreadnought: A History of the Modern Battleship* (London: Michael Joseph, 1965), pp. 1–12, 33–42.

13. Elting E. Morison, *Admiral Sims and the Modern American Navy* (New York: Russell and Russell, 1968), pp. 80–81, Chapters 8, 9, and 12.

14. Bradley A. Fiske, *From Midshipman to Rear Admiral* (New York: The Century Co., 1919).

15. U. S. Naval History Division, *Destroyers in the United States Navy* (Washington, D.C.: Government Printing Office, 1962), pp. 6–8; John D. Alden, *The American Steel Navy* (Annapolis, Md.: U. S. Naval Institute, 1972), pp. 149–155.

16. Richard K. Morris, *John P. Holland* (Annapolis, Md.: U. S. Naval Institute, 1966); Alden, *op. cit.*, pp. 179–185.

17. George van Deurs, *Wings for the Fleet* (Annapolis, Md.: U. S. Naval Institute, 1966); Archibald D. Turnbull and Clifford L. Lord, *History of United States Naval Aviation* (New York: Arno Press, 1972), pp. 1–44.

18. Jack Sweetman, *The Landing at Veracruz: 1914* (Annapolis, Md.: U. S. Naval Institute, 1968).

19. John A. DeNovo, "Petroleum and the United States Navy Before World War I," *Mississippi Valley Historical Review*, March 1955.

20. Kenneth A. Davis, *F.D.R., The Beckoning of Destiny 1882–1928* (New York: G. P. Putnam's Sons, 1972), pp. 322–323.

21. William F. Halsey and Joseph Bryan III, *Admiral Halsey's Story* (New York: Whittlesey House, 1947), p. 18.

22. Hanson W. Baldwin, "The End of the Wine Mess," U.S. Naval Institute *Proceedings*, August 1958.

23. Melvin I. Urofsky, "Josephus Daniels and the Armor Trust," *The North Carolina Historical Review*, Summer 1968.

24. Walter Millis, *Road to War* (Boston: Houghton Mifflin Co., 1935).

25. Sprout, *op. cit.*, pp. 334–346; Francis Duncan, "The Struggle to Build A Great Navy," U. S. Naval Institute *Proceedings*, June 1962.

26. Beers, *op. cit.*, Part II, *Military Affairs*, Fall 1946; Fiske, *op. cit.*, pp. 561–589.

27. Joseph K. Taussig, "Destroyer Experiences During the Great War," Part I, U. S. Naval Institute *Proceedings*, December 1922; Josephus Daniels, *Our Navy at War* (Washington, D.C.: Pictorial Bureau, 1922), pp. 54–56.

28. Morison, *op. cit.*, Chapter 19.

29. Tracy B. Kittredge, *Naval Lessons of the Great War* (Garden City, N.Y.: Doubleday, Page & Co., 1921), pp. 419–420.

30. Daniels, *op. cit.*, pp. 57–58.

31. Thomas G. Frothingham, *The Naval History of the World War* (Freeport, N.Y.: Books for Libraries Press, 1971), Vol. III, Chapters XVI–XIX; Dudley W. Knox, *A History of the U. S. Navy* (New York: G. P. Putnam's Sons, 1948), p. 400.

32. Arthur J. Marder, *From the Dreadnought to Scapa Flow* (London: Oxford University Press, 1970), Vol. IV, p. 43 and Vol. V, pp. 124–127.

33. Harrod, *op. cit.*; "The Yeomanettes of World War I," U. S. Naval Institute *Proceedings*, December 1957.

34. John D. Alden, *Flush Decks and Four Pipes* (Annapolis, Md.: U. S. Naval Institute, 1965).

35. Ray Millholland, *The Splinter Fleet* (Indianapolis: Bobbs-Merrill Co., Inc., 1936); Alexander W. Moffat, *Maverick Navy* (Middletown, Conn.: Wesleyan University Press, 1976); William S. Sims, *The Victory at Sea* (Garden City, N.Y.: Doubleday, Page & Co., 1920), pp. 208–209.

36. Taussig, *op. cit.*, Part II, U. S. Naval Institute *Proceedings*, January 1923.

37. Sims, *op. cit.*, pp. 122–141.

38. R. B. Carney, "The Capture of the U-58," U. S. Naval Institute *Proceedings*, October 1934; Daniels, *op. cit.*, pp. 59–60.

39. Daniels, *op. cit.*, pp. 62–64.

40. Sir Arthur Hezlet, *The Submarine and Sea Power* (New York: Stein and Day, 1967), pp. 94–95.

41. Marder, *op. cit.*, Vol. V, p. 111.

42. Robert C. Duncan, *America's Use of Sea Mines* (White Oak, Md.: Naval Research Laboratory, 1962), pp. 47–66; *The Northern Barrage and Other Mining Activities* (Washington, D.C.: Office of Naval Records and Library, 1920).

43. Turnbull and Lord, *op. cit.*, Chapters VIII–XIV; Theodore Roscoe, *On the Seas in the Skies* (New York: Hawthorn Books, Inc., 1970), pp. 104–108, 110–112.

44. Robert D. Heinl, Jr., *Soldiers of the Sea* (Annapolis, Md.: U. S. Naval Institute, 1962), pp. 195–204.

45. J. W. Bunkley, "The Woozlefinch: The Navy 14-inch Railway Guns," U. S. Naval Institute *Proceedings*, May 1931.

CHAPTER 8—THE LONG ARMISTICE

1. Arthur J. Marder, *From the Dreadnought to Scapa Flow* (London: Oxford University Press, 1970), Vol. V, pp. 190–191.

2. Quoted in *American Sea Power Since 1775*, Allan Westcott, ed. (Philadelphia: J. B. Lippincott Company, 1947), p. 333.

3. Harold and Margaret Sprout, *Toward a New Order of Sea Power* (Princeton, N.J., Princeton University Press, 1943), pp. 51–54.

4. *Ibid.*, p. 55.

5. *Ibid.*, p. 69.

6. *Ibid.*, pp. 70–72.

7. Stephen Roskill, *Naval Policy Between the Wars* (New York: Walker and Company, 1968), Vol. I, pp. 212–217.

8. Sprout, *op. cit.*, pp. 96–98; Thaddeus V. Tuleja, *Statesmen and Admirals* (New York: W. W. Norton & Co., Inc., 1963), pp. 22–23.

9. Quoted in Sprout, *op. cit.*, p. 109.

10. *Ibid.*, Chapters VIII–XIII; Ernest J. Andrade, Jr., "The United States Navy and the Washington Conference," *The Historian*, May 1969; Thomas A. Bailey, *A Diplomatic History of the American People* (New York: Appleton-Century-Crofts, Inc., 1946), pp. 688–699.

11. Samuel Eliot Morison, *The Two-Ocean War* (Boston: Little, Brown and Co., 1963), pp. 24–25.

12. Dudley W. Knox, "The United States Navy Between World Wars" in Samuel Eliot Morison, *The Battle of the Atlantic* (Boston: Little, Brown and Co., 1947), p. xxxvii, cited hereafter as *Atlantic*.

13. *See* annual appropriations chart in George T. Davis, *A Navy Second to None* (Westport, Conn.: Greenwood Press, 1940), pp. 473–474.

14. David A. Rosenberg, "Officer Development in the Interwar Navy: Arleigh Burke—"The Making of a Naval Professional, 1919–1940," *Pacific Historical Review*, November 1975; Davis, *op. cit.*, p. 472; Gerald E. Wheeler, *Prelude to Pearl Harbor* (Columbia, Mo.: University of Missouri Press, 1963), pp. 105–129; Ernest J. King, *U. S. Navy at War, 1941–1945* (Washington, D.C.: U. S. Navy Department, 1946), p. 5.

15. Patrick Abbazia, *Mr. Roosevelt's Navy* (Annapolis, Md.: U. S. Naval Institute, 1975), Chapter I; Morison, *op. cit.*, pp. 11–12.

16. Davis, *op. cit.*, Chapter XIII; Morison, *op. cit.*, pp. 3–13.

17. Waldo H. Heinrichs, Jr., "The Role of the United States Navy," in *Pearl Harbor as History*, Dorothy Borg and Shumpei Okamoto, eds. (New York: Columbia University Press, 1973).

18. Charles M. Melhorn, *Two-Block Fox: The Rise of the Aircraft Carrier, 1911–1929* (Annapolis, Md.: U. S. Naval Institute, 1974), pp. 4–5, 85–86.

19. Richard K. Smith, *First Across!* (Annapolis, Md.: U. S. Naval Institute, 1973).

20. Melhorn, *op. cit.*, pp. 28–38.

21. Morison, *op. cit.*, p. 9.

22. Quoted in Roskill, *op. cit.*, p. 248.

23. Burke Davis, *The Billy Mitchell Affair* (New York: Random House,

1967) cited hereafter as *Mitchell*. Quotes from Mitchell are in Morison *Atlantic*, p. xliv.

24. Archibald D. Turnbull and Clifford L. Lord, *History of United States Naval Aviation* (New York: Arno Press, 1972), Chapter XVIII; Davis, *Mitchell*, Chapter 7; Melhorn, *op. cit.*, Chapters 4 and 5.

25. Moffett is quoted in Davis, *Mitchell*, p. 110; Edward Arpee, *From Frigates to Flat-tops* (Lake Forest, Ill.: Edward Arpee, 1953), pp. 83–87.

26. Melhorn, *op. cit.*, pp. 100–101; Turnbull and Lord, *op. cit.*, p. 207

27. Clark G. Reynolds, *The Fast Carriers: The Forging of an Air Navy* (New York: McGraw-Hill Book Company, 1968), pp. 14–18; Gerald E. Wheeler, *Admiral William Veazie Pratt, U. S. Navy* (Washington, D.C.: Naval History Division, 1974), p. 275, cited hereafter as *Pratt*; Melhorn, *op. cit.*, pp. 113–115.

28. Arpee, *op. cit.*, Chapters 10–13; Turnbull and Lord, *op. cit.*, pp. 281–283; Roskill, *op. cit.*, p. 528.

29. Robert D. Heinl, Jr., *Soldiers of the Sea* (Annapolis, Md.: U. S. Naval Institute, 1962), pp. 255–260, 299–305; Jeter A. Isely and Philip A. Crowl, *The U. S. Marines and Amphibious War* (Princeton, N.J.: Princeton University Press, 1951). Chapters II and III.

30. Abbazia, *op. cit.*, p. 9; Wheeler, *Pratt*. pp. 365–367.

31. Davis, *op. cit.*, pp. 358–359.

32. *Ibid.*, p. 361; Morison, *op. cit.*, pp. 20–21.

33. Quoted in Bailey, *op. cit.*, p. 742.

34. Richard Hough, *Dreadnought: A History of the Modern Battleship* (London: Michael Joseph, 1965), pp. 201–205, 212.

35. Edward P. Von der Porten, *Pictorial History of the German Navy in World War II* (New York: Thomas Y. Crowell Company, 1976), pp. 17–18; Morison, *Atlantic*, p. 4.

36. Abbazia, *op. cit.*, Chapter 5; Morison, *Atlantic*, pp. 13–16.

37. Morison, *Atlantic*, pp. 27–30.

38. James MacGregor Burns, *Roosevelt: The Lion and the Fox* (New York: Harcourt, Brace and Company, 1956), pp. 437–442; Abbazia, *op. cit.*, Chapter 7; Morison, *Atlantic*, pp. 33–36.

39. Bailey, *op. cit.*, pp. 773–776; Morison, *Atlantic*, pp. 36–38.

40. Morison, *Atlantic*, pp. 24–26; Abbazia, *op. cit.*, pp. 108–109, 152; Westcott, *op. cit.*, p. 306.

41. Knox is quoted in Westcott, *op. cit.*, p. 356; Abbazia, *op. cit.*, p. 189; Morison, *Atlantic*, pp. 49–55.

42. Quoted in Abbazia, *op. cit.*, p. 318.

43. Abbazia, *op. cit.*, Chapters 20, 23, and 25; Morison, *Atlantic* pp. 79–81, 92–98.

44. Morison, *Atlantic*, pp. 45–49; *Command Decisions*, K. R. Greenfield, ed. (Washington, D.C.: Office of Military History, 1960), pp. 14–20.

45. Samuel Eliot Morison, *The Rising Sun in the Pacific* (Boston: Little, Brown and Co., 1948), Chapter IV, cited hereafter as *Rising Sun*.

46. *Ibid.*, pp. 80–87.

47. *Ibid.*, pp. 76–79; Roberta Wohlstetter, *Pearl Harbor: Warning and Decision* (Stanford, Cal.: Stanford University Press, 1962), pp. 246–263.

48. Morison, *Rising Sun*, pp. 88–94.

49. *Ibid.*, pp. 94–95; Walter Lord, *Day of Infamy* (New York: Henry Holt and Company, 1957), pp. 44–49.

50. Lord, *op. cit.*, pp. 66, 70–71.

51. *Ibid.*, pp. 89–90.

52. Morison, *Rising Sun*, pp. 98–125.

53. *Ibid.*, pp. 125–126.

CHAPTER 9—"THE WAY TO VICTORY"

1. E. B. Potter, *Nimitz* (Annapolis, Md.: U. S. Naval Institute, 1976), p. 16, cited hereafter as *Nimitz*; John Toland, *But Not in Shame* (New York: Random House, 1961). pp. 131–132.

2. E. B. Potter, "Chester William Nimitz 1885–1966," U. S. Naval Institute *Proceedings*, July 1966.

3. Samuel Eliot Morison, *The Two Ocean War* (Boston: Little, Brown & Co., 1963), p. 35, cited hereafter as *War*; Samuel Eliot Morison, *The Rising Sun in the Pacific* (Little, Brown & Co., 1948), p. 256, cited hereafter as *Rising Sun*; Samuel B. Griffith, *The Battle of Guadalcanal* (New York: Ballantine Books, 1966), p. 277; Potter, *Nimitz*, p. 32.

4. King is quoted in John B. Lundstrom, *The First South Pacific Campaign* (Annapolis, Md.: U. S. Naval Institute, 1976), unnumbered page, pp. 197–205; Morison, *Rising Sun*, p. 257.

5. Morison, *Rising Sun*, pp. 389–398.

6. F. C. van Oosten, *The Battle of the Java Sea* (Annapolis, Md.: U. S. Naval Institute, 1976); Morison, *Rising Sun*, pp. 271–380.

7. Walter G. Winslow, "The Galloping Ghost," U. S. Naval Institute *Proceedings*, February 1949.

8. Samuel Eliot Morison, *Strategy and Compromise* (Boston: Little, Brown & Co., 1958), pp. 71–74.

9. Bernard Millot, *The Battle of the Coral Sea* (Annapolis, Md.: U. S. Naval Institute, 1974); Morison, *War*, pp. 140–147; Alan Westcott, ed., *American Sea Power Since 1775* (Philadelphia: J. B. Lippincott, 1947), pp. 398–404; Potter, *Nimitz*, pp. 63–77. Ernest J. King, *U. S. Navy at War: 1941–1945* (Washington, D.C.: United States Navy Department, 1946), pp. 45–47.

10. Quoted in Walter Lord, *Incredible Victory* (New York: Harper & Row, 1967), p. 3.

11. Potter, *Nimitz*, p. 79.

12. *Ibid.*, pp. 91–107; King, *op. cit.*, pp. 47–49; Morison, *War*, pp. 147–163; Westcott, *op. cit.*, pp. 404–416.

13. Lord, *op. cit.*, p. 66.

14. Thomas B. Buell, *The Quiet Warrior: A Biography of Admiral Raymond A. Spruance* (Boston: Little, Brown & Co., 1974), pp. 129–140.

15. Sidney L. James, "Slaughter of Torpedo 8," in *The United States Navy in World War II*, S. E. Smith, ed., (New York: William Morrow & Company, Inc., 1966), pp. 271–276.

16. Clarence E. Dickinson, "The Target Was Utterly Satisfying," in Smith, *op. cit.*, p. 280.

17. Buell, *op. cit.*, pp. 144–150.

18. King, *op. cit.*, pp. 49–52; Morison, *War*, pp. 164–167; Westcott, *op. cit.*, pp. 419–422.

19. King, *op. cit.*, pp. 29, 153–154.

20. Richard F. Newcomb, *Savo* (New York: Holt, Rinehart and Winston, 1961); Morison, *War*, pp. 167–177; Westcott, *op. cit.*, pp. 422–426.

21. Morison, *War*, p. 167.

22. *Ibid.*, pp. 177–182; King, *op. cit.*, pp. 53–54; Westcott, *op. cit.*, pp. 420–431.

23. Morison, *War*, pp. 182–189; King, *op. cit.*, pp. 54–56; Westcott, *op. cit.*, pp. 434–438; Potter, *Nimitz*, pp. 195–197.

24. Quoted in Potter, *Nimitz*, p. 198.

25. Morison, *War*, pp. 190–208; King, *op. cit.*, pp. 56–61; Westcott, *op. cit.*, pp. 438–448.

26. Morison, *War*, pp. 208–214; King, *op. cit.*, pp. 61–63; Westcott, *op. cit.*, pp. 448–451.

27. Clark Reynolds, *The Fast Carriers: The Forging of an Air Navy* (New York: McGraw-Hill Book Company, 1968), pp. 51–59; King, *op. cit.*, pp. 214–215; Oliver Jensen, *Carrier War* (New York: Pocket Books, Inc., 1945).

28. Barrett Tillman, *The Dauntless Dive Bomber of World War Two* (Annapolis, Md.: U. S. Naval Institute, 1976).

29. King, *op. cit.*, pp. 20–25, 29–30, 152–153.

30. *Ibid.*, pp. 196–200; Reynolds, *op. cit.*, pp. 20, 128–130; Potter, *Nimitz*, pp. 128–129; E. B. Potter and Chester W. Nimitz, *Sea Power* (Englewood Cliffs, N.J.: Prentice-Hall, Inc., 1968), pp. 639–648.

31. Samuel Eliot Morison, *The Battle of the Atlantic* (Boston: Little, Brown & Co., 1947), pp. 125–135, cited hereafter as *Atlantic*; Edward P. Von der Porten, *Pictorial History of the German Navy In World War II* (New York: Thomas Y. Crowell Company, 1976), pp. 249–250; King, *op. cit.*, pp. 77–80.

32. Quoted in Von der Porten, *op. cit.*, p. 251.

33. Quoted in Morison, *Atlantic*, pp. 200–201, 229–231; Dudley W. Knox, *A History of the United States Navy* (New York: G. P. Putnam's Sons, 1948), pp. 450–457.

34. Quoted in Felix Riesenberg, Jr., "Atlantic Slaughter," in Smith, *op. cit.*, pp. 125–126; Malcolm F. Willoughby, *U. S. Coast Guard in World War II* (Annapolis, Md.: U. S. Naval Institute, 1957), pp. 192–204; Morison, *Atlantic*, pp. 233–237.

35. Quoted in John J. Forsdal, "Wipe the Oil Out of My Eyes," in Smith, *op. cit.*, p. 130; Morison, *Atlantic*, pp. 135–157; King, *op. cit.*, pp. 80–81.

36. Alfred Price, *Aircraft versus Submarine* (Annapolis, Md.: U. S. Naval Institute, 1973), pp. 114–150; Sir Arthur Hezlet, *The Submarine and Sea Power* (New York: Stein and Day, 1967), pp. 179–190; Morison, *Atlantic*, pp. 311–375.

37. Sir Peter Gretton, *Crisis Convoy* (Annapolis, Md.: U. S. Naval Institute, 1974), pp. 147–153; Von der Porten, *op. cit.*, p. 269.

38. Price, *op. cit.*, p. 147.

39. Morison, *War*, pp. 370–373; Knox, *op. cit.*, pp. 524–525; Potter and Nimitz, *op. cit.*, p. 564.

40. Hezlet, *op. cit.*, pp. 228–240; Morison, *War*. pp. 558–564; Von der Porten, *op. cit.*, pp. 319–337.

41. Morison, *War*, pp. 215–263, 349–357; King, *op. cit.*, pp. 82–88.

42. Morison, *War*, pp. 384–395; King, *op. cit.*, pp. 135–137.

43. Cornelius Ryan, *The Longest Day: June 6, 1944* (New York: Simon and Schuster, 1959), pp. 233–235; Morison, *War*, pp. 395–406; King, *op. cit.*, pp. 137–142.

44. Quoted in Westcott, *op. cit.*, p. 551.

45. Quoted in Knox, *op. cit.*, p. 514.

46. Morison, *War*, pp. 264–298; King, *op. cit.*, pp. 63–70; Potter, *Nimitz*, pp. 235–256.

47. Morison, *War*, pp. 295–317; King, *op. cit.*, pp. 70–74.

48. Potter, *Nimitz*, p. 295.

49. Quoted in Donald Macintyre, *The Battle for the Pacific* (London: B. Batsford Ltd., 1966), p. 165.

50. Buell, *op. cit.*, pp. 263–280; Morison, *War*, pp. 338–345; King, *op. cit.*, pp. 106–112.

51. Westcott, *op. cit.*, p. 497.

52. Edward P. Stafford, *The Big E: The Story of the U. S. S. Enterprise* (New York: Random House, 1962), pp. 347–354.

53. Clay Blair, Jr., *Silent Victory: The U. S. Submarine War Against Japan* (Philadelphia: J. B. Lippincott Co., 1975), pp. 775–776.

54. *Ibid.*, p. 778–779.

55. Morison, *War*, pp. 493–500; Blair, *op. cit.*, pp. 67–69.

56. Morison, *War*, pp. 501–512; King, *op. cit.*, pp. 201–203; Hezlet, *op. cit.*, pp. 210–227; Ellis A. Johnson and David Katcher, *Mines Against Japan* (White Oak, Md.: Naval Ordnance Laboratory, 1973), pp. 21–38.

57. Morison, *War*, pp. 421–423, 419–432; King, *op. cit.*, pp. 117–120.

58. Hanson W. Baldwin, "The Sho Plan—The Battle for Leyte Gulf," in *Sea Fights and Shipwrecks* (Garden City, N. Y.: Hanover House, 1955), pp. 134–182, includes notes by Halsey and Kinkaid; Morison, *War*, pp. 436–451; King, *op. cit.*, pp. 120–124.

59. Morison, *War*, pp. 441–451; King, *op. cit.*, pp. 121–122.

60. William F. Halsey and Joseph Bryan III, *Admiral Halsey's Story* (New York: Whittlesey House, 1947), p. 217; Morison, *War*, pp. 463–464; Potter, *Nimitz*, pp. 334–335.

61. C. A. F. Sprague and Philip H. Gustafson, "They Had Us On The Ropes," in Smith, *op. cit.*, pp. 864–871.

62. Amos T. Hathaway, "Small Boys—Intercept!" in Smith, *op. cit.*, pp. 872–874; Morison, *War*, pp. 451–463; King, *op. cit.*, p. 122.

63. Potter, *Nimitz*, pp. 335–340; Morison, *War*, pp. 463–470; King, *op. cit.*, p. 123.

64. Halsey and Bryan, *op. cit.*, p. 220

65. Morison, *War*, pp. 513–557; King, *op. cit.*, pp. 173–180; James H. Belote and William M. Belote, *Typhoon of Steel: The Battle for Okinawa* (New York: Harper & Row, 1970); Hanson W. Baldwin, "The Greatest Sea-Air Battle in History," in Baldwin, *op. cit.*, pp. 297–310.

66. Quoted in Belote, *op. cit.*, p. 102.

67. Quoted in Baldwin, *op. cit.*, p. 305.

68. King, *op. cit.*, pp. 188–195; Morison, *War*, pp. 564–577.

CHAPTER 10—CHALLENGING YEARS

1. *The New York Times*, April 6, 1946.

2. Quoted in Richard K. Smith, *Cold War Navy* (Falls Church, Va.: Lulejian & Associates, 1976), Chapter II, pp. 10–11.

3. John W. Spanier, *American Foreign Policy Since World War II* (New York: Praeger Publishers, 1973), pp. 22–44; Harry S Truman, *Memoirs* (New York: Doubleday & Co., 1956), Vol. II, p. 101.

4. Smith, *op. cit.*, Chapter 5; Naval History Division, *The United States Navy: Keeping the Peace* (Washington, D.C.: Government Printing Office, 1968), pp. 23–24, cited hereafter as *Peace*.

5. *Report of the Secretary of the Navy, 1946* (Washington, D.C.: Government Printing Office, 1947), pp. 3, 22–27, 32–37.

6. Naval History Division, *Peace*, p. 20.

7. Quoted in Demetrios Caraley, *The Politics of Military Unification* (New York: Columbia University Press, 1966), p. 100.

8. Quoted in Naval History Division, *Peace*, p. 20.

9. Smith, *op. cit.*, Chapter 4, pp. 2–3.

10. Richard G. Hewlett and Francis Duncan, *Nuclear Navy: 1946–1962* (Chicago: University of Chicago Press, 1974), pp. 23–35.

11. Caraley, *op. cit.*, pp. 3–20.

12. Quoted *Ibid.*, p. 151*n*.

13. *Ibid.*, pp. 153–182.

14. James A. Field, Jr., *History of United States Naval Operations: Korea* (Washington, D.C.: Government Printing Office, 1962), pp. 28–29.

15. *Ibid.*, pp. 29–30; Smith, *op. cit.*, Chapter 4, pp. 4–7; Russell F. Weigley, *The American Way of War* (New York: Macmillan Publishing Co., 1973), pp. 376–377; Paul Y. Hammond, "Super Carriers and B-36 Bombers: Appropriations. Strategy and Politics," *American Civil-Military Decisions*, Harold Stein, ed. (Birmingham, Ala.: University of Alabama Press, 1963), pp. 465–567.

16. Weigley, *op. cit.*, pp. 377–379; Field, *op. cit.*, pp. 29–32; Smith, *op. cit.*, Chapter 4, pp. 7–20.

17. Field, *op. cit.*, pp. 33–34.

18. *Ibid.*; Malcolm W. Cagle and Frank A. Manson, *The Sea War in Korea* (Annapolis, Md.: U.S. Naval Institute, 1957).

19. Field, *op. cit.*, Chapter VII; Cagle and Manson, *op. cit.*, Chapter 3.

20. Quoted in Robert D. Heinl, Jr., *Victory at High Tide* (Philadelphia: J. B. Lippincott Company, 1968), pp. 6–7, cited hereafter as *High Tide*.

21. Robert D. Heinl, Jr., *Soldiers of the Sea* (Annapolis, Md.: U.S. Naval Institute, 1962), p. 550; Field, *op. cit.*, pp. 181.

22. Quoted in Heinl, *High Tide*, p. 102.

23. Arnold S. Lott, *Most Dangerous Sea* (Annapolis, Md.: U.S. Naval Institute, 1959), Chapter 16; Field, *op. cit.*, pp. 229–242; Cagle and Manson, *op. cit.*, Chapter 4.

24. Quoted in Caraley, *op. cit.*, pp. 88–89.

25. Hewlett and Duncan, *op. cit.*, pp. 215–220.

26. *Ibid.*, pp. 186–193; Clay Blair, Jr., *The Atomic Submarine and Admiral Rickover* (New York: Henry Holt and Company, Inc., 1954).

27. Hewlett and Duncan, *op. cit.*, pp. 370–371; Herbert J. Gimpel, *The United States Nuclear Navy* (New York: Frederick Watts, Inc., 1965), pp. 58–59.

28. Hewlett and Duncan, *op. cit.*, pp. 371–372; Gimpel, *op. cit.*, pp. 96–107.

29. Hewlett and Duncan, *op. cit.*, pp. 308–310, 314–317.

30. Quoted in Smith, *op. cit.*, Chapter 5, pp. 7–8.

31. *Ibid.*, Chapter 15; *Time*, August 4, 1958.

32. Smith, *op. cit.*, Chapter 15, pp. 19–20.

33. *Ibid.*, Chapter 16; Jonathan T. Howe, *Multicrises: Sea Power and Global Politics in the Missile Age* (Cambridge, Mass.: The MIT Press, 1971), Chapters 7 to 11.

34. Quoted in Howe, *op. cit.*, p. 218.

35. Smith, *op. cit.*, Chapter 18; Elie Abel, *The Missile Crisis* (Philadelphia: J. B. Lippincott Company, 1966).

36. Quoted in Smith, *op. cit.*, Chapter 18, p. 8.

37. Quoted by Stewart Alsop and Charles Bartlett, "In Time of Crisis," in *The Cuban Missile Crisis*, Robert A. Devine, ed. (New York: Quadrangle Books, 1971), pp. 59, 61.

38. For the early history of the U.S. Navy's role in Vietnam see Edward J. Marolda and G. Wesley Price III, *A Short History of the United States Navy and the Southeast Asian Conflict 1950–1975* (Washington, D.C.: Naval Historical Center, 1984), pp. 1–4.

39. Weigley, *op. cit.*, p. 460; Spanier, *op. cit.*, pp. 234–251.

40. Eugene G. Windchy, *Tonkin Gulf* (Garden City, N.Y.: Doubleday & Co., 1971).

41. Elmo R. Zumwalt, Jr., *On Watch* (New York: Quadrangle Books, 1976), p. 35.

42. Charles K. Merdinger, "Civil Engineers, Seabees, and Bases in Vietnam," in *Naval Review* (Annapolis, Md.: U.S. Naval Institute, 1970); R. L. Schreadley, "The Naval War in Vietnam 1950–1970," in *Naval Review* (Annapolis, Md.: U.S. Naval Institute, 1971).

43. Malcolm W. Cagle, "Task Force 77 in Action off Vietnam," in *Naval Review* (Annapolis, Md.: U.S. Naval Institute, 1972).

44. Edwin B. Hooper, "The Service Force, Pacific Fleet in Action," in *Naval Review* (Annapolis, Md.: U.S. Naval Institute, 1968).

45. F. O. McClendon, Jr., "Doctors and Dentists, Nurses and Corpsmen in Vietnam," in *Naval Review* (Annapolis, Md.: U.S. Naval Institute, 1970).

46. Cagle, *op. cit.*; U.S. Pacific Command, *Report on the War in Vietnam* (Washington, D.C.: Government Printing Office, 1968), pp. 14–54.

47. Peter B. Mersky and Norman Polmar, *The Naval Air War in Vietnam* (Baltimore, Md.: Nautical and Aviation Publishing Company of America, 1986), p. 30.

48. John B. Nichols and Barrett Tillman, *On Yankee Station: The Naval Air War over Vietnam* (Annapolis, Md.: Naval Institute Press, 1987), p. 55.

49. *Ibid.*, p. 18.

50. Mersky and Polmar, *op. cit.*, p. 192.

51. Nichols and Tillman, *op. cit.*, p. 53.

52. *Ibid.*, pp. 57–58.

53. Edward J. Marolda, "The War in Vietnam's Shallows," *Naval History,* April 1987.

54. Naval History Division, *Riverine Warfare* (Washington, D.C.: Government Printing Office, 1971), pp. 38–53; S. A. Swartztrauber, "River Patrol Relearned," in *Naval Review* (Annapolis, Md.: U.S. Naval Institute, 1970); Schreadley, *op. cit.*

55. Stockdale told his story in *In Love and War* (New York: Harper & Row, 1984).

56. " 'Mayday' for the *Mayaguez*," U.S. Naval Institute *Proceedings,* November 1976.

57. Thomas W. Ray, "The Bureaus Go on Forever . . .," U.S. Naval Institute *Proceedings,* January 1968.

58. Zumwalt, *op. cit.,* Chapters 7 to 11.

59. Paul B. Ryan, "USS *Constellation* Flare-up: Was It Mutiny?," U.S. Naval Institute *Proceedings,* January 1976.

60. Sergei G. Gorshkov, *Red Star Rising at Sea* (Annapolis, Md.: Naval Institute Press, 1974), p. 141.

CHAPTER 11—"THE VIOLENT PEACE"

1. For naval affairs under Carter see Paul B. Ryan, *First Line of Defense: The U.S. Navy Since 1945* (Stanford, Calif.: Hoover Institution Press, 1981) and Robert W. Love, Jr., *History of the U.S. Navy: 1942–1991* (Harrisburg, Pa.: Stackpole, 1992), pp. 670–701.

2. Ryan, *op. cit.,* p. 183.

3. Claytor is quoted in Jan S. Bremer, *U.S. Naval Developments* (Baltimore, Md.: Nautical and Aviation Publishing Co., 1983) p. 29.

4. Harry G. Summers, *On Strategy II: A Critical Analysis of the Gulf War* (New York: Dell, 1992), p. 87.

5. *Ibid.,* p. 91.

6. Thomas B. Hayward, "The Future of U.S. Sea Power," in *Naval Review* (Annapolis, Md.: U.S. Naval Institute, 1979.)

7. Bremer, *op. cit.,* p. 30.

8. Letter from L. Edgar Prina in U.S. Naval Institute *Proceedings,* November 1987.

9. For a discussion of the Maritime Strategy, see the special supplement to U.S. Naval Institute *Proceedings,* January 1986; for criticism see Jack Beatty, "In Harm's Way," *Atlantic,* May 1986.

10. James D. Watkins, "The Maritime Strategy," special supplement to U.S. Naval Institute *Proceedings,* January 1986.

11. Philip Gold, "600 Ships to the Defense," *Insight,* September 14, 1987.

12. Benis M. Frank, *U.S. Marines in Lebanon, 1982–1984* (Washington, D.C.: Government Printing Office, 1987).

13. Ronald H. Spector, *U.S. Marines in Grenada 1983* (Washington, D.C.: Government Printing Office, 1987).

14. Robert E. Stumf. "Air War with Libya," U.S. Naval Institute *Proceedings*, August 1986; W. Hays Parks, "Crossing the Line of Death," U.S. Naval Institute *Proceedings*, November 1986; *Time*, May 5, 1986.

15. William H. Nelson, "Peacekeepers at Risk," U.S. Naval Institute *Proceedings*, July 1997; John L. Byron, "The Surface Navy Is Not Ready," U.S. Naval Institute *Proceedings*, December 1987.

16. Washington *Post*, September 28, 1991.

17. Quoted in Thomas G. Paterson, J. Gary Clifford, and Kenneth J. Hagan, *American Foreign Policy: A History Since 1900* (Lexington, Mass.: D.C. Heath, 1991), p. 719.

18. For the events leading up to the Iraqi invasion of Kuwait see Norman Friedman, *Desert Victory* (Annapolis, Md.: Naval Institute Press, 1991), Chapters 1, 2, and 3.

19. For the naval buildup, see *The U.S. Navy in "Desert Shield"/"Desert Storm"* (Washington, D.C.: Department of the Navy, 1991), Chapter 2.

20. Friedman, *op. cit.,* p. 88.

21. *Ibid.,* p. 87.

22. For the marine buildup, see Edwin H. Simmons, "Getting Marines to the Gulf," U.S. Naval Institute *Proceedings*, May 1991.

23. Friedman, *op. cit.*, pp. 102–105; Douglas M. Norton, "Sealift: Keystone of Support," U.S. Naval Institute *Proceedings*, May 1991.

24. Quoted in Rick Atkinson, *Crusade: The Untold Story of the Persian Gulf War* (Boston: Houghton Mifflin, 1993), p. 30.

25. *Time*, January 28, 1991.

26. For the air campaign see Friedman, *op. cit.*, Chapters 8 and 9.

27. Atkinson, *op. cit.*, p. 150.

28. *Ibid.* p. 151.

29. Friedman, *op. cit.*, Chapter 12; Edwin Simmons, "Getting the Job Done," U.S. Naval Institute *Proceedings*, May 1991.

30. Quoted Summers, *op. cit.*, p. 274.

31. Washington *Post*, March 17, 1991.

32. For the naval side of Desert Storm see Friedman, *op. cit.*, Chapter 11, Stan Arthur and Marvin Pokrant, "The Storm at Sea," U.S. Naval Institute *Proceedings*, May 1991.

The **Naval Institute Press** is the book-publishing arm of the U.S. Naval Institute, a private, nonprofit, membership society for sea service professionals and others who share an interest in naval and maritime affairs. Established in 1873 at the U.S. Naval Academy in Annapolis, Maryland, where its offices remain today, the Naval Institute has members worldwide.

Members of the Naval Institute support the education programs of the society and receive the influential monthly magazine *Proceedings* and discounts on fine nautical prints and on ship and aircraft photos. They also have access to the transcripts of the Institute's Oral History Program and get discounted admission to any of the Institute-sponsored seminars offered around the country.

The Naval Institute also publishes *Naval History* magazine. This colorful bimonthly is filled with entertaining and thought-provoking articles, first-person reminiscences, and dramatic art and photography. Members receive a discount on *Naval History* subscriptions.

The Naval Institute's book-publishing program, begun in 1898 with basic guides to naval practices, has broadened its scope in recent years to include books of more general interest. Now the Naval Institute Press publishes about 100 titles each year, ranging from how-to books on boating and navigation to battle histories, biographies, ship and aircraft guides, and novels. Institute members receive discounts of 20 to 50 percent on the Press's nearly 600 books in print.

Full-time students are eligible for special half-price membership rates. Life memberships are also available.

For a free catalog describing Naval Institute Press books currently available, and for further information about subscribing to *Naval History* magazine or about joining the U.S. Naval Institute, please write to:

Membership Department
U.S. Naval Institute
118 Maryland Avenue
Annapolis, MD 21402-5035
Telephone: (800) 233-8764
Fax: (410) 269-7940
Web address: www.usni.org